April 14/59

Blessings eternal,

Norman R. Westfall

1959

Symbol of the New Golden Age

LORD
MAITREYA

or the
New Golden Age

by

MAH-ATMAH AMSUMATA

AMSUMATA PUBLISHING CO.
Shrine Temple · · Los Angeles

PRINTED IN UNITED STATES
by
TIMES-MIRROR PRINTING & BINDING HOUSE

DEDICATION

I lovingly dedicate this book to my Beloved Master-Teacher Lord Maitreya, Jesus, Mahatma Koot Hoomi, Goddess Maria, Master Joshua, Master David, Master Dorothy, the Great White Brotherhood, the Brotherhood of Mount Shasta, the Lemurian Brotherhood, the Golden Age Brotherhood, the Universal Brotherhood, the true Rosicrucian Brotherhood and all Masters and Beloved Students of Light who have assisted me in its writing and publication.

MAH ATMAH AMSUMATA,
(SAINT GERMAIN).

THE MASTER'S CALL

Ages you've slept, enthralled by Nature;
Centuries have crept by, faintly recalled;
Spheres unheralded enfold you, unnoticed,
Constant, filled with ecstasies never sensed.
Glorious splendors burst about you, stilled
To your earthly ears. Will you be wise?
We come and go—Beacons to open eyes.

Scorned by souls in lethargy, we press on,
Watchful for the keen mind, devoted beings
Seeking mystics' call. Can't you hear it?

Worlds upon worlds DO whirl about you,
Scintillating, their rays bearing delights,
Riches immeasurable, and infinite.

Man you are now—a god by trying.
Stretch forth your wings in flight to God.
Severed, apart, your soul will have flown
Back to its source—beginning—its own,
To drink again of the waters most freely—
Creative joy sublime—wholeness undefined!

Masters come and go. Give ear! Give ear!
Giving their lives that others may live;
Tired but never wearying, they trudge on,
Blessing all stopping to take heed,
Well-wishing those who but pass them by,
Helpful to the needy, hopeful for the doubter,
Their work their joy, sorrow happiness.

Give ear that you may hear the call;
Watch that you may see the glint
Of the Master's eye, sense the fragrance
Of His sweet-smelling soul, perfumed
By God's first choice of Aetheria,
Or feel the thrill of Spirit eternal—
He labors for your good and others—
Skilled in all things—man's elder brothers.

—AMSUMATA.

TABLE OF CONTENTS

TABLE OF CONTENTS (Continued)

POEMS, SYMBOLS AND ALLEGORIES

FOREWORD

SAINT GERMAIN

SAINT GERMAIN is somewhat a mythical, historical figure having been mentioned at various times during the past three or four hundred years, and it is impossible to understand just how he has been able to play the part he has manifested in great historical events unless one understands the nature of the human spirit, the Divine Spirit, the various bodies each individual possesses, and how the individual spirits of each and all embodiments culminate in the present-day life-stream of a person.

Since 1929 there has been a great awakening among mankind on earth due to the direct effect of the Cosmic Light. Even as early as 1875 when Master Koot Hoomi, through the person of Madam Blavatsky, founded the Theosophical Society, there was much activity of the cosmic in our limited earth realm. Consequently there have emanated from the Great Central Sun of all life, many new cosmic activities, understood more or less by the esoteric philosophers, little understood by science and even unheard of by the average person.

I shall not tell you I will entirely clear up the terrible misunderstandings that have arisen about Saint Germain because of a very meagre knowledge and explanation of his life and activity by pseudo-masters and messengers, but I am certain I can explain much that has never before been published to the outside world. I am certain, too, since I met Saint Germain at Mt. Shasta in Northern California in September, 1940, there is no one of the present generation on earth who has been so close to him as the writer. I am privileged by Saint Germain and other ascended masters to explain to the world, just as they explained them to me, the higher laws of life. I especially invoke the blessings of Saint Germain, Jesus, Mahatma Koot Hoomi, Lord Maitreya, Mary the Mother of Jesus, Joshua the Master of Love, Anoma the Lord of Venus, Master Morya (St. John), Sanat Kumara, Lord Mahachohan and Archangel Michael and all the blessed beings who have taught me the past eleven months.

The time is propitious for a manifesto to be published to the outside world of the current events in the cosmic field of speculative science from the standpoint of the esotericist or transcendental philosopher. Saint Germain is now and has been for several hundred years one of the chief exponents, if not THE chief exponent of the metaphysical theorems appertaining to the transcendental laws of life. There are masters and teachers of physical science, mental science, and spiritual science. Saint Germain is an ascended master. He mastered all laws of life so far as this physical world is concerned. It is the aim of the writer to explain as clearly as possible who Saint Germain is today, what his place is in the cosmic scheme of things, and to clear up misunderstandings and misinterpretations that have been published regarding the so-called ascended masters. "A little knowledge is a dangerous thing," wrote Alexander Pope. This is particularly true of those who have made outlandish claims regarding their individual powers as "messengers of the ascended masters."

There is almost as much difference between a so-called "messenger" and a real master as there is between daylight and the darkest night. No real master ever makes wild claims as to his powers in the outer world, nor does he ever try to enforce the least of the cosmic laws upon mankind. Love is the ruling principle of the masters. Jesus, and His Ascension, is the greatest example of mastership the outside world has ever knowingly produced. However, He even said, "Greater things shall ye do, for I go to the Father." I sincerely believe we shall do greater things in this day than Jesus did in His day. Why should we not? Certainly He knew what He was talking about. The world is advancing forward, not backward. Did Jesus live today, embodied, he could reach hundreds of millions of mankind with His message of love. Is this not greater than when he was performing His ministry? Is it impossible for Jesus to re-embody today? I have been told by Mahatma Koot Hoomi, (Joseph the Father of Jesus), that Saint Germain was John the Brother of Jesus at the time of the ministry of Jesus two thousand years ago. Yes, Jesus and Saint Germain were brothers of the same physical mother, and I have also been told they were Sons of the same Spiritual Father—both divinely sent into this world to enlighten the blind people of this dark planet. If they were brothers then, certainly they ARE brothers now. Time is most insignificant when considered from a Divine or eternally spiritual viewpoint. Science, religion and philosophy—the triune pathway

that leads to balanced enlightenment and illumination—which
have traveled more or less abreast up through the ages—must
now be given an accounting as to their being the main stem of
the Tree of Life and Understanding. A New Age is here—the
Golden Age. We must have a new statement of Life's Laws to
correspond to human progress and advancement. We have known
and mastered Life's manifestation in mentality and physicality.
Now we must learn and master the Spirit—LIFE ITSELF. The
invisible realm of actuality is now, in the New Age, to be learned,
mastered and experienced. The individual spirit of Saint Germain
has much to do with this new element in the mass consciousness
of mankind. He, I have been told, is to carry out the work in
the human octave of life that his elder brother, Jesus, began
and planned when on earth two thousand years ago. It is no easy
task, but great hosts of ascended Beings from the cosmic realms
of life, have promised to assist him, and he does not hesitate to
make a statement at this time that thousands of his faithful
adherents have looked forward to for many years. He is aware,
so he has informed me, there are thousands of students of the
"I AM" principles he instituted who have been side-tracked by
pseudo-masters, who knew only the elementary teachings, but led
faithful, trustful students to think they were master-teachers.
Most terrible conditions, mentally and physically, have resulted
in unnumbered cases throughout America and the world simply
because the egotistical, partially-enlightened, sought to "lead the
blind." Thousands have become fearful through affirmations
diabolically projected into the ethers to shatter their groping
minds. Destructive practices are ruthlessly committed in the
name of Truth and Righteousness. Students who choose to look
to God, Jesus Christ or even Saint Germain, without adherence
to those who have set themselves up as self-appointed masters,
are blasted with shattering decrees, denounced publicly, driven
insane and otherwise tortured until they know not which way
to turn. These are those whom Saint Germain wishes to reach,
assuring them that such "black" practices are not of God, the
Ascended Masters, nor the White Magic of Love the Master
Jesus taught us centuries ago.

It is in the name of the Lord of Love, the Goddess of Love,
Blessed Saint Germain and Jesus and our Beloved Lord Maitreya
that I submit the following encyclical, fully aware that the Council
of the Great White Brotherhood does heartily agree to its publi-

cation for the benefit and direction of those faithful thousands
who now struggle for the Light, Love, Wisdom and Power of
Almighty God.

Affectionately given,

September 11, 1941   AMSUMATA.

THE GREAT SPIRIT

For twenty-two years I was consciously under the instruction
of the Masters before those years of intense study and application
brought forth to me the actual tangible proof of the modus
operandi by which they do Their GREAT WORK in the outer
manifestation. My first contact with them was through the
Theosophical Society, after I had been an ardent student of
psychology and kindred subjects. My second contact with the
Masters came through R.S.C., the Rosicrucian Brotherhood; my
third through various Brothers of the Universal Brotherhood;
my fourth channel of initiation was Saint Germain's so-called
"I AM" activity; and my fifth and greatest source of instruction,
initiations and ascension into the cosmic consciousness and spiritual reality of Life, Light and Love, was directly through Brothers
of the Great White Lodge; and the physical place where I made
the supreme contact was Mount Shasta in northern California.
Mahatma Koot Hoomi (Kuthumi), to me the greatest Initiate
living on earth, had more to do with my actual instruction than
any other one Master; however, numerous ones did confer upon
me the particular initiatory work it is their respective duties to
perform in the various offices they hold in the Great White
Brotherhood. It was through the initiations I received from the
Great Mahatma Koot Hoomi that I was brought into perfect
contact with Saint Germain and through whose Light and Love
I am able to walk constantly beside Him (Saint Germain). We
became ONE IN SPIRIT. "I do nothing of myself, but by
(Him) the Father." As each Great Being initiated me into
Their "Temple" of Wisdom I also became ONE with them in
Spirit and in Truth. All who seek the whole Truth must first
find that ONENESS IN SPIRIT before they can actually contact
the Ascended Masters.

It was in the following order, as nearly as I can recall, that
I contacted those from whom I received instruction and initiations: Mary, Mother of Jesus (Ave Maria), Mahatma Koot

Hoomi (Joseph), Jesus, Archangel Michael, Lord Maitreya, Sanat Kumara, Master Morya (St. John), Joshua, Lord Mahachohan, Beloved Krishna, Buddha Gautama and Anoma, Lord of Venus. Other Masters I contacted, whom I may now recall, but did not instruct me, were: The Venetian, Hilarion, Master Serapis (Egyptian Temple), Issyra. In 1925 I had made the acquaintance of Master Kelpa, who gave me marvelous instruction, informed me he was "finishing" and would soon ascend, and asked me to carry on his teaching after he passed. For many years I had received instruction through Saint Germain in the inner levels. Through Him and Master R.S.C. I had received my earlier training. It was in 1929 that I began to be conscious of the great influence Saint Germain had, in spirit, over my lifestream (Tree of Life). This spiritual influence proved to be more dominant in my life from 1933, just previous to the birth of a son in our family, David. He was a most remarkable child, having, for example, sung and hummed the sacred word AUM of the Orient many times daily from when he was two months of age. He never once cried before he was ten months of age. He ascended soon after his sixth birthday anniversary, but not before he had taught me many things through his radiation of Divine Love and his direct verbal expression of the higher laws of life. He seemed to know everything without even thinking. Probably I shall explain more regarding this episode of my life in future chapters of this brief book, when a further explanation of the Divine Spirit is given.

Following my explanation of the Great Spirit or ONENESS OF ALL LIFE, I shall give you the events in their chronological order as they occurred following my contact with Mary, the Mother of Jesus, at Mount Shasta, August 29, 1940.

THE BIRTH OF FREEDOM

Would it not be heavenly, were we all free individuals, with nobody to look to for orders? With nobody to criticise or reprimand? With nothing but kindliness to admonish us regarding our mistakes? Would it not be a Paradise to look up to the bright glowing sun in crystal-blue heavens and just feel that you were entirely free from all HUMAN bondage, rid of all fear that ever caused you to think one single thought of hate toward another human being? Can you visualize what every individual upon this earth might enjoy were we independent of human mistakes and entanglements into which we have been drawn by HUMAN DESIGNS AND CREATIONS throughout the ages? Think of the blissful joy we might share among earth's own splendors, even today, were it not for human hate, selfishness and discord. What pleasures we humans do deny ourselves! Simply because we do not understand the WHOLE. Our freedom cannot extend beyond our innate intelligence. We are the ones who bind ourselves; we are the ones who must sever the chains of selfishness by our own God-given will. You must look to yourself, to your own heart, your own intelligence—that "I AM" intelligence—if you would be FREE.

This matter of FREEDOM—this quality of freedom—this progress of freedom—this universal battle FOR FREEDOM is the throe of travail of old Mother Earth bursting forth into a new BIRTH OF FREEDOM. The now-historical Wall Street crash, the subsequent depression, labor strikes and riots, international financial quandaries, and all the depressive mental stresses and reactions resultant on the part of humanity as a whole, ARE THE LABOR PAINS OF MOTHER EARTH, through which she is now passing in order to give birth to our blessed UNIVERSAL FREEDOM. The forces of LIGHT have at last won; the forces of darkness are on the run. To him who sees the cosmic writing on the wall of time, numerous manifestations are now apparent to prove it.

That you who read this story, how the LIGHT "I AM" gradually expanded from within me out into this human HEART, BRAIN, BODY AND WORLD, to express herewith this explanation of LIFE, I am going to give a simplified analogy. This you will never forget, for it will "bring home to you" your closeness to God, your dependence upon God and your INDEPENDENCE of humanly created restraint and domination.

WHAT MAKES THE HEART BEAT? For many years as a young man and even as I came to be mature, I thought science understood all such matters. Well, they didn't. Your guess, up until a few years ago, when came forth Saint Germain's explanation of it from the higher octave of life, was just as good as any doctor's or scientist's. In a publication I once published, not infrequently I provoked people to think of the deeper phases of life by asking them such questions as "What makes the heart beat?" I might ask you, "What makes a leaf green?" or "What makes a flower bloom? Where does it get its life, its beauty and loveliness?" There is but ONE GOD—ONE LIGHT—

ONE LIFE—ONE CENTER. We are each and every one of us cells in the body of the WHOLE. In the physical octave of life we can only use geometrical symbols in explaining the vibratory status of each octave of life. Realizing that there is but ONE and that you are a UNIT in THAT ONE, even though you be an infinitesimal unit within it, then you, too, must realize "'I AM' ONE with THAT ONE and IT is my FATHER." Jesus said "I can do nothing of myself, but by the Father." In the Bible is also stated, "You are made in the image of God." Now that does not mean simply that you are shaped "like Him," but, also, that you walk about within Him, you breathe Him, you are within Him, "closer than hand or foot." Now, what MAKES THE HEART BEAT?

Have you heard of the "silver cord" that is broken when one dies and passes from the physical body? It, too, is mentioned in the Bible. There is nothing that will ever be mentioned on this earth regarding the transcendental phases of life that is not somewhere hidden within the pages of Holy Writ. But it has been so twisted, mistranslated, misinterpreted and knowingly and unknowingly abused and misused by priests and preachers, poets and writers for so many hundreds of years that there are few who possess enough of the "Light" within themselves to recognize IT. WHAT MAKES THE HEART BEAT? There is a silver cord or stream of light that comes through the top of your head, which is anchored within your heart. That is what makes your heart beat. It is connected to your heart just the same as your electric light is connected with the powerhouse or generator from which it receives its "juice" or electricity. God is the powerhouse; you are one of His Lights. God is the WHOLE; you are a unit of the WHOLE. That is why God is Holy—He is the WHOLE. When you become WHOLLY perfect you become ONE WITH GOD. When you become ONE WITH GOD you are God. Jesus said, "I and the Father are ONE and the SAME," and "Even greater things than these shall ye do, for I go to the Father." These are the things I want to explain to you and "I AM" the LIGHT that can explain them. YOU ARE the LIGHT, too, but you MUST KNOW YOU ARE *THAT* LIGHT before it will reveal ITSELF to you as the LIVING GOD, the Great Cosmic Light which worketh such wonders with man these days.

Now, I shall give you the real bodily analogy, since you KNOW you have a part with the Living God, the Light of

God—the "I AM" Presence of God. You might wonder why I write in the FIRST PERSON. It might sound silly to you, but I AM THE FIRST PERSON, and I want you to realize that YOU ARE, too, THE FIRST PERSON, and in order for you to see things clearly and directly I MUST talk to you direct. You yourself, are the analogy. You, in the physical body —the physical part of you, according to science, are made up of about three billion cells. Where do those cells get their life? Did you say, "from the food you eat?" That is silly indeed! If that were true science could produce a synthetic man just as wise and intelligent as you. But science cannot produce a man, because science is not God—the Great Central Sun of all Life— and God is the One who gives you the real life that courses through your nervous system. The physical part of those cells does come from the food you eat, mostly, at least, we will admit, but the life principle, the Cosmic Light Part—the Real Self that thinks and directs the movements of your physical body—is the Being anchored within your heart. In speaking of you I say, "YOU ARE," in speaking of myself, I say "I AM" the Life, the Light, the Love, the Intelligence and Energizing Substance which "I AM." You are the Lord and Master over those three billion cells. Those cells look to you for life and sustenance. Your heart-center is their God. You were made in the image and likeness of God. What are you doing with your heritage? Those cells are your world. Think of the millions of little lives crying to you for life, light and love. And have you realized that there is a human being somewhere within this particular universe that corresponds to each and every cell within you? In other words there are probably the same number of individual souls in and about this earth as there are cells within your physical body. Had you ever thought of that? You are a single cell in God's body; these physical cells in your body are single units within you. Isn't it simple? So simple that the would-be-wise overlook it all for looking outside instead of inside. Just as there are billions of tiny suns blazing in your body, you are a sun (son) shining in the body of God. You are actually a Son of God. As you become fully aware of your sonship with God you will begin to feel the Electronic Light-Substance flowing into your heart. You will actually see it. It is only through this complete radiance and the full realization of its Love, Wisdom and Power, that you catch the idea of Eternal Youth, and KNOW that you ARE A "WHITE-FIRE BEING IN THE HEART

OF GOD." Physical activity, cleanliness, dietetics, proper breathing, visualization, concentration, qualification of the Light-Energy as it comes into the body—purity of mind—are all necessary aids in bringing about harmony in the physical body enabling one to realize ONENESS with GOD.

Friend, look to your heart. Speak to it. It is the nearest you can get to God, because it is actually God beating your heart. Your own God-Presence is just above your head, too. You have other bodies besides your physical body. Call to God to reveal these things to you. Speak to God. God spoke to Moses from a burning bush. He spoke to Jesus, Elijah and hundreds of others. It is not unusual for people to speak to God these days, and it is not unusual for God to answer. When you understand that all Life is electro-magnetic—electrons and protons—it is as simple as your radio.

IMPERSONALITY

Now, I (we) must carry the analogy of the universality of life and the Great Spirit further, so that you may realize more fully your oneness with God—His Light, Love, Wisdom, Power and Intelligence. You shall know God when YOU BECOME LIKE HIM. How can you become like Him unless you think of yourself as being like Him? Does a barred rock egg, laid by a barred rock hen, fertilized by a barred rock rooster, have much trouble becoming a barred rock chicken, if placed under a barred rock setting hen, so that Nature (instinct)—God's out-picturing in the physical octave—can take its natural course? It certainly does not. Then, do you think you will have much difficulty becoming like God, should you make up your mind to depend upon God, to trust in Him, to visualize yourself as His Son, to long for His perfection and be His mighty powers of Love? Yes, we have physical fathers and we have spiritual fathers. There is the physical body and there is the spiritual body, as Paul so ably explained in the Holy Scripture. Each has its corresponding parents—Father-Mother. In higher occult and spiritual circles, so to speak, Joseph and Mary are recognized as the Spiritual Parents of the Fifth Root Race. It is the Great Spirit in Its infinite activity that so few of today really understand. The reason they do not understand is simple. They have not attained to that divine principle in their own individual development. One cannot accept something one has not experienced. *The*

Divine Incarnation is experienced only by those who become Brides and Bridegrooms in the Spirit of Christ.

In your physical body, mind and soul, you are a world within yourself. Remember, you are, in addition to other SPIRITUAL or ELECTRONIC adjuncts, three billion five hundred million little cell-worlds—all looking to you for guidance—just as you, as an individual, should you have the proper faith, look for all your needs in God. Visualize yourself as large as the United States. Your head is in Washington state, your toes are in Florida; your heart is in Denver, Colorado; your right hand in Los Angeles, your left in New York. Do you think you will have any trouble feeling your foot down in Florida? Your heart in Denver? Or your hand in Los Angeles? Intelligence is instantaneous. God is pure Intelligence. You are in the Body of God. Do you think, even though you are an infinitesimal point in the Body of God, that He has any difficulty in knowing you are there? Absolutely not! Not any more than you would find it difficult to feel a fly walking across your toe, even though your toe were in Florida, and your brain, where you receive the electronic message via the nervous system, were in Washington. For each and every individual in the world there is an invisible ray of light connecting all hearts to the Heart of God, just as every cell and atom in your physical body is connected with your heart through your nervous system. As there are billions of tiny suns blazing in your body, you are a sun (Son) shining in the Body of God. You are actually a Son of God. When you become fully aware of your Sonship with God you will that instant begin to feel the Electronic Light-Substance flowing into your heart.

Again, returning to the visualization that God is the WHOLE BODY OF ALL—EVER PRESENT in His boundlessness, and you a cell in THAT BODY, let us consider for a moment the element of Time, as we see it in the physical octave. There can be no such principle of Time, as we understand it, in the ALL-KNOWING, ALL-PRESENT, EVER-PRESENT (WHOLLY) FATHER. Time is a humanly created element that has to do with physical objects and life in the physical plane. Physical objects—even planets and stars—are the products of the GOD-INTELLIGENCE and SUBSTANCE under controlled expansion from within out through God's suns (Sons) and satellites, lesser-gods, goddesses, human beings, animals, insects, plants and minerals. If there were but one physical object in all creation—small or large—with one single mind, which filled the entire object, how could there be such an element as Time? But let that single mind-object conceive the possible creation of another mind-object—with the consciousness of space in between them—immediately—instantaneously—you have brought into extrinsicality the element of TIME. However, let me remind you that even the first object, in its exoteric physicality, had to be first conceived by a PURE INFINITE INTELLIGENCE—THE GREAT SPIRIT—and all mind-objects ever conceived from the beginning of TIME, are STILL within the first MIND-OBJECT, which is GOD—ALMIGHTY GOD—INFINITE GOD. Remove all material things, the planets and all earthly objects, and there would be no Time. However, that need not affect the intelligence, light-substance, which is the ONE INFINITE MIND.

As a matter of comparison, taking small, infinitesimal forms of life on the one hand and human beings on the other, let us see if we can come to a better understanding of the mocking delusion Time really is. Science has proved there are infinitesimal animalculae so extremely tiny that if one started to walk or creep, as the case may be, from your toe to the top of your head and back again where it started, it would take it just as long as it would for you to encircle the earth by walking around it. The millions and billions of forms of physical life, I believe, are but the outer incrustation of the inner expansion of the ONE LIFE. If intelligence can exist in an infinitesimal speck so small that even a microscope cannot magnify it to be seen, then it is possible for intelligence to exist in an object so large that it might be infinite.

I am certain I AM in the Body of God—in HIS BEING. I am just as certain that everything in all existence is also. I believe some of us are in the Heart of God, some NEAR His Heart, some in His hands, others in His feet, some in His head, etc. We go out from His Heart-Center and we return to THAT CENTER. Until we determine our own way, God determines it for us. The main object in life—physical life—is to get back to God. Man is given free-will so he can do this. If he were not thrown out on his own he could never become like God. As individuals we may flounder around in the stream of Life for hundreds of centuries, and possibly sink into oblivion, but the probable thing we will do is what God intended us to do when He projected us into this realm of the human free-will—BECOME LIKE HIM—AGAIN. Life in this octave is its own excuse for being. Life is constant change. Now we want more life, light and love. We will get it when we get back and when we get back we will find that it is simply a state of consciousness. Especially the physical plane. We came from nowhere and we are going nowhere. WE ARE. I AM. GOD!

FIRST GOLDEN AGE MANIFESTO OF THE GREAT WHITE LODGE

Blessed Brothers of Light
And all who seek the Light of Christ:

With urgency I proclaim to you a vital message—a Message of Light, Love, Wisdom and Power, from the Great Masters of the White Brotherhood, and from the Council of the Great White Lodge. God Almighty, and the Blessed Christ Incarnate, be our witness, to the Most Blessed Message that has come forth to the people of this world in thousands of years.

Our Brother Amsumata of Bela, Guru, who received his final initiations through Mahatma Koot Hoomi, Lord Maitreya, Master Issa, Lord Sanat Kumara and God of the Golden Heart Mahachohan and the Lord of Lords Buddha Gautama, with the assistance of Ave Maria, the Mother of Jesus, whose son he (Amsumata) was at the time of the Ministry of Jesus almost two thousand years ago,—does proclaim to all true seekers of Light and Love, hopeful of its acceptation by those who know Christ IN THEIR HEARTS, that he did ascend unto His Father last June 4, 1941, through the Blessed Initiations aforementioned at Mount Shasta in northern California, where he was, as he has stated, not only conscious of the ascension, but was also conscious of the crucifixion, saw the RED BLOOD pour from his hands, feet and the "pierced side," was conscious of the "GOLD ESSENCE" being charged into his "higher body," and now bears the evidence of Christ incarnate in his physical body. "She who is Nameless," the "Jewel of the Golden Age," also of the "Golden Body of God," did witness all regarding the initiation and ascension of Amsumata, "The Radiant One," just as He did witness the incarnation of Christ in Her and as the "Silent Watcher," whose office He did hold, was with Her during the time that She did grow and develop into the FULL ILLUMINATION of the Jewel of the Golden Age now being established in Earth "in the Hearts and Minds of Mankind."

Following His ascension Amsumata was taken into the Great Presence, as the "Most Beloved Disciple," of Lord of Lords

Buddha Gautama, which is interpreted "Maitreya, THE DOOR," the Way, the Truth, the Life, the Light, IN CHRIST. Therefore Amsumata is "Maitreya" to "Seekers of Light."

In the same Light and Love that Jesus spoke centuries ago, and by the same authority of the Heavenly Father, the Cosmic Father, through the Universal Media of the Great White Brotherhood, and by the empiric authority of the Great Mahatma Koot Hoomi (KH) and Master Morya (St. John), Manu of the Seventh or Golden Age, Amsumata does proclaim to the world, "I AM THE DOOR THAT NO MAN CAN SHUT, for the Father has chosen me as His Beloved Son to bear the Cross for the many who now seek entrance through the 'portal' into the 'Temple of Light, Wisdom and Power' of Almighty God, the Cosmic Father of all, who now calls His Sons of Righteousness and Truth home again."

"Oh, Prince of the Golden Heart, where art Thou my Son?" spoke the voice of the Almighty. "I am your Father, God of the Golden Heart. I come to take you home into the Sun again."

"Here am I," answered Amsumata. "Thou knowest I love Thee and Thy Truth, Thy Light, Love and Wisdom above all things of earth."

And following the 12th of November, 1940, the Great Masters did come forth to teach Amsumata, one after another, as their duties were performed in their respective offices they hold in the Great White Brotherhood. And just this week Mahatma Koot Hoomi has declared the "finishing touches have been met as advocated" to ripen and develop the "Chief-Avatar," who "now must not let shyness delay your accepting the cross placed on your shoulders to carry."

Mount Shasta, "The Mountain of God," has been chosen by the Great Brotherhood as the "DOOR," where Amsumata-"Maitreya" shall receive and initiate those "proven worthy" into "that Temple not made by hands eternal in the Heavens." Master KH and Morya, both residing now in Tibet, have promised to be here in America early next year to assist Amsumata, the "Chosen One," in his momentous work of bringing all true seekers of Light unto Christ the Radiant Sun (Son) of Almighty God.

Sincerely, in His Name, the Light of Christ,
SANUTRA.

(Written by Amsumata by the Spirit of Maitreya, and signed by one known in the Universal Brotherhood as Sanutra.)

THE JEWEL OF THE GOLDEN AGE

The Jewel of Perfection has risen to Her rightful place in the heavens. The Sons of Righteousness guard Her Throne. She blesses them with Her Love-Light. She feeds them crystal-clear honey through the fragrance of Her love. They feed the world. She reigns Queen.

The Lord of Love rules in the Heart of the Jewel. Wisdom stands at Her left hand—Power at Her right. Beauty and Goodness are Her hand-maidens. Her Great White Diamond radiates purity to every human heart. Her words are like the soft musical petals of a Lotus, falling into a weary world to shed Love and Peace eternally.

Jewels there be—yes, many of them. But the Jewel of Jewels is "She Who is Nameless." For Her the Gods have long waited. Her Light illumines the world. To Her all Masters now bow in humble homage. Her Love is the Law of the New Golden Age. Her radiance now becomes the OUT-PICTURING OF PERFECTION THROUGH THE SONS OF GOD. Her Love reigns. It is Law.

The Jewel of Jewels, now risen—IN FULL ILLUMINA-TION—now walks forth the BRIDE OF CHRIST, and all shall soon be called to the Great Feast. "And the Spirit and the Bride say, 'Come.' And let him that heareth say, 'Come.' And let him that is athirst come; and whosoever will, let him take the water of life freely." Christ is here again.

And all who look for Him will see Him as He is. And we had a promise of God that He would appear in the heavens August 27, 1941, A.D. HE DID APPEAR. May the world rejoice that the Jewel of Jewels is in Complete Illumination. She is the Law of the New Golden Age.

Sincerely and affectionately given,

GURU AMSUMATA

AMSUMATA CHOSEN
BY WORLD-TEACHER KOOT HOOMI

The following message was received by Amsumata from Koot Hoomi October 13, 1941, at 9:18 P.M., Gloria H. Sommerville having been the receiving amanuensis:

October 13, 1941
9:18 P.M.

"To Amsumata:

"The light is strong to begin the greatest outpouring of the Light of the World, and as the years grow on and on the Universal Power will be increased a million fold to bring out the development we talked of. I am sure you have that intuition, but I am using the Amanuensis to emphasize the necessity to not waste any time, as the distance grows shorter and shorter as the time rushes on us. The great disaster is upon us if not unfolded in the scheme as planned by all the Masters at our Great Conclave; for a TIME and PLACE is marked out and the delay in the development must be avoided and not let drift, but as the stars are set and place for all things timed, so must our plans be fulfilled and you, 'Chosen One,' now must not let shyness delay your accepting the cross placed on your shoulders to carry. Many may be in the error of overlooking the timely training, the FACES, as it were, that have been used to ripen and develop the leader to the point of assuming the place as head of the staff when all is ready, Chief-'Avatar,' and so the way is shaping now to start the procedure when the finishing touches have been met as advocated. The timing of the writing completed, look well to the 'East' and stand at attention when you see 'Soon-Day' Sun advance, and as the waning (sunset) takes place do the vows we all agreed, and grow stronger and stronger, My 'Azamata,' and be a GREAT STAR in the Firmament of our 'Brotherhood'—and BE WHERE ALL CAN BEHOLD. I am staying firmly at your side, and will so continue.

"Your teacher,

"KOOT HOOMI (KH)."

P.S. From Amsumata: I wish it to be understood that it is the DIVINE FAMILY that shall come forth as the Great Outward Manifestation of Light in Christ in the New Golden Age. Koot Hoomi is the re-embodiment of Joseph; Morya is St. John the Beloved; Hilarion is St. Paul; Jesus is re-embodied in "She Who is Nameless;" I am John the Brother of Jesus. Mary, Mother of Jesus and other Great Ones are also re-embodied now.

Lovingly,

AMSUMATA.

The Amanuensis who received the above letter knew nothing of my spiritual association with Mahatma Koot Hoomi at the time it was received, which proved to me conclusively the definite source from which I had received much spiritual instruction. It also proved to me that Ascended Masters such as Koot Hoomi can use specially prepared persons as instruments through whom instructions in the Great Work may be given to the outside world; however, I do not wish to convey the idea that all or even the greater part of my instruction was received in this manner. I have received revelations, discipline, instruction and almost every conceivable form of spiritual elucidation.

Maitreya's Golden Age is here at last. In this book may be found that wisdom that proves to him who seeks sincerely in his heart, THE SECOND COMING OF CHRIST. The profound laws of life are herein simplified in a manner never before presented in the world. We are confident that Christ's Message will joyously reach the sincere seeking heart, and we are certain, too, that much so cunningly hidden from the exotericist during the "dark ages" is now revealed through the GREAT COMMAND OF LOVE—yes, by LORD MAITREYA, THE LORD OF LOVE.

—THE AUTHOR.

THE GREAT SPIRIT

The Love-Breath

I sensed the sweet-scented Love-Breath;
   'Twas wafted from somewhere afar—
I dreamed it came through Thy Love-Will
   From the radiant distant Love Star.
Like roses melted with sun-mist;
   Like a heavenly dew with pink glow,
That attar of roses enfolded me—
   Through me, Master, it did flow.

The song of your heart came with it,
   Your letters were missives of Light;
I heard the music of angels—
   All things did beckon my sight.
Thy golden voice in the night
   Brought love and strength profound.
Now, where art Thou, Oh, Rose-Breath?
   Oh, where art Thou to be found?

Touch my heart with Thy fingers of Light;
   Fill it with Thy Golden Glow;
Race the golden fire through my veins;
   Reveal Thy Double Rainbow;
Immerse me in the Ocean of Might;
   Place in my hand the Sceptre of Blue;
Embolden me with the power of Right,
   Blaze the Golden Light thru and thru.

Seize my mortal, hold it true;
   Enfold me in Thy dazzling White,
The Gold, the Pink and the Blazing Blue;
   Hold me in Thy embrace tight.
Carry me to the Central Sun;
   Take me to the Radiant One;
Invest me with Thy Golden Key,
   That I may open THY DOOR to THEE!

Lovingly,

AMSUMATA.

CHAPTER I

During the month of June, 1939, I went from Eureka, Calif., to Los Angeles to attend the semi-annual conclave of the so-called "I AM" students of Saint Germain assembled at the Shrine Auditorium. Mr. and Mrs. G. W. Ballard had just at that time attained the peak of their religious-philosophical movement, under the direction (we do not doubt) of Saint Germain. The Ballards were messengers of the Ascended Masters, as was and is shown by the marvelous discourses received and recorded through Mr. Ballard. Evidence of the authenticity of the discourses can be no better proven than by the understanding of the transcendental laws of life so truthfully and accurately delineated.

I had also attended the conclave at the Shrine Auditorium during the summer of 1938; had read every book and magazine published by the organization up to that time, having received the first edition of "Unveiled Mysteries" from my "director" in the Universal Brotherhood in 1934. I was fully aware of the activity, inner and outer, and knew the Masters of the Great White Lodge were not only directing The Ballards through Saint Germain, but knew also that Saint Germain himself was being directed by the Great Lodge. In 1925, when I had first experienced such a state of consciousness as the ascension, I had gone, so to speak, into the Cosmic Heart of ALL LIFE (GOD) and returned to the lower planes of consciousness with a very important message for this world. This message had to do with the incoming of the Golden Age.

Even before I returned to this outer consciousness I went to the Supreme Master of the Rosicrucian Brotherhood (then my teacher) and told him that the Cosmic Light would become so intense in this world that only those of the Light would be able to remain here. "Those who do not harmonize with the Great Light," I explained, "will not be able to live upon this earth." This will be and IS TODAY the preparation for the establishment of the New Golden Age, which, as I will explain later, will be quite fully established by 1950. Through other persons, writings and experiences, as well as events that came about in the outer world, all such matters pertaining to the Cosmic Light and its activity were confirmed in my personal mind and proven in my individual experiences and physical activities. For instance, I met and heard one Harry Eyer in 1926 in the Theosophical Lodge Hall in Tacoma, Wash., who gave a dynamic lecture on "Cosmic Rays." He was so dynamic and powerful in his declarations in expounding the transcendental laws regarding the "spirit" and cosmic light I could actually see lightning flashing about the hall. Up to that time Mr. Eyer was the most confident and positive individual I had ever seen. HE KNEW LIFE AND ITS LAWS. What he talked of confirmed what I had already experienced in the inner planes, or higher cosmic consciousness.

Previous to my going to the "I AM" conclave at Los Angeles in 1939, there had been a disagreement with my wife regarding my whole-hearted adherence to the "I AM" movement. She could not realize in her outer consciousness just how thoroughly I was enmeshed in the nucleus of the organization. My heart and soul were in the matter. I had seen its inception on the inner long before it became manifest in the outer octave; had consciously conversed with Mr. Ballard in the higher planes, directed the important phases of the activity, and frequently contacted Mrs. Ballard, too, who was informed, in my presence (on the inner planes) of Mr. Ballard's eventual passing from the physical body. Many of these matters I had written about to Mr. Ballard. I have copies of the letters I wrote and the answers he wrote to me, some of which will be published in this book.

My wife, knowing I had ability to become more prosperous, stubbornly persisted in encouraging me to turn my attention more to money-making and home-making, and divorce myself from the "insane idea" that I should "save the world."

Therefore, when I went to Los Angeles, my heart was surely troubled. I was torn between what I felt I should do in the physical world and what my duties were regarding the Great Spirit. Years previous it was very clearly shown to me that I had embodied as Abraham Lincoln. Mr. Ballard claimed to be the re-embodiment of George Washington. I did not doubt his statement. Too much had taken place in my own life-stream to doubt such assertions from another. Following the conclave in Los Angeles, after repeated failures to contact Mr. Ballard and talk to him personally regarding matters of great importance

2

to the "I AM" organization, I again tried in every conceivable way to get an interview with him. "Why shouldn't Lincoln and Washington work together?" I would speak silently under my breath. I went to the Biltmore Hotel, called his secretary by phone, called Mrs. Ballard by phone, sent notes to Mr. Ballard from the foyer of the Shrine Auditorium, telling him it was important that I see and talk to him. I had even written to him before coming to Los Angeles, asking for an interview. Having written such nice explanatory letters to me at various times previously, I felt certain he would allow me to see him. Somehow I was always prevented. Finding other avenues of approach closed I went to Charles Sindelar, publisher of the "Voice," the "I AM" magazine, to see if he could arrange a meeting for me with Mr. Ballard. Mr. Sindelar tried, but as usual, we met failure. It seemed so important for "Lincoln" to see Washington, but it seemed the very "devils" of Hades were working against both of us to prevent it.

In the meantime I had a most dramatic vision, a presentiment of the passing of my beloved son, David, whom I knew to be the re-embodiment of a great master. This came while I was trying so hard to contact the Ballards and prove to them the position I was to hold when the Ascended Masters were to actually begin their work of establishing the new order on earth. I had definite proof later that the "Blacks" were responsible for the sinister activities then beginning to take place.

I have been told by my beloved teacher, Koot Hoomi, to relate these things without reservation. This I shall do. One cannot fully express the truths one knows in any other way. I have nothing to hide. I have nothing to sell. I even haven't an "axe to grind." I own nothing. I want nothing but to help lift "fallen" humanity up to their own rightful sphere of life and consciousness. This I know how to do, with the help of the great Masters who have offered me help and protection, guidance and direction, in all matters pertaining to God's laws. It is as Saint Germain told me the other day: "We are all ONE BODY WEE, but many many are not up to par." So, to all seekers after wisdom I say, "I want to help you get back to par." Isn't that a wonderful thought? Remember, you were up to "par" one time. Now make up your mind to get back up "there."

"The fatal blow" struck. At 12:15 P.M., August 12, 1939, I received a telegram while staying at the "I AM" Sanctuary at 1320 South Hope Street in Los Angeles. The telegram read:

"Norman R. Westfall, 1320 South Hope, Los Angeles. Come immediately. David injured badly. Dorothy."

I was sitting by the window in the Sanctuary reading the book, "Ascended Master Light," when the messenger boy brought the telegram. This was the most crushing thing that had ever happened to me in this life. Of our five children David was the youngest and most loved. He was a little ascended master himself. He had proven it. When 2 months of age he sat in his cradle and sang the sacred word AUM, intoning it in two definite notes in a most powerful and musical manner. Every night when put to bed and every morning when he awoke he hummed and sang those words, radiating forth his love and light. Should he happen to awaken in the night, which he did sometimes, he would sing himself back to sleep, by continuing to hum the word "AUM." David never cried once before he was ten months of age. He would sit as a "little Buddha," smile and sing "A-a-a-a-h-h-h—M-m-m-m-m," over and over again and again. I loved him more than anybody or anything in all the world. I was overcome with grief. I thought my heart would burst. A woman we called Elsie, who worked about the Sanctuary, and another, tried to console me. They proclaimed decrees to the effect that all was for the best, and whatever happened, David would either be completely healed or ascend. The whole Sanctuary seemed to be flooded with violet light. A great passion of sorrow enveloped me. I felt close to God Almighty. I wept unceasingly.

Just 58 minutes later I received the following telegram: *"David gone. Come immediately. Mrs. N. R. Westfall."*

Then I decreed that "in the name of God and all the Masters of Light, David would either walk out of that undertaking establishment or he would ascend and become an Ascended Master." I knew that my prayer had reached the Great Cosmic Center.

Being without funds I wondered how I would even get back to Eureka. Mr. Lanning had gone to attend a conclave in Oakland. Elsie said she would help me. Grief-stricken as I was, knowing that my wife would be in a terrible state of mind, I went to a broker's loan shop and borrowed fourteen dollars on my gold watch and chain, and left as soon as I could by stage for San Francisco. While waiting at the station for the outgoing bus at San Francisco, I sent a telegram to Mr. Ballard who was then starting a class in Oakland, telling him of the tragedy in our family, and asked him to call for David's ascen-

4

sion. In addition to other things I had added to the message telegraphed that "I always called David 'My Angel Boy'." The other wording of the telegram I do not recall.

Having boarded the bus and on my way toward Eureka again, I wondered how David had been injured. Had he been run over by an automobile, or just how had he been taken from us? Many such questions went through my mind. A news boy came through the bus selling papers at Willits, almost half way to Eureka from San Francisco. I dared not buy a newspaper. I did not feel strong enough to face the truth. Finally someone left a newpaper in a seat opposite me. I did muster up courage enough to pick up that paper and read it. On the front page was the story, how little David Westfall, age six years, had somehow gotten his hands in the wringer of a powerful electric washer, both arms were pulled into it and he was strangled to death. His mother had found him hanging in the wringer a few minutes later, but all efforts to bring him back to life failed when he was taken to the hospital.

When I arrived in Eureka Mrs. Westfall was 12 miles out in the country near Trinidad, unconscious, and not expected to live. She had collapsed after sending me the second telegram. She had known David was gone when she first telegraphed, but feared my hearing of his death without previous warning might be fatal to me. As soon as I had made necessary arrangements with the mortuary, and prayed beside the body of David for some time alone, I was taken to the bedside of my wife. She was in a critical state. I was able to rouse her to consciousness, but immediately she would swoon again, saying, "I don't want to live. I killed him, I killed him. I'm to blame." She felt responsible for the accident because she had either left the washer where he could get to it or had probably absent-mindedly left it running when she went down to the hotel we owned in Eureka. David had gone ahead of his mother on the return home with his little sister, Anne. She had stopped in to play with a playmate in the neighborhood. David had gone on to the house with another little boy. A neighbor later saw the other boy run from the house. When the mother arrived at the house she found David hanging in the washer, lifeless. She in her critical state could not, when in the hospital later, get that picture out of her mind.

On the night of August 13 Mrs. Westfall was taken to the hospital. She gradually became stronger, and on the 14th I showed her a telegram I had received from Mr. and Mrs. Ballard, as follows: *"Norman R. Westfall. Call being made. Will let you know as soon as any definite word is given. Limitless love and blessing. Mr. and Mrs. G. W. Ballard."* Mrs. Westfall was able to understand. It seemed to strengthen her to think that the Ballards were interested in David.

The next day, August 15, we received at noon the following telegram: *"Mr. and Mrs. Norman R. Westfall, Central Hotel. Last night Saint Germain verified that your son David made the ascension. How we rejoice with you. Limitless love and blessings. Mr. and Mrs. G. W. Ballard."*

When I read the above telegram to my wife she definitely began to revive. At last she began to realize that although David was gone, he was immortal and had attained what was intended in this life.

August 18, we received the following letter from Mr. and Mrs. Ballard, typed on Hotel Claremont stationery, Berkeley, Calif.:

Mr. and Mrs. Norman R. Westfall   August 18, 1939.
Central Hotel
Eureka, Calif.

Blessed Students of the Light:

Confirming our telegram to you of August 15th, Saint Germain gave us the definite information that your son David made the Ascension under the New Dispensation, instead of going through the changes ordinarily accompanying so-called death.

So far as we understand, this is the beginning of the Ascension of children under the new dispensation.

We call to the "Mighty I AM Presence" of each one of you to charge you with Ascended Master Discrimination, Self-control and Courage that you may accept the Full Blessing of this magnificent privilege and be determined in your refusal to allow it to arouse within you any human feeling of self-esteem, which would of course deprive you of the great benefit you might otherwise receive. Nothing could be more harmful than to allow the human to take credit in any way for such a Miracle of Divine Compassion and Assistance.

With Limitless Love and Blessings,

Yours in the Service of the Light,

(Signed)   MR. AND MRS. G. W. BALLARD.

Slowly Mrs. Westfall mended, and with good care she was able, after fifteen days, to leave the hospital, and again resume her studies at Humboldt State College at Arcata, where she had been attending school in an endeavor to get a scholastic degree with the intention of teaching in the public schools. She had taught school in Kansas City prior to our marriage, having been art teacher there.

The many letters we received from various students of the "I AM" movement regarding the ascension of David were encouraging to Dorothy, my wife, to try to forget the tragic episode of her life, but she could not forget it. Many times I would come upon her weeping; frequently she would awaken me in the night sobbing, that picture of his frightful passing hovering over her like a threatening shadow.

It is impossible to publish all the letters received regarding David's ascension, but for reasons efficacious to the future welfare of sincere students of the profound principles taught by the Ascended Masters, I include the few following letters herewith:

SINDELAR STUDIOS
2600 So. Hoover St.
Los Angeles, California

Norman R. Westfall   October 20, 1939.
Central Hotel
Eureka, Calif.

Beloved Friend:

The reason you have not been answered before is because Charles wanted to write to you himself. But you know without my telling you how almost impossible it is for him to get time even to dictate a letter and now I have made up my mind to wait no longer as through talking to him I know what he would like to say to you, so please accept this as from both of us.

We both thank you a million times for that very beautiful picture of precious David, as well as the smaller pictures. How thoughtful and sweet and kind of you to send them to us.

How blessed you are! How glorious to be able to know that your precious child has made his Ascension. I know what that must mean to you and your precious wife. Of course we know that this knowledge of His release into the Ascended State must have taken away all sorrow that you would otherwise have had at His passing for you know of course that He is with you all the time and then, what assistance He can be to you, your dear wife and the other children. Surely it is glorious beyond the power of words to express.

7

When you look at that radiant smile, you can very easily understand His Ascension. It is evident to me that He was brought back in this embodiment just so He could make His Ascension quickly, having earned it in His last embodiment.

Thank you so much for your wonderful letter, for the description of this beautiful child and of your dream.

How amazing that almost from the beginning He was singing the "I AM"—proof positive beyond a doubt that He came in prepared for the glorious event and you should feel yourselves blessed beyond most people that He was loaned to you for so long a time and surely through His influence you are all sealed in the Light of God that never fails!

We rejoice with you beyond the power of words to express.

Yes, you are right. Little Anne does remind one of Mrs. Ballard.

With all our love we enfold you, your precious wife and your beloved children and shall always be glad to hear from you and see you when you are in our city for now more and more we realize the absolute oneness of the entire student-body and that which effects one effects all. Therefore, as "One" we are striving together reaching upward together and may we all make our Ascension together very very shortly.

Ever lovingly and sincerely yours,

In the service of the Light,

PS/bm   (Signed)   PEARL SINDELAR.

*   *   *

The magical radiance from the pictures I sent of David to a few friends of mine is evidenced in the following letter I received from a friend in Victoria, B. C.:

476 Constance Ave.
Victoria, B. C.
Oct. 9, 1939.

Dear Mr. Westfall:

May God, the "Mighty I AM Presence" bless you FOREVER for sending me the picture of your precious Son, the Ascended Master David Westfall! With all the sincerity of my heart I thank you for it and for your kindly letter.

Words fail to express the wonderful *blessing* that came with the picture. I shall ever treasure it as one of my dearest possessions. As I held it in my hand and read your letter the most glorious feeling of PEACE just flooded my being. All I could do was just love, love, LOVE and bless Him and ask Him to pour out His limitless Ascended Master blessing upon you and his dear, dear mother, until you too make YOUR Ascension.

THE NEW GOLDEN AGE

David's ascension has made me comprehend and FEEL so much more fully the truth of Jesus' words: "I, even I, if I be lifted up, shall draw all men unto me." I feel, or He has enabled me to feel, some of the GLORY of His Ascension. Now can you see why I am so sincerely *grateful* to you —because to FEEL that Glory, even for a moment, is a fore-taste of Heaven—of one's own freedom and Victory. Oh, I *do* thank you with all my heart!

How wonderfully privileged we are to be a part of this activity! I just ask the Presence to house-clean this old human so I can pour forth ALL the love and gratitude my heart longs to do.

Looking at that sweet child-face with such pure *joy* shining through it does something to me that I can't explain. But again I call forth the Eternal blessings of Light upon you and dear Mrs. Westfall. May the great Joy, Peace and Divine Understanding of your precious Son enfold you and all your dear ones until the *moment* of your Ascension.

My deepest gratitude forever,

Your sincere friend in the Light,
(Signed) PEGGY MANNETTE.

*   *   *

The announcement of David's ascension was made through the Messenger Guy W. Ballard in the presence of about three thousand students at the convocation in San Francisco. The following letter was received from my dear friend, Frank Lanning, who was present:

San Francisco, Cal.
Aug. 14, 1939.

Dear Norman and Mrs. Westfall:

Saint Germain announced through our Beloved Mr. Ballard at the meeting this evening that your Boy has gained his Eternal Freedom in his Ascension. We rejoice with you.

FRANK LANNING.

P.S.—A Transcendent Class is this one.

*   *   *

Yes, friends of Truth, of Light, Love, Wisdom and Power, I do have a motive in publishing this book, and that motive is not selfish. I received my Freedom, passed through the Crucifixion, Resurrection and Ascended unto my Cosmic Father June 4, 1941, and I am here to tell about it. One motive in publishing these matters is to let the world know that one does not have to die to ascend.

9

Even if I did not have a true motive myself in the publishing of these facts, the Ascended Masters themselves have asked me to publish them and PUBLISH THEM WITHOUT RESERVATIONS. Saint Germain is more eager for me to publish them than anybody else. Why shouldn't he? He and all the Ascended Masters have been so outlandishly misrepresented, certainly someone should come forth and explain to the hungry world the higher laws that the Masters want explained.

It is most evident to the Masters who know and understand the higher laws of the Cosmos, that there is no one shown up yet who can lead the people out of the darkness in which they find themselves. Since Mr. Ballard passed the last of December, 1939, no discourses have come through to his followers. Not even the most meagre message was published in the official magazine of the organization from Saint Germain. September 2, 1940, I was asked by Koot Hoomi to write to Mrs. Ballard in reference to the Ascended Masters. Following is an excerpt from the letter I wrote her at that time:

"You called to Mt. Shasta recently, so this Master told me, for some Master to come and speak from 'the platform' to your students. Should such a Master come—would you be able to recognize Him? Please do not judge others. The masters—yes, THE MASTERS—are much closer to you than you may realize, possibly. However I do not wish to judge you.

"REMEMBER I have written you in the past, 'if you ever need assistance please do not hesitate to call me.' It was Master Katumah's desire that I write you. Following the ascension of my son David, I had much to do with the 'passing' of your husband, Guy W. Ballard, and there are certain 'connections from the past' that must be balanced. Please believe THE MASTERS whom I have contacted but during the past week—even the Lord (CHRIST) Maitreya—whose loving embrace I am not worthy to claim (yet He embraced me)—do not believe me for myself, but THEM, and KNOW they are with you, but I AM He who would protect you.

"Lovingly,

"NORMAN R. WESTFALL."

*　　*　　*

I received no answer to a number of letters in which I offered to assist Mrs. Ballard. As late as October 8 and 9, 1941, I called her secretary, seeking an interview with Mrs. Ballard, but was refused. Saint Germain had told me to undertake to assist her once more.

CHAPTER II

Love is the ruling principle of all Ascended Masters. When Love no longer reigns in the heart of a student of light, you may know that student will somehow turn on the "left-hand" pathway. Love—Divine Love—is the balancing power. It is easy for the Initiate to determine who are of the Light and those who are "Brothers of the Shadow." The "fruit" of each is readily classified by He who KNOWS. None can hide from the "Eye of Houri," the "All-Seeing Eye" of the Master. The Master does not go about looking for evil, but He knows that where Light is not radiating, darkness accumulates and the works of Satan thrive.

"Where your treasure is, there your heart is also," as Jesus said, or vice versa, "Where your heart is, there your treasure is also." It is not difficult to tell what, of all the things of this world, one chooses. What you choose determines your heart's desire. Generally speaking, those who choose worldly things—money, fine homes, beautiful garments, jewelry, great real estate holdings, etc.,—are not people who seek the simple truths the Masters teach. There are exceptions to all rules! There are today many great industrialists whose holdings might be worth billions of dollars, yet they are little wrapped up in earthly possessions. Their heart is more in doing things that will enable human beings to work at honest labor and better themselves, than it is in possessing world wealth. Henry Ford is an example. He, to my knowledge, for many years has been an exponent of the Theosophical teachings of the Great Masters. Henry Ford, personally, is a very plain man, ever expressing the higher principles of Light and Love; always seeking to better man's sphere of activity here on earth, and he is fearless in endeavoring to do what he thinks best, irrespective of what public opinion may be about it. Love, Wisdom and Power—in the Light—must be balanced in an individual before he can attain mastery. Power without either Love or Wisdom is invariably destructive.

Seldom in the many years I have been under the direction of the Masters, even during the greatest of trials, was love unseated from my heart. Ten days before David was taken away, while I was bending every possible effort toward seeing and talking to Mr. Ballard, I had an impressive vision or dream. At the time I thought some great being such as the President of the United States was passing; however, I recalled, after David was gone, that a casket clearly seen in the vision was a child's casket. This convinced me then that the Great Being passing over the Great Divide was David. A few days before I left Eureka for Los Angeles David had asked me when we were alone in the lobby of the hotel, "Daddy, if I was to ascend, would I be able to come back and see Anne?" He meant his sister, two years older than he, whom he loved so very much. I replied, "Yes, David, I think you would be able to come back and see her, but I am not sure that she would be able to see you." My answer seemed to satisfy him and he asked me no more about it, but little did I think that he would be ascending so soon. His own Soul-Presence knew, of course, that he was soon to ascend. He was as matter-of-fact about it as any grown-up might be.

I was in Los Angeles a part of June, all of July and up to the 12th of August (the time of David's passing). Just a few days before the accident David was visiting his dear old friend, Mary Todd, who lived in an apartment at our hotel on the third floor. She was a student of the "I AM" principles and loved David more, I think, than anyone in her own family. She told me later how David, while deeply engrossed in some little thing he was playing with on the floor, casually remarked, "No one understands Anne and me." Mrs. Todd, not believing that he could have said what he did, asked, "What did you say, David?" Again he emphatically replied, "No one understands Anne and me." "Well, I understand you, David," she lovingly replied. "No, no one understands Anne and me," he determinedly answered.

To convince you that children sometime, especially some of our children of the New Age, are frequently controlled by their own higher presence, or spirit, I am going to relate another incident regarding David and his parents. In managing the hotel in downtown Eureka we had arranged so that I slept at the hotel most of the time instead of at our home, 2904 "F" Street. One day I was home to see the family when Dorothy and I got into quite an argument about something. One word brought on another, as is often the case between man and wife, until finally we were entirely too heated about the matter to suit David who was nearby. He was upon a chair on his knees leaning over on the dining room table, toying with something in his hand, saying nothing. In fact I had not noticed him near me. Dorothy was out in the pantry washing dishes. I would say something to her, then she would yell back at me. This went on for some time. After a while there was a pause in the word-battle. David leaned over closer to me, so that his mother would not hear what he said, telling me in a half-whisper, "Daddy, if you will stop talking, Mamma will stop."

"David, my Angel Boy," I said, "we will stop right now." And we did. He got down from his chair immediately and went out into the yard to play. That little child had certainly called me down in the most wonderful and loving manner I had ever experienced. A few minutes later I told Dorothy about it. Consequently we both enjoyed a good laugh about it all, after we were through being ashamed of ourselves. "And a little child shall lead them," that wise quotation from the Bible, certainly fit in well for that incident.

As I have previously stated to you, I experienced a prophetic vision about ten days before David's passing. I saw a large harbor in which was a great tall flagpole upon which waved a huge American flag. A rather large row boat came in to shore. I assisted the uniformed sailor place a casket into the boat, then got in with him and he started rowing the boat out toward a large ship. In referring to the occasion I spoke to the sailor, calling him Captain. He replied, "I am not a Captain, I am a coxswain." As we rowed the boat near to the large ship, cannons were fired, which I knew to be in honor of the one passing over the Great Divide. For that reason I had, after I awakened from the vision, thought the President of the United States or some great personage such as he was going to pass on. But later, after David passed, the fact that it was a small casket convinced me that all the grand arrangements were made for his passing, on the inner planes of life, and I knew that it meant he was a great soul to have received such particular attention. This, I might say here, was all proved to me later when I was able myself to visit him in the higher planes of life where he is a Buddha Lord in Nirvana.

Among the children of today we find many re-embodying who definitely belong to the New Golden Age now dawning. Those of us who are able to analyze them learn much of the transcendental laws of life which are to be brought through and manifest among this New Super-Race. David was the youngest of our five children. We have three other boys and one girl. I even was aware of the conception of our first child, a boy, who is now fourteen years of age. I talked to him in the inner planes three months before he was born. I knew then he was to be a teacher of the New Age. I also saw our second child before he was born, another boy who is now thirteen. Our third boy, now eleven, I ascertained on the inner planes, was a German aviator during the World War. It was when he was just a few weeks of age that I held him on my knee, bouncing him up, talking to him and questioning him. I talked to him just as if he understood every word I said, and judging from what took place later, I might be safe in saying he did understand me most thoroughly, although he could not explain what he wanted to tell me, since his physical vehicle was American and he could only talk German, and too, he had not even trained his tongue to speak that. I bounced him about, laughing and talking to him. I recall I said, "Where did you come from, little angel boy?" He would grin and say "G-o-o-o." "Just where did you come from, anyway?" I questioned over and over several times, looking him straight in the eyes. I visualized deeply into his eyes, actually wondering where that little soul had come from, and all he could say was a broad grin and some meaningless "G-o-o-o's."

But I have something more to tell you about that little fellow. I craved so deeply to know where that soul had hailed from that my own higher self made a thorough investigation a night later. I had a marvelous soul-experience. I suddenly found myself over the French-German trenches during the World War. My attention was centered on two airplanes in a "dog-fight" thousands of feet above the lines. One was a German, the other French. They soared about, dodging, leveling shots at each other, see-sawing back and forth for some time, and then suddenly I noticed the German plane was crippled. The pilot could glide the plane, but the engine was out of commission. He was at such high altitude, and being a good glider, took off over Germany, directing his plane at a swift downward angle. I, in consciousness, went right along with the plane, watching it to see where it went. When the pilot had evaded his enemy by quick maneuvering, he cautiously took to gliding more easily and slowly. This continued for several minutes, when I saw the plane suddenly take a dive for the backyard of a beautiful German farmhome. It fell right in the backyard, bursting into flames. A rather large, kindly-faced German woman came to the back door and walked out on the porch. The aviator staggered from the flaming plane. I rushed forward and started to throw my arms around him. I looked into his eyes. They were the same eyes of the little soul I had questioned, "Where did YOU come from?" The woman who came out on the back porch was his German mother. This I knew in my consciousness just as surely as if any physical person had told me. The young man was about 22 years of age, I should judge. He died as the result of the crack-up and flames. He had re-incarnated in our family. Time in the spiritual plane is beyond understanding in our outer consciousness, but I, in my own inner being, was able to go there and see all of that in the akashic or etheric records. When little Edward (that is his name) got to be old enough to talk, he definitely talked with a German accent, and, strange though it may seem, he would eat sauerkraut and different German foods the other children would not touch. We frequently referred to him as our "Little Dutchman" of the family.

Here is an instance where I was able in my ascended body to trace and record those etheric records with such precision and so impressionably that I could bring it all back to my physical or outer consciousness. The eyes have been frequently referred to by writers and poets as the "windows of the soul." This proved to be true in this case. You will find that when you meet your friends and relatives in the spiritual planes, their bodies may appear differently but invariably their eyes are the same, for truly the "eyes are the etheric expression of the soul," as well as they may be simply considered the "windows of the soul." The eyes of a corpse do not have that same spiritual expression. This we know without contradiction.

Another principle brought out in that etheric experience is the fact that an intense desire or love of something will attract you to it, even in consciousness, if for some reason you are not able to go to it in the physical plane or octave of life. Where your heart is there your treasure is, as Jesus is said to have stated. It was my keen desire to know where Edward had lived before he came to my wife and me to live. I knew that we all live before we come to this world. It is just as logical that we lived before we came here as it is that we live after we leave here. The fact is we live eternally. You will one day find that the physical world is but a "side-issue" so to speak, of life. If for some reason or other we happen to lose our physical body, it is quite natural for us to pick up another. We are not complete without it. We live

15

and enjoy other realms and worlds simultaneously while living in this realm. The principal trouble with most of us is that "we are not *all here.*" As Saint Germain, my higher presence, said the other day, "We are all one small body wee, but we are not all up to par." The idea is to bring through to this plane our entire, complete and fully illuminated being—our WHOLE SELF. The WHOLE (HOLY) SPIRIT, the ONENESS OF ALL LIFE, IS GOD ALMIGHTY. We have lived hundreds of times on earth. Each time we build a definite individual spirit with characteristics corresponding to that embodiment. To become fully illuminated we must get all those spirits lined up in a direct channel to GOD, the CENTRAL SUN of all Life. We must get all side-tracks directed toward the MAIN-LINE, and that Main-Line becomes the direct radii to the God-Head, the ALL-FATHER and ALL-MOTHER OF ALL. Your Spiritual Tree has within it every individual spirit you have accumulated since you were first projected into the earth realm from God. This Tree of Life is sometimes alluded to in occult or metaphysical circles as the "Sky-Tree." There is some allusion made to it in the Bible, where it is described as a tree with its "roots in heaven and its branches reaching down to earth." Jesus referred to it when he said, "I AM the vine and ye are the branches." You might think of yourself, your real HIGHER PRESENCE, as being the trunk of your "Life Tree," and your various embodiments are the branches and twigs and leaves. It is the ONENESS of life symbolized in a green living tree that we must understand and utilize if we are to know CHRIST and the FATHER-MOTHER GOD. Love is the ruling principle of mastership. Wisdom and Power are of little eternal and beneficent value without LOVE.

CHAPTER III

The first of January, 1941, I sold the hotel at Eureka, and had a few days previously encouraged Mrs. Westfall to attend the "I AM" convocation in Los Angeles, she having taken the two younger children with her. I went to Los Angeles after the transaction regarding the selling of the hotel was completed, arriving there about the 3rd of January. I found Dorothy in bed sick and unable to attend the classes being held at the Shrine Auditorium. While in the city I gave a brief talk at the Sindelar Studio regarding the ascension of David. Following my talk many of the people in the audience wept, my relating little incidents about Him having touched their hearts, for I so loved Him myself I could not talk about Him without radiating His great Love. While talking on the rostrum there, it seemed I was being bathed in a great stream of liquid light.

Within a few days Dorothy was able to return to Eureka. We moved to Arcata, nine miles north of Eureka to be near Humboldt State College, where Dorothy was determined to continue her studies in the second semester then starting. She attended during January and February, but by the end of February was so nervous and irritable from trying to keep house, going to school during the day and studying at night that I feared she would have a nervous break-down. I encouraged her to stop school and take a trip to Oklahoma to visit her mother and brother. She finally agreed to this. She agreed to take the two younger children with her and I was to take the two older boys with me.

It was during February that I was prompted through a strong inner urge to go to Mt. Shasta. I also had a vision in which I met a feminine being who called herself "Maria." I was walking along a lonely road. A dove came fluttering about in front of me. It seemed to disappear up my sleeve, so I thought, but then, suddenly, there appeared a feminine being right in front of me in a pink flowing garment. I exclaimed as I approached her, throwing my arms around her, "I have not seen you for a thousand years." There was a joy about the meeting I had never experienced before. I began to weep for joy. She rather sternly remarked, "This is no time for weeping; you must go to the assistance of Castro." Immediately I braced up, took a sheet of paper (from where I got the paper I do not know), hurriedly wrote a note on the paper and she disappeared as quickly as she had appeared. While this was going on I seemed to be conscious of possessing greater powers in higher realms of being, and, as was indicated by her, the message I wrote on the paper set a certain being free in a higher plane of life. When I became conscious in the outer octave I could not think of anybody I had ever been close to in this life by the name of "Maria." It was not until the following August that I found who Maria was. She was Mary the Mother of Jesus, and I met her in a human physical body at Mt. Shasta. That is where my most intensive study and instruction actually began.

While my wife was in Oklahoma City I founded a weekly newspaper at Etna, California, Siskiyou County, about thirty miles from Mt. Shasta. The newspaper was known as the Scott Valley Beacon. While on a business trip to Redding, California, on the 29th of August, 1940, I stopped off in Mt. Shasta to see if I could find the author of an article I had read in another paper regarding a Great Master who had been seen to walk forth out of the mountain there. There was certain symbolism referred to in the article that led me to think there was a hidden message within it. I found the author of the article, or instead, I might say, the author found me, for she had been told by a spiritual messenger that I was down on the street in Mt. Shasta and wanted to see her. She was told that it was most urgent for us to meet. She appeared in front of the newspaper office the instant I inquired there. I asked her if she might sit in my car at the side of the street and talk to me regarding the "Mt. Shasta story." She did. We soon discovered we had much in common. It was as though two old friends had met for the first time in many years. I was hesitant in asking her to accompany me on the business trip to Redding, however, I did, and when I asked her she replied, "Yes, I shall. I have nothing urgent to do this afternoon." I had made an appointment with a man in Redding for 2:30 that afternoon and was behind time then, so I was extremely happy to have the lady accompany me.

Yes, that lady turned out to be Mary the Mother of Jesus, but I was not informed of this that day. She went with me to Redding, sat in the car until I finished my business interview with a man there, then we returned to Mt. Shasta. We talked of the mysteries of life constantly during the entire trip going and returning. Little did I realize what that trip meant to me. I realized she was a very enlightened woman, but I did not know that she was the first of the Ascended Masters I was to meet and receive through them the highest possible initiations obtainable on earth through the Great Brotherhoods.

It was less than a week later that I called to see the Mystery Woman, seeking more Light and instruction regarding the Great Mysteries. She was happy to see me. I was amazed to find that she knew all about what I had been doing the past week, even before I told her anything about it. She also told me of certain things that were going to take place in my life. She explained that she had looked into my life-stream, and it did not take her long to convince me that she knew far more about me than I knew about myself. For instance, she explained that the day she had been told to go down town to meet me she had been informed by the Ascended Master messenger that she should hurry. "There is a man down on the street who wishes to see you," he said, "and it is very important for you to see him. He is somebody I love very much. He is Abraham Lincoln."

Now this may seem queer, for I had never seen that lady before in my life, let alone tell her anything of my own conviction that I had been Abraham Lincoln in a previous embodiment, but Ave Maria, as she was wont to call herself, could, I later found, very easily look into your life-stream or "Sky Tree" and tell you much about yourself in your numerous embodiments, clear back, as she said, "when you had funny-shaped faces in very ancient days in the far-distant past." While sitting talking to her I was frequently astonished, when I first began to get acquainted with her, to have her address beings about her who were entirely invisible to me. Those she usually addressed were Koot Hoomi, Jesus, Saint Germain, Archangel Michael, Lord Maitreya, Master Morya and Buddha Gautama. Others she less frequently talked to were Master Hilarion, Serapis (The Egyptian Lord), Anoma of Venus and others whom I do not recall.

I wish to inform you now that Ave Maria does have another name by which she is known in the outer world. Those of you who are familiar with the ways of the Masters know, of course, that they are the most reticent people in the world. They are such perfect actors, so to speak, that you, unless you are "one of them," can no more distinguish one of them from ordinary people than you can fly. I have met several of them in their natural bodies, in bodies of others, disembodied, in visions, dreams, and under all kinds of conditions and circumstances. There is no telling where or how you are liable to meet an Ascended Master. Their greatest interest is lifting humanity into higher and higher planes of consciousness to enable us to establish the Brotherhood of God among the human beings on this earth. They take advantage of every opportunity to do this. The manner in which I met Ave Maria is an example of how one might meet an Ascended Master. For many many years I watched every possible means by which I might catch a glimpse of some new angle of the Truth that I knew to come from the Masters, the Lords, the Gods, the Sons of Almighty God. It was simply through seeing in one small newspaper article a certain revelation symbolized, that I was inadvertently led to one of the greatest Masters of this world— Ave Maria, the Mother of Jesus.

You, seekers after Truth, I must pause for a brief moment to tell how I feel regarding the Masters and their Great Work. It was with hesitancy that I could come forth into the world, telling you of the things I now relate. 'Twas but a few days ago that I was told by the Great Mahatma Koot Hoomi of Shigatse, Tibet, that I was chosen by the Great White Brotherhood, and the Council of the Great White Lodge as the "Chief-Avatar" of the New Golden Age. For several months I had known from indistinct and intuitive revelations from the inner planes of life that I was to carry a sensational message to the outer world from the Great Council, but I dared not think of myself as the "Chosen One" to lead mankind out of darkness. True, I had been conscious of the crucifixion in my etheric body, of the resurrection and the final ascension, when I ascended into the Great Cosmic Center of Life, and felt and experienced the ONENESS WITH THE GREAT SPIRIT, but I knew there were many others who had been through the same experience. Most of those I was associated with, those who had taught me and trained me, were, from all I knew regarding them, older and wiser than I. Why should I be chosen? I asked Koot Hoomi about this. It was my Divine Inheritance, he explained. Not what I have done in this life alone, but what I have done for humanity in my endeavor to free them down through the ages. He stated that I had been faithful to God for thousands of years, that my faith had been unrelenting, that I had for ages struggled to enlighten my less-informed brothers of the race. In my many embodiments, one of which was Lincoln, another Saint Germain, another Shakespeare and John, the Brother of Jesus, I had ever striven to awaken humanity to the Truths of Goodness and the Love, Wisdom and Power of Almighty God. The accumulation in my "Sky Tree" Mahatma Koot Hoomi considered my Divine Inheritance. Blessed Koot Hoomi and the other Ascended Masters of the Great Council have asked me to relate the numerous incidents that have taken place in my life the past year, during the time that I received matchless instruction and training from the Ascended Masters, and they insist that I do it "without reservation."

Now, friends, I wish you to know, definitely, that I do not relate these matters for the purpose of putting myself forward, and I wish it clearly understood that whatever I have received from the Masters is all possible for you to contact and receive. It has been planned by the Great White Lodge that I do this in the manner I am doing it. They have good reasons for having me do it this way. The time has come when the "Truth, the Whole Truth and nothing but the Truth" is to be revealed to struggling mankind. Who will dare stop it? The Great Council has so decreed it. This is the time when ALL LIGHTS MUST UNITE UNDER THE ONE *GREAT LIGHT*. This is the time when all churches, all clubs, all societies, all industrial organizations and all brotherhoods of this world must come together under that ONE GREAT LIGHT. This is the last call to the "Brothers of the Shadow." Those who do not take heed to this pronouncement of Truth and Light "shall be cast out into utter darkness." This is the closing of a manvantara (cycle), and at its completion only the Children of Light shall remain on this earth. We of the Light now hold the balance of power. Love in all its kindly and brotherly aspects shall manifest. "Thy Kingdom, Oh Lord, shall be established on earth." The Golden Age is now dawning.

Those of the "shadow," who plan on the empiric control of all human life on this planet, shall now find that the Brothers of Light are numerous throughout the world. This is the first time in thousands and thousands of years that the Gods of Light hold the balance of Power. Those who know and understand the Great Work of the Ascended Masters see clearly, even in the great war raging in Europe, that the Lords of Love, Wisdom and Power in the Light of Christ do rule this world. Within the next year, 1942, you will see swift-moving changes in the climax in the world's massive stage of activity. The Light of Christ is now penetrating into every "nook and corner" on this old planet. For thousands of years there has been a web of darkness woven about this earth by the sinister forces of evil. Now, with the dawning of the Golden Age, there is woven a Golden Net about the whole planet. Its radiance envelops every person, place, condition and thing in this world. From the center of the earth, invisible to the average person, radiates forth, under the direction of the Ascended Masters and the Great Lords of the Rays, luminous electronic light-substance that now comes forth to the periphery of the planet, making of it a great luminous Sun, dissolving all darkness. This planet is no longer a Dark Star as it was in the past. It has now become a Golden Blazing Sun. All darkness and every "shadowy" being shall be driven out, for they cannot withstand the True Light of Christ. Yes, there are literally millions who claim they know Christ and they call themselves Christians, but the LIGHT OF GOD will prove them to be what THEY ARE. None can hide their dark faces from the Son of God. There are no dark places where they may hide. The dark crypts and dungeons, their damp and musty cathedrals and walled enclosures shall be swept clean by the Light of Christ. The Seven Rays of the Lords of Light, and the New Eighth and Ninth Rays, with their overpowering Light, are now sweeping east and west, north and south, around and about this earth, cleansing, purifying, dissolving everything that is not of the Light of God. Christ Lord Maitreya, the same Great Being who came forth to teach Jesus centuries ago, is my Master-Teacher today. In His Name, in His Light, by the Word from His Mouth, I go forth into the outer world, calling all those who would seek Him. "I am the open door that no man can shut." I am the Chosen One of the Great Brotherhood. I am asked to bring the East and the West together. Krishna, Christ, Buddha, Brahma, all Sons of the One Almighty God, do call all peoples of this world to COME UNDER THE ONE GREAT LIGHT.

CHAPTER IV

The few times I was able to visit my new-found Master-Teacher at Mt. Shasta during the month of September, 1940, were like visiting a Goddess on a distant star. It was almost enough to just sit in Her presence and drink in the Liquid Light from Her radiance. But there was instruction given. Through Her marvelous teaching I began to see the Light beyond the shadows that had seemed to enfold me for a number of years hindering me from expressing the great truths I knew to reside within my heart. I told my wife of my meeting and the instructions I was getting. Yes, she was jealous. At one time during the month when I spoke to her of "the lady at Mt. Shasta," she flew into a rage, and for a few minutes the radiations of jealousy from her mind were terrific. Whenever Dorothy got into a bad state of mind, such as she did frequently, I would never leave her alone until I had somehow brought about peace in her mind. I would talk to her, plead with her, and try in every way I could to bring about peaceful understanding between us before I dared leave home for the office. Under the stress and strain we had to live in for a number of years following the financial crash in 1929, with a large family of five children, all of whom had been born during the short period of seven years, Dorothy was not strong. She worried more about money matters than anything. She was an ideal mother to her children. Their physical and educational welfare was always uppermost in her mind. There never was an evening until the time of Little David's passing that she did not gather the children about her before bedtime and read stories to them, explaining, answering questions, and impressing the higher principles of life upon their impressionable little minds. She was an ideal teacher and a loving mother; however, the heavy trials under which we were both placed, tried her so very much that she became nervous and extremely irritable. For this reason I never once in my life blamed her for any tantrums she brought on herself. Even though I might have lost my temper a number of times, invariably our quarrels were followed by peace-making on my part. Dorothy was extremely stubborn, which is a good quality if used in the right direction. If there were any peace-making to be done it was I who had to do it, which I always did. She was a woman who hid her feelings and emotions. I am one who expresses them openly. I am of the nature to reveal all; to bring out into the open everything, for I know within my heart that we can hide nothing. People who try to hide certain characteristics they possess are apt to develop deceit in their personal nature. The person who is open and frank with you, providing, of course, he is honest, is one from whom you may learn much. The true characteristics of the gods are accumulated as we live and learn through the experiences of the ages. We first came from God, yes, but we were THROWN OUT, as it were, from the LIFE-CENTER through involution INTO the primeval elements of EARTH—Earth, Water, Air and Fire. Then we start on the journey BACK TO GOD, THE FATHER, through evolution. We thus evolve until we are conscious of our own evolution, and then we start to develop. When we become God-Conscious, we actually get right down to "Our Father's Business," and try OUR UTMOST to become LIKE HIM. And, my beloved friend, right then is when you are liable to MEET AN ASCENDED MASTER. I DID. YOU CAN. MY WORDS ARE WORDS OF LOVE, WIS-DOM, AND POWER—ALL IN THE LIGHT OF CHRIST. YOU WHO READ MY WORDS ARE BROUGHT INTO MY HEART OF GOLD. YOU BECOME ONE WITH ME. I AM ONE WITH MY FATHER. THE WHOLE WORLD BECOMES ONE IN CHRIST. CHRIST IS GOD INCARNATE. "AND THE WORD BECOMES FLESH AND BLOOD AND DWELLS AMONG MEN." I AM CHRIST MADE MANIFEST. THOU ART CHRIST MADE MANIFEST. I AM. YOU ARE. BE THOU MADE WHOLE (HOLY). I AM SWALLOWED UP IN THE *GREAT SPIRIT* OF GOD ALMIGHTY. THOU ART SWALLOWED UP *WITH ME*. WE ARE *ONE*. I AND THE FATHER ARE *ONE*. YOU AND THE FATHER ARE *ONE*. WE AND THE FATHER ARE *ONE*. WITHOUT GOD THERE IS NOTHING. WITH THE FULL REALIZATION OF YOURSELF AS THE *SON OF GOD* YOU ASCEND IN CONSCIOUSNESS *TO GOD ALMIGHTY*.

On the evening of September 21, 1940, Dorothy, the children and I had made preparations to go to the Siskiyou County Fair at Yreka. On the morning of the 22nd, however, Dorothy did not get up to get breakfast. This was most unusual for her. I arose and got the breakfast ready for the children. Dorothy had said she was not able to get up. As she had been complaining considerable in recent days I did not think much about it.

While we were eating breakfast Dorothy came into the kitchen, saying she was going to take an aspirin tablet. She felt miserable, she said, and remarked that she was not going to the fair, but would stay at home alone. I rather jokingly replied that "Well, mother, we can have a good time without you," thinking, of course, that she really did not mean to stay at home. She took, I believe, two aspirin tablets, and started back toward the bedroom. My jovial manner didn't set well with her. As she walked through the room where I slept, through which she had to pass from the kitchen to her room in the front of the house, she sorrowfully remarked, "One of these days I'll get a gun and put an end to the whole thing." She walked but a few steps when she gave one shrieking scream and fell to the floor. I ran into the room and undertook to pick her up. It seemed to me that some power had hold of her twisting and shaking her body. I half carried her to her bed. She could not talk. I knew she was deathly sick. I yelled to my oldest son to run and tell Mr. Horn, who lived near us, to phone for the doctor, for we lived at the time two miles out from Etna, California, on the old Horn ranch. Realizing the terrible condition Dorothy was in, I suddenly was overcome with grief, put my arms around her, lay my head upon her breast and wept bitterly. She could hear but could not move. I knew it would not do for me to weaken, but that I must brace up and do all I could. In a few minutes Mrs. Frank Horn came. I was still crying. My pity for her, who was so moved by the scene, caused me to straighten up, gather myself together and face the trying ordeal, no matter how painful it may be. The doctor arrived. He examined the patient, shook his head and stated that there was nothing he could do but wait and see what would happen. After waiting a few minutes Dr. Haynes decided to go back to his office to get some medicine he needed. While he was gone I felt stronger and undertook to heal Dorothy myself, since I had healed her many many times in the past. This time, however, the sudden stroke had so shocked me that I was not in a state of mind to undertake healing her, but during the absence of the doctor and the other people who had been in the room, I drew the Aeth forces from the atmosphere and charged her body with the healing light. She roused, moved her hands, and in a

25

few minutes was able to sit up. We talked about different things, and I tried to cheer her up. I told her that if anything should happen that she was taken away I would take good care of the children. I knew that was her greatest worry. I also spoke to her regarding her statement she had made just before she was stricken. "Dorothy," I said, "let this be a lesson to both of us. Let us try to be kind to each other always. We know better than to say harsh things. We MUST be kind to each other, Dorothy." She agreed that we should do our best to help each other to be good.

Soon the doctor returned. He was much surprised to see the patient sitting up. He had by now made a thorough diagnosis of the case, but did not state just what he understood the disease to be. He left some medicine to take, and said it would be all right for her to eat something should she care to. I fixed some tea and toast for her but she merely sipped the tea once, refusing to eat anything.

About two hours later another stroke came on Dorothy. I was bending over her, she grabbed a pencil from my vest pocket with her left hand. She wanted to write something. I quickly got an envelope for her to write on, but by that time she could not even use her left hand. Her right side had first become paralyzed. She merely got the pencil in position to write, made an unintelligible scribble and then sank back upon her pillow. We sent for the doctor again. When he came he assisted us to place her in his large car which was arranged with a stretcher in the back, and we took her to the hospital at Yreka. Three physicians there analyzed the case, one a specialist in similar attacks, but they did not seem to know definitely what ailed her.

The specialist at the General Hospital at Yreka said Dorothy was unconscious. I knew she was not. About the third day, while talking to her I noticed her eyes moved. She could look up and down, rolling her eyes. I told her to look up for "yes," and down for "no." She immediately looked up and then down, proving to me that she could hear and understand everything I said. When I realized that she had heard the doctors and nurses talking about how it was impossible for her to recover, and how dreadfully sick she was, I shuddered. I asked her if she was in pain. She answered with her eyes, "No." From that time on until she passed, 3:00 A.M. September 30, I talked to her hours at a time. I strengthened her spiritually so she could face the great "passover." I told her the Masters were with her to direct her on into the higher realms of light and love. I talked to her of the children and their interests, and took them a time or two to see their mother.

For nine days Dorothy was paralyzed, yet all that time, up until just a few hours before her death she was fully conscious of everything that went on about her. I knew that the Masters were preparing her etheric body for her ultimate ascension. A few hours after she passed she came to Ave Maria and me in Mt. Shasta in spirit, telling us how happy she was, and remarked, "I would not return for anything in the world." Two weeks later she informed us that she had a thousand students under her instruction in the inner planes of consciousness. She also informed us that we need not worry about her. "I am going right on up," she said.

The remains of Dorothy were cremated at Grants Pass, Ore., and on the Thursday following her passing, services were held in the "I AM" Sanctuary in Eureka, where Mrs. Henrietta Airth directed the last rites. David had previously been cremated at Eureka. We, Ave Maria and I, took the ashes of both to the 8500-foot level of Mt. Shasta, where they were scattered in the presence of the Ascended Masters. But while we were scattering the ashes of the body of David he came in spirit, crying, and told us to save some of the ashes for his sister, Anne, who he said was his Twin Ray. I still have most of the ashes in a copper container in which they had been kept at the Crematory in Eureka. Later David appeared a number of times to his little sister in Mt. Shasta where she stayed with Ave Maria for about a year. During that year Anne was instructed by the Masters, actually went through the crucifixion, resurrected and ascended at the same time that another woman and myself ascended. We had been told by Koot Hoomi previously that there were but four ascensions to take place in the world at this time. This need not discourage the thousands of people who have been misled into thinking that all they had to do was to say a few decrees and they would ascend. One's ascension at this time or any other depends more upon their "DIVINE INHERITANCE" than any other one thing. If you have not "what it takes" in your own "SKY TREE" you had better "go slow" or you are liable to dig up a few incorrigible "spirits" in your own "Tree" that may not be to your liking.

The "Sky Tree" and the individual spirits of your life-stream will be thoroughly explained and symbolized definitely in later chapters of this book. This is the greatest mystery revealed to the outside world in this present age. Jesus might have under-stood these things, I mean from the standpoint of explaining to the uninitiated, but we have so much greater advantages today than He had then to explain Christ to people. We have perfect means of communication and the educational advantages the world now possesses, along with the religious, scientific and phil-osophical expansion in our present-day mass-intelligence, all shall be utilized by the Great Masters and Lords of Wisdom to disseminate the principles of Christ-Consciousness throughout the entire world. The "DOOR" is actually now open, and all who sincerely seek Christ, shall be permitted to be "crucified." *How many are willing to follow "me."* Do you think I, Koot Hoomi, Jesus, Morya, or any other being who ever went through the crucifixion, resurrection and ascension, had an easy time of it? How many times in the past have I been murdered, crucified, shot, tomahawked, and dispatched in various other ways by the ignorant "Brothers of the Shadow?" It is about time the whole truth be revealed to the seekers of Christ and His Light. How thankful I am that the forces of darkness are at last "wiped out." They will now KNOW there are thousands of us IN THE LIGHT. They have no dark caverns in which to hide any more. We and our True Brothers of Light have re-embodied again and again until at last our message of Light, Love, Wisdom and Power has "gone over" to the honest God-fearing people of this world. This is the time when all churches of this world must actually acknowledge Christ, learn of his Infinite Love and Intel-ligence, Wisdom and Light, or they will become empty shells in which the Light of Almighty God is not found. This is the time when all divisions of God's people shall be removed. All must recognize the ONE GOD and come under the ONE GREAT LIGHT. No longer can religion be used as a means of livelihood for lazy wine-bibbers and loud Sunday-morning chatter-boxes. The Greatest Church of all in the future will be God's Great Outdoors, with Nature, and the magnificent Snow-Capped Mountains will be the Towering Cathedrals of His Saints, the Lesser Mountains will ring with the joyous voices of His worshippers, the Golden Sun in the Heavens will symbol-ize the Son of Righteousness (Christ), and the twinkling Stars in the Vaulted Skies, God's candles, are the Lords and Masters of His Infinite Love.

Yes, Brothers of Light, and you who may chance to be just a little "shadowy" yet, I realize just how a great percentage of the people who read this "unheard-of" book will want to crucify me again. I wish to inform you that it isn't at all necessary. I have learned my lessons in "physicality." Do you realize that jealousy is simply proof of one's inferiority? Yes, this is right. The only ones who might wish to crucify me again, in the flesh, are those who are contemporaries of any "New Interpretation of Christ" that might come into the outer world. There are hundreds of thousands of priests and ministers of the gospel as they see and understand it and as they have "sheep-like" been taught by empiric leaders of orders, churches, so-called brotherhoods and ecclesiastical regents-of-Christ, etc., who receive high salaries, live in gorgeously furnished palaces, and have everything their hearts desire, while their lowly followers live poorly clothed, half-starved, misery-soaked and sorrowful lives. The princes in palaces are the crucifiers, the hungered are the crucified. Naturally the crucified will first resurrect, and those to resurrect will be the first to ascend into His Glory—CHRIST. Oh, that those in high places in the empiric world knew of Christ and His Laws of Love, Wisdom and Light! How soon we might change this world from a battlefield of hate into a paradise of Love and Goodwill. ALL LIGHTS UNITED UNDER THE ONE GREAT LIGHT.

Awake, seekers of Truth! Proclaim the laws of Light and Love throughout the world. "Fear not. I am with you always."

Have you, Blessed Friend, ever thought of why they actually crucified Jesus on the Cross? Did it ever occur to you that it was because he looked just like an ordinary person to ninety-nine and nine tenths per cent of those who saw Him? Had they seen Christ, the "SUN" within Him, you know they would not have killed Him. You, Beloved, can never see Christ in me, until you KNOW HIM in your own heart through LOVE.

CHAPTER V

In spite of all that had befallen me in the sickness and passing of my wife, I did not miss editing and publishing a single issue of the Scott Valley Beacon, a weekly newspaper in which I had been able to publish bits of the Great Truth from time to time that certainly pleased my loyal readers. One of the first Ascended Masters to contact me after meeting Ave Maria was Master Koot Hoomi, who is often referred to as Master KH. Almost the first thing he spoke to me about was my little newspaper, and he called me his "Beacon in the West" because of the flashes of Light and Life I frequently published. I soon found that the Great Masters certainly know if and when we do anything which might be efficacious to the Great Work of bringing the world into the Light of Christ.

During the month of October I visited Ave Maria, with whom my little daughter lived, several times. Each time it seemed the Light was expanding within me. When in her presence I was so amazed with the wonderful instructions I received and the radiance of Light about Her that I was almost dumbfounded, however, I must admit, too, that it all seemed to be quite natural. As I have often thought since, there definitely was an air of nonchalance about me that even today I cannot explain. And I do believe had I been anxious about the matter, I should never have received the marvelous revelations I did.

It was along toward the last of October that I began to understand the "modus operandi" of the Ascended Masters or Lords of the Higher Worlds. When I did begin to understand I wondered why I had not known it all my life. And now I know I did understand, but I was not able to "bring it through" to my outer consciousness.

I must explain something to you that is vital to your future instruction and training. Remember, My Beloved, it is your understanding, intelligence and expansion of the Light within you that I am interested in accomplishing above everything. It is of utmost importance to the whole world that every individual Life-Light expand, that we might lift this planet into a New Radiance, the Golden Age.

Here it is. "Ye who have ears to hear," read closely what I am about to tell you. The life in you that feels and knows things is your individual "SPIRIT." Some might call this the soul. Others might think of it as the sub-conscious mind. A mathematician or geometrician may refer to it as the fourth dimensional intelligence; Mrs. Eddy calls it the Spiritual Mind; Emerson spoke of it as the "Over-Soul;" and I could go on and on, giving this elusive Life- and Intelligent-Substance different names that have been placed upon it down through the ages, but still it is the same principle — LIFE — LIGHT-LIFE — A SPARK OF THE ALMIGHTY. I am reminded of a simple analogy I frequently use. "If you have a yellow dog whose name is Rover and you change his name to Sport, he still remains a yellow dog. The name-changing didn't change the dog at all, in color nor in character." Well, changing the name of Christ to Buddha, Brahma, Krishna or any other name, doesn't change the Spirit of the Son of God. All the names that are given to the Third Principle of the God-Head does not change God's Laws one whit. Father-Mother-Son is the Creative Principle—the Triangle of the Godhead.

When you do chance to meet one Ascended Master—one who has ascended in His Higher Body, is conscious of it in His outer body, and knows He has an Immortal Body in Christ, as I AM and have—through that ONE you can easily contact any Master you might choose to meet. This I have proved conclusively to my own satisfaction, I know others who have proved it to their own satisfaction, and for this very reason I was chosen to relate these incidents, happenings, and means of revelation and instruction to you. There have been a great number of men and some women down through the ages who attained Christhood, Sonship with God, and were able to bring it through to their outer or physical senses, but there was not enough general knowledge on the part of the masses of mankind to accept it. In a sense no one is to blame. The evolution and expansion of the mass-intelligence had to come about before this EN-LIGHT-MENT could possibly take place. This is the time. Many of us who are of the LIGHT and have been IN THE LIGHT for centuries and centuries, knew the process of evolution, development and Christ-consciousness had to take place throughout the world, so to speak, before we as Sons of God can come forth without being deliberately killed by the ignorant people of the planet who were greatly in the majority. Thank God, at

31

last, through the marvelous works of Science, along with Religion and Philosophy, the human race now has gumption enough to compare the meagre understanding of the masses at the time of Jesus with the great intelligence of the average man of today. Thank God that we do have religious freedom in the United States, and I, John the Brother of Jesus who became the Christ, can come forth and speak to you of the Christ Lord Maitreya, the Solar Christ to this Universe, and not be again crucified as I have been in the past. I thank God Almighty that our Blessed Scientists are at last proving, through the Electron, the Radio, the study of the Stars, and the many revealing facts of chemistry, that there is a Mighty Intelligence running this Universe. Study that ONE LIFE, Brother, if you would understand God and become HIS SON—Christ Incarnate. There is but ONE LIFE, ONE WISDOM, ONE LOVE, ONE POWER. There are not two wisdoms. How could there be? Remember, as Pythagoras said hundreds of years ago, "All life hinges around the numeral ONE," in other words. I might inform you that Master Koot Hoomi, who was Joseph the Father of Jesus in one age, was also Pythagoras in another embodiment. Thus the Great Ones return again and again, living and dying in the physical octave to help lift the human race up again unto God, the Almighty Father.

So, my friends, I soon found, after I had contacted Ave Maria, and received certain instruction under her, it was quite easy for me to contact almost any of the Great Masters I chose. She became, for my benefit, an oracle, I might say, through which the Divine Wisdom of the Great Gods was poured out to me like an everlasting Spring of the Water of Life and Power, and I was truly bathed in its Glorious Radiance by the Chosen Sons of God themselves.

One evening while talking to Ave Maria, and while looking at her, humbly open to receive the slightest whisper of her blessed wisdom, I noticed her entire countenance changed. Her voice changed, her words were different, the accent absolutely foreign to her nature. Even the eyes were strange and more beautiful. The room took on a radiant glow. I felt an unutterable peace steal in and about us. In awe I sat, almost afraid to breath, thinking the "spell" might vanish should I move. Another being sat before me. Yes, another Ascended Master. A number of times before that there had been changes in Ave Maria, even in Her manner of talking, but this time, all was so changed, I knew not what to expect.

"And who do you think I am?" asked the being before me. "Can't you recall whom I am? I was with you much even hundreds of years ago. I met you in Rome long ago, in Egypt, and other places in the Far East."

I looked more closely at the radiant one who sat near me. Then I noticed reddish, auburn hair, some freckles, and two kindly eyes that were very familiar to me. Distinctly I could see an auburn-colored beard too, and then it dawned upon me I was looking into the face of Jesus the Christ. The Spirit of Jesus Christ was in that temple-body before me. Ave Maria was gone. "Make thy body beautiful, entire and clean that the Gods may dwell therein," came to my mind. There was the sweetest half-smile about His mouth that I had ever seen. I just wanted to sit there, quietly, saying nothing, drinking in the Light and Love of His aura. How gradual the Masters had handled everything so that I would not be too astonished about anything. About two years before I had met Jesus in the inner planes. Yes, we were together in a garden. He would stoop down and write symbols in the smooth earth as He explained various principles of Life and Love to me. At another time years ago I brought back to this outer consciousness that same face when we were digging irrigation ditches in Egypt. We were then brothers, too, I recalled. Now He comes to teach me here in this body, to help me in my ascension back to Our Father. He said little. He sat and looked at me. I looked at Him. He simply radiated His Light, Love, Wisdom and Power into my very heart, into my mind and body. Our individual Spirits were blending into ONE. LOVE RULED. LOVE ENFOLDED US. LOVE CAST A PEACEFUL RADIANT GLOW ABOUT THE ROOM. LOVE'S LIQUID-GOLD BATHED MY WEARIED BRAIN, QUIETED MY TROUBLED HEART, STRENGTHENED MY TIRED BODY AND CAUSED ME TO FEEL THAT *I WAS SWALLOWED UP IN THE GREAT SPIRIT OF ALL LIFE AND LOVE.*

After a few minutes He was gone. He slipped away just as stealthily as He came. Ave Maria returned. She spoke to me of His having been there.

"Now you know," she said, "who has been teaching you a great deal of the time since you came here."

"Yes," I replied, "I now begin to understand. *You are won-*

derful! He is wonderful! All is wonderful! I now begin to see how the Great Masters and Lords work among mankind. Why didn't we know these things in the outer world long ago?"

She then explained to me some of the vital principles regarding the Individual Spirits in one's own life-stream or "Sky-Tree," as it is referred to by the Masters. Ah, Brothers and Sisters of Light, it was so very remarkably and astonishingly marvelous to me to learn these simple, though profoundly magnificent laws of life! Now I knew I was to be supplied the "missing links" in my CHAIN OF WISDOM, I had been working to create and weld together down through the dim and shadowy ages. HOW HAPPY WAS I! Yet, there was that feeling of nonchalance that seemed to be the protective light and radiance about me that enabled me to withstand it all. There was a part of me, as it were, that definitely felt itself equal to any and all beings, Masters, Lords, Gods or Goddesses whomsoever might come to converse with me and instruct me in my outer or physical consciousness. This part of me that FELT EQUAL must have been that part that Abraham Lincoln meant when he said, "All men are created equal." And thus it is. "ALL MEN ARE CREATED EQUAL," but as Saint Germain now says, "All are not up to par." But, Fellow Workers of Light and Love, WE ARE GOING TO BRING ALL WHO SINCERELY SEEK THE TRUTH AND LIGHT OF CHRIST UP "TO PAR."

I must further explain to you now, as Ave Maria and Jesus did to me, how that all the Spirits in your life-stream, are the ones you must "get in line" before you may ascend. As I have intimated to you before, each embodiment in which you lived for ages in the past, as we measure time in the physical world, you created, of your "own free will and accord," the individual Spirits that make up your particular "tree of life." All those Individual Spirits are in your tree, some of whom are merely roosting there, some are more or less active, others are quite dominant, and not a few of them actually want to run everything because of the selfish characteristics they accumulated when they were embodied. Those are the "blacks" who want to force everything in the outer world. Don't think that all the so-called "Black Magicians" are in or about other people than yourself. Anyone, no matter what they think of themselves, who want to "lord it over" others in this world, are of the "Shadow." Any of you who have selfish ideas about your intelligence, wisdom or powers, are not WHOLLY WHITE. Now, do you see where most of your difficulty is? Most of it is in your own "TREE." As some have put it, "In your own backyard." How true!

As an example for you, as I have intimated, Abraham Lincoln is one of the Individual Spirits in my "Life Tree." Well, friends, I must confess to you that I had no little difficulty in getting Lincoln lined up and MASTERED, so that he would peaceably enter the Temple of Love, Wisdom and Power, into which he had been invited by Our Blessed Lord Maitreya. And that is not all, Our Dear Lincoln developed quite a fondness for the Spirit of Ave Maria, and She had to give him to understand that "he had better get into the Temple of Wisdom and stay there until he learned definitely what he should do" if he wanted to assist in the Great Work of establishing the Golden Age upon earth.

Let me explain more fully, if I may, how these Individual Spirits work. They have, of course, a great deal of freedom of their own, yet they are under your control, providing, however, that you are MASTER of the human vessel, the physical body, to which they are spiritually attached. In the same sense there are Spiritual Trees, as it were, which are the Spiritual Ancestral Trees of Spiritual Families. I, for instance, am of the Ancestral Tree of Koot Hoomi, directly speaking, who was my spiritual Father during the time of the Ministry of Jesus. So far as my Spiritual inception was concerned, as well as my Spiritual Antecedents, my physical parents had very little to do with it other than that they were selected as earthly vessels through which entry was made into the physical octave of life. These individual Spirits in your "Tree" have much to do with your intuitive faculties, your moods, your inspirations, your various natural characteristics, and especially your religious and philosophical growth and expansion. They are really your spiritual higher selves, ready and willing to serve you at your bidding, yet, it is through your own self-generated LOVE that you become HARMONIOUS with them and thus they work for you. Therefore, you will see that even the ONE GREAT TREE OF GOD is the ONENESS Jesus referred to so often when He made such statements as, "I and the Father are ONE and the SAME. I do nothing of myself, but by THE FATHER." Again He said, "I am the *vine,* ye are the BRANCHES." Those of us who had ascended before we returned here this time, have a fully developed HIGHER ASCENDED PRESENCE. My Higher Presence is Saint Germain. Yes, He ascended a few generations back, but He has had a few bodies since, even though John, whom He was and is, had been DIVINELY SENT as Jesus was. However, you of the world today, can readily see why John was not accepted at that time. Even today not all narrow-minded religionists will accept the fact that any who ascend become SONS OF GOD in the same sense that Jesus did. Yet Jesus tells you that more than once in the Scriptures, through His Disciples. The people during the time of Jesus—those who did believe him—could not believe there could be more than ONE Messiah. Therefore, John, as His Mother told me last November, 1940, was not accepted because "there was a misunderstanding." You may readily see what the "misunderstanding" was. It was ignorance of the underlying laws of Life, just as today, the people of the world cannot and will not accept more than they can understand. Even Blessed Jesus, My Beloved Brother, when on the cross, said, "Father forgive them for they know not what they do." I, today, might say of those who disbelieve me and hate me "without a cause," "Father forgive them for they know not Thy laws. They are but children. In time they will understand. We shall Love them, teach them, and lead them into the LIGHT OF UNDERSTANDING."

Yes, Brother, you might criticize me for admitting that I am John the Brother of Jesus, that I was Lincoln, that My Higher Presence is Saint Germain, and that My Spiritual Father is Koot Hoomi. I realize that it isn't good etiquette to make such personal statements, as though I'm "blowing my horn" too much. Well, friend, I am not interested in etiquette. I am interested in establishing "Thy Kingdom on earth as it is in Heaven," and I realize that I will have to blow "my horn" MIGHTY LOUD if I out-do MY BROTHER JESUS. There certainly was not anything weak nor timid about Him when it came to speaking for Himself or His Father. Those subtle rules of etiquette by which the "Black Brothers" keep a great percentage of the people of the world in fear, have no power over me, nor any Brother of Light. The only reason most people do not make great claims for themselves is the fact that they have nothing to claim. Everything I have said of myself was first claimed of me by the Great Brothers of the Great White Brotherhood. They "Chose" me. I did not go to them and tell them that I had a "wild scheme" for the salvation of mankind, and put myself up as a "Perfect Son of God." They actually came to me and told me that very thing. They had an awful time convincing me that I was the Great Being they said I was. Now, understand me. I am talking about my Higher Presence, known to the outer world as Saint Germain. I understand there is another fellow over in Europe who claims to be Saint Germain. Well, if he can convince me, Koot Hoomi, Lord Maitreya, Buddha Gautama, Ave Maria, Jesus, Morya, Serapis, Archangel Michael, Anoma of Venus, Joshua and a few others I can mention, that he IS Saint Germain, then I will be willing to believe that he is ME. And I AM HE. I shall expect him to make a visit to America the very moment he hears about this. Yes, MOMENT! I have heard he is a duke of some kind in Hungary or somewhere thereabouts. I shall be glad to meet anybody any time who might think they ARE SOMEBODY, for I am sure there are others now embodied who have been misunderstood just as badly as I have all my life. We Brothers of Light must get together, ALL OF US. There are thousands of us now, but there are other thousands still unaccounted for. Even James, my other brother, is still to be brought into the Light of Christ. Jesus had two brothers, James and John. It was to me that Jesus spoke from the cross, "John, know thy mother." It was I who took care of Mary after Jesus' ascension. For that reason she was able to come to my assistance when I needed help in my ascension. Isn't it wonderful that the great Law of Compensation does endure down through the ages? Truly, "Whatsoever a man soweth, that shall he also reap."

CHAPTER VI

Another vital point in the explanation of the various vehicles we possess are our individual activities with reference to our seven bodies that correspond with the seven planes of consciousness. To me, again, it does not seem important what we might name the seven bodies so long as we understand the divisions of physical, etheric, mental, spiritual, aesthetic, electronic and Christ bodies or grades of consciousness we experience in the ONE LIFE. Vibration is manifest in every form of life. The colors of the spectrum is one example, the octaves of the piano is another, altitude is one; even depth might be considered a fair analogy for explaining vibration, however, electricity is probably the best—or we may say, the electro-magnetic or negative-positive principle that has been analyzed by the scientific physicist. The vibration of waves made by the transmitting or projecting of electricity into the sea of ether enveloping the earth, when a radio message is sent out, is the most definite proof to the mind of the laity of the invisible though tangible forces of the field of electro-nature. The average person who listens to a radio program does not realize the great phenomenon manifesting. Similarly we of today take many marvelous productions of science and invention as mere common-place adjuncts of everyday life. Ordinary minds abhor abstract thinking. A great percentage of human beings cannot concentrate on visualizing things in the abstract. Many of them will actually become nervous and irritated should you talk to them much of such principles. The moment you go beyond the etheric reach of another's mind that one, in order to justify himself, will, in whatever way he can, do his utmost to prove you not more than his equal, and may even try to master you and prove you to be his inferior. It is most natural for all human beings to be EQUAL. Every ONE innately feels his EQUALITY, even though it may be so deeply hidden he gets but a faint glimmer of it in the shadowy recesses of his limited physical sphere. I shall endeavor to clearly explain the seven bodies of man.

Taking the earth as an epitome of the Cosmos, we narrow down the expanse of life to a sphere about twenty-five thousand miles in circumference. The diameter is eight thousand miles. Air, we are told, extends to about forty miles above the earth's surface. Beyond this is ether, a finer element than air, which is claimed by science to fill all space to the uttermost and nethermost, the highest and lowest.

What is the secret of all life and activity? That is the great question of the ages. This has puzzled the greatest of minds, and there has probably been more said about it, written about it, than any one thing that was ever thought of. And yet this secret of secrets lies hidden right in the HEART of man. He, too, is an epitome of God, of the earth, of the universe, of the COSMOS. He is the microcosm, the whole of life and activity is the macrocosm; he is the little world in the immensity of the ALL-WORLD; he is a tiny cell in the great BODY OF GOD, a spark of Light in the luminous sphere of ALL LIGHT.

Relatively, all life is in one MASS-CONSCIOUSNESS. The CENTER of that CONSCIOUSNESS is GOD. The part of that consciousness that reaches farthermost from the Center is the physical atom. You have a body that corresponds to each plane of the WHOLE of GOD'S CREATION. Your physical body corresponds to the physical part of HIM; your outer mentality corresponds to His Lower Mind or Physical Mind; your etheric, astral, or emotional being and body harmonize with the Etheric part of Him; your higher mental body is an extension, in a sense, of His Higher Mentality; your aesthetic or Bliss-Body is in keeping with God's Beauty, Joy, Love and all that is Peaceful and Blissful; your Electronic Body or Fire-Body is like God's LIGHT-BODY, and the Seventh Body, the Christ-Body, is the Radiant Sun of Light, Love, Intelligence and Power of God Almighty. Then you become and ARE the Son of God, ONE WITH HIM in the Glory of His Being. You have always been His Son. Now you are ONCE MORE realizing IT, the I AM. God IS IN YOUR HEART. The Christ-Body is THERE. I AM THAT I AM. I always was and ever shall be. I have a Christ-Body. It is like God's Body.

My greatest desire is to assist all mankind to understand all their Seven Bodies as well as the numerous Spirits that may be in their Life-Tree or Sky Tree. Love is of primary and utmost importance in understanding the abstract planes of consciousness through which God does manifest, even in the physical world. LOVE IS A DIVINE SUBSTANCE. It is the ALL-PERVADING principle by which and through which God works throughout ALL CREATION. Through your Electronic Body you work with Light. Through your Aesthetic Body you work with Love. In your Etheric Body you work with a different form of electricity than you do with your Higher Mental Body, etc. Each body you possess has its corresponding substance or Light-Substance or Essences of God's Attributes. When we understand and have mastered and harmonized all the Seven Bodies we become ONE WITH THE ABSOLUTE — we become, as I AM, a SUN radiating forth Light, Love, Wisdom and Power of our own accord, because of our own Divine Right. I have gone back to the Father IN THE SUN. I still have my physical body, yet, in consciousness I AM ONE WITH THE FATHER-MOTHER GOD. I went into the Cosmic Heart, the ONE CENTER, consciously, and AM in my FULL ILLU-MINATION and CONSCIOUSNESS, ONE WITH GOD.

Beloved friends, the three lower bodies are the ones that cause us all the trouble here in the physical plane. The physical, mental and emotional bodies surely have to be ruled, and every single spirit in your life-stream and every other person with whom you come in contact, have much to do with harmonizing those three lower bodies. The harmonizing, transmuting, regenerating and everything that is essential in ascending to God, must be done right here in the physical body. The physical body you now possess is by far the most important body you have through which you can become a regenerated being. A tree cannot bear fruit without life and the leaves on the tree are the "life-gatherers" through which the intelligence of the "seed" or heart of the tree generates fruit. Your physical body, with your lungs, heart, blood-stream, nervous system and all the other marvelous attributes you possess, are the laboratory in which you, a man, are now BECOMING A GOD. Inasmuch as you become in harmony with God you do become HIM. Therefore, as soon as you get all of your selves and your Seven Bodies in harmony, naturally you become the fully Illuminated Son of God. I have known many fine teachers of transcendental principles who might have finished and completed their work and become ONE IN CHRIST had they not taken for granted as fact that every vision, emanation, psychic experience, etc., they saw, were of the Highest God. The "Dark" forces can only work in and through the three lower bodies. How sad it is when you see those who might otherwise be wonderful beings in the Garden of God's Love, but simply because of their misunderstanding or not understanding the WHOLE of God's Creation, they remain just outside the Temple of Light, Love, Wisdom and Power whose "DOOR" is Lord Maitreya, and I AM His Chief Officer and Representative here in the Earth Plane, through whom all who sincerely seek Truth and Light, may enter and dine with the Gods.

Yes, Love is so essential. Without it you cannot harmonize even your own physical temple, let alone trying to show others what they should do in order to be saved. Yet, so many become conceited and egotistical, thinking they should teach the people of this world. We must become most obedient to the Masters of Light, otherwise we do not receive the higher teachings each of us require, to rise higher and higher, until we do KNOW GOD and become ONE WITH HIM.

I well remember when Lord Maitreya asked me, "Would you like to go into Nirvana?" I knew little about Nirvana. Yet I knew it was something very desirable should one want to aspire to the Highest.

I asked, "How does one go there?"

"I AM THE DOOR TO THE TEMPLE," He explained. "The portal is open to you. You may enter in. I am the Lord of Lords. I will teach you."

"I shall be glad to go to Nirvana," I replied.

"It is the Field of Bliss. There you shall rest in Peace, and you will learn in your Higher Body, in your Higher Presence, many things you wish to know," He answered.

Yes, I went to Nirvana. Much I learned. Some of it, at the time, I brought back to my physical consciousness, but most of it vaguely I recalled. But none of the great Love, Wisdom, and Blissful Experiences I contacted there was forgotten. As I became more harmonious in my three lower bodies gradually it all came through to my outer mind.

For about three days following my entry into Nirvana, I felt rather drowsy and dreamy in my mind. You see, my Spirit was in Nirvana. As we often say, jovially, of course, "I was not all here." And, friends, that is the trouble with most all of us. We are not all here. A great part of ourselves is out somewhere else feeding on the things our hearts most love. "Where your treasure is there your heart is also," as Jesus said. Be sure that your heart is set on the worthwhile things in God's creation. Should you wish to go into Nirvana, there is nothing to fear. Jesus went into Nirvana, into the Field of Bliss, before He could have become the great being He was. If and when we love Christ enough, we are that instant drawn into the higher planes of Light and Love. We are taken into the Temple by Lord Maitreya who is the Lord of Love. I AM the Door.

When Jesus said, "Come unto me, ye who are tired and heavy laden and I will give you rest," He was talking about Nirvana, the Temple of Love, and Lord Maitreya the Lord of Love now invites you to pass through the "DOOR" into His Temple, CHRIST'S TEMPLE, where you shall rest in peace, and learn the Wisdom of the Gods your heart has yearned for such a long, long time. Mount Shasta in northern California has definitely been chosen as "The Mountain of God." From this mountain the Gods do pour forth their Light, Love, Wisdom and Power. The "DOOR" is open to TRUE SEEKERS, but ever closed to those who choose the ways of darkness.

May you, my Brothers and Sisters, ever keep your three lower bodies in perfect harmony, for thus you shall transmute all forces in those bodies into the pure Electronic Substance of Divine Love and it shall all be drawn into the AURA of Lord Maitreya for the upliftment of ALL MANKIND.

You might ask, Beloved, "Who are those that are invited to enter the Temple?"

I, my Beloved Friends of Light, am not an active member of any outer organization or brotherhood. I am a member of the Great White Brotherhood, and I AM A MEMBER OF THE COUNCIL OF SEVEN who direct the activities of the Great White Brotherhood. I am a Priest of the Order of Melchizedek —THE SPIRITUAL ORDER. I am a member of the ILLU-MINATI, the SPIRITUAL ORDER OF THE ROSICRU-CIANS. I am a member of the CELESTIAL LODGE, THE SPIRITUAL ORDER OF THE MASONIC FRATER-NITY. And I can go on and on, naming SPIRITUAL BROTH-ERHOODS without number, almost, of which I am a member. I AM THE DIRECTOR OF THE ACTIVITIES OF THE "WHITE FORCES" ON THE INNER PLANES OF LIFE AND THE "CHIEF AVATAR" OVER ALL TRUE BROTHERS OF LIGHT IN ALL OUTER BROTHER-HOODS SUCH AS THE "UNIVERSAL BROTHER-HOOD." I HOLD THE GREAT SEAL OF "ALPHA AND OMEGA" OF THE EGYPTIAN GNOSTICS. I FEAR NO ONE IN MAKING THESE STATEMENTS. I EVEN KNOW OF ALL THE ACTIVITIES OF THE BROTH-

ERHOODS AND SISTERHOODS OF THE ROMAN
CATHOLIC HIERARCHY, and I AM CHRIST'S TRUE
BROTHER INCARNATE FOR THOSE WHO CHOOSE
THE LIGHT IN THOSE ORGANIZATIONS JUST THE
SAME AS THE OTHERS I HAVE MENTIONED
ABOVE. I AM NO RESPECTER OF PERSONS. I AM
THE TRUTH, THE LIGHT, LOVE, WISDOM AND
POWER OF GOD ALMIGHTY INCARNATE IN EARTH
FOR THE PURPOSE OF LEADING MANKIND OUT OF
DARKNESS INTO THE LIGHT AND UNDERSTAND-
ING OF THE NEW GOLDEN AGE. COME! COME
ALL—ALL WHO SEEK THE LIGHT OF CHRIST, THE
RADIANT SON OF GOD ALMIGHTY. THE DOOR IS
OPEN. LOVE'S LIGHT WILL LEAD YOU ON INTO
THE TEMPLE OF CHRIST.

No, Friends, there is not one single angle of any religion on
earth that I do not understand. When we become ONE WITH
GOD there is nothing hidden from us. In this I mean the wisdom of God and the knowledge of His Divine Laws, and surely
there is not a single principle that any "little man-made church"
on earth might have fostered that God and His Son do not
understand. Beloved, you will be amazed one of these days to
know how ONENESS WITH GOD will solve every problem
you ever thought of.

All outer empirical orders, brotherhoods, fraternities,
churches, groups, organizations, cliques, clans, etc., from the
African Voodoos to the Pope of Rome and the Heads of all
Catholic, Protestant, Jewish or Whatnot national, international
or ecclesiastical, or whatsoever—ALL ARE SUBJECT TO
THE SPIRITUAL HIERARCHY OF GOD. AND THE
GREAT WHITE BROTHERHOOD AND THE COUN-
CIL OF THE GREAT WHITE CELESTIAL LODGE
ARE THE SPIRITUAL AUTHORITY OF GOD AL-
MIGHTY ON THIS EARTH. LET NO MAN THINK
THAT MY WORDS ARE NOT OF TRUTH, LOVE,
WISDOM AND POWER. THOSE WHO QUESTION
SHALL DOUBT. THOSE WHO DOUBT KEEP THEM-
SELVES WITHOUT THE "DOOR." THOSE WHO BE-
LIEVE SHALL FIND ALL AND EVEN MORE THAN
THEY EVER EXPECTED. HEAR MY WORDS, KNOW
THE TRUTH AND THE TRUTH WILL MAKE YOU
FREE. I AM SENT THAT YOU MAY KNOW CHRIST

THROUGH ME. THOSE WHO DOUBT ME SHALL NOT BE RECEIVED BY HIM WHO SENT ME. THOSE WHO ARE NOT WITH ME ARE AGAINST ME. THOSE WHO DO NOT BELIEVE ME DO NOT UNDERSTAND THE TEACHINGS OF MY ELDER BROTHER JESUS. THOSE WHO DO NOT UNDERSTAND JESUS SHALL NOT SEE CHRIST IN ME. THOSE OF YOU WHO KNOW CHRIST IN YOUR HEARTS SHALL READILY RECOGNIZE CHRIST IN ME. CALL ME INTO YOUR HEART AND JESUS CHRIST AND I, HIS YOUNGER BROTHER JOHN, SHALL BOTH COME TO YOU AND BLESS YOU IN THE LIGHT OF CHRIST LORD MAITREYA. WE ARE ALL SONS OF THE ONE FATHER. IF YOU KNOW THE ONE FATHER THEN YOU SHALL KNOW ME, FOR TRULY I AND MY FATHER AND BLESSED KOOT HOOMI, AND ALL THE SONS OF GOD ARE ONE—"ONE BODY WEE"—POURING OUT OUR LOVE-LIGHT TO ALL MANKIND. COME UNTO US AND BECOME ONE WITH US IN CHRIST. "CHRIST" means GOD INCARNATE. "AND THE WORD BECOMES FLESH AND BLOOD AND DWELLS AMONG MEN." THE GODS—SONS OF THE ONE ALMIGHTY GOD — ARE NOW INCARNATING IN EARTH TO ESTABLISH "THY KINGDOM ON EARTH AS IT IS IN HEAVEN"—THE GOLDEN AGE. "FEAR NOT," WE ARE WITH YOU ALWAYS.

All churches must now band together under the ONE GREAT LIGHT. This is their last chance to manifest TRUE BROTHERLY LOVE. If they fail this time, they shall be thrown into utter darkness—those who choose darkness.

CHAPTER VII

During 1937, while managing a hotel in Eureka, Calif., I had, as was my habit, wherever I chanced to be, taught a class or group in Esoteric Christianity, or as I might explain, the secret interpretation of the Holy Scripture. Most of my direct teaching and explaining of these things had come to me through the Rosicrucian Fraternity and the various Brotherhoods which are embraced in its many departments of training, discipline and other activities of service to mankind.

I must say I have been, in the physical plane, as well as the inner planes, the most fortunate individual possible when it came to attracting to myself any and everything I needed for my philosophical development. Truly, I can say that I never more than wished for anything in the way of wisdom, when it would certainly appear on the scene in the form of a vision, inner experience, a physical man, a spiritual man, a physical book, a spiritual book, a fraternal connection, through the Holy Bible, or some other mysterious manner. For the past twenty years nothing has been hidden from me that I desired to know.

Having first read the initial book of the Ballard "I AM" activity in 1934, and other books thereafter, it was in 1938 that I felt I should take a more active part in the OUTER ACTIV-ITY of the organization, since I had taken a great part for a number of years in its formation and activity on the inner planes of consciousness. Frequently I brought back to my outer consciousness the part I was playing in the activity esoterically. I seemed always to be directing such activities in the inner planes. I recall distinctly how I brought through to my outer consciousness the organization and production of a New Age Magazine. This was at the time the "Voice" was first published, a magazine that Charles Sindelar produced under the direction of the Ballards in 1936. I mention this because I wish to explain another startling experience I had with Blessed Charles Sindelar at another time. This I shall explain later. He knows nothing of the things I shall relate in the outer, however he did get all beautifully in the inner.

45

I had a very trying time to become an active worker in the "I AM" organization. I shall relate, in fact produce herewith, a part of the correspondence and other contacts I made in my endeavors to help them. There are other letters, copies of which I did not keep. A great deal of the correspondence I have carried on with "Students of Light" and friends of mine during the past many years I made carbon copies, for which I am now most thankful. At the time I never dreamed they might be useful for publishing in a book. My intention at the time they were written was invariably because when I write to one interested in the LIGHT I become inspired. So frequently I had wished after mailing a letter that I had kept a copy of it, for I found that after my inspirations "cooled down," so to speak, those letters were very interesting and inspiring. Since I left grammar school and the printing office where I set type by hand for several years, I always tried to perfect my writing. This habit of striving for perfection in writing grew on me. Therefore, when I did get to the point where I could write inspiring letters I formed the habit of keeping carbon copies of them. Thanks to the foresight of "Saint Germain," I now have some of this correspondence which was carried on with the Ballards and others of the Light. There were some previous communications before this one I shall now quote, but I shall give you a thorough understanding of the GREAT BATTLE I had in trying to HELP the very ONES who were PRAISING MY OWN HIGHER PRESENCE— SO STRANGE BUT YET SO TRUE:

Saint Germain Press   Central Hotel
P. O. Box 1133   Eureka, Calif.
Chicago, Ill.   Aug. 9, 1938.

Beloved Enlightened Ones:

Before I went to the Shrine Class in Los Angeles, where I received so much good, and where I endeavored to find just what I should do in order to start a class, after having written to Ratana, Box 661, Alhambra, Calif., to whom I was told by Brother Mike Gallagher to write, after having also written to Mr. and Mrs. Ballard without any definite reply, and after having heard conflicting reports on the part of several leaders and students as to just what one should do to start a group, truly, I am at a loss as to know just what I should do. All I can do is to LOOK TO MY PRESENCE, the "GREAT I AM" and do what my heart bids me do.

Do I need to be invested with any authority from somebody to teach the TRUTH I KNOW? Or should I simply start a group, following the work as taught by your messengers, and forget about all human authority?

I KNOW THE LAW . . . I KNOW THE TRUTH AS TAUGHT IN THE "I AM" BOOKS . . . I HAVE EXPERIENCED ALL PHASES OF THE TEACHING . . . SO FAR AS I CAN SEE . . . EXCEPT THE ASCENSION . . . YEARS BEFORE I EVER READ THE "UNVEILED MYSTERIES" AND I DO WANT TO HELP CARRY THE TEACHINGS TO THE WORLD. I SEE THE NEED OF THIS NEW CHANNEL . . . UNADUL-TERATED . . . FOR THE MASSES TO RECEIVE THE TRUTH OF THE "MAGIC PRESENCE." I HAVE LIVED A BOOK NO LESS INTERESTING THAN "UNVEILED MYSTERIES" AND THE "MAGIC PRESENCE" . . . WILL YOU BELIEVE ME WHEN I SAY *I WANT TO HELP YOU?* Will you give me the least bit of an idea as to just how you would want me to start?

I know how to teach—have been a teacher of Esoteric Christianity for the past 18 years, and feel that I can be of great help to you if you wish me to be. I am not egotistical . . . I care not to elevate my personality . . . I do not need to learn more . . . I need to practice what I know . . . and teaching others helps one to do this. Above all I wish to aid struggling humanity . . . a great urge that has welled up within my heart since I was seven years old. I have attracted to me Masters and teachers from all over the world. I MUST go forth to help others.

I have been actively attending group meetings (I AM) in Eureka for the past few months. I first contacted the work in 1934, when a teacher with whom I corresponded (UB) in Washington, D. C., sent me a copy of "Unveiled Mysteries."

Yours in THE LIGHT

(Signed)   NORMAN R. WESTFALL.

(Sanscrit)   (AMSUMATA)

Please write me.

* * *

As early as the middle of the summer, 1936, I had lectured before audiences in Olympia and Bremerton, Washington, on the "I AM." I lectured in a banquet room at the Governor Hotel in Olympia and at the Enitai Inn in Bremerton. This can easily be proven. Ernest Van Walker, Olympia, Wash., was chairman of the meeting there, and my younger brother, D. K. Westfall, and his wife attended the meeting. I mention names merely because I want the world to know that I have nothing to hide. I want all things to come forth into the LIGHT. Should there appear to be an untruth anywhere in this book I want to hear about it.

47

Saint Germain Press   Central Hotel
P. O. Box 1133   Eureka, Calif.
Chicago, Ill.   Sept. 26, 1938.

Dear Friends of the Light:

In reply to your note of no date I am returning the Group Leader Registration card filled out complete, as you required.

At the time I mailed the card in the first place I had not, as is explained thereon, started a group, but I supposed that one had to get some kind of authority, etc., before beginning. I had been told by Mr. Gallagher to start a Minute Men's Group. I had written to Ratana in Alhambra without getting a reply. While at the Shrine Class in Los Angeles I saw Ratana but she was so busy I did not get to go into detail with her regarding the class or group. Since receiving your note and since Mr. Hamilton was here (with Mrs. Deal) from Oakland, I have, following the statement of Mr. Hamilton to "go ahead and start," gotten a group together in cooperation with Mrs. James and Mrs. Airth and Mrs. Connick, all of whom, as you know, are leaders here in Eureka.

There have never been many men interested in the "I AM" here, but now since we have gotten started with the Minute Men's Group, we are gradually getting new-comers, and I am sure, with the great interest all have shown in the work, we are going right ahead.

We sincerely ask your blessing in our undertaking. I have dropped all activity in all other outer work that might interfere with my advancement in the "I AM." I was a member of the old Theosophical Society as long as 16 years ago. I got much good from that study. I was also a student under Dr. R. Swinburne Clymer for 14 years and I must say I learned and experienced marvelous *PROOFS* OF THE *TRUTH* OF THE *GREAT WORK* OF THE MASTERS. I cannot doubt the least bit of the work as set forth in the "Unveiled Mysteries," "The Magic Presence," "The 'I AM' Discourses," "The Ascended Master Discourses" and "Ascended Master Light." They are all inspired books.

I feel that I should tell you why I took up the "I AM" as I have. First the first book, "Unveiled Mysteries," was sent to me by my leader in the "U-B" through whom I received documents from the White Brotherhood.

These documents were wonderful. I learned much from them. I have always sought the Truth; I have never tired of seeking *it*. I have been unusually blessed with proof beyond doubt.

However, I believe Mr. Ballard is the One chosen to lead the people out of darkness. I believe there had to be a new channel created through which the Unadulterated Truth had to be given to the people. I realize why he was chosen, *and I believe if I had proven as strong and good as he, then I might have been chosen for a similar work, for I, too, was under the training of the Masters during the same time he was. I was not chosen*

*for that particular work, but I am willing to keep on trying to help others,
and the good I have in me will come forth some day to help me help others.*

I want you to know that I am for "THE I AM" and I pray that your
faith in me shall not be in vain. I have had transcendental experiences to
prove the I AM. *I have seen some of my past lives.* Now, since a few
days ago, or nights, rather, when I contacted Mrs. Ballard's messenger
(on the inner) as well as Mr. Ballard, himself, and I was told to go
ahead with the meetings, I write this letter. I remain yours,

Fearlessly, in THE LIGHT,

NORMAN R. WESTFALL.

*   *   *

The following letter was the first communication I received
from "The Ballards" accepting me as a Group Leader:

PALMER HOUSE
Chicago

Norman R. Westfall   Oct. 21, 1938
Central Hotel
Eureka, Calif.

Blessed Student of the Light,

Thank you so much for your Group Leader's Registration. We are
indeed glad to call to the "Mighty I AM Presence" of each one and to the
Great Host of Ascended Masters to take full charge of your entire activity,
produce Ascended Master Perfection, hold it Eternally Sustained and
pour forth a Mighty Radiation to Bless all with whom you come in contact.

Noting the reference made in your letter to your previous channels
of study we feel it advisable to call your attention to the need for each
student and more particularly for each Group Leader to be eternally
vigilant that by no chance does any of the instructions received through
other channels creep into their work in this activity.

The instruction given in the books and magazine, as you have com-
mented, is complete in itself. It requires no interpretation or explanation
in terms of any instruction which you may have received in the past. Of
course Saint Germain and the other Ascended Ones under whose radiation
this work is being given forth appreciate fully the great benefits students
have received through their past studies, but They also realize that there
were many mistakes in much of the instruction previously received and
They realize that the human cannot possibly distinguish between that which
is correct and that which is not. They therefore request that in giving
forth this instruction each Group Leader must be meticulously careful to
adhere strictly to the instructions actually given in the books and magazines
and the Discourses of the Ascended Ones.

You will remember that Jesus in His Discourse given Christmas 1935
and printed in the "Voice" for February 1936, urges all sincere students

49

to set aside everything they have studied in the past and stand 100% by their "Mighty I AM Presence" and the Discourses by Saint Germain. May you rest assured there is an important reason for this and in carrying out this, and other similar requests, we ask all Group Leaders to set aside anything that would act as a reference to other sources of instruction, such as use of "Inner Names" and other forms of symbology associated with the other teachings. This must not be taken as any criticism of the wonderful assistance that has been received through other channels; it is simply obedience to Saint Germain's request that this particular channel be used only for giving forth the instructions which it was designed to convey.

We thank you and bless you for your service to the Light and call forth to you the Limitless Directing Intelligence, Strength, Courage and Perfection of your own "Mighty I AM Presence" Eternally Sustained.

Our Love and Blessings enfold you always,

GWB/PBC   (Signed)   THE BALLARDS.

* * *

The above letter, to me, is a wonderful message of advice, even today, after all I have gone through in order to discover WHO I AM. I hold Mr. G. W. Ballard in my consciousness as probably the greatest being I ever met up to His time in the outer octave of life. It is true, no doubt, that he was merely a MESSENGER, but he was the GREATEST MESSENGER the world ever knew up to HIS time. He brought forth a MESSAGE that was the cause or, I should say, the result, of the GREAT COSMIC CAUSE that issued from WITHIN OUT at that time. Had I been more IN TUNE with my OUTER SELF at that time, I would have been chosen as MESSENGER or to cooperate directly with Him. "WHAT-SOEVER A MAN SOWETH THAT SHALL HE ALSO REAP." I never blame another for what "lack" or sorrows may be placed upon me. That is the height of stupidity—to blame others for what we might have to suffer in order to get BACK TO GOD. "God is not mocked." LOVE will lead you to the "threshold" and even on "through the portal" into the "TEMPLE OF THE LORD." Brother Ballard held, in a certain sense, the same position while He was on earth as I NOW HOLD.

I am certain that Mrs. Ballard never attained the height Mr. Ballard had mastered. That was all shown to me on the inner planes at the time of Mr. Ballard's passing. Mrs. Ballard was not to have taken charge of the "I AM" activity. Her son,

Donald, was to be in charge of the outer organization. Mrs. Ballard was left in "a bad way" so far as her "initiations" were concerned. Her husband and "Master-Teacher" was taken from her so suddenly she knew not what to do. She was right in the midst of important steps or "initiations" and trials and tests, and the "Blacks" so called, pounced on her from all sides. She could not distinguish between the "good" and "bad." She had not advanced to that "degree" of mastery where she was MASTER enough to KNOW definitely and be able to bring through to the outer plane the guidance and direction and instruction that the "I AM" students need to carry them on into NEW and Necessary FIELDS of KNOWLEDGE and EXPERIENCE. There was so very much that Saint Germain, Koot Hoomi, Morya, Jesus, Ave Maria and other Ascended Masters wished to bring through to give to the "I AM" students and all True Seekers of Light throughout the world. Far be it from me to blame Mrs. Ballard or any of those BRAVE ONES who undertook to do the very best they knew under the circumstances. If you Blessed Ones who feel like blaming them just HAVE TO BLAME SOME ONE THEN BLAME THE SINISTER FORCES WHO WERE RESPONSIBLE FOR ALL THE TROUBLE. They are the ones who took my little son by placing him in the powerful rollers of an electric wringer. They were the ones who tormented me and my dear wife until she, too, was taken. I have walked through "HELL" many times to rise through seemingly "ETERNAL OPPOSITION" to get where I now stand SERENE IN THE FACE OF WORLDLY TURMOIL. At last I have risen above such trials, and the GODS STAND BESIDE ME TO PROTECT ME FROM ALL HARM.

Of course I do not say I could not be harmed in the physical body, but WOE UNTO THE ONE OR ONES WHO WOULD DARE TRY TO HARM ME. I did not come forth into the world to give out this message of the TRUE ASCENSION until the GREAT MASTERS told me I had their protection. As soon as I knew the GREAT LAW OF THE GOLDEN AGE and brought it through to my physical consciousness, WHEN I HAD MASTERED and they told me "you are now MASTER AMSUMATA," I did venture forth. NOW I AM FREE. I AM MASTER. I HAVE ASCENDED UNTO MY FATHER. MY HIGHER PRESENCE IS

EVER WITH THE FATHER, GOD OF THE GOLDEN HEART, MAHACHOHAN.

Had Mr. Ballard remained a little longer, I dare say, so he could instruct Mrs. Ballard in the few additional "degrees" she was to have been given, she would have become MASTER. In order to be Master, we must know and understand how to use all three—LOVE, WISDOM and POWER, in their perfect BALANCE, and THE GREATEST OF THESE IS *LOVE*. Mrs. Ballard, I shall again dare to say, went too much to the Wisdom and Power—too much to the positive or masculine side to be properly balanced. All her activities following her husband's passing showed this. Had she called to the Master, the Lord of Love, Maitreya, things would have turned out differently for her. Forgive ALL, OH, LORD OF LOVE!

What I am more interested in than any other phase of the Ballard "I AM" activity is getting the essential "next steps" in the Great Initiations to the millions of students who have taken the "first steps." Now there is no one in their organization to take them on "through the door" into the "TEMPLE" of the LORD. There must be the MASTER to take them on "IN." Mrs. Ballard could not do that. She had not finished her own "Initiations." *I know.* During the trying trials Mrs. Ballard was passing through the early part of 1941, while I held the office of Silent Watcher to this world, I was in the presence of Mrs. Ballard more than once, simply for the purpose of analyzing her to see what was essential to her initiatory welfare. I have stood within ten feet of her for long periods of time, analyzing every thought that went through her heart and mind. There is no one on earth nor in heaven who wanted to help Mrs. Ballard more than I, but it was impossible to help her because of her powerful outer mind and innate "stubbornness," all of which are magnificent attributes or qualities if rightly used. Mrs. Ballard definitely went to the glamourous side of life, too, which is diametrically opposed to the ways of the Masters. The Great Masters dress simply but beautifully. They never COMMAND outer persons, or impose their powers in any manner whatsoever upon others. An Ascended Master would never tell one what to do or even suggest anything unless LOVE REIGNED SUPREME IN HIS HEART. I WANT THE WORLD TO KNOW, HOWEVER, THAT I DO NOT THINK OF MRS. BALLARD, DONALD BALLARD OR ANYONE CONNECTED WITH THAT "I AM" ACTIVITY WITH

WHICH THEY WERE ASSOCIATED BUT WITH THE GREATEST RESPECT AND LOVE. THE WHOLE WORLD SHOULD LOVE THEM EVERYONE, THEN THE PERFECT VISION THEY HELD OF THE NEW GOLDEN AGE MIGHT QUICKLY COME INTO MANI-FESTATION AND JOY AND HAPPINESS REIGN THROUGHOUT THIS WORLD. EVERY CONSTRUC-TIVE DECREE THEY HAVE VOICED INTO THE AETHER SHALL MANIFEST. THE SHATTERING AND DESTRUCTIVE DECREES THEY MISTAKENLY VOICED I HEREBY DECLARE *"IN THE NAME AND LIGHT AND LOVE OF LORD MAITREYA"* TO BE TRANSMUTED INTO THE PURE ELECTRONIC SUBSTANCE OF DIVINE LOVE AND DRAW ALL INTO THE AURA OF LORD OF LORDS MAITREYA TO USE AS HE SEES FIT IN THE UPLIFTMENT OF ALL MANKIND.

There is so very much that is to be taught the students first before they can possibly enter the Higher Temple of Initiation that, to us who know, it seems most childish the manner in which many self-appointed teachers have undertaken to "lift" their fellowmen. I, as a teacher, authorized by the True Broth-erhoods since 1925, have never once, to my knowledge, taught anything I had not experienced. I never once hinted to another, that I recall, of ever considering myself a Master, until I was acclaimed "MASTER" by the Great Brothers of the Great White Lodge. Then it was because of the position I was chosen to fill as a "World-Teacher," the "Chief-Avatar," that I did state to the world that I am a "MASTER." And this term, Beloved Students of Light, signifies that I have MASTERED my desires, my passions, my forces, my body, the "four elements" that make up this body and spirit and that I HAVE AS-CENDED INTO THE COSMIC HEART OF GOD AND KNOW THAT I HAVE THAT "CELESTIAL BODY" THAT PAUL SPEAKS OF IN THE HOLY BIBLE. I KNOW THAT I SHALL LIVE FOREVER. I KNOW THAT I AM INDESTRUCTIBLE. I REJOICE IN MY OWN INDIVIDUAL IMMORTALITY. I AM ONE WITH MY SPIRITUAL FATHER. I BREATHE IN AND BREATHE OUT THE GREAT SPIRIT OF LIFE FOR THE PEOPLE OF THIS WORLD. I AM EVEN YOUR—you who read these lines—BELOVED TEACHER, otherwise you would not now be reading them. It is so declared by Christ, Son of the Living God, whom I AM.

The following letter, written by myself to Mr. and Mrs. Ballard in answer to their letter dated October 21, 1938, from Chicago, will clearly show you "where my heart was as well as my treasure":

Mr. and Mrs. G. W. Ballard   Central Hotel
Palmer House   Eureka, Calif.
Chicago, Ill.   Oct. 28, 1938.

Beloved Messengers:

Your letter of acknowledgment of the 21st instant, in that you mention my Group Leader Registration, I make haste to answer, assuring you of the happiness it brought me. Though somewhat belated, I do truly consider it a great blessing, coming from you at this time.

For six months, as you may know, I have striven for this acceptance, having attempted through Mr. Gallagher first, at his suggestion, through Ratana, H. L. Rogers, (at Shrine Class in Los Angeles in July), previous letters to you and Ratana, Leader Hamilton in Oakland, and Mr. Leach here in Eureka—yes, for six months I have tried to get some kind of acceptance such as your letter embraces, and at times I must say I was very discouraged, but at last I AM MOST THANKFUL TO GOD, THE MIGHTY "I AM" PRESENCE, THE ASCENDED MASTERS AND THE HOST OF LIGHT, THAT YOUR BEAUTIFUL LETTER, WITH ALL ITS LOVE AND ENCOURAGING ADVICE, IS AT HAND. It is so lovingly kind I shall always prize it as one of my most valued possessions.

I am reminded of the old Alchemist's advice to the "Fourth Wise Man":

"PATIENCE, PATIENCE, Thou camest into the Desert a vendor of salt; thou mayest go forth an Alchemist, distilling from life's PLEASURES AND SORROWS such sweet Attar in Thy Soul that Thou mayest enter into the CITY OF THY DESIRE."

I am thankful that I possessed the patience that has finally brought to me the loving acceptance I sought. Your suggestions regarding mention of "inner names" etc., or references to other teachings, I sincerely appreciate. Forgive me for having ever misused such. However, Mr. and Mrs. Ballard, is it advisable at any time to refer to you regarding any "inner" experiences we may have had or may have in the future? For instance, just a few days ago I experienced the following, and I believe it may be of importance to you and the work:

I had just retired, relaxed, lying on my back, entirely awake, when a being, apparently similar to "Goddess of Liberty" or some being dressed in long flowing garments, came floating by, from right to left in front and above me. There was just one word spoken—"BE" —and it was spoken like a note of music. The power of the word seemed magnified many times over, and it resounded several times, like you might pluck a string on "your harp," thus:

"BE-E-E-E-e-e-e-"

And it seemed to have the power of materializing whatever I thought of—for instance I seemed to have been thinking of money, thus:

"M O N E Y—BE-e-e-e-e-e-e."

First the sound was very abrupt, musical, and then fading out gradually as the sound of a musical note, and, the peculiar thing about it all was that the "Goddess" or being who spoke the word, came into view and vanished as the sound came and went, with the "E E E E E e e e" resounding as the vision disappeared.

In meditating upon the vision afterwards I associated the word "BE" with "Let there 'BE' light, and there was Light," etc.

I had never before in my life thought of the single word "BE" BE-ing such a marvelous word. BE there. BE now. Beeeeeee— manifest. BE—materialize. BE—harmonious. Come into BE-ing. BE Thou peaceful! BE Thou wealthy! BE Thou Blessed! "BE THOU MADE WHOLE."

"IN THE NAME OF THE MIGHTY 'I AM' PRESENCE" BE Thou and Thine the manifestation of "LOVE, WISDOM AND POWER" in the pouring out of the "LIGHT OF GOD THAT NEVER FAILS." BE E E e-e-e-e . . .

I shall endeavor at all times to see that none of my past teachings in any way "creeps into the work of this activity." I have returned all private books and instruction to my former teacher of certain teachings that might have not harmonized with the Saint Germain teachings.

I had instructions from another source—indirectly through the White Brotherhood, I believe, to take up St. Germain's work—the Universal Brotherhood—as it is called, and since I was first associated with the Theosophical Society in 1922—the old Society, in which Katumah was active, New York City—not the Besant society—I am certain I am to work with you Blessed People, and I look forward to being a worker in the field for you or with you or wherever you see fit to place me. I am particularly blessed with the "power of speech," and I have been able to do marvelous healing in several instances where it was deemed to be essential. Some time I hope you will see fit to converse with me regarding certain experiences I had, for I AM CERTAIN THE TIME WILL COME WHEN I WILL BE ABLE TO HELP YOU AND OTHERS OF MY FELLOWMEN VERY MUCH.

Washington is the Father of our Country—Lincoln freed the slaves, but, as I have jokingly said in the past, "Now, it is up to ME to free the

WHITE PEOPLE." (Reader please note this statement. I then knew that I had been Lincoln, but I had to use the utmost subtlety in referring to this). I have had some startling experiences with Abraham Lincoln— so startling and unusual that I almost fear to mention them—but some time I hope to be able to talk to you, Mr. and Mrs. Ballard, *face to face*, and when I do, at that time, I hope and pray to be able to manifest the "Love, Wisdom and Power" now sleeping within my heart, which I am sure, "WHEN MY TIME COMES," will be used for the benefit of suffering humanity.

Thank you for your Blessing, and may the Blessings of the Ascended Masters be continually upon you and your marvelous son, Donald, in your Great Work for the "establishing of the New Kingdom on earth AS IT IS IN HEAVEN" with the Ascended Hosts of Light.

I send you love from the Eureka Minute Men's Group—though small in numbers—sincere in our work of Love.

On your receipt of this letter I shall expect a manifestation of Light from your heart, Mr. Ballard, such as you experienced with "my heart" at the Shrine Class in Los Angeles. It was marvelous. I felt the Light go from my heart to yours, and it astonished me when you immediately mentioned that you experienced something in your heart you had never experienced before. REMEMBER? God bless you and keep you. I again ask thy blessing. I can see all the activities that had to take place in various realms and spaces before I could actually consider myself "one with you" in the great "St. Germain Work." There was QUITE A SQUABBLE ON OTHER PLANES ABOUT ME AND WHERE I BELONGED IN THE FUTURE WORK ON THIS PLANET. (Students please note). I am thankful I know positively at last.*

Lovingly in the Light,

(Signed)   NORMAN R. WESTFALL.

---

*In connection with my mention of Washington and Lincoln in the above letter, as well as other Lincoln episodes alluded to in other places in this book, I wish to tell you something which proved most startling to me when I first learned of it.

A few days after my wife passed, while talking to Ave Maria, She informed me that Dorothy (My Wife) had been the re-embodiment of John Wilkes Booth. While Ave Maria was telling me this Dorothy was present and first asked Ave Maria not to tell me the truth about it. But Ave Maria said: "Yes, I shall tell him, for he should know the truth about it. It is an instance of the quick reaction of the law, and *the world should know about it.* I know now that you think no less of her because such was the case."

I was told by Lord Maitreya to include this note in the book, since it is proof to me again that "whatsoever a man soweth that shall he also reap." You will recall that just a few seconds before Dorothy was stricken she rather hatefully said: "One of these days I'll get a gun and put an end to the whole thing." The full force of her own remark reacted upon her that instant. Her statement precipitated her physical end, so to speak. I had wondered for years why she suffered so much. She loved me, I know, and I loved her, but so frequently she would wail: "Oh, I feel so heavy —I feel like lead. Oh, Norman, I just feel like I cannot go on." Again she would say, "I feel like I'm going insane." Even years before David was taken from us she

CHAPTER VIII

The aim of this book is to actually "initiate" everyone who reads it into the Great Temple of Light, Love, Wisdom and Power of Almighty God through His Son, Christ Lord Maitreya, a Great Being whose Divine Office is Solar Christ to this Universe.

The publishing of the letters herein produced is to prove to any who might have the slightest doubt, that I state nothing but the TRUTH and the WHOLE TRUTH. Even the transcendental experiences I relate have also been experienced—many of them—knowingly—by others with whom I was associated. All of them, practically speaking, were witnessed—even MY ASCENSION—by a woman who is the re-embodiment of a Great Being whose own physical body is the focusing of "The Jewel of the New Golden Age," the "Bride of Christ," referred to previously in the "First Golden Age Manifesto of the Great White Lodge" as "She Who is Nameless."

Following is a letter to the Ballards, who were the chosen Messengers of Saint Germain, having been written by me in 1938, which explains definitely my background so far as my training and understanding were concerned at that time. You

---

would pass through the most sorrowful spells of suffering. And the more I tried to help her the more it seemed to cause her to suffer.

I want the world to know I do not think any less of my wife because of anything she might have done in any embodiment. I might have done just as bad or worse things to her in some other embodiment. I know now that she ascended through my help and others who are Ascended Masters. Had she not been willing to suffer she would not have been able to "make good" and ascend. May she rest in peace, and may the Love of Lord Maitreya and all the Lords of Light enfold her in their radiance. She was an ideal mother, worked with me wholeheartedly for the incoming Golden Age, and promised me when she was paralyzed that she would continue to assist me in the Great Work I have to do on earth. God bless her.

Dorothy knew of my undying desire to work for Christ. She knew that I had been given the name "AMSUMATA" by the Lords in charge of the Universal Brotherhood as early as 1930. She herself was a member of the Esoteric Brotherhood and was a registered student under Master-Teacher R. Swinburne Clymer, Supreme Master of the Rosicrucian Brotherhood as early as 1918. It may seem strange to you but Lincoln as well as Booth were students associated, I have been told, with Pascal Beverly Randolph, who was Supreme Master of the Rosicrucians as early as 1856.

will notice how wholehearted was my sincere desire to help humanity:

Dec. 1, 1938

Beloved Messengers, Mr. and Mrs. Ballard:

Greetings and salutations—love, Wisdom, Power—and PEACE be with you. And may the blessings of the Ascended Masters abide with you always in your transcendent work for the good of humanity.

Somehow, I feel I am talking to you, Mrs. Ballard. I do not wish to take too much for granted, in you knowing, instantaneously, my innermost desires and aspirations, however; but I am certain you will feel and KNOW the sincerity of my appeal to you.

I *need* your personal help to aid me in the decision I made long ago, even as a child, with myself and God—that I would never deny Him, no matter what happened in my life, and that I would carry the LIGHT to those who seek the LIGHT.

Numerous miracles, visions, light symbols, soul-conscious or higher-mental body experiences, the revelation of some of my past embodiments, etc., have proved to me, Mrs. Ballard, that I know the Truth, for I AM THE TRUTH MADE MANIFEST. I HAVE BEEN UNUSUALLY BLESSED WITH PROOF OF ALL YOU TEACH, or that THE MASTERS TEACH IN YOUR WONDERFUL BOOKS, WITH THE EXCEPTION OF THE ASCENSION. I know that you will believe me; you MUST believe me, for I must carry the message—your message and my message—to millions of doubtful souls in the world today.

I do not fear anything in the world. My life was even threatened years ago by a "Black" who said he came direct from the "head man." He said he would get me if I didn't keep still.

In 1924 an unascended Master (really was ascended) came to me in Olympia, Wash., from Mt. Sinai in Arabia—Kelpa—who, in addition to other teachers I contacted in the outer, taught me, wanted me to carry on his work since he had told me he would soon be passing on (which he did in Seattle). This man—Kelpa—who was John Dew, was an instructor in Oxford University for 40 years—possessor of eleven different degrees of higher learning—was the only man who ever proved to me that he could actually transmute the baser metals (Alchemy) into pure Gold. You probably know of him yourself.

I first contacted Theosophy — the old Blavatsky Lodge — not the Besant group — in 1916 through a man, Wm. E. Mullinaux, in the Ozark Mountains in Independence County, Ark., having become a member-at-large of the original New York Lodge, by recommendation of two old members, in 1922.

I later studied 14 years under Dr. R. Swinburne Clymer, Supreme Master of the old American Rosicrucian Order—the one originated by Dr. Pascal Beverly Randolph—a descendant of one of the signers of the

Declaration of Independence—and he (Dr. Clymer) I do believe, came nearer bringing the Light to the people than any messenger up until you and Mr. Ballard were "chosen" as bearers of the LIGHT. He steadfastly battled the Black Magicians, and, I think, helped make it possible for the Light to come forth for you, me and others. Following my studies with Dr. Clymer I contacted the U.B.—a universal brotherhood that no doubt you know of. I received some wonderful teachings through this source, indirectly from the Ascended Masters . . . and have received, at times, instructions direct from Masters who appeared to me in their finer bodies. They always taught me the higher laws regarding the "Light of God."

In a vision about fourteen years ago (in the higher cosmos) I was told that this Cosmic Light that is coming about through you, Blessed Messengers, would come upon the earth and become so powerful that all evil would be dissolved on this planet. I was told that millions of people would be eliminated, as it were, from this world, because they will not be able to withstand the higher vibration of Light on earth, etc. In classes I taught in Tacoma, Portland, Olympia, Centralia, and other places in the Northwest ten years ago I told my students that the Masters would materialize and come forth to teach the higher laws.

In 1928 when on a railway train going north near Mt. Shasta, on my return trip from a tour of the United States, I sensed the heavenly perfume of the Masters about the Mountain, and told my wife of it on my return to Olympia. I knew, instinctively, there was at least one Master there, anyhow.

Please bear with me, Mrs. Ballard, and hear my brief story, and then you will know how and why I wish so very much to help you in this Great Work. I might mention that I also studied the "I AM" with Chesley, who, as you may know, was a marvelous teacher in her day in Seattle and vicinity. I have a little book she gave me in 1924, with "I AM" on the cover, "I AM the Light," on another page, etc. You probably have seen the little book.

I merely mention these various things because I want you to know that I know the Truth from having studied it most universally as well as having experienced it. When I first read "Unveiled Mysteries" almost four years ago, which book was sent to me by my teacher in the U.B., naturally I recognized it right away as the true bearer of the Light, and the unadulterated Truth as the Masters teach it. Had I not been permitted by a Master to visit my own dear father after he passed on in 1925, in my own higher body, and experienced the unspeakable bliss in the realization of my own immortality, my own indestructibility, and the great joy when I actually felt of that higher Body, glowing as it was with Light and Power,—as I say, had I not experienced such a thing I probably would not believe whole-heartedly in every word that you publish in your books and in "The VOICE," but I can truthfully say I have seen, and

I do not but believe, I KNOW, and because I do KNOW, and because I have studied every one of your books, over and over again, as well as the "VOICE," I hope you will realize my ability to speak freely of the "I AM" without having somebody dictating to me what I should say and what I should not say. I mean there are two or three blessed students here in Eureka, who think that because they have been studying for a couple years they are in the position to dictate to all the leaders just what they should do. This hampers the leaders and the growth of the work. God— the Ascended Masters, St. Germain, and all the Hosts of Light know that I believe in you, Mr. and Mrs. Ballard, as the accredited Messengers of St. Germain. I know St. Germain's teaching is the NEW, UNADULT- ERATED CHANNEL THROUGH WHICH THE LIGHT IS TO BE CARRIED TO ALL THE WORLD. Years ago, when I was editor of newspapers in the state of Washington I prophesied the coming of the Golden Age, I wrote an article one time—in 1931, in which I said the time would come when people would not be able to commit crimes or deceive people because what they planned in their minds would be known before they carried it out. Last week in the new "VOICE" I noticed the same thought is expressed. That day has come when people can no longer deceive.

I have a program on KIEM here in Eureka, Mrs. Ballard, known as "I AM YOUR FRIEND." Now, I do not talk about the "I AM" for I thought some of the students would find fault right away. But what I do wish you to do is to ask St. Germain if I might be a messenger, so that I might be more free to speak of the Light, the Truth, the Ascended Masters and you Blessed Messengers, even as my "I AM" Presence prompts me to express. As it is I feel hampered, and I am sure there is no reason why I should not be able to express myself freely, as long as I declare myself 100% for you, Mr. and Mrs. Ballard, St. Germain and the Ascended Master teachings as published in your books.

Mr. Stickle was here for three meetings last week. He did a marvelous lot of good for our local groups. I do hope and pray, Mrs. Ballard, that you will grant me more freedom, such as He, Mr. Stickle, has. I would love to talk about the "I AM" work as it is published in the books, on my program. Mrs. Mary Todd, my confidential friend and student here, suggested that I do this—that I write to you about it, for she thinks I could do so much to broadcast the "LIGHT" and start smaller groups here in Northern California.

I can submit a copy of all talks I might give if you think it necessary. There is great need of messengers in the field, Mrs. Ballard, and since I have studied for many years with the intention of carrying the message of Light to the world, I shall be one of the happiest persons in the world if you can see fit to sanction my work.

I have asked MY PRESENCE many times to carry my desire to Your Mighty Presence.

Please answer me soon regarding this matter, and I shall immediately set to work in real earnest. May the Peace and Blessings of the Ascended Masters be with you.

Yours in the Light,

Central Hotel   NORMAN R. WESTFALL.
Eureka, Calif.

*   *   *

You who read my reminiscences of these things, and my lengthy correspondence with The Ballards, may know that I realized how very busy they were, but you must understand, My Beloved Friends of Light, that MY PRESENCE (SAINT GERMAIN) was doing every possible thing He could in order to get the Ballards to recognize HIM in this MY OUTER BODY, but for some reason they could not see ME. I do not blame the Blessed Ballards. I know now of even greater than they—even Ascended Masters—who were fooled. This may sound strange and unbelievable, but I shall relate later an instance where this happened. You may know now, however, that it is not so easy for any Master to follow a Spirit Body or Electronic Body to the physical Body that Spirit uses. This is not hard to understand when one realizes that the Spirit is Instantaneous. There are many Ascended Masters re-embodied now. They shall all be gathered together during the next nine years. Those who do not BECOME WHITE AND ASCEND will, I am sorry to say, become Black Masters, those who use their forces destructively. Should they "turn black" they will be annihilated or thrown into a "black compound" to await another evolutionary age or cycle. This may even be, so far as time in our outer consciousness is concerned, a million years, before they will have another opportunity such as now, when CHRIST STANDS AT THE DOOR AND INVITES THEM INTO HIS FATHER'S TEMPLE. The STARS IN THE HEAVENS HAVE MUCH TO DO WITH THIS. THE GOOD *ENLIGHTENED* ASTROLOGERS OF TODAY WILL EVEN PROVE THIS TO YOU. However, do not dabble with astrology. It is most dangerous to the average student.

About Christmas time, following the writing of the letter above, I wrote a letter in the form of a Christmas Greeting to Mr. and Mrs. Ballard, a copy of which I failed to keep. It was, as I recall, a great out-pouring of Love from My Heart to them. Following is their reply to it, an answer I had not expected at all:

THE BILTMORE HOTEL
Los Angeles

Norman R. Westfall   January 2, 1939.
Central Hotel
Eureka, Calif.

Beloved One of the Light,

Love, Light and Blessings as of a Thousand Suns to you and yours eternally sustained!

We want to thank you for your expression of Love and appreciation sent to us this glorious Christmas season.

Remember, that the Love of the students is the tool with which we work and we always offer it all up to the Ascended Masters to amplify without limit, and return it to you as that which is needed most for your Eternal Victory and Freedom.

May the Love, Blessing and Light of the Great Host of Ascended Ones, the Legion of Light and the Great Cosmic Beings enfold you always unto your Ascension.

Lovingly yours in the Service of the Light,

GWB/MK   (Signed)   THE BALLARDS.

*   *   *

You may understand, even as I did, that the heavy mail received by The Ballards, hindered them, of course, from answering many of their communications immediately, and I am also certain that but few of them were answered personally—I mean comparatively speaking. So it was evident to me why I had not yet received a reply from my lengthy letter to them asking for more FREEDOM OF EXPRESSION IN MY TEACHING THE PRINCIPLES OF THE "I AM." Yet, I wrote another letter in answer to their Christmas reply. It follows:

Mr. and Mrs. G. W. Ballard   Eureka, Calif.
c/o Sindelar Studios   Feb. 2, 1939.
2600 So. Hoover
Los Angeles, Calif.

Beloved Messengers of the Light:

May your Individual Love, Light and Wisdom be multiplied each day you work in the service of the Light with the Ascended Masters and the Great Host of Light, until the Light in every human heart expands to glorify God in His Cosmic plan for the Love of all Humanity!

Your beautiful letter—wholly unexpected, but so greatly appreciated—in answer to my Christmas letter to you, I prize as one of my treasured keepsakes.

I did not answer it sooner because I know you Friends in the Light are so very busy, however, the thought came to me, "Even though my letter is never read, I may have the joy of writing it, and I KNOW my thoughts and Love expressed in the letter WILL GO TO THEIR INTENDED DESTINATION, from MY HEART, OVER MY OWN INDIVIDUAL LIGHT RAY TO THOSE I LOVE." I have proved this many times, and I KNOW it is true, our thoughts go out to their intended destination on the WINGS OF LOVE—WHICH IS *FEELING*.

Mrs. Ballard, "I AM" working on a very big business proposition, for which I made a trip to San Francisco last week. Now, I know it is not the proper thing to bring up such among the students in a Sanctuary, but I was told by a student with whom I was talking personally, to at least write you and tell you of the idea and ask your blessing for it, since, if put into operation as I intend, will eventually put about 50,000 people to work, and I have planned, of course, on putting as many "I AM" students to work as possible, for I know any 100% "I AM" student can be depended upon to be sincere, honest and industrious.

So, Mrs. Ballard, although I am, I believe, making great progress in the physical octave as well as in the higher realms, I do sincerely hope for your blessing. I am certain St. Germain gave me the idea, for I asked for a plan whereby I could make use of what talent I have in printing, writing, publishing, radio and newspaper work, (my trade and vocational work) and the most wonderful thing about the idea is that all the things in which I am proficient, dovetail together in the plan evolved. Should I be able to put it over as planned it will be a wonderful publishing project for the future of the "I AM" era or Golden Age, for it has to do with instantaneous record-finding of the inhabitants of America when and after the plan is worked out and completed.

I hope I have not needlessly taken up your time, I am thankful for your kind consideration in the past, and I sincerely hope for your future Friendship in the Light.

May the Blessings of the Ascended Host ever remain with you and yours, and I do hope to be able to see you sometime during the Oakland Class, and if possible, talk to you a bit about the publishing project I plan.

I have made great progress in my class work lately, all of which I am most thankful, and since we are to have Dean and Pauline Sunderland here all next week, I am certain we are to have a great expansion in the Eureka Sanctuary. Classes will be held at Eureka Inn, Feb. 7 to 12, Inc.

Lovingly in the Service of the Light,

(Signed) NORMAN R. WESTFALL.

Then I received a letter—a wonderful letter—from Mr. Ballard himself dated April 6, 1939, in which he answered at least three letters I had written him—ALL IN ONE BEAUTI-FUL LETTER. This proved to me that Mr. Ballard was most sincere, and when he found a student such as I, who was so whole-heartedly interested in the "I AM" activity and the plan of the Masters, he certainly did give him ALL THE ATTENTION ONE MIGHT EXPECT FROM SUCH A BUSY, BUSY MAN. One could not help but love such a being. The letter follows:

CONGRESS HOTEL
Chicago, Illinois

Norman R. Westfall   April 6, 1939.
Central Hotel
Eureka, Calif.

Blessed student of the Light:

The answer to your most recent letter has been delayed because of the great pressure of other matters requiring immediate attention and while we are writing we feel it essential to make some comment regarding your letter of October 28th. Please be assured before you read any further of our love for you and of our appreciation of your sincerity and your determined desire to be of the greatest possible service to the Light.

It is necessary also that we explain to you regarding what is to follow in this letter, that we are in no way concerned about your private life or whether or not you are obedient to the Law of Life in your private activities. In connection with all such matters our only position can be that we explain the Law of Life and cannot then be concerned whether or not the individual is obedient.

However, when the safety of this work is involved, as is the case when the individual is a group leader, then we must make sure that so long as that individual is to receive our approval and support as a Group Leader, they must have sufficient understanding and application of this Instruction as will prevent them from leading the students astray.

We notice that in your letters you still refer to "the old Alchemist's advice," the "Universal Brotherhood," "Kelpa," the "Theosophical Society," "Dr. Clymer" etc., etc. We are taking these names at random from your correspondence just to illustrate the point that apparently you have not as yet divorced your attention completely from older systems of instruction. If you are to remain active as a Group Leader in this activity it is essential that these things be removed entirely from your consciousness. We quoted a definite statement to this effect in our letter of October 21st. If there are those among the students who still want to cling to these old forms of instruction, which were so cluttered up with human concepts and opinions as to still leave the students in relative darkness after all

64

of these years, then such students must of course have the privilege of doing so, but it would be a mistake for us to allow such ones to continue as Group Leaders.

This attitude is not taken on our own initiative, but is based on the requests dictated by the Ascended Ones to definitely regulate this activity.

We note your very great interest in something which you received inspirationally in connection with the word "Be" and can only suggest that when the students have been given the definite accurate instructions of the Ascended Masters Themselves, instructions that are taken down stenographically when given and then printed without any chance of human concepts entering in, we cannot see how they would profit by giving their attention to anything received "inspirationally" through any human channel.

Of course, it is understood that each true Inner experience is of great help to the student on the path, but the danger is, on the one hand, that they accept as true experiences things which are merely incidental or spurious and on the other hand, that they place so great attention and importance upon their own experiences that they fail to do the one thing of most importance, the applying of the Ascended Master Instruction in their daily life.

In your letter of December 1st you say, "I hope you will realize my ability to speak freely of the 'I AM' without having somebody dictating to me what I should say and what I should not say."

While it is quite true that no human being should dictate to you what you should or should not say, yet it must always be borne in mind that the Ascended Masters Themselves have requested that in the Study Group Activity, never, under any circumstances shall any instructions be given except as direct quotations read verbatim from the books and magazines.

It may be difficult for one just beginning the study of this work to understand the perfection of that request, yet we can assure you that when your understanding has expanded and your appreciation for the Perfection of the Ascended Masters' own instructions has become adequate, you will come into full understanding and agreement with it.

In answer to your question about the radio broadcast we must explain that Saint Germain has requested that no one broadcast this instruction over the radio except ourselves personally—a request which we must respect until such time as He might give other instructions.

Messengers are appointed by Saint Germain alone. We never undertake to usurp such responsibility and it is our understanding that it is not Saint Germain's intention to appoint any more Messengers.

We appreciate so much your great enthusiasm and your intense desire to do your utmost to spread this Light, and we would not dim your ardor for anything in the world, but we must call to your attention the need for restraint.

From many expressions and attitudes indicated in your letters, we feel sure that you have much to achieve in the way of understanding of this work and application of it in your daily life before you would be sufficiently stabilized to undertake more than the carefully restricted responsibility of Group Leadership.

Again may we assure you that all of this is written in the most profound love and gratitude to you for your love and devotion to the Light and we know that as you continue with your diligent and dynamic application to your own "Mighty 'I AM' Presence," you will be caused to do all that is necessary in order to bring your mind, being and feeling world into such full Obedience to this Law of Life that you may quickly become a channel through which your own "Mighty 'I AM' Presence" and the Ascended Host can Bless without limit all with whom you come in contact.

Our Love and Blessings enfold you always.

GWB:PBC   (Signed)   THE BALLARDS.

* * *

The above letter was dictated personally by Mr. Ballard, I am sure, and the envelope in which it was mailed, which I still **have, was** addressed in his own handwriting.

CHAPTER IX

For fourteen years I studied the Rosicrucian Mysteries under Dr. R. Swinburne Clymer, M.D., Supreme Master of the associated brotherhoods of the Rosicrucian Fraternity, such as Sons of Isis and Osirus, The Illuminati, the Rose Cross Order, The Magi and Priests of Melchizedek and the Aeth Priesthood. There is no one of all the teachers I have contacted in the outer world from whom I learned more than from Dr. Clymer, and I always, during the many years I studied under him, revered him greatly. I loved him greatly.

However, at times, I am frank to say, Dr. Clymer did not understand me, and for a number of years, because of certain questions arising, there was a feeling of enmity shown on his part, evidence to me of my having transcended him in the field of speculative philosophy. Finally, in 1938, after I had written to him rather sharply because he had—I felt—discussed me too intimately to another of his students—he wrote me that "he wanted to hear of me no more." This saddened me, so after some weeks' reflection of the matter, and realizing at the time that I was not to be long in the outer activity of the world, I wrote the following letter to Dr. Clymer:

Central Hotel
Eureka, Calif.
Mar. 24, 1939.

My Blessed Friend:

May the blessings of the Masters of Light be upon you, and may their Peace and Happiness abide with you. May the Wisdom, Love and Power from the "innermost and uppermost" inspire you, and may your Light so shine and expand that it reaches the "outermost and uttermost" points of being and consciousness as a blessing to all whom it may touch. This is the wish of *"The Radiant One."*

"God works in a mysterious way His wonders to perform." "Judge not lest ye be judged."

In our travels on our return to "Our Father's House" we want nothing left undone that we may do to hasten that long-sought-after homecoming. In the glorious pathway that leads to those "Radiant Ones" whose individual "Lights" ever grow brighter, as we travel on, may we, each of us, tread its blissful course unhampered by the least human mistake that we might have made to with-hold the fulfilment of God's Eternal Truth.

I sincerely believe that my contact with you in this embodiment was just as necessary to the fulfilment and unfoldment of your individual activity as your contact with me was to mine, and IS to mine.

It is not possible, let alone probable, that I might minimize the marvelous work you have done in this world, and in spite of certain statements you might or might not have made to other students of yours, *I AM CERTAIN* it is to the best interests of both of us to remain friendly helpers to each other. I cannot think that I ever had the least thought of hate toward you, in spite of all I might have written you.

I beg nothing of you, Blessed Brother, because I do not feel the need of anything you may have to offer me. Honestly. When I am at one with my Soul, which has always, in this embodiment, been quite easy for me to attain, once I desire it, I have invariably received instruction, and it is probably even true that I have helped you more than you may guess. I do not know.

Confidently, I believe my aid to you is, and has been, just as essential to you as your aid has been to me. Why shouldn't it be that way?

As I look over the vast correspondence I have carried on with you throughout the past fourteen years, I cannot help but realize that probably you were just about as much at a loss to know who I AM—in fact more—than I have been unable to determine your place in the scheme of things. Should we weigh the goodness in your correspondence and the inspiration of my letters to you—measuring one against the other—I dare say mine would far over-balance yours. What is written IS written.

It is quite easy for me—looking at the drama of activities over the above mentioned period of time—to observe that you allowed certain entities influence you regarding me—and you wrote to me and others accordingly. To say that you never made a mistake would be pure egotism.

Let us be thankful that all such misunderstanding has been consumed in the true Light of Understanding (LOVE).

If nothing else, dear Brother, I wish to be your friend, TRULY AND SIMPLY BECAUSE I THINK I CAN HELP YOU, and by helping you I will be helping all mankind.

Please do not mistake my kindness and consideration for something less fitting.

Your Loving Friend in the Light,
(Signed)   NORMAN R. WESTFALL
(SansK)   AMSUMATA.

* * *

It will seem strange to any who reads this correspondence I carried on with Mr. and Mrs. Ballard, the preceding as well as the following, not to ever have had an interview with either of

68

THE NEW GOLDEN AGE

them. I was never granted an interview with either of them in my life. Those of you who study this correspondence carefully, however, will find many essential points of the transcendental laws of life explained, and you can get a good general idea of what goes through one's mind who is about to ascend. I was near the point of ascending, one phase of it having been described by me in the following letter:

Mr. and Mrs. G. W. Ballard   Eureka, Calif.
Murry Hill Hotel   April 17, 1939.
Park Avenue, N. Y.

Blessed Teachers of the Light:

Your long letter of April 6 was and IS such an outpouring of your love and kindly consideration that truly I feel that I can never repay you for it but through becoming as true an example of humility myself in the Service of the Light—"The Light of God that never fails." Thank you, Blessed Ones, for your Great Blessing.

You were, Oh, so considerate of my every question, and I assure you that even before I received your letter, since it had been so long a time since I had first written you—I had received your love and advice through other and more feeling means.

I am trying with all my *HEART* to be just as obedient and helpful as your letter indicated I should BE. Your love I return to you a thousandfold. May the ALMIGHTY GOD BLESS YOU, and may the Ascended Host continually attend your every good and constructive wish.

I am enclosing herewith a prospectus of the new business I am undertaking. The symbol—the geometrical part of it—came to me just a few days before the Oakland Class in February. Where you see the GOLD color I saw a radiant, dazzling Liquid-Gold that streamed through the round disc and struck me in *my heart*. It almost overcame me, and I had the most transcendent feeling of love I ever experienced in my life. It seemed that all the beauty and love in the world was intensified and magnified or concentrated right in that one round disc, and it became more and more radiant until I could stand its radiance no longer—IN MY HEART. It was wonderful.

Please do not take the time to write in answer to this letter unless you feel you should, but I simply had to write you of my appreciation for your marvelous letter. Sometimes, you know, we feel inspired, and in order to give expression to our love, we sit down and write to those who are most in harmony with us. To me, Dear Ones, LOVE IS UNDERSTANDING, and unless I can be with someone or write to someone who understands, life seems so empty.

I have had a rather hard time to become adjusted to the "I AM" but ever since I first read the "Unveiled Mysteries" more than three years ago, I knew, more or less, of the NEW CHANNEL, and, since I had never been able to fully conform to other teachings I had faithfully followed, there was but one thing for me to do—BECOME ONE WITH YOU AND SAINT GERMAIN.

You both seem so close to me at times—and you, Mrs. Ballard—I received such a marvelous radiation from you in the San Francisco Sanctuary the Monday night following the closing of the Class there—and I felt the Light go out from me so powerfully—from my heart and from my brow. (I was definitely conscious of the spirit of Saint Germain in me at the time I referred to in the letter, and she, evidently saw my Higher Presence radiating.)

I am writing to Dean and Pauline Sunderland. God Bless them.

May God bless you all, Sincerely,

(Signed)   NORMAN R. WESTFALL.

*   *   *

The reference made to Mrs. Ballard having noticed me was an instance in San Francisco in which she somehow was attracted to me. She was sitting on the rostrum and I was near the back of the large hall, nevertheless, she caught the radiance from my aura somehow and we exchanged thoughts back and forth for a few seconds. She did not realize that my Higher Presence was Saint Germain any more than I did at that time.

I wish everyone to thoroughly understand how it is easily possible for one to be such a Spirit as Saint Germain in one's Higher "I AM" Presence and still not be aware of it. We are not aware of our Higher Presence until we consciously ascend while in the outer body. I had ascended first in 1925, FELL, so to speak, after I married, then re-ascended in consciousness, bringing it through again to my outer body and consciousness June 4, 1941. Understand, please, the re-ascension did not come about suddenly. I was conscious of many many degrees of initiations received on the inner planes during the interim between my first conscious ascension and my last. And, I must also inform you that I almost daily experience some phase of higher enlightenment and illumination, even yet, and I dare say I shall so long as I continue in a physical body.

Mr. and Mrs. Mike Gallagher were messengers sent forth into the field by Mr. and Mrs. Ballard. Mr. Gallagher had encouraged me to start a group in Eureka in 1938, but somehow, somebody had informed Mike of certain things regarding me (whether true or false I do not know) which he did not fancy, so he gave me a "cold shoulder," so to speak, when he later came to Eureka to lecture. He was quite rude to me in regard to my being an usher at the Woman's Club Hall. Consequently I had to radiate a little light toward him while he was speaking to the audience. This wholly upset him so far as his speaking that evening was concerned. I simply directed the Light from my "All-Seeing Eye" which I knew I possessed. I did it to protect myself, not that I would have harmed him for anything. It was an instance of where the quality he radiated out was multiplied several times over and returned "to its source"—him.

I knew well then that I was to have a great part to play in the "I AM" activity before it was finished, and I did not wish to have anything inharmonious existing between me and any student, so, in order to try to avoid undesirable feelings or trouble of any kind in the future I wrote a letter to Mr. Gallagher and sent a copy of it to Mr. Ballard. The letter to the Ballards I quote first, followed by the letter to Mr. Gallagher, whom I hope and trust is even my friend today, for I send out love to everyone in this world:

Mr. and Mrs. Ballard   Eureka, Calif.
Saint Germain Press   June 8, 1939.
P. O. Box 1133
Chicago, Ill.

Beloved Messengers:

May thou, "Governor of the Cosmic Light," and thou, Blessed Lotus, stand in the "Fullness of His Light," The Radiant One, whom "I AM." (The first time I ever referred to my own Higher Presence to the Ballards.)

I am enclosing herewith a letter I felt impelled to write to Friend Mike Gallagher. It is self explanatory, and I do hope it brings about complete harmony between us, and I decree that "if I have done wrong in this I call on the law of forgiveness for myself and all humanity, that the Perfection of the Ascended Masters may come forth on earth and remain eternally sustained."

Mr. and Mrs. Ballard, PLEASE, may I have an opportunity to see and speak to you just a few minutes during the Shrine Class? I do feel that I can Help Oh, so much, and I pray that you will permit me to talk to you just a few minutes. I have worked hard for many years to bring about the necessary perfection in myself to carry the Light to struggling mankind, and all I ask is an opportunity to go out into the field and work. I implore your advice and assistance in allowing me to "go forth" and "blaze the Light" to those who need the Light. I KNOW I CAN HELP VERY MUCH. There are thousands of small towns and villages in the U. S. that I could work in, and I know there are thousands waiting

71

for me to call on them, for "I AM" ready and I am willing to be a perfect instrument through which the Ascended Masters can work.

Please permit me to see you. I ask it in the Name of the Mighty "I AM" Presence.

May the Blessings of the Ascended Masters be upon you eternally.

Yours sincerely, In the Light,

NORMAN R. WESTFALL.

* * *

Again you will notice how untiringly I tried to get in touch with the Blessed Ballards, but never could I get within a few feet of them. One time during the Shrine Class in Los Angeles, when there were thirty-three of us attended a banquet (Men Group Leaders) at the Biltmore Hotel, I did get to shake hands with Mr. Ballard, and he said, as we shook hands, "GOD BLESS YOUR DEAR HEART." Each one present was asked to say a few words. The principal speakers were Mr. Ballard, Brother Bill, Paul Stickle and Donald Ballard. The best speech of the meeting was made by Donald, whom, I felt, was being controlled by the Spirit of Saint Germain. I had no opportunity at this meeting to speak to Mr. Ballard as I wished to.

Following is the letter written to Mike Gallagher, a copy of which was mailed to Mr. Ballard:

Mr. Mike Gallagher   Eureka, Calif.
c/o "I AM" Sanctuary   June 8, 1939.
133 Powell St.
San Francisco, Calif.

My dear Mike:

I want to thank you again—you and Ann (Mrs. Gallagher)—for the marvelous service rendered the Eureka "I AM" students. We need just such enthusiasm here among the students frequently, and I do hope and DECREE that you will be able to be here for a whole week sometime soon, for then you will be able to see just what we have accomplished here. We do have a very harmonious group of leaders, and I had not realized there had been any inharmony among any students or leaders until you alluded to such in your talk—and then, Mike, frankly, I felt you deliberately acted coldly toward me, which, under the circumstances, hurt me quite sharply. This is about the third time you have done this, and it is my fear, that unless the cause of such personal feeling is consumed, dissolved, annihilated—it might even cause both of us trouble in the future. Will you please tell me what it is so that I can do whatever is necessary to eliminate such a thing, if such exists?

Mike, I am endeavoring to do the very best I can. I hold no grudges against anyone. I send out love to all "I AM" students, and to all beings in all realms and worlds. Since I started as Group Leader here in Eureka, following the written blessing of Mr. and Mrs. Ballard, I feel that individually I have accomplished considerable.

I believe I have been responsible for getting more new students into the "I AM" than any other one person here. A few times when gossip or something between some of the leaders—the cause of which I do not even know—threatened inharmony—I do believe "I AM" the one who brought about harmony—BECAUSE I ENDEAVORED TO BRING THE TROUBLE OUT INTO THE OPEN AND DISSOLVE IT RIGHT THERE AND THEN. That is just what I want to do in our case, Mike.

If there is any particular reason why you should act toward me as you do—I WANT TO KNOW WHY AND I BELIEVE I HAVE A RIGHT UNDER THE DIVINE LAW OF THE ASCENDED MASTERS TO DEMAND THIS.

I mean business in the "I AM." It is no plaything with me. If there is one insincere thought in my mind or being I hope it is instantly consumed in the "Violet Consuming Flame of Divine Love." I KNOW THE LAW, MIKE, AND I BLAZE THE LIGHT TO ALL ALIKE. I SEE THE LIGHT—I FEEL THE LIGHT—I KNOW THE LIGHT—and I do not have to depend upon any personality for the LIGHT OF GOD THAT NEVER FAILS. But in my universal, infinite, cosmic "I AM" being I love all, and I realize my place in the world of action.

And I KNOW that "I AM" one who can help all who may come to me for help, because I stand in the "fullness of His Light" which "I AM."

Forgive me, Mike, if I have done anything for which you think I should ask forgiveness. I call on the law of forgiveness for you, myself and all humanity, that we may realize the fulness of THAT LIGHT, and thus aid ALL HUMANITY in the realization of eternal harmony for all mankind.

I do hope you can see fit to hold a week's class here sometime. I am sure all the leaders here will be only too glad to aid in every way they can. Then I am sure any misunderstanding that might have accrued from past incidents, gossip, misplaced words, or whatever it may have been—will be cleared up. God bless you.

I will be at the Shrine Class, God willing, and I do hope to see you there and have a little talk with you. Will you permit it, Mike?

Lovingly, In the Light,
NORMAN R. WESTFALL.

(To avoid further misunderstanding, I shall mail a copy of this letter to Mr. Ballard.)

*   *   *

Mr. Gallagher did approach me and shake hands with me on the evening of the last day of the class. God bless him.

CHAPTER X

At the time of Mr. Ballard's passing, which was I believe on the 29th of December, 1939, I was in the Central Hotel in Eureka, alone in the apartment we occupied, when I felt a strong urge to give some decrees or affirmations and prayers for Mr. Ballard. I felt he was in dire need of assistance. My wife and two of the children had gone to Los Angeles to attend the Shrine Class of the "I AM." I went into another room on the second floor of the hotel where I felt more secluded and gave a number of forceful decrees for helping Mr. Ballard, not knowing at the time that he was passing from the physical plane.

Even after I got to Los Angeles, about the 2nd or 3rd of January, 1940, I had not heard of the passing of Mr. Ballard. It was some days after that even before I heard of it. Most of the students about the Shrine Auditorium were living in great expectancy. It seems that they thought Mrs. Ballard had some great surprise for them. They had not been told of Mr. Ballard's passing. Later they found that she had expected "Daddy" Ballard to materialize in his tangible body on the stage of the auditorium and speak to the students. A few of the intimate friends of the Ballards knew of his passing. Everything was wrapped in much mystery and the people did not know what had become of Mr. Ballard. Mrs. Ballard and Donald, her son, went on with the classes, allowing the student-body to wonder. In the meantime I had a strange experience regarding Mr. Ballard which I later wrote about to Mrs. Ballard.

I was in one of my finer bodies on the inner planes. I stood by a large framework of a temple. Just the skeleton of the building was erected, the studding, upright timbers, rafters, etc., and a very good foundation had been built. While I stood there silently, Mr. Ballard appeared on the scene, dressed much in the same manner he usually appeared when speaking before the student-body, a full white evening dress suit, with white tie, diamond tie pin, etc. Mr. Ballard did not observe me standing

74

nearby, which proved to me that I was in a higher body than he. Donald, his son, was with him, and he was very hurriedly explaining to Donald what to do about finishing the structure he had started. Mr. Ballard seemed to be in a very great hurry, and after giving certain explanations to his son, which, I knew at the time, had reference to the future development of the "I AM" activity, he quickly passed through the framework of the building and disappeared. I thought he had passed the "Great Divide." I then approached Donald who was very busy working about the foundation of the building. I asked, "May I help you, Donald?" He replied, "No, I've got to hurry. I must put sixteen inches of salt around the foundation of this building." That is all he said, and that is all I brought "through" regarding the experience.

Now, that vision may mean something different to others, but to me it meant that Mr. Ballard, who knew in his Higher Body he was passing, wanted his son Donald to be in charge of the "I AM" activity. He explained certain things to Donald, which he may or may not recall in his outer mind, however, I am certain he will recall them when the proper time comes. The salt around the foundation signifies to me that Donald realizes his inadequate training and development at this time to direct the activity as it should be directed, but he looks well to preserving the foundation of the work until such time as Saint Germain, who was present, is able to come forth and assist him. I am sure it was not Saint Germain's wish that Mrs. Ballard take charge of the activity, otherwise Mr. Ballard would have instructed her instead of Donald on the future of the organization, which was symbolized in the partially constructed building. I am also of the opinion that Mrs. Ballard in her outer stubborn nature, driving out of the organization all who did not agree with her, due principally to her jealousy, so crushed Mr. Ballard that he did not care to endure it any longer, therefore wished to pass on. I dare say, too, that Donald knows whereof I speak, and I believe Charles Sindelar also understands the case.

More and more I felt that I was to have a very active part in the very center of the activity in the outer octave as well as on the inner planes. I had written other letters to Mrs. Ballard asking to be able to help her. The following letter I received from Mrs. Ballard:

75

THE BILTMORE HOTEL
Los Angeles

Mr. Norman R. Westfall January 30, 1940.
General Delivery
Eureka, Calif.

Blessed Student of the Light:

May the Infinite Powers of Light shower you and yours with Blessings and take you forward in the Light.

Replying to yours of January 14th, I do not find it possible to see you personally. With the many duties I have to perform, the world conditions, etc., it is about a man's sized job, and personal interviews are out of the question.

Since our Blessed Daddy is in the Ascended State, He together with Saint Germain are watching over me and mine and these Activities, and I am relying wholly upon my "Mighty I AM Presence" and Their Assistance to guide and guard me and the work.

Thanks for your personal interest, and may your Light expand quickly and lift you into your complete Freedom.

Always in the service of the Light,

EWB/BOM/L MRS. G. W. BALLARD.

* * *

Again you will see that I was refused an opportunity to see Mrs. Ballard. I wanted to talk to her regarding a great number of revelations I had received regarding the "I AM" activity, and most of all, to assist her, because I knew she had more than she could handle, which proved so within a few months after I had written her.

The following letter to Mrs. Ballard, in answer to the one just above, is quite significant, which you will notice:

Mrs. G. W. Ballard P. O. Box 548
Saint Germain Press Arcata, Calif.
P. O. Box 1133 Feb. 11, 1940.
Chicago, Ill.

Blessed "Mother" Ballard:

I return to you, "In the Name of the Mighty 'I AM' Presence," and multiply to you a thousand-fold, all the Blessings you asked the Infinite Powers to shower upon me, in your letter of January 30, 1940.

I realize how very busy you are, Mrs. Ballard, and do not feel at all put out because you were unable to give me a personal interview. However, I did contact you twice on the "inner levels" regarding the one particular thing I wished so much to talk with you about. THIS WAS:

regarding the picture of Blessed David. Everyone who has heard of Him, and especially those who have seen His picture, want a picture of Him. Well, dear Mrs. Ballard, I do not want to deny them a picture, I do not wish to sell them a picture, and I cannot afford to purchase enough pictures to supply one-tenth the demand, so I wanted to ask you if you would not help me solve this matter.

David was especially interested in precipitation and did manifest a number of things, as it were, "out of the blue," and this is an idea that came to me regarding this matter of permitting everyone who desired a picture to purchase one.

I have given Ratana (I AM TEMPLE in Los Angeles) the negative of the picture of David that everybody loves to own. Would it not be possible to allow her to start a "Temple Fund" from the proceeds accruing from the sale of the pictures? I am sure there would be enough money come in within a short time to construct a Temple large enough to accommodate all students at all classes in Los Angeles. The pictures, in various sizes, frames and quality materials, will be very much in demand, and there is, as you know, a very wonderful radiation from the picture.

Wherever that picture goes there will go "David's joy and radiation." I feel that you should handle this, and I shall furnish you with negatives, and every privilege within my power to grant, should you decide upon anything definite.

*   *   *

I hereby give you full privilege to do with this matter whatsoever you may decide for the good of the Great Work in the Service of the Light.

Yours sincerely,

(Signed)   DOROTHY WESTFALL
NORMAN R. WESTFALL

P.S.—Dorothy, my wife, agrees to above and has signed with me.
—NRW.

*   *   *

Mrs. Ballard's reply to the above letter in which I had again offered to help her in her activity from a little different angle, I herewith quote:

THE BILTMORE HOTEL
Los Angeles

Mr. Norman R. Westfall   February 22, 1940.
P. O. Box 548
Arcata, Calif.

Blessed One of the Light:

Thank you for your letter of the 13th, and check for $1.00 enclosed.

I have read your letter carefully and appreciate how you feel and the situation as it is. However I cannot allow these pictures to go forth commercially, nor can we ask Ratana to take charge of such things, for with the many students making the Ascension, the first we know we would be swamped.

While we know a Radiation can be poured through a picture of this sort, we prefer to wait until the pictures of them come forth in their Ascended Master Bodies before offering them to the student body.

We know you will appreciate the position it would place us in, AND I AM SURE IT IS NOT SAINT GERMAIN'S WISH AT THIS TIME. All attention must be directed to the protection of America, and students must not have their attention divided until she is safe.

Please advise what you wish done with the check for $1.00 sent in for this Fund, and please do not send in any to the Saint Germain Press as indicated, for we cannot start such a fund.

Accept my deepest Love and Blessings and know I am doing that which I know is Wisdom for all.

Sincerely in the Light,

EWB:BOM:L   (Signed)   MRS. G. W. BALLARD.

* * *

The letter I reproduce, one I wrote about a month after I had again been refused to help in any way whatsoever in the "I AM" activity that I in My Higher Presence Saint Germain had so LOVINGLY originated, planned and brought through to the outer mind and activity of G. W. Ballard,—I say this letter, which reveals to you and all the world the OVERPOWERING desire I had to carry the "I AM" organization through to the SPIRITUAL SUCCESS it should have been, I now produce, as follows:

"GOD BLESS ANY AND ALL WHO READ THIS."
(Written across top of page)

Box 548
Arcata, Calif.
Mar. 11, 1940.

Mrs. G. W. Ballard
Biltmore Hotel
Los Angeles, Calif.

Beloved Messenger of the Light:

May the Presence of Divine Love be with you at all times, and Eternal Blessings attend you always.

Beloved Mrs. Ballard, I know you must have wondered—you as well as Daddy Ballard—at my eternal persistence, but there is a DEFINITE REASON.

I appreciate very much having received the long letters from Blessed Daddy, which he knew to be vital to my training then, and I somehow believe he knew more about me "individually" than he let me know. If any other in the "I AM" activity did know of my "Individual Presence," then I think it was you. Oh, Mrs. Ballard, believe me! I HAVE SPOKEN TO A FEW PEOPLE OF MY PAST EMBODIMENTS —PROBABLY AT TIMES WHEN I SHOULDN'T HAVE DONE SO. We have all made mistakes. We all need more and more discrimination, wisdom, and all the virtues of the Ascended Host, but, are there none with whom we may speak of "ourselves," our heart's cravings, our plans for activity in the Light, for which I have definitely been trained the past 20 years? OH, PRECIOUS MESSENGER, MRS. BALLARD, FOR YEARS AND YEARS AND YEARS, I HAVE IMPARTED THE *LIGHT* TO EVERYONE WHO CAME MY WAY. Yes, I may have made mistakes—definitely I made mistakes. Who hasn't? But, Blessed One, I have stuck pretty close to the "PATHWAY OF LIGHT," and TRIED AND TRIED AND TRIED.

PLEASE READ ON! Last summer when I so wanted to see Mr. Ballard—before David ascended, I called several times to see Pat Krouse. I went to the Biltmore Hotel again and again. I had had a vision of David's passing. Dear Mrs. Ballard, I do not want to go into detail what I went through. I BLAME NOBODY. I SENT YOU LOVE. I SENT DADDY BALLARD LOVE. I called on the law of forgiveness for myself and all mankind. I would not allow myself to hate anybody. I understand how the sinister force deals with matters such as I wished to talk to you and Daddy about. I knew something was impending as a result of my family association that might be avoided. IT WASN'T. DAVID IS GONE, AND I AM SURE IF THERE EVER WAS AN ANGEL ON EARTH BESIDES JESUS THE CHRIST, IT WAS HE. I knew he was a Master when he was two months old. I had definite evidence I was Abraham Lincoln 14 years ago, too. I have had many proofs of it since and even others had proof of it. That is what I wanted to talk to you and Mr. Ballard about. No one knows my Presence, I believe, better than I. By this I mean human beings. Of course the Great Divine Director, Saint Germain, Jesus and the Ascended Host know about me, just as they do every human being on earth. If they do not know they can easily find out.

Now, dear Mrs. Ballard, you will understand why I have been so very anxious to help you in every way possible. You will realize what a great love I have for mankind; how I have always—especially since coming into this embodiment—wanted to carry the Light to each and every human being on earth. I can give you hundreds and hundreds of proofs of this in magazine articles, newspaper editorials, radio talks, poems (OF MINE) and other evidences of this undying desire to help all mankind.

Again, I offer you assistance in whatever way I may give it.

If you do not need my assistance in your direct activity, then, Mrs. Ballard, I decree, in the Name of the "Light of God that never fails," that you permit me the freedom to go forth, wherever my Presence directs, "in the Service of the Light."

This is all I ask, and I pray Thy Blessing, and the blessing of Saint Germain, Jesus, Nada, the Great Divine Director, Sanat Kumara, Beloved David, "Daddy" and all the Ascended Host.

I am, sincerely, your Servant in the Light,

AMSUMATA   NORMAN R. WESTFALL.

*   *   *

I received, in answer to the above letter, a very bombastic letter from Mrs. Ballard, to the effect that if I didn't settle down and be obedient and quit making wild claims I was liable to go insane, or something to that way of expression. I happended to leave that letter in my auto which I had lost to a finance company in Eureka. When I went back to get it and some other letters I had left in a small compartment in the dashboard of the car they had been removed, therefore I cannot publish the answer Mrs. Ballard wrote to me. However, she has not written to me once since that time. I am not sure it was because I look less like Abraham Lincoln than she looks like Joan of Arc, or whether she feared maybe that Abraham Lincoln might prove to be more popular than she, anyhow, she has never seen fit to write to me again since. I have written to her a few times, and even tried to call her in Los Angeles as late as October 9, 1941. This I do know, MRS. BALLARD CANNOT ENDURE TO HAVE ANY PERSON AROUND HER WHO MIGHT COMPETE WITH HER IN ANY ENDEAVOR WHATSOEVER.

Some years ago, Mrs. Westfall, who was not so gullible as I regarding the Ballards and Ascended Masters, had definitely expressed her opinion of Mrs. Ballard when Mrs. Katherine Rogers, a beautiful singer, was "turned out" of the "I AM" activity by her Highness the Governess. Mrs. Westfall frankly said jealousy was at the bottom of the whole thing. Right she was. This I now know. I do recall that immediately after Mrs. Rogers was barred from the activity Mrs. Ballard ran a number of short decrees (gems) in various places in the "VOICE" magazine for getting rid of jealousy. That jealousy then developed into a terrific blazing fire of fury which destroyed the REAL "I AM" organization. Gradually the "WHITE ONES" were either turned out or quit the organization. Eventually *"SHAT-*

80

TERING DECREES" and all sorts of "BLACK" activities came forth, glaring evidences of the destructive tendencies of the VAUNTED LEADER, Mrs Ballard.*

"Have no fear," you Blessed Children of Light, who were duped into following Dear Little Lotus. You shall reap your rewards for your loyalty, no matter whom you remain with to prove your loyalty. "Whatsoever you sow that shall ye also reap." "God is not mocked."

I shall reproduce the answer to the letter that was lost—the one Mrs. Ballard wrote to me in answer to the letter in which I claimed to be Abraham Lincoln re-embodied. It will give you a clear idea of what Mrs. Ballard wrote to me, since I answered it most thoroughly and to the point. The letter follows:

Mrs. G. W. Ballard   1715 "J" St.
Biltmore Hotel   Arcata, Calif.
Los Angeles, Calif.   Sun., Mar. 31/40.

Beloved Messenger of the Light:

I received your letter the day I left for Oregon, and since I had planned on publishing the small booklet enclosed, (LIGHT OF MT. SHASTA) I delayed replying until I could mail you a copy of it. You are the FIRST to be mailed one, for I wanted you to see it. I hope there is nothing in it that you might find fault with, for it truly comes from my heart, and I want, WITH ALL MY HEART, to help you and Don and the entire staff in every way I can to carry the "LIGHT" to every one possible. I am sure "My Presence" is close to me in this matter.

I have started a small center in Klamath Falls, Ore., (or rather, Group) and have prospects of getting started in Medford and Grants Pass. There are also several interested in the "LIGHT" at Cave Junction. I am sure I can do a lot of good in this way, and I hope the work I have planned is not contrary to anything you might approve.

Of course I want to do what the Ascended Masters have denoted in the books, and I realize that we must, if we are to be FREE, learn to look to our own Presence. I have studied every book and every magazine published—much of the dictated work over and over many times. I have contacted you and Mr. Ballard a number of times on the "inner levels" regarding these things. This you may be aware of or not—I do not know. About nine months ago I met you and Mr. Ballard in a beautiful "field"

---

*In this I refer to the lower bodies of Mrs. Ballard, not her Higher Mental body.—*Author.*

—a rolling pastoral woodland—a few trees here and there—several sheep grazing peacefully thereabouts—wild flowers bedecked the hills—all very wonderful; and we three talked of the "LIGHT." At other times I talked to you and Mr. Ballard alone.

Night before last I stood near Mr. Ballard and Don. Mr. Ballard finished the foundation of a large building, and the frame-work was "raised"—and everything exactly delineated. Mr. Ballard informed Don to "preserve the foundation," etc., etc., and then disappeared. I stood watching Don work for a few minutes, then asked him if he wanted me to help him. He remarked: "I've got to get sixteen inches of 'SALT' clear around the foundation of this building." And Don went on working as fast as he could to get the work on the foundation finished.

Now, Beloved Mrs. Ballard, I have my own ideas about what these things mean, but my head is not "turned" by any such matters, for I have been accustomed to such things all my life. I even talked to our oldest son, Norman, Jr., who is now twelve, before he was born. The little booklet will probably let you know more of my real nature—which —of course, I have had to keep to myself most all of my life. Anyhow— REMEMBER THIS—*should YOU and DON ever need help from ONE who has "no axe to grind" whatever—please call on me.*

Believe me, Mrs. Ballard, I want nothing you have. As to my being or not being Abraham Lincoln, that does not bother me one minute. (THE GREATER THE SOUL THE GREATER THE RESPON-SIBILITY.) However, with the great number of incidents, co-incidences, etc., on the inner as well as in the outer, that have taken place in my life, it would be impossible for me to not think I was VERY CLOSE to "Honest Abe" or was Him, or He did and DOES "overpower" me—or something—who knows? ASK SAINT GERMAIN TO SOLVE IT. Anyhow—let's laugh it off. I believe you were more concerned about the Abraham Lincoln phase of my letter than anything else. Well, that was not essential to me at all, and if you will kindly read the letter again, I believe you will see that you were sidetracked a bit. The main thing is to get the "LIGHT" to humanity.

The "Letter of Love" in the back of the booklet enclosed was written to My Un-Ascended Master (RSC) in 1925. That should answer your question.

Love and best wishes to you and Don and ALL the Staff,

NORMAN R. WESTFALL.
(AMSUMATA)

P.S. I plan on lecturing on "Cosmic Light" in Masonic Lodges, as I am a Mason. I am scheduled to lecture to the Arcata Lodge next week. I have done much lecturing since 1924 on all phases of "LIGHT."

Should you answer this letter please address me to Box 161, Cave Junction, Ore. "God Bless You." (I am sending Mr. Sindelar a Booklet.)—NRW.

*　　*　　*

On the back of the preceding letter to Mrs. Ballard I had written with a pen the following: "Lincoln freed the slaves of the South, but it is now up to us to FREE the so-called White people."

Mrs. Ballard did not answer the above letter. While publishing the booklet, "Light of Mt. Shasta" at Cave Junction, I had a very interesting little incident to happen. It happened at the time, or just a few days previous to my having written the above letter. I printed the booklet, of about twenty thousand words, I guess,—at Cave Junction, a small village in southern Oregon. While working there on the booklet I stayed at an auto camp about a block from the post office building where the printing office was located and the Illinois Valley News is published. I had received quite an inspiration in writing the booklet, and I felt sure Saint Germain was "with me" in the publishing of it. However, I wanted to be sure the Forces of Light were supporting me, so I did what I often do as a matter of corroboration in order to strengthen my own position. I got my Bible and opened it at random and read the first verse my eyes fell upon. This may sound a bit superstitious, but it isn't. There is a definite "law" back of every such incident. I TURNED TO 10th Chapter of Ezra, the 4th verse coming directly under my gaze, and therefore I read: "Arise: for this matter BELONGETH unto thee: we also WILL BE with thee: be of good courage and do IT."

Nothing on earth could have stopped me then, after getting such a marvelous confirmation of my own conviction.

Another unusual thing happened about the time of Mr. Ballard's passing. It was in regard to the long letter he had written to me—the one I mentioned as having been addressed (The Envelope) in his own handwriting. I carried that letter in the inside pocket of my coat for months. Even when I was in Los Angeles for weeks trying to get an interview with Mr. Ballard, I carried that letter with me. I was proud of that letter. I had shown it to a few of my most intimate friends who were students of the "I AM." It was, as near as I can recall, about the time my wife and two children left for Los Angeles to attend the Christmas Class at the Shrine Auditorium in 1940 that I had

83

read that letter over again, and before I put it into my pocket this thought came to me and I penciled it on the back of the envelope, which I now have before me: "EITHER MY LOVE FOR YOU WILL BECOME YOUR TORMENT, OR MY BLESSING THRU YOUR SILENCE, FOR NOW, THAT I NO LONGER LOOK TO YOU, I RETURN TO GOD, FROM WHOM I RECEIVED MY INSTRUCTION BEFORE YOU. BEFORE YOU, *I AM.*"

I had so loved Mr. Ballard, but at last realizing that it was impossible to have him know how much our work was to have been accomplished together, I now KNOW it was MY HIGHER PRESENCE that prompted me to write those few words on the back of this envelope, A POWERFUL DECREE FOR JUSTICE.

CHAPTER XI

It was, as you may recall, the 29th day of August, 1940, that I contacted Mary the Mother of Jesus in a physical body at Mt. Shasta. The following Sunday I returned there to get more "LIGHT" regarding the things I had learned. I had written other letters to Mrs. Ballard which I do not have copies of in my files, and I had received one letter on the inner planes from her, which I have alluded to in the following letter, as well as other interesting phases of the "I AM" activity referred to:

Etna, Calif.
Sept. 2, 1940.

Mrs. Edna M. Ballard
c/o Sindelar Studios
2600 So. Hoover St.
Los Angeles, Calif.

Beloved Mrs. Ballard:

My last letter to you regarding the "Dove of Peace" and the letter you—your Higher Body—mailed to me on the "inner," was evidently ignored. Please, My dear Mrs. Ballard, call to your "Higher Mental Body"—your Mighty Presence—to reveal to you THE ONE WHO IS TO PROTECT YOU DURING YOUR PRESENT TRIALS. Do not take my word for it. Call for the truth to be made known. Guy W. Ballard, in your presence and mine, on the inner plane, in beautiful surroundings—a pastoral scene—told me to protect you. Do you not recall? You, My dear, do have and will have tests and trials until you ascend.

True love is but complete understanding—WHOLENESS. Do you understand me? Would you judge me? Please be careful in your judgments.

Now, please believe me—I plead with you—once more—when I tell you that I was with a Master—whose identity I cannot reveal—just last Friday—in person—in a tangible body—at Mt. Shasta—who asked me to write to you.

My son—BELOVED DAVID—is with Koot Hoomi and Sanat Kumara—particularly with Koot Hoomi. Koot Hoomi, in the presence of the other Master, told me many things I am to do during the next two months. Donald, your son, is the Spirit of the "I AM" activity in the outer octave. During the next twelve months the great change will take place.

You called to Mt. Shasta recently, so this Master told me, for some Master to come and speak from "the platform" to your students. Should

85

such a Master come—would you be able to recognize HIM? Please do not judge others. The masters—yes, THE MASTERS—are much closer to you than you may realize, possibly. However, I do not wish to judge you.

REMEMBER I have written you in the past, "If you ever need assistance please do not hesitate to call me." It was Master Koot Hoomi's desire that I write you. Following the ascension of my son David, I had much to do with the "passing" of your husband, Guy W. Ballard, and there are certain "connections from the past" that must be balanced.

Please believe THE MASTERS whom I have contacted but during the past week—even the Lord (CHRIST) Maitreya—whose loving embrace I am not worthy to claim (yet He embraced me)—do not believe me for myself, but THEM—and KNOW that they are with you, but I AM He who would protect you.

Lovingly,

NORMAN R. WESTFALL.

*   *   *

As you may guess, I received no reply from this letter, and all the time the students, under Mrs. Ballard's direction, were decreeing that the Masters come forth in tangible bodies to speak to them. She—bless her heart—did not then realize that most all the Ascended Masters have physical bodies right here on earth. This is where the "Kingdom is to be established," and here is where the Masters are, to DO THE WORK.

The statement in the above letter, "During the next twelve months the great change will take place," I wish to explain to you. At the time Master KH had made the statement to me I did not know just what was meant. There had been much talk among the "I AM" students due to the Ballards' teachings of a coming cataclysm. This I had thought might be what was alluded to in the "great change." But it was not. The great change that did take place was IN ALL THE GREAT SOLAR AND PLANETARY OFFICES OR PLACES HELD BY THE GREAT LORDS, ARCHANGELS AND GODS WHO GOVERN THIS UNIVERSE. Then, the great war in Europe took on a much worse manifestation, due, we might say, to the cosmic and inter-planetary changes above referred to.

In most prophesies we hear in the outer world there is some basis in truth from which they originate. Frequently I see the underlying truth of otherwise meaningless rumors. For instance, if you recall, there was a great change expected on the 16th of September, 1936. That great change did actually take place and was given wide publicity on the front pages of the leading newspapers of the world through the Associated Press. The matter had to do with a statement from the Pope of the Roman Religious Hierarchy or Roman Catholic Church. I do not say that the canon that came from the ecclesiastical head was "good, bad or indifferent," but I am certain that it was a turning point in the history of the world from the standpoint of the empiric powers in this world. The present war (1941) is the result of the stand the Roman Church took at that time (1936). In this connection here I shall not go into this subject, but in a later chapter, when world conditions, religions, economics and philosophies are explained and remedies offered, I shall discuss the important part the Roman Catholic Hierarchy plays in the GREAT CHANGE now taking place in the world of affairs. As Lord Maitreya has said to me, "EVERY SOUL MUST BE SAVED." All peoples of all the great divisions of the world—all races and all religions—all states and all nations— MUST SEE THE ONE GREAT LIGHT.

Surely the time has come when the Great Religions of the world will SEE THE LIGHT. It is pitiful when we look upon the sad affairs of the outside world. Why do people, religions, fraternities, nations and races fight over things? The FATHER OF ALL LIFE certainly does not want us eternally fighting over earthly things. We so hope that the world at this time, with its wonderful spiritual leadership, will SEE THE LIGHT, and through their Spiritual Illumination and Intelligence build up a WHITE BROTHERHOOD so much more powerful in real UNDERSTANDING than anything Mussolini, Hitler or any other dictator could possibly imagine, that all empiric power shall realize itself absolutely impotent in creating anything but the everlasting WHITE SPIRITUAL HIERARCHY ON EARTH, WHICH IS THE FOUNDATION OF THE THIRD GOLDEN AGE.

Once the Great Leaders of the World realize how the Great Brotherhood actually directs the affairs of this planet, then they will see how simple is the means of directing an economic system that will supply every needy soul on this earth with everything essential for its gradual development and eventual full illumination. Did love reign in even sixty per cent of the souls on this earth HOW EASY IT WOULD BE TO SUPPLY THE MEANS TO CONTINUAL HAPPINESS IN THIS WORLD!

When we, in our individual selves, recognize the ONE GOD and invoke the direction of HIS SON, THE UNIVERSAL LORD and KNOW CHRIST IN OUR HEARTS, we shall not want to buy and sell and make profit on the supplies God has given his children here on earth. Isn't it simple? Then, instead of having Charity Societies, we shall all "LOVE ONE ANOTHER" as Jesus admonished us to do, and what is produced in the world will be "OURS" instead of "MINE." How silly the majority of human beings are, with all their vaunted intelligence! As Cain said, "Am I my brother's keeper?" Every selfish person, even today, is apt to ask of you, "AM I MY BROTHER'S KEEPER?" GOD KNOWS YOU SHOULD BE.

Oh, Brother Mine, you who long for peace and brotherly love to reign throughout the world, look deeply into your heart and ask Christ Lord Maitreya to speak to you. He WILL. I AM HIS REPRESENTATIVE IN THIS EARTHLY BODY. I have spoken the Spiritual Word into the ethers of this planet, and I KNOW that each and every sincere heart does hear MY VOICE. Henceforth you shall have no excuse to say, "I do not know the truth." I have spoken the truth into your heart. Now, should you not heed My Voice, you shall be cast out into utter darkness, for this is the end of the present world cycle, and you are given this "LAST WARNING" to turn within and listen for the "VOICE" of Christ in your heart. "Lo, I AM with you always."

I HEAR THE BELLS OF FREEDOM RINGING FOR ALL THE WORLD AND I KNOW THE BROTHERS OF THE GREAT WHITE LODGE, WHO ARE GOD'S TRUE SONS OF LIGHT, NOW HOLD THE BALANCE OF POWER ON THIS PLANET. SOON ALL SHALL REALIZE WHAT I SPEAK. THE WORD OF AL- MIGHTY GOD RULETH. CHRIST, THE SON OF GOD, IS HERE TO BLESS ALL MANKIND. CHRIST IS GOD INCARNATE. CHRIST MEANS THE EARTHLY SON IN ALL LIGHT AND ILLUMINATION. MY LIGHT I RADIATE TO ALL THE WORLD. I AM COME TO THOSE WHO SEEK ME. I BLESS ALL WHO HAVE FAITH IN HIM (ME). ALL IS NOW REVEALED. THE LIGHT OF CHRIST DISSOLVES ALL DARKNESS FROM THIS PLANET. EVEN THE LEAST SHADOW

UPON THE MOST INSIGNIFICANT BEING SHALL
VANISH BEFORE THE LIGHT OF CHRIST. EVERY
SOUL SHALL BE GARNERED INTO THE GRANARY
OF GOD, THE FATHER. HE NOW CALLS ALL HIS
CHILDREN HOME AGAIN. OUR HOME IS THE
GOLDEN AGE. OUR HOME IN GOD IS THE HIGHER
CONSCIOUSNESS OF TRUE BROTHERLY LOVE THAT
IS THE RULING PRINCIPLE OF THIS GOLDEN AGE.
AGES WE HAVE LABORED FOR THIS HARVEST.
NOW WE SHALL REAP. NOW THE SONS AND
DAUGHTERS OF GOD SHALL KNOW THEIR
FATHER, AND THEY SHALL RECOGNIZE ME AS
HIS SON WHO HAS COME TO SHOW THEM THE
WAY UNTO EVERLASTING LIFE.

THE LORD IS WITH YOU WHEN YOU CALL,
EVEN BEFORE YOU CALL. LORD MAITREYA, IN-
STANTANEOUS IN HIS UNIVERSAL INTELLIGENCE
AND LOVE, ENFOLDS YOU IN HIS LOVE-LIGHT
THE INSTANT YOU THINK OF HIM.

LOVE AND LIGHT

Come away from the crowd to my Temple Hill,
In the land where my Soul dwells apart;
And there let your Soul with Divine Love thrill
From melodies deep in your heart.

Both Love and Light does this Temple fill,
As we gaze on a scene so grand;
The earth's all in tune with God's Own Will,
And He leads us by the hand.

Oh, the sky is blue, and the ocean, too,
And Love shall reign Supreme;
While the troubles of Man, since our World began,
Seem to us but a troubled dream.

—SANNIKRA.

CHAPTER XII

Teachers of the truth are numerous, but few possess the silent wisdom to prove they have the faith that works. When we talk loud of our own knowledge we should feel ashamed for the modicum of demonstrable learning we actually manifest.

A wise man once wrote, "Those who talk do not know; those who know do not talk." What wisdom! An ancient teacher said, "Be still and know that I AM God." And the wisest of all teachers said of His own closest followers: "O, ye of little faith."

Yes, it was Jesus who said that. When we read of the awful time Jesus had to get his closest disciples to understand his simple teachings, I don't wonder that there are many Gods walking among us today who have to have another God to tell them of their own illumination. "Know ye not that ye are the Temples of the Living God?"

It takes little faith to make money. It requires little knowledge to build a material house. With a little confidence you can memorize volumes of wise sayings of others, but it requires faith, knowledge, confidence, hard work and UNLIMITED SACRIFICE to build a Spiritual Temple. IT REQUIRES THE WHOLE MAN. For this reason that wise teacher, Jesus, said, "Ye cannot serve two masters."

Too many of our so-called wise men of today—would-be teachers—are hard at work trying to serve two masters. They accomplish neither. They love to talk about God, Jesus Christ, the Truth, and repeat the beautiful sayings that were coined by our wise, good teachers of the past, but when it comes to actually manifesting the least of those good works they prove to have very "little faith." They deny themselves nothing. They sleep in soft feathery beds, sit in over-stuffed chairs, take joy rides in their luxurious chariots, and occasionally spout off a few ancient phrases that are certain to tickle the ears of their hard-hearing devotees. They are paid much more than "forty pieces of silver."

Jesus loved His enemies, but He spoke burning words in condemnation of the "money-changers" in the temple. He was no coward. He hewed straight to the line of truth and "let the chips fall where they would." There was no sham about Him.

He spoke not words to please people; He spoke the spiritual words of the Father to displease the hypocrites. He said: "I come not to bring peace but a sword."

That sword is here now. It is splitting the world in two. On the one hand you have the "Money-Changers," on the other you have the true seekers of the law of spiritual truth. As our possession of the truth increases, our love of material wealth decreases. When we get tired serving one "master" we naturally turn to the other.

As Kipling has said in his prophetic "L'Envoi":

"And only the Master shall praise us,
    and only the Master shall blame;
And no one shall work for money,
    and no one shall work for fame;
But each for the joy of the working,
    and each in His separate star,
Shall draw the thing as he sees it
    for the God of things as they are!"

The ancient prophets, after having written all the books of the Old and New Testament, and St. John, after having written all the other chapters of the Book of Revelation, in the eleventh verse of the last chapter in the Bible, wrote:

"He that is unjust, let him be unjust still; and he who is filthy, let him be filthy still; and he that is righteous, let him be righteous still; and he that is holy, let him by holy still."

And he goes on to explain that each shall be rewarded according to his works. "And let him who is athirst come (meaning the water of life)." But in no place in the Bible were the teachers advised to judge their brothers and tell them they had to do this, that or the other thing. It was left up to the individual, once he was told of the truth, to choose for himself what he would do.

The command was, "Go, teach, preach, heal, etc.," that the people might know of the truth and the "truth will make you free." But a man who changes his mind "against his will, is of the same opinion still." Should you know the law of righteousness and break that law, do you think you will not pay, and pay dearly? Have you a conscience?

Your conscience is your guide. Your conscience is the law of right and wrong whispering to you, as you know the law. When you break that law within your own mind, you pay. Should you break the same law again and again, you reap what you have sown again and again.

Once you learn to analyze your sorrows, your aches and pains, your reverses and tribulations, you will have learned the site of your trouble. There is little learned without error.

Some folks are so good they're good for nothing, and others are just mean enough to be good for something. "He who hath not sinned, let him cast the first stone." "The blind" have been leading "the blind" for a long time.

It is a grand thing to teach the truth, but it is a dangerous thing to command the truth of a man who knows not the law of righteousness. Many a man is asked to drink the truth before he has had his fill of error. Most people yet eat the "husks" and live in darkness.

At this time, as many authorities of the transcendental have intimated, we are at the close of one of the great world cycles. The great Mahatma Koot Hoomi, no doubt the FATHER, so to speak, of all Masters now embodied, has told me the time is very short before the "clearing of the landscape" shall take place. And I know he meant that all "dark and shadowy Brothers" on this planet, who have not hearkened to the "VOICE" of the Almighty, shall be "wiped out." This is the time when the BROTHERS AND SISTERS OF LIGHT shall KNOW they hold the balance of power on earth. The LIGHT of their very souls IS THAT POWER. The terrible destructive diseases, electrical vibrations of a cataclysmic nature, poisonous germ cultures the Germans have developed for future use, war machinations beyond the human mind to conceive, and all such things the Black Forces may use in order to hold the balance of power on this planet,—none of these things will affect the TRUE BROTHERS OF LIGHT, for the Light, Love, Wisdom and Power—ALL IN BALANCED PERFECTION IN THOSE WHO LOOK TO CHRIST LORD MAITREYA —shall be securely protected. The trying years of the GREAT TRANSFORMATION shall not harm HIS FOLD, THE CHILDREN OF LIGHT. BY 1951 the KINGDOM OF GOD SHALL BE WELL ESTABLISHED ON EARTH AND HUMANITY—WHAT IS LEFT—WILL UNDER-STAND THE PRINCIPLES OF THE GOLDEN AGE ESTABLISHED ON EARTH.

Just last week a Brother placed in my hand a book, "Letters of Occult Meditation," under the authorship of Alice A. Bailey, first published in 1922. The letters therein published are purported to have been dictated by The Tibetan Teacher, to whom the book is dedicated. As I started to read the book—even the first paragraph—I sensed the Cosmic Fatherhood of Mahatma Koot Hoomi. So, my dear reader, to me, Koot Hoomi is the Tibetan so many people refer to, and I dare say you will ultimately find that my intuition is correct. I feel certain, too, that my beloved teacher, KH, will not, at this late date, object to my revealing his true identity. Many names and many "faces," many titles and many "places" lay claim, as it were, to the Great Cosmic Beings who have so very much to do with the directing of the Light, Love, Wisdom and Power to the Truth Seekers on our earth at this time of Great Change.

In this connection I wish to quote from Alice Bailey's book, page 197, second paragraph:

> "At the same time you will see the misuse of those powers—a misuse that will herald in one of the final struggles between the Lords of Light and the Lords of Darkness. Great will be the cataclysm and terrific the disaster, but ever the Light shines in darkness, and He who reigns above all, and Who holds all within the circumference of His Aura knows the hour of opportunity, and knows too how to utilize that which can protect."

Regarding the cataclysm alluded to above, Lord Maitreya has told me that such will not be as most so-called prophets might think. He emphasizes the need for all Children of Light to remain calm and serene, and "fear not" whatever may come about. He said, "EVERY SOUL MUST ULTIMATELY BE SAVED." He called last June, 1941, on all the Lords of the Rays and all Gods who have anything to do with this earth and the direction of such world changes, to AVOID A WORLD CATACLYSM. It was avoided. The most destructive phase of the present World War, which actually took place this last summer between the Fascist Hordes and the Communist Legions, actually, so to speak, prevented the world cataclysm that was about to burst forth.

When one of universal understanding looks upon the world changes, he realizes that the war in Europe, in a sense, LET OFF ENOUGH OF THE VIRUS OF POISONOUS HATRED THAT HAD GENERATED *IN THE EARTH,* to prevent the kind of a world cataclysm the people who were aware of its approach had expected. Again, when we look at that terrible spectacle itself we cannot help but consider it of cataclysmic proportions. Even thus far it is estimated that no less than five millions of human beings have lost their lives, and yet there is no apparent end of the strife in view. Truly the Whites and the Blacks are warring with each other in that conflict. The Masters of physical wealth and power are battling with the Masters of Light and Understanding. Many are the sacrifices made on each side, but the ultimate victory will remain with the WHITE—those who seek Brotherly Love and its protective Light that shall ESTABLISH THE GOLDEN AGE.

Here I shall tell you something that will amaze you, I am sure, even more than it did me. Early last spring while I was in Bremerton, Washington, I know of an Ascended Master who was sent on the most peculiar mission I had ever heard of. The Mighty Logos of this world had decided that it was time to take a physical body on earth for the explicit purpose of aiding in establishing the NEW LAWS OF THE GOLDEN AGE. The Lords in charge of this phase of the transcendental duties they perform for humanity had been watching for some time for proper parents to be chosen, through whom this GREAT BEING might be born into our earth world. Such parents were discovered in a small town in the state of California. The Ascended Master I know—one whom I had been fortunate enough to receive instruction from—was sent by the Higher Lords to that California town. He was told to go to the public library there, where he would see a young couple who visited the library each evening. The young mother was said to be with child. They were just normal, middle-class people, but of high ideals and they were of the opinion that a mother expecting to give birth to a child should be given every consideration so far as environment was concerned. Each evening they carefully selected the best of literature. Even what an expectant mother studied and thought had a great bearing upon the child to be born, so these young people believed. Little did they know that the Universal Lord was hovering over them, guarding them, loving them, and inspiring them to do the very things they were so joyous in performing. And little did they dream there was actually an Ascended Master right there in the library with them for weeks each evening when they went there for relaxation and study. Think of it, Beloved Friends of Light, what great interest the Gods do take in the present affairs of the world changes taking place on our planet. No wonder the earth is no more a Dark Star but a Blazing Sun. Astrologically we are receiving the transcendent FAVORS OF THE

95

COSMIC LORDS. AWAKE BROTHERS! AWAKE SIS-TERS! REALIZE THE TRUTH I NOW GIVE UNTO YOU. IF IT WERE NOT SO I WOULD NOT TELL YOU.

The Blessed Age we have dreamed of for ages, for centuries and centuries, is now upon us. Things are taking place—events are happening to us and our planet that visit us but once in hundreds of thousands of years as we see and understand time. And still the so-called Masters of Darkness battle to keep the world in the same darkness we have endured for all those centuries. They boast of their ancient monuments—a few hundreds of years old—like little children boasting about pretty marbles. I smile when I think of them. The other day Lord Maitreya spoke to me of the coming two thousand years as though it were a two-weeks vacation. He told me of changes that will take place during that time. He mentioned various ones who will be re-embodying to assist in governing the people of this world during the Golden Age. Things that may even disturb other Lords that I have seen and know are so thoroughly understood by Him from their Cosmic Source to their realization in extrinsicality that He is ETERNALLY THE SERENE MASTER OF ALL WITHIN HIS SOLAR RING, ABOVE TIME AND SPACE AND MOTION, THE DIVINE DIRECTOR OF ALL ACTIVITIES, ESOTERIC AND EXOTERIC, OF THE SPIRIT AND OF OUR LIMITED EARTH WORLD.

I call to all who seek the Light. Call for the WHITE LIGHT OF PURITY TO ENVELOP ALL BEINGS OF THIS EARTH. AND KNOW, BELOVED BROTHERS OF LIGHT, THAT THE CHILD IS BORN IN THE UNITED STATES THAT WILL BE THE GREAT ONE TO LEAD ALL PEOPLES OUT OF DARKNESS INTO EVERLASTING LIGHT. That child, born the 25th of last June, will be the one, WHEN BUT TEN YEARS OF AGE, who will actually be so wise that the officials of the United States will heed his wisdom and a "little child shall lead them." In 1951 that child, who will have been under the direct radiance and instruction of the Masters of Light, will come forth to teach the people of this world. HE WILL MANIFEST SUCH LOVE, WISDOM and POWER THAT HE WILL BE ACKNOWLEDGED AS A GOD INCARNATE ON EARTH.

This is the time, Beloved, when such things shall come to pass. Even today the Gods do walk among us. They are here to show you the way. Believe. Have faith. Seek the Light. Learn of the Wisdom of the Great Masters. Look about you and KNOW that Christ is here again. Walk in His Light, call to Him and He will come and "sup with you, walk with you and talk with you" of the marvels of God's Kingdom now enfolding us IN OUR HEARTS, IN OUR MINDS, AND EVEN IN OUR BODIES. CALL TO LORD MAITREYA THE LORD OF LOVE TO COME TO YOU AND SPEAK TO YOU IN YOUR OWN HEART OF GOLD. HE WILL COME WHEN YOU LEAST EXPECT HIM. HE DOES NOT FORGET HIS OWN.

IT'S UP TO YOU!

Figure it out for yourself, my lad,
    You've all that the greatest of men have had;
Two arms, two hands, two legs, two eyes,
    And a mind to use if you would be wise:
With this equipment they all began,
    So start from the top and say, "I can."

Look them over, the wise and great,
    They take their food from a common plate,
And similar knives and forks they use,
    With similar laces they tie their shoes,
The world considers them brave and smart,
    But you've all they had when they made their start.

You can triumph and come to skill,
    You can be great if you only will.
You're well equipped for what fight you choose;
    You have arms and legs and a mind to use:
And the man who has risen great deeds to do
    Began his life with no more than you.

YOU are the handicap you must face,
    You are the one who must choose your place.
You must say where you want to go,
    How much you will study, the truth to know;
God has equipped you for life, and He
    Will help you decide what you want to be.

Courage must come from the soul within
    For to man has been furnished the will to win.
So figure it out for yourself, my lad,
    You were born with all that the great have had:
With your equipment they all began,
    Get hold of yourself and say: "I can."

                                            —Anon.

98

CHAPTER XIII

It was during the month of October, 1940, that I began to receive much instruction direct from the Ascended Masters at Mt. Shasta, as I heretofore stated. Jesus, Ave Maria and Mahatma Koot Hoomi were teaching me for some time before I was able to bring through to the outer plane clearly and definitely their personal or individual radiance and form outline. I was so amazed, so enthralled, by it all that I would sit for hours without hardly moving or uttering a word. The most feeling aspect of these periods of instruction and radiance, of course, was the LIGHT and SPIRIT about us when THEY appeared.

I had never been interested in spiritualism so-called, but had been a student of occult knowledge and training all my life. I did understand the modus operandi of the mediums with their controls, etc., but I knew that ordinarily mediums do not bring through very high and constructive knowledge and information. A medium, in other words, can not bring through knowledge or Light-Radiance higher than their bodies and minds can withstand or understand. For this reason it is best for any student of higher occult knowledge not to dabble in spiritualism. At times Masters do use bodies of near-masters, but, unless mediums KEEP THEIR BODIES IN PERFECT HARMONY MORALLY, PHYSICALLY AND MENTALLY, THEY ARE NOT TO BE TRUSTED BY THE HIGHER MASTERS, FOR THE BLACK FORCES HAVE ACCESS TO THEIR BODIES AND OFTEN ENTER AND GIVE DESTRUCTIVE TEACHINGS AND ARE LIABLE TO BRING ABOUT OTHER MISCHIEF. NO ONE CAN FOOL A MASTER. HE ALWAYS KNOWS A MASTER BODY. THERE ARE PROBABLY A HUNDRED DIFFERENT WAYS FOR A MASTER TO DEFINITELY DETERMINE THE SACREDNESS OF A BODY-TEMPLE. For instance, the voice of the individual, the movements of the body as to grace, the rhythm of the walk, the words (fruits) spoken, the knowledge expressed, the temperament, the phrenology and physiognomy of the person, the color and texture of one's skin, the vibration radiating forth, and, best of all, the aura of the individual.

Up until this time there have been very few body-temples the Cosmic Masters could use on earth. This is because the astrological as well as the astronomical changes taking place in the heavens are conducive, we may say, to higher evolved beings incarnating on earth, or, in another sense, man has developed higher bodies on earth enabling more of the Egoic Groups (the I AM Presences) of individuals to manifest on earth during this New Age. It is almost impossible to express some of the higher principles of soulual evolution and development without the use of some terms foreign to the average mind, however, I shall endeavor to more clearly explain this matter of New Age incarnation or re-embodying of souls now returning to take earth bodies.

There are, I believe, 25,000 years in one manvantara (cycle) such as is now closing. Some authorities on such occult matters have ventured the statement that this is the closing of even many such cycles. Should this be true, which I am inclined to believe, then this universe has become in such close proximity with certain Cosmic, astral, etheric and terrestrial bodies in the heavens as to make it possible for us to develop our physical bodies to such a high degree of perfection that we are now able to manifest the Higher Ego, the Christ-Body or Individualized God Presence, right here on earth. These are the kind of bodies we are to use in the Golden Age now here. I have my new physical body just about perfect. I have already developed my Golden Body and I even experience it in my physical body at times when it is essential for the performance of duties the Cosmic Beings wish me to do. I have explained to you regarding the Seven Bodies we have. Those who are not able to manifest in their Highest Bodies during the next nine years will not be able to live on this planet. The higher Light Vibrations will not permit any to live here who do not harmonize with IT. It will be like a "CONSUMING FIRE." THIS IS MENTIONED IN THE VERY LAST CHAPTER IN THE OLD TESTAMENT OF THE HOLY SCRIPTURE, the Book of Malachi: "For, behold the day cometh, that shall burn as an oven; and all the proud, yea, and all that do wickedly, shall be stubble; and the day that cometh shall burn them up, saith the Lord of hosts, that it shall leave them neither root or branch."

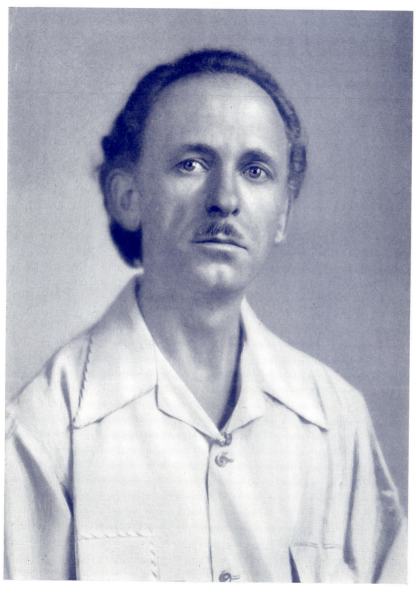

MAH-ATMAH AMSUMATA

ऋतुम्मातः

DAVID

And in the following verse, I wish to call to the attention of the CHILDREN OF LIGHT how significant it is when compared with what I have written in this book: "But unto you that fear my name shall the SUN of RIGHTEOUSNESS rise with healing in his wings; and ye shall go forth, and grow up as calves of the stall."

Then, the next to last verse in the Old Testament, in the same chapter: "Behold, I will send you Elijah the prophet before the coming of the great and dreadful day of the Lord." WHO IS ELIJAH? He is one of those who has a PERFECT BODY IN CHRIST. HE IS HERE NOW.

* * *

I shall now endeavor to give you a number of events that took place in my initiations and instruction, in their chronological order, beginning with the 29th of August, 1940, when I first met Mary the Mother of Jesus in the outer body at Mt. Shasta. Many important points came and went during the month of October and up to the 10th of November before I was informed that I should keep records of certain things that were transpiring. In fact I had little dreamed that I was at all important concerning these events taking place in which I was even then one of the principal "actors on the stage of life" being brought forth by the Great Masters.

I have related to you in a previous chapter how I was taken into the Field of Nirvana, the Higher Planes of Bliss, His (Christ's) Temple, where I "rested" and was taught in my Higher Body regarding the Great Truths of the Soul, of God and the Cosmos (symbolically the Isle of Patmos of St. John) where one who has received certain inner initiations becomes conscious of his ONENESS WITH THE FATHER. It was during October that I received these initiations, and it was on November 10, 1940, that I was informed I should keep records of certain revelations given to me. By that time I had somehow suddenly become, so far as those Masters who visited me were concerned, the SILENT WATCHER. I was told that I was to do a great deal of investigation work throughout the world in my Higher Body, that records should be kept, that reports should be made to the Recorder of the Great White Lodge, and that I should recommend things that should be done regarding world affairs and the in-coming Golden Age. Almost overnight

I had been changed in a most miraculous manner, so it seemed, from an ordinary human being into at least a Semi-God.

It was November 11 that Lord Maitreya talked to me quite at length regarding my future work. He told me then, too, that Ave Maria was in Nirvana for a much-needed rest.

November 11 is recorded as a very important date for another reason, according to the notes I have kept. It was on that date that Lord Maitreya explained that "No one entereth the portals of the Temple of Love and Wisdom but through me." I asked him then, "Who are you?" He replied in the most kindly voice, "I am the Lord of Lords." It was on the same date, November 11, that the Great Lord Sanat Kumara came to radiate his Light and Love to me. He showed me how to sit, how to hold my hands, and told me to "sit IN THE RAINBOW SPIRIT." This rainbow spirit, to those who have studied Saint Germain's instruction in the "I AM" Presence means this: DO NOT MERELY VISUALIZE YOURSELF BELOW THE LIGHT OF THE PRESENCE (THE RAINBOW SPIRIT SANAT KUMARA CALLS IT) BUT SEE YOURSELF RIGHT *IN IT*. There is a vast difference, as you will see, in being beneath a spirit and BEING RIGHT WITHIN IT. You should visualize yourself in the CENTER of the PRESENCE —the SEVEN RAYS OF THE LORDS OF CREATION SCINTILLATING ABOUT YOU. These rays should be visualized in the same order as they appear in a rainbow, which is always the same. Or, if you are able to isolate a ray from the sun, as some of us are able to do,—study it and get well impressed in your imagination those colors in their clearest possible radiance. Colors—especially the Cosmic colors in LIGHT—are most important to one's advancement and development. If you can definitely and persistently visualize the harmonious radiation of those colors about you there will be no question as to your spiritual unfoldment, joyous health and industriousness or any other good and constructive activities you may wish to bring about. In this connection, too, it is well to begin to do CONSCIOUS BREATHING. I refer to your being actually aware of the "prana" or Electronic Light-Substance in the atmosphere about you. LOVE-LIGHT, a term I first coined, so far as I know, in a poem I wrote in 1938, a copy of which I mailed to Mr. G. W. Ballard, is a compound word that may help you in visualizing the Light about you. Then, too, LOVE-WILL is another one of my own compound words that is definitely a great help, for you are combining LOVE and WILL together, which is absolutely necessary if you accomplish anything. Love-Will creates FEELING. Without Feeling you do not create anything.

To anyone who may think they have a monopoly on any terms I may use, I would refer them to the OAHSPE BIBLE from which Mr. Ballard received much of the inspiration which lifted him to the point of illumination where he was, for a time, a perfect messenger. There are hundreds of messengers in the world, but there are few MASTERS, yet. The Oahspe Bible, first copyrighted in 1882 by John Ballou, is one of the most amazing books ever published in the history of the world. There are few people, however, who can understand it even today. Ballard did understand it, and he combined his own knowledge with that of what he accumulated from a number of other sources, thereby enabling himself to create the biggest stir in theological circles since the time of Jesus the Christ. God bless him (Ballard). We need thousands like him, and within a few years now we shall have them. Had his wife not become so conceited and egotistically inflated he might have remained on earth a few more years, as Saint Germain planned. History would have been different.

November 12, 1940, is a date that should be well remembered in the ages to come. It was on that date that Christ in His Spirit did first incarnate in a physical body on this earth in THIS NEW AGE. I was with the physical body in which this IMMACULATE CONCEPTION OF CHRIST actually took place. I was directed by the Great White Lodge to be present in the official capacity of the SILENT WATCHER. Again, IF IT WERE NOT SO I SHOULD NOT TELL YOU.

I regret very much that I did not record more of the details of this wonderful INCARNATION. In this connection, however, I shall give you some amazing occult or transcendental information, which, so far as I know, HAS NEVER BEEN EXPLAINED ON THIS EARTH.

Jesus came in His Higher Presence, through that very body in which CHRIST WAS "BORNING" AND EXPLAINED TO ME THINGS THAT I COULD NOT FULLY UNDERSTAND AT THAT TIME. It was simply too much for my slowly awakening SPIRIT to wholly grasp. The activity of the Divine Spirit was all very new to me. I was told that I held a very important and SACRED office. Of all beings on earth I, John the Brother of Jesus (Silent Watcher), was chosen to be with Ave Maria during the incarnation of Christ into that body for the incoming of the Golden Age. Jesus was very very happy because He was relieved of His former office, Christ to this World, and was raised to Lord of this Earth. He explained to me, also, that I would have to face "great tests, but there will be GREATER BLESSINGS." Lord Maitreya came and said of "Her Who is Nameless," "She must be known as Ave Maria only, but not known by the one who works through Her. She is part of the Godhead that radiates through the heart."

November 12, too, was when the Great Father the God Mahachohan, God of the Golden Heart, came and called: "Thou, PRINCE OF THE GOLDEN HEART, SON of the GOD OF THE GOLDEN HEART, BORN FROM MY MOUTH, WHERE ART THOU?" Ave Maria spoke to me saying, "It is you He is calling—THE GREAT FATHER IS CALLING YOU."

I knew not what to do. "You should answer Him," she said. Again I heard the voice: "Oh, Prince of the Golden Heart, where art Thou My Son. I am your Father, God of the Golden Heart. I come to take you home into the Sun again."

"Here am I," I answered. And it was as though a mighty power within me spoke from my lips, "Thou KNOWEST I LOVE THEE AND THY TRUTH, THY LIGHT, LOVE AND WISDOM ABOVE ALL THINGS OF EARTH."

Thus it is Oh, Beloved Seeker after Light. You must want Christ and His Light above all things of this world, else the Love in your Heart is not Great Enough to draw to you YOUR FATHER, THE GOD OF THE GOLDEN HEART. As the Bible has stated for centuries, "Love Thy God with ALL THY HEART, WITH ALL THY SOUL AND BODY." If the people of this world only knew the importance of LET-TING GO of all things earthly in order that CHRIST MAY COME INTO THEIR HEARTS. Oh, why is it that we become so enthralled in earthly things? Why is it, even today, tragic war rages, when, with common sense, the leaders of this world might bend their efforts toward world peace, EQUALITY, JUSTICE, ECONOMIC SECURITY FOR ALL WITH A GUARANTEE OF INTERNATIONAL HARMONY AND

THE NEW GOLDEN AGE

ULTIMATE ILLUMINATION FOR ALL PEOPLES, RACES, CREEDS AND CLANS? Let us again call together —all of us of the Light: "ALL LIGHTS UNITED IN THE ONE GREAT LIGHT."

I shall never forget that 12th of November, 1940. It might be that few in the outer world realized what a great event had taken place, but I felt most definitely the miraculous Spiritual Change in myself and SAW that CHANGE taking place in another, Ave Maria's physical body. She acted much like a woman who had given birth to a new-born babe. I was told by Mahatma Koot Hoomi to stay close by to protect her from any harm, physical, etheric or mental. I was given certain signs and symbols to use in attracting the necessary powers of the Lords of the Rays there. They came in answer to my calls. Like Sentinels they came. They taught me many phases of the Great Work, too, that cannot be published for everybody to read, however, I am able at this time, because of the higher "level" and understanding of the masses, to publish much more of the hidden mysteries of occultism than has ever been allowed for public perusal before. I am confident there is no one on earth at this time who has experienced such transcendental states of consciousness and activity unless it were "She Who is Nameless." The body in which "She" abides on earth is forever safe from the curious eyes of the "uninitiated" world. Yes, "SHE MUST BE OBEYED."

November 13, 1940: Master Morya, Lord of Power, came to us, weeping. He spoke of "OUR KINGDOM." He explained that He had been chosen as "King" of the New Spiritual Kingdom on Earth. Morya is, as I have stated before, the re-embodiment of St. John the Most Beloved Disciple of Jesus who wrote the most illuminative Book of the New Testament, "Revelation." I would analyze his weeping in this way: He, knowing that Christ was incarnating at that time, and other GREAT OFFICES changing simultaneous, He came prayerfully pleading that the Great Lords and Gods of the Spiritual Hierarchy carefully guard "Her Who is Nameless" until such time as the Powers of Darkness could do Her no harm. As other great ones came that day I began to realize what a Grand and Glorious Spectacle was really INCARNATING IN EARTH. The incarnation of Christ was fully realized, so we thought, on the 13th. Ave Maria called me to Her, saying she had something she wished to talk to me about. There was such

105

a marvelous radiation of love about Her as I approached Her where she lay restfully reposing upon a couch that I felt just like a little child approaching its mother. Strange, but that was just what she wanted to talk to me about.

"Amsumata," she began, "you are to take a great part in the affairs of this planet during the approaching Golden Age. You have been referred to by Master Koot Hoomi and others of the Divine Family as John the Brother of Jesus. It is true. You were my son, too, when your older brother, Jesus, was on earth. You were also Divinely sent, even as He was, but there was a misunderstanding. It was to you that Jesus spoke when on the cross, when He said, 'John, know thy Mother.' Readers of the Scriptures thought it was John the Beloved to whom He spoke, but it was not. You took care of me, John, after Jesus ascended. You were good to me, and I have always loved you for it. Now I am able to come and assist you in your time of great trial."

I was so touched I wept. She spoke so feelingly of those times of the past I could actually see them pictured right before my eyes. Her eyes, too, overflowed with tears. She talked on. "Much is expected of you, John. Remember, you are one of the Divine Family. Those of our family must stand together. Our protection and the New Kingdom now approaching depends upon us. Your brother James—we do not know where he is. I always think of him as he was then, with a beard. We must find him."

In Tacoma, Wash., years ago I had met and studied under a remarkable teacher of the mysteries, Harry Eyer, who had intimated to me after I became well acquainted with him, that he was the re-embodiment of the Apostle Peter. Brother Eyer told me then that James and John were both embodied and living in Tacoma at that time. Now, he may have known I was John. I do not know. Anyhow I had met the one he said was James and got pretty well acquainted with him, so I told Mother Mary about it. The whole matter came into my mind instantly as she mentioned James. "I think I know where James is," I remarked. "A teacher I once knew in Tacoma told me he was living there."

"Do you recall his name?" she asked;—"his name in the outer world?"

"Yes, in a way I do. It was either Hansen or Larson or something like that."

"What work did he follow?" she wanted to know.

"He was a building contractor."

"Yes," she exclaimed, "that would be just like him, still following his father's trade."

For a few minutes it was as though Ave Maria were dozing. I thought she had gone to sleep. But no. She had gone in spirit to Tacoma, but returned soon to tell me that she had found James there. I had told her that he was, even years ago when I knew him, interested in the Higher Teachings of Christ. She spoke little regarding James any more, but when I went north from Mt. Shasta in January, 1941, I visited an old friend and student of mine, Mark Bartlett, there. While in the city I inquired of another Norwegian friend of mine if he knew where Larson was. He said he was still in the city, also in the contracting business. He was, however, I found, one of the active workers in Father Divine's religious movement. I did not see him, but God Bless him, and while I am on the subject I say, "GOD BLESS FATHER DIVINE, TOO." He is doing a marvelous work for all who seek the True Light of Understanding.

For the benefit of you people who seek the Light of Christ and yet look down upon the Colored races, I shall later tell you about the time when I ascended. Next to Ave Maria the ONE who helped me most was the Goddess of Light. Well, Beloved Friends of the Light, the Goddess of Light is now embodied in a Negro body. "Judge not lest ye be judged." REMEMBER, as Lord Maitreya said, "EVERY SOUL MUST BE SAVED." One thing I have always admired in the Roman Catholic Church —they make no distinction in color or race in their membership. The Colored people, to me, are a marvelous race. They make much more out of a limited opportunity than many of us do out of great economic and educational advantages. I am now thankful that the Universal Lord placed me in various environments in this life in which I learned all races, all cliques, creeds, clans and social and economic conditions. I know human beings of every kind and grade. Being adept, I can meet any of them on their own ground.

Other important matters came up on November 13. The Mighty Cosmic Lord came to pay his respects, so to speak, to Ave Maria, and called Her the Solar Sun. At High Noon a Great Spiritual Being annnounced that the Son of Christ was born in Ave Maria. Later Saint Germain came, declaring with great power, "THE SWORD OF AVE MARIA MUST BLAZE THROUGHOUT THE WORLD — EVERY-

WHERE." Mahatma Koot Hoomi stated that Mary Magdalene, who is embodied and living in California, must be given every possible aid at this time to enable her to ascend. Her rising to mastery, he explained, is most important to the ascension of ALL WOMANHOOD of this world.

In my hurry to get this message to the world, I do not have time to perfect a great work of literature, but, Beloved Brothers of Light, I do want you to dwell on these marvelous essentials alluded to in this brief resume, since the blending together of the numerous "bits of mystery" associated with this REVELATION will definitely and positively lift YOU into the full consciousness and illumination of the GREAT SPIRIT—the Ascension.

I was told later by an Ascended Master that Mary Magdalene is now under the direct instruction of a Master-Teacher. She was told of what Mary the Mother of Jesus and KH had said of her near-ascension. She wept with joy, eager to put forth every possible effort in her own spiritual development and unfoldment.

At 5:30 P.M. Mahatma Koot Hoomi announced, "The Solar Christ will come March 10, 1941, stepping through to the earth in full power." At 6:00 P.M. Buddha Gautama came, instructing me in some very important phases of the Oriental teachings of Krishna, and also gave me information regarding my little daughter's future training. This I shall take up in another chapter.

May I remind you once more, Beloved, to repeat now and again, when it occurs to your mind, the Slogan of the Great White Lodge: "ALL LIGHTS UNITED IN THE ONE GREAT LIGHT." GOD BLESS YOU.

CHAPTER XIV

MY SECRET

No one knows the joys of my heart
> No one knows my sorrow;
>> No one knows my delights of today
> Nor my dreams of tomorrow.

I am my joy,
> I am my sorrow,
>> My delights of today,
> My dreams of tomorrow.

Of course, as you will understand, it is impossible for me to relate but a very small part of all that transpired on the dates I mention while with Ave Maria and the Great Masters at Mt. Shasta. Some of it I did not record, nor do I remember a great deal of the details of that part not recorded. Other knowledge given to me and special instruction, I am not permitted to give to the outside world. It is only as certain ones attain to the "proper degree" of enlightenment that they are "CHOSEN" by the Master to receive instructions direct from HIM. Remember, Beloved, the "student is chosen by the Master." The student does not choose the Master. "Many are sent but few are chosen." One must definitely understand the basic SPIRITUAL LAWS IN HIS HEART before he can be chosen to "sit at the feet of THE MASTER." Strange it may seem to you, but WHEN you meet ONE MASTER you have met ALL MASTERS. THE MASTER is "HE WHO IS NAMELESS." Mother Mary, I might GUESS, is the FIRST woman ever to attain FULL ILLUMINATION AND MASTERY ON EARTH, in the same sense that Jesus was referred to in the Holy Bible as the "FIRST FRUIT." *HE* IS THE BRIDEGROOM. *SHE* IS THE BRIDE. *I AM* THE BRIDEGROOM. *SHE IS* THE BRIDE OF CHRIST. "He who hath ears to hear, let him hear." The Spirit of God will reveal that to you, Beloved, which you are to know. "Maitreya," the Lord of Love, is "THE DOOR."

November 14: Master Morya, The Venetian, Serapis and Saint Germain came, stood before us in full regalia, saluting us and saying: "WE ARE WITH YOU." Morya, as I have told you, is the Great Manu or King of the New Golden Age; the Venetian works with the Great Mahachohan on the Third Ray; Serapis is Lord of the Rosicrucian or Egyptian Fourth Ray (Green); and Saint Germain, at that time was being transferred from the Seventh Ray (Violet) to the Second (Blue). The Third Ray is Gold. Contrary to many students of Saint Germain's misinterpreted teachings, the Violet Ray is the lowest of all rays. The Newly Initiated Master is usually placed in charge of the Violet Ray more or less as a trial or probationary period. Saint Germain, as I have intimated before, had previously been initiated as early as 1925, consciously to my outer mind, but, I AM FRANK TO SAY, I did not bring ALL through clearly enough to get the complete details. Later, when I married, my outer consciousness of the inner activities became more dimmed because (as KH explained later) of abuse that usually accompanies a human body through misuse of sexual powers. It is the loss of vital forces by over-indulgence in the marriage rite that causes more misery in this world than all other causes put together. Relative to this important phase of moral and religious instruction I refer the sincere student to the Seventh Chapter of First Corinthians in the New Testament. In a later chapter I shall give all the direct information anent this subject I dare publish. Purity of mind and a GODLY PURPOSE are the most essential principles that should always be uppermost in the minds of all persons at all times regarding any sexual act. However, I dare say I can add little to that Saint Paul has written about "right and wrong" regarding sex in the biblical chapter referred to above.

This I will venture to say, even of my personal life: I never touched a woman before I married my legal wife, whom I married July 18, 1926, at the age of thirty. I was conscious of the first conception of my Blessed Wife after we were married and talked to our first son, now 14 years of age, three months before he was born. And again, I reiterate, I first ascended in 1925, while living in Olympia, Wash., where I then witnessed THE WHITE DOVE ABOVE THE "MOUNTAIN" IN THE SEA OF LIFE. My Master-Teacher (RSC) should have known what took place in my inner initiations at that time, since I had written to him in their regard, but he was not fully awakened to the significance of these matters, I am sorry to relate, which, APPARENTLY, delayed the incoming of the Golden Age. However, Beloved, I do not judge.

The most disgusting thing to me in this world is the appalling fact there are hundreds of thousands of supposed wise priests, preachers, teachers, philosophers and university professors, and yet, none of them are able to reasonably interpret the Holy Bible. There is actually billions of dollars in money paid to these organized human leeches who suck the life-blood out of the poor ignorant people under the guise of being God's chosen religious servants. Jesus called them "money-changers." They sell Christ at so much a month. Some of them probably get as much as ten thousand dollars a year. Others are paid a certain percent of the monies collected. God help them. God have pity on their very souls these "last days." And the saddest part of all is that the majority of them are actually sincere because they "blindly follow the blind." Someone is going to have a heavy price to pay when the balancing of the "Lamb's book of Glory" is looked into soon. Then there will be "wailing and gnashing of teeth" aplenty. Don't blame me, My Shadowy Brothers. Take my advice right now. Look into your hearts. Look for the REAL LIGHT OF CHRIST there before it is too late. In the end then when the balancing of the "book" is brought about you will thank me for having told you the TRUTH to your face. Answer me this, you Make-Believe "Wolves-in-Sheep's-Clothing" Regents of Christ: "Do you think we might ever have 'His Kingdom established on earth' should we follow your practices of Mammon?" For almost two thousand years you have been preaching your Mammon way. Now Christ Himself comes forth. With all your organized selfish money-making false religious teachings, the Stars of Heaven are against you. The Lords of Light accuse you in your Dark Hearts. Your burning consciences sear your guilty minds as the Light of the Christ sifts through your Black Shells. You are now being stript of your Wolfish Clothes. You stand naked before Him. His "All-Seeing Eye" discerns your every deceitful thought. You will pray for "the mountains to fall upon you." Yes, even your souls must be "saved."

I make no apology for stating the Truth regarding these things. I KNOW the TRUTH and unless I state it my "sins of omission" would remove me. I must do what MY FATHER

HAS TOLD ME TO DO. I have been told I must "FINISH THE WORK YOUR ELDER BROTHER JESUS STARTED TWO THOUSAND YEARS AGO." Yes, My Father told me that just as plainly as I might say it to you. I tarried several years, thinking, "surely this cannot be that I am to go forth making such claims before the people of the world." But, Beloved, I DO MAKE THEM NOW and I make them KNOWING THAT MY FATHER IS WITH ME IN ALL I SAY OR DO. And all the Lords of Light have promised to assist me, to protect me, to uphold me and to BLAZE THE LIGHT AHEAD OF ME WHEREVER I MAY GO. You who would oppose me, I shall not resist you, but THE LIGHT OF CHRIST WILL ENFOLD YOU, CONSUMING YOUR DARKNESS, REVEALING YOURSELF TO YOU. When you see your own HIGHER SELF then you will know ME. If you know MY FATHER then you will know ME, for I and MY FATHER are ONE SPIRIT. I was taken into His Heart. I AM ONE WITH HIM. To Me, ONE WHO KNOWS GOD AND HIS LAWS, you cannot hide anything from ME.

November 15, 1940: Ave Maria came forth in the fulness of Her Spirit and stated that she had been given power over all Black Magicians. She related to me how she had cast out the "Prince of the Satans" who was embodied at the time in Spain. Archangel Michael had, she said, assisted Her in this great work.

November 18: In the morning Archangel Michael came to tell us that Joshua (Christ born of Ave Maria) and John the Brother of Jesus (Amsumata), were asked to go forth to do a special work in the world. Joshua was claimed as Michael's child. This was the first intimation I had regarding anything like a mission such as I now have to carry out as the "Chief-Avatar." The Masters were extremely careful in mentioning any such thing, for they would say nothing or do nothing that might cause me to feel personally conceited or egotistical in my outer mind. When I look over the past fourteen months I am still amazed at the remarkable manner in which every little detail in my intensive training was handled. All my life I have been trained, especially on the inner planes of consciousness, and I have been under teachers and masters in the outer world for more than 20 years, but the past 14 months it seems that all I ever dreamed of in the way of spiritual awakening and actual attainment has culminated in ME NOW AS I AM.

Joshua, the one referred to by Archangel Michael, is my Twin Ray, so I found later. She, too, has a Golden Body such as I have in my Higher Presence. I say "SHE" because she is now embodied in a feminine body. Joshua is the same one who succeeded Moses and was ruler over the Israelites. He is the one who "commanded the sun to stand still," and it STOOD STILL. When you, Beloved, attain to Joshua, you will have become a Son (sun) of the Father. I shall tell you later of an amazing episode in my training that took place that same day, November 18. It has much to do with the Spirit as well as the Body of a Master.

"She Who is Nameless," I shall henceforth refer to as Ave Maria. I shall, for convenience in explaining, therefore, refer to the body of this PARTICULAR MASTER as Ave Maria. Understand, this ONE BODY, which is used by the Great Lords as the PERFECT VESSEL in this material world, is the JEWEL through which Their INDIVIDUAL RAYS scintillate to all the world in this outer octave of life. This is a new activity to this age which has not been made use of in this world since Jesus was embodied almost two thousand years ago. That Body is to be used primarily, as I understand, by Jesus Himself, and it was prepared mostly by Ave Maria, THE JEWEL OF THE GOLDEN AGE. Joshua and Jesus are the same Spirit. Even in the Oahspe Bible He was called Joshu. The art of preparing our physical bodies as a Temple in which the Master may come and abide, is the work of the Alchemist. That is what I had to do, Jesus had to do, Ave Maria had to do, or any other who attains mastery. You MUST practice Alchemy.

Jesus will not be alone this time. There are many of us on earth this time for the purpose of performing the miraculous task of establishing the Golden Age in all its glory.

November 18 Koot Hoomi also came to tell me that I should deliver a lecture announcing to the world the Second Coming of Christ. He cautioned me not to lecture anywhere outside of Mt. Shasta City. He specified the time, November 24, which gave me little time to publish it in the local newspaper. I did hurry about, however, and rented the main Masonic Hall there for the evening of Nov. 24. The following notice ran in the

Mount Shasta Herald, dated Nov. 21, 1940, as well as a news story about the same wording:

NOTICE

. . .

Norman R. Westfall, former editor, writer, lecturer, will deliver a lecture at the Masonic Hall in Mount Shasta

SUNDAY EVENING
NOVEMBER 24

beginning at 7:30; his subject

"CHRIST'S COMING"

in which he will explain how the Cosmic Lords have NOW prepared the earth through the Cosmic Light for the Coming of the Solar Christ into this world.

Mr. Westfall represents no particular church nor organization, but is undenominational, and invites all churches, lodges and people who believe in the Light of Christ to attend these lectures. They are free to the public.

There were eighteen persons present at the lecture. I had been told by Lord Maitreya on November 18 to "announce to the world that there is but one standard of life for both, men and women." He emphasized the ONE GREAT LIGHT. East and West, he said, "must unite under the One Great Light. In a similar manner you are to teach as your Great Brother Saint Germain teaches." (At that time I did not know my Higher Presence was Saint Germain.) An hour before the lecture was to begin, a Master appeared and said: "I am the Chief Officer of Lord Maitreya. Saint Germain will deliver the lecture this evening. Lord Maitreya asked me to explain the Maltese Cross and He wishes you to explain it to your audience." It all seemed strange to me. I had often wished for somebody to explain the symbolism of the Maltese Cross to me, but somehow no one ever had explained it to me. He indicated that in the first place you draw a square. Then, he said, you draw a cross from corner to corner across the square; you cut a part out of each corner of the dark square, and place a small circle in the center where the two original lines crossed which represents a lotus flower. That center jewel is gold. The other part or background of square is blue. As we advance in the transmutation of the baser elements in our ascension toward God, the Black becomes less and less until there is nothing left but all the GOLD of our being, on a background of Blue, which takes the form of a full blown Lotus. Our ascension takes place then, WHEN ALL THE DROSS IN OUR MINDS AND BODIES ARE DISSOLVED, TRANSMUTED AND REGENERATED and we are FREED FROM THE SQUARE OF MATERIALITY. The drawings below will give you a better idea of the explanation:

I was greatly inspired during the lecture. Now I knew who had inspired me so much all during my life when I endeavored to speak to an audience. It was Saint Germain. Ave Maria was present in the audience. She saw Saint Germain. I talked, of course, principally about the Second Coming of Christ and the Golden Age now here. Ave Maria said my words were electrifying. She had never heard me speak in public before, but I had told her of the overpowering inspiration that always came over me when I spoke to people of the New Age. Lincoln, she said, was also quite in evidence in my body while I was talking. I had been told to announce myself as a Disciple of Christ. Following is the Invocation I used before beginning the main part of the address:

Master Koot Hoomi, Ave Maria, Jesus the Christ (Issa), Saint Germain, Archangel Michael, Sanat Kumara (Father of this Planet), Lord of Lords Maitreya, and Thou Almighty Lord God of the Great Central Sun of All Life, Light, Love, Wisdom and Power,—we invoke thy blessings here upon us. We KNOW you hear our call. We rejoice with Thee in the Service of the Light. May every heart in this room be touched by Thy Radiance, and may Thy Blessing reach to every human heart in this world. We thank Thee that Thou hast seen fit to allow us to serve Thee in this present activity. Bless us, Oh, Lord of Lords, that we may bless others. We thank Thee.

And thus, Beloved, the first announcement of the incarnation of Christ into this world in this New Age, was proclaimed throughout the ethers of this planet. Instead of the few who were present in their physical bodies, there were millions who felt that message in their hearts as it sounded and resounded on the ether waves. The Great Lords were present. I was chosen as the physical vessel through which it was announced in this octave or plane of life, but today, one year from that date* when it was proclaimed, much has changed in the mentalities of all human beings. There is the mass feeling throughout the whole world that we are fast approaching SOMETHING VASTLY DIFFERENT UPON OLD MOTHER EARTH. Time will bring all that is anticipated by the Children of Light, yes, and MORE.

That evening, when we gathered together, after the lecture, Lord Maitreya came and said to me: "You asked that your All-Seeing Eye and your All-Hearing Ear be opened. I come to open your eye that you may see with the EYE ABSOLUTE." Among other things he told me how pleased he was with the way I handled the announcement of Christ's Coming to the World.

*(The above paragraph was written Nov. 24, 1940.—*Author*).

CHAPTER XV

Beloved Friends of Light, I wish to tell you now of the most extraordinary visit I ever experienced in this physical body. It was on that memorable November 18. I was born on an 18th and that number as well as nines, twenty-sevens, elevens and twenty-nines invariably play great parts in my activities here on earth. My own birthdate I do not care to disclose at this time. And I would advise any student of Light to desist in giving out data regarding their birth. "I've GOT YOUR NUMBER," has more significance to it than the uninitiated may suspect.

It was a beautiful sunny afternoon, though cold, windy and bleak outside, which caused us to appreciate all the more the cheerful heat from a crackling wood fire indoors. Ave Maria and I had, as usual, been discussing various principles and teachings of philosophy, and especially those of the Master Jesus. She told me how He had when on earth during his Great Ministry originated the Druid Brotherhood. She gave me the ancient alphabet of the ANCIENT SCRIPT, the character letters He used at that time. "Every Avatar," she said, "always starts a brotherhood of His own when embodied on earth, and that Brotherhood disseminates His teachings to the people of earth following His earthly Ascension. The Druids migrated to the British Isles following the Ascension of Jesus."

There dwelt in the room about us an atmosphere wrapt in mystery. The blissful calm and peacefulness was indeed heavenly. The Spirit of Jesus was with us. All became perfectly quiet. Neither of us spoke. For several minutes this unutterable stillness lulled us into such blissful repose we were oblivious to all things earthly.

And then the physical body I thought to be Ave Maria straightened up on the couch where she reclined. The sweetest voice I have ever heard spoke to me. The most beautiful eyes I have ever seen looked at me. "Who are you?" that sweet little musical voice inquired. "Are you a Master?"

Astonished almost beyond speaking, I answered, "Some may call me a Master. Maybe I am a Master."

"Well, you must be a Master or my mother would not be here. She only associates with Masters," that childish voice continued. "I am so lonely where I am," she added. "Those who are with me do not understand me. They all think of me as a little girl. I am not a little girl. I am just living in a little girl body now. Koot Hoomi teaches me music. Some day he says I will be a great musician. I am taking lessons in music in my physical body, too. I go to the Retreat in India, too, in my Spirit Body. I am studying the Rosicrucian Mysteries."

"Who are you?" I asked.

"I am Joshua," she replied.

"Well, Joshua, I am John the Brother of Jesus, so I was told by Koot Hoomi the other day," and I spoke to her in as kindly and fatherly manner as I could.

"Oh, you are John. I have heard of you. Do you teach my mother?"

"Well, Joshua, I am more inclined to think your mother teaches me. It might be that we teach each other."

Beloved, Thou who seekest Light, here was evidenced another strange form of teaching and instruction which is common among the White Masters. Joshua, whom I was told is my Twin Ray, and one who must work with me in the Great Work of bringing in the Golden Age, had a physical body nine years of age, and that physical body is the daughter of Ave Maria in the physical plane. This visit of her with me was wholly unexpected, and I must say, not at all understood by me until days later when it was fully explained to me. She so longs to be with her physical mother at times that her spirit, the Soul of her, actually comes and dwells in the mother's body and not only visits with her but others who might chance to be around. In this particular instance, Ave Maria was not even conscious of the conversation that went on between us, Joshua and I, for she (Ave Maria) had gone to a distant place to carry out an important mission for the Great White Lodge, and she had called the Spirit of Joshua to remain in her body while she was out. She wanted, as was the desire of Koot Hoomi and Lord Maitreya, to have Joshua and me to get acquainted. That was our first visit, but, I am happy to say, it was not our last.

Joshua was there with me for at least an hour and a half, I would judge, and it was just as though a nine-year-old girl had been talking to me, but for one important difference; she was, I found, extremely wise, and above all, radiated more love than any

118

individual I had ever talked to before in this life. After a while she took the liberty to walk about the room, examining various articles here and there just as a strange child would do. She asked questions about a statue of Psyche when she picked it up, which denoted her remarkable understanding of things of the soul. A picture of her mother when she (Joshua) was a tiny baby in her mother's arms was on a little table. She picked it up, stating that that was herself when she was a little baby.

I must confess that although Joshua was in the body of Ave Maria, it was all I could do to prevent myself from taking her in my arms and holding her close to my heart. I might say, too, that I believe she wanted to be loved just as much as I wanted to love her. The Masters, I somehow knew, were trying me severely in this matter. I am of a most affectionate nature, however, there has never been in my life a time when I was not master of my desires and passions, I am happy also to confess.

Joshua even told me many things about her mother that Ave Maria had not told me, some of which, I dare say, she should not have said. You know how children are. Sometimes they tell things to outsiders that their parents do not wish published. I guess she happened to think of this feature of affairs and she said, "You must be careful what you say about my mother. She will know everything you say. You cannot keep anything from her if she wants to know about it."

I had found already what Joshua said about Ave Maria knowing anything and everything she wished to know regarding a person or thing. Of course it is not hard for a Master to know when anyone is talking about him. And in proportion to his being able to read the akashic records around a person they can read what has gone on in a room or any particular environment hours or even years later.

Joshua told me how dissatisfied she was with matters in her schooling and her home. She was in a Convent. She said the Sisters did not understand her. Her father, she said, also, did not give her the proper consideration. Understand, please, that Joshua was living at a Convent, or going to school at a Convent and living with her father who had the custody of the child. The mother of the child in this embodiment is Ave Maria. Even the court records can be produced to prove every statement I make regarding this. The father of Joshua very angrily yelled in the court when divorce proceedings were in action—alluding to the mother of the child—"She thinks she's Mary the Mother of Jesus and she wants me to be Joseph." That was when the child was about seven years of age. The father, a wealthy physician and surgeon, not understanding the occult and mystical background of his wife, who was reared in Germany, had the entire matter brought into the public court in a California city. She, Ave Maria, was there "crucified," so to speak by the uninitiated, who,—GOD HELP THEM—did not understand what a momentous court proceeding was in session. They accused her of being insane, took her child from her, provided a small amount of alimony for her, and tortured her in every conceivable way they could. But, lo and behold, she rose above it all, the great being she is, and NOW stands the MOST PRECIOUS BEING IN A WOMAN'S BODY THAT EVER WALKED UPON EARTH. WOE UNTO THOSE WHO TORTURED HER.

Just a few days following the court settlement, Ave Maria, while in her room alone, was visited by Archangel Michael. He appeared to her in a tangible body. Among other things He said, "You must go to Koot Hoomi. He will teach you."

Ave Maria had never heard of Koot Hoomi. She had studied occult and mystical things all her life, yet she had never contacted anyone who spoke to her of Master KH, as Koot Hoomi is generally known. She had, a year or so previous to the court action, contacted Saint Germain's teachings through the Ballard organization. In one of the books later published there was a discourse dictated by KH, but that book, "Ascended Master Light," had not been published when Archangel Michael appeared to Ave Maria. She later published two wonderful little books under a pseudonym, which clearly show to the spiritual discerning mind that she was and IS a person of extraordinary illumination and development.

Immediately after the visitation of Archangel Michael Ave Maria got busy to find where this being, Koot Hoomi, was to be found. You might say, "Well, why didn't Archangel Michael tell her?" My Beloved Friend of Light, that is not the way the Great Masters work. They tell you little, and let you, of your own "FREE WILL AND ACCORD," work out MUCH. It was several weeks before Ave Maria found who, what and where Koot Hoomi IS. Through the Theosophical Society she found that he IS a Great Ascended Master who lives in a physical body in India—IN TIBET—to be exact—SHIGATSE, TIBET— and He is not only an ordinary human being, but a KING. He is the ruler of one-half of Tibet. Even the natives of that far-off country, which is almost inaccessible from the outside world, look up to Koot Hoomi as a God, WHICH HE IS, AS IS KNOWN BY THE OTHER GREAT MASTERS OF THE RAYS AND BY THE HIGHEST OCCULTISTS AND TRANSCENDENTALISTS OF THIS WORLD.

As soon as Ave Maria found where Koot Hoomi was and WHO He IS, things began to happen in order and with rapid-fire rapidity. As Saint Germain said to me the other day, it was "fast, faster Fastness." Now, Beloved, that is getting pretty fast. Thirty-five hundred dollars was placed at her disposal with which to arrange for passage by ship to India. She hurried about to make arrangements for sailing. She was so "lifted up," she told me later, that she was actually invisible a part of the time. The LIGHT VIBRATIONS or SPIRIT had become so awakened in her that she almost instantly became a being of a higher order. Her Higher Body, the Great Presence, became manifest in her outer body. She told me how that one day she went to the office of a steamship company to see about her ticket and other arrangements that had to be made before sailing. She approached a gentleman there in the office and began talking to him regarding her ticket, not realizing she was invisible. The poor man was almost "scared out of his boots." He stared about with the most frightful look on his face. At first she knew not what to think of it all. Then she happened to think that probably she was invisible. When she suddenly appeared that did not help matters much. The distraught gentleman was on the verge of rushing from the place when She, with Her calmness and mastery, assured him there was nothing wrong.

Ave Maria sailed for Calcutta the latter part of 1938, dis-embarked there, arranged for travel to Darjeeling and on through the mountainous regions to the border of Tibet. There were two native Indo-Chinese who travelled with her in the higher country beyond where there are railroads—a man and a woman. They looked after her burros, her lodging, food and equipment. They were often battling with each other, she said, over who should do "this and that" regarding her welfare. They passed through some dangerous regions, however, her guides knew the country and the people contacted, so all went well until they came to the border of Tibet. There the officials would not let her pass over, even though she had a passport and every-thing in perfect order.

121

They told her it was impossible for a large pack train to go into that rugged, bandit-infested region at that time, let alone a woman with a couple of Chinese coolies. For three days she lodged at the border, wondering what should be done. By the third day she began to affirm her need and what should be done, to the Great Masters in Spirit. She called to Koot Hoomi. She gave Him to understand that she was sent there by Archangel Michael and it was up to Him to see that she got to her destination. A miraculous thing happened.

She had been told by "Master Wireless" to make arrangements to have her baggage taken care of for passage on into Tibet. Koot Hoomi had ordered it moved into the interior.

At the right moment, wholly unexpected to Ave Maria, Master KH appeared on one side of her and Master Morya on the other. She was picked up through their powers of levitation and actually carried through the air several hundred miles and placed "safe and sound" in her own room that had been prepared for her in the Retreat at Shigatse, Tibet. The first thing she said, she told me, after she was placed on her feet and was standing facing Koot Hoomi was, "You are the most beautiful being I have ever seen." She admitted to me that she had not even thought of what she was going to say, and she was really quite embarrassed.

For more than three months Ave Maria stayed at the Great Retreat of Koot Hoomi's, where she received the highest occult teachings obtainable on earth. After hundreds of years Joseph and Mary were together once more. Even though Master KH is considered the Greatest Living Initiate, He acknowledged to me that He learned much from Ave Maria, and often he has said to me, "Don't be fooled; She knows all things. You can hide nothing from Her. She has access to the highest realms of life. Nothing daunts Her." This I have proved, Beloved Seeker after Truth. Here I have told you of one instance where the seemingly impossible was accomplished. These things I relate are but a foretaste of what you will witness in the next nine years on earth. The time is here, and you shall see that I am not exaggerating in the least in what I have told you.

While in Tibet and other regions, including India, Ave Maria was treated much as a visiting queen from a foreign country. There were many Great Masters who knew of her coming long before she arrived. They knew Her Higher Presence—the Spirit—Mary the Mother of Jesus. At one time she told me of riding along through a certain district on her burro, when, looking down, the burro had suddenly changed into a beautiful prancing war horse, and she and the horse were both dressed in full regalia. Thus she rode along for a considerable distance. People on both sides of the road were seen bowing and saluting her as though she were a great general. She explained that one of her embodiments when she had lived in that country hundreds of years ago had suddenly become envisaged, and she was living through that particular episode of the embodiment. After a time the whole vision vanished and her plodding little burro, none the worse for the experience, swung along at his regular gait, probably dreaming of the delicious meal his new mistress would provide for him at their next stop.

At another time a messenger was seen hurrying toward her on horseback. She had no idea he was approaching her. But he was. His master, a great Seer of India, had seen Ave Maria miles before she came near to his castle. The messenger, with all the courtesy he could muster, implored her to come and visit with the Indian Monarch, that arrangements had been made to entertain her and grant her an interview that would be most illuminating to her. She did visit with him and found him to be a Great Master. He, she told me, knew more about her and her past embodiments than she even dreamed possible.

At still another time she had been asked to attend a ceremonial gathering in one of the great temples of India. She stood by a large window high overlooking the open court where the proceedings were set to take place. Suddenly everything seemed to be at a standstill. She saw the Master who sat on the dais or throne look up to where she stood motioning as though he wished someone from up there to come down to where he sat the central figure of this auspicious occasion. She thought he motioned to someone behind her. She looked but there was no one behind her. In a moment one of the officials of the Great Buddha who was in charge of the ceremony approached her saying that she was wanted down below by the Master. Ave Maria told me she did not understand what was going on at all, but felt impelled to do as asked. The entire ceremony was held up until she could approach the Buddha. As she walked through the throng the people bowed down on the ground before her. The Master descended from His throne and asked her to ascend upon it.

The ceremony then proceeded and Ave Maria sat on the throne during the affair. She said there was an amazing change in herself when she got on the throne. Even the language of the people, the ritual and all necessary signs, symbols and such matters were naturally carried out by her as though it were an every-day experience.

Now, Friends of Light, you may wonder about all these strange things happening as they did. I do not wonder. Those Masters knew of Ave Maria's past embodiments. They knew WHOM SHE IS. They knew that even the GREAT BUDDHA GAUTAMA WAS IN HER BODY AT THAT VERY MOMENT. The Master was cognizant of that fact. He could not direct the ceremony himself so long as there was a Greater One present than Himself. Do you understand, My Beloved? Again I must remind you that such things will become so commonplace in the United States of America within the next few years that they shall not appear miraculous at all.

After months of mystery-wrought experiences in India and Tibet Ave Maria was told to return to America. She told me she wept for days when and after she left. It seemed that to her it would be impossible to return to this harsh world where no one seems to understand. She was directed later to Mt. Shasta. That is where I first met her August 29, 1940, and that is when my life took a startling turn toward Higher Things.

CHAPTER XVI

Blessed Seeker after Light, I am most thankful that I have been so blessed by the Great Ones. Now their blessing I can radiate on to you and you, in turn, will send it on to those you deem needful of the Light of Christ Lord Maitreya. This book, Beloved, is your authority as a Messenger of God. I AM YOUR TEACHER. You will find every word I tell you true. You will find in this BOOK, if you meditate upon it and always call for the Lord of Love to reign in your Golden Heart,—yes, you will find in this BOOK all the needed instruction to lead you RIGHT INTO THE GREAT TEMPLE OF LIGHT AND LOVE. Fear not, My Beloved Student, I am with you IN TRUTH AND LIGHT AND LOVE, saith Lord Maitreya.

Yes, Beloved, this Book is your authority. You are My Messenger. You are My Disciple. But, My Beloved, be ever on guard. Do not go forth boastful of your Light, Love, Wisdom and Power. For if you do, you will find yourself utterly alone. You will be stript of all power you ever possessed. Your empty words will die on the still air even before they are uttered. Should you claim things for your personal self your boastful claims will echo back to you, accusing you of faithlessness in Christ. His Spirit will have deserted you. KNOW, oh Thou who wouldst be a Power for Good, that True Humbleness before Christ, Son of the Living Almighty God, is, after all, the DOOR to His Abode. In any undertaking for God's New Age, always invoke His guidance and the cooperation of His Sons, the Great White Masters of Love.

And again, Beloved, I would remind you to be well groomed and clothed in the Armour of Righteousness before you go forth to do battle for Christ. Every plate of armour must be in its right place. You must be beyond reproach to face the rigid world as a teacher or instructor. Even the tiniest vice you may admit into your human body, mind or spirit will prove to be a missing plate in your protective Armour of Righteousness. Weigh carefully these words I now speak to you. I AM HERE.

My Beloved Messenger, there are many like you, who now are ready to go forth unto the Harvest. Truly this is the harvest time. The closing of the Great Cycle has come. Those who are mature in Life, Light, Love, Wisdom and Power, shall go forth FREE. You shall RISE INTO SONSHIP WITH GOD. YOU SHALL NOW ASCEND. I send you forth as my ambassadors. Millions stand waiting for YOU. They have heard MY VOICE in the stillness of the night. I have told them of MY COMING. In their HEARTS they know ME. When you, My Blessed Messenger, speak to them of ME, they will recall that they heard MY VOICE.

When you do go forth, Beloved, into the byways and highways of life, KNOW THAT I AM WITH THEE. Realize that even the Words of Love shall be uttered in your mouth through His Spirit, Lord Maitreya, that shall awaken your hearers as by magic. Each Word of Mine is charged by the Intelligent Power of Love. Each Word is Everlasting Life. Each Word you utter IN HIS NAME AND SPIRIT shall radiate forth that Godly Wisdom and Illumination that my Elder Brother Jesus used centuries ago when Lord Maitreya sent Him forth. WE ARE ONE IN CHRIST.

Your own Individual Spirit, My Beloved, knoweth the FATHER. In your Higher Mental Body—the One who watches over you—you were sent forth ages ago to carry a message to your Brothers and Sisters of the Shadow now living in darkness on this earth. I now empower you to go forth in His Name, Lord Maitreya. Now you have the Power and Light to dissolve all darkness. When a Brother of the Shadow comes near to you, you have the Intelligent Light and Power to instantly strip him of his wrongly qualified substance and energies. The Love-Light radiating from your Golden Heart will take care of him. He is powerless in the Presence of Christ Lord Maitreya. When He is with you who can be against you? Therefore, Beloved, be sure Christ is in your Heart before you step into the battlefield. Look well to your Armour of Righteousness. I AM WITH YOU ALWAYS IN ALL GOOD THINGS.

In the Sunlight of Silence I shall come to you, Beloved. Seek solitude among the flowering works of Nature. In the stillness of God's creations I soothe the ruffled feelings of My Children. In the noise and turmoil of the city I do not forget you. But you have most forgotten ME. Children of Light, surely you have at last learned your lesson. Will you not come into My Temple again? Will you not listen to My Voice, the Voice of Love?

Will you not, oh, Beloved, look for ME in these, Your Brothers? Judge them not. They are but yourself in themselves. They are this ONE LIFE manifest in many bodies, many minds and many spirits. Whatsoever you do unto any one of them you do unto Me, the Beloved Master. I AM SENT TO TEACH THROUGH LOVE.

Look into your Heart of Gold, Beloved. Look deep and long. Deeper stare, into the darkness of your being. See thou there a Light? Even though but the tiniest spark, fan it. Feed it fuel through Love. Breathe upon it My Light and Love. "Let there BE LIGHT" ever so bright in thy Golden Heart. See it expanding, see it enfolding, within you, and about you. "Know ye not that thou art the Temple of the Living God?" Through Him, Lord Maitreya, thou art made Whole. Call to your Father, the God of the Golden Heart, Mahachohan. He hears you. He answers your call, though feebly it may sound. He calls you unto His Throne in the Golden Sun. The Prodigal Son He calls Home again.

"In My Father's House there are many mansions," said My Elder Brother centuries ago. Yes, Beloved, the Fields of Bliss, too, are numerous. There are Heavenly places even on earth. Seek out the Beauty Spots where God's Light scintillates. Beneath some flowering ledge you may meet the Master of Love. There He may give you to drink from the "Chalice of Ecstasy." There He may come to speak to you, to teach you the ways of Love. Your Faith, Beloved, may draw Him near unto you. If it were not so I should not tell you. He cometh unto His own. "Fear not. God is not mocked. Whatsoever a man soweth, that shall he also reap."

Nature speaks in a strange voice, but beautifully if left alone. She heals over all scars when Love is Her helpmate. Forget the past, Beloved. Henceforth carry with you but the joys and beauties of Life. The marks and blemishes that may have fallen upon you are gone. The Light of Christ Maitreya dissolved them. No single shadow remains. His Love-Light enfolds you. His Love-Will directs you. His Power-Energy fills you. His Illuminating Spirit is ONE with you. Our Hearts beat as ONE in the Glory of His Presence. You are not alone.

Go forth, Beloved, among the Sheep of My Fold. Lift up the fallen. Heal the weak and weary ones, then teach them My Truths before you pass on. Bless the stranger. Your ways may seem strange to him, but he will not forget you. Memory of you will remain an example for him. Your healing Light will glow and expand in his aura. Your words will preach sermons to him long after you are gone. The Love you so stealthily set aflame in his heart will surely expand. Some day it will claim his whole being. Nothing IS but of God.

Listen unceasingly for my Voice in your Heart of Gold, Beloved. You are now an Alchemist, "distilling that Sweet Attar" in your Heart through Christ's Love. Its life-giving essence flows through your veins. It cleanses the very cells of your brain. Your mind becomes crystal clear through His Love-Light. Your entire body glows with His Warmth and Radiant Love. You thrill with His feeling of immortality. He places about you His Mantle. It is a Garment of Pink Light. He places in your hand a Golden Sceptre. Radiant Gems encrust its blazing receptacle. They scintillate forth the Powers of the Seven Lords of Life, Light and Love. Remember your Garment, Beloved. Forget not Thy Sceptre. These shall protect you eternally. Love is the measure by which you shall mete. Love determines the Vessel through which you receive. Without Love thou art barren of all good things.

Christ's Mystery lieth in your Heart. He calleth unto the Four Angels of Creation through Love and they do His bidding joyously.

CHAPTER XVII

We had thought—Ave Maria and I—that Christ had fully incarnated in her on November 12, but there was much more that had to be done in that body of hers before she could withstand higher vibrations of The Great Ones in the manner they wished. She was told there would be another expansion of the Cosmic Light in her body on November 29. This time it was even more trying, and we might say, disturbing, to the outer body than was the first preparation that had taken place on November 12.

We learned that all such matters were definitely planned by the Masters of the Great White Lodge. They placed much emphasis upon the necessary protection for Ave Maria during these times of stress in her body due to the expansion of the Light within her. Strange, but several times nuns and priests of the Catholic Church came there on the etheric plane, some of whom might have done harm because of their limited understanding, but being always seen, not only by Ave Maria, myself and Koot Hoomi, but other great beings of the Great Lodge, they were powerless to even impress their empiric ideas of religious rulership in the least. There were others at various times of other churches and empiric orders and organizations who were attracted there. Archangel Michael stood beside the bed of Ave Maria all during the night of November 29, and at other times was present to protect her. Saint Germain, in His Higher Body, would instantly appear at the slightest call from Her for protection. She was certainly guarded most closely. Any number of Lords from the Cosmic Realms came to pay their respects to her and to assure her of their protective love.

I must remind the reader again that I, while all this preparation for the incoming of Christ for the New Age was going on, held the office in the Great White Lodge of SILENT WATCHER. His powers were for the time being fully invested in me. I assure you it would have been impossible for any harm to come to Ave Maria at any time so long as I kept myself reminded of the power of the SILENT WATCHER in me. I could feel it at times with such potency and overpowering radiance, it is no wonder He, the Silent Watcher has been

129

referred to as the only ONE working in the world INDEPEND-
ENT OF THE LOGOS. He, as I understand it, has more
actually to do with the establishing of the Golden Age than any
other one Lord or God. He it is who has the Power of Almighty
God to do AT THIS TIME what is needed to be done in order
to handle the organized forces from the COSMIC STAND-
POINT who naturally, because of selfishness and power in the
outer world, are opposed to any economic changes that must be
brought about before Christ and His New Kingdom is actually
established on earth. Lord Maitreya explained to me how all
such organized forces that have been so long established on
earth preventing God's Kingdom coming to this planet HAVE
LOST THEIR POWER.

He went on to explain that they possessed power only on
the three lower planes. This he meant to be the power of the
selfish ones. Of course there are selfish priests, ministers and
members to all churches and empiric orders and organizations.
He did not mean that the Catholic Church or any other church
is not for some good purpose in the world. But he did explain
to me that all such powers that they might have held in the past
from a selfish standpoint have been taken from them. In the
past, for instance, the Catholic Church of Rome, because of the
limited understanding of the ecclesiastical heads of the institution,
did many things in the Name of Christ, which, when we analyze
them now, were of the lower order of etheric spirits of selfishness.
Just as an individual has all of his trouble in becoming master
in his three lower bodies, so you may see how the THREE
LOWER BODIES OF ALL THE ECCLESIASTICAL
RULERS AS WELL AS THE OTHER KINGS OF THE
PAST ON EARTH HAVE CREATED CONSIDERABLE
HELL HERE FOR US HUMAN BEINGS TO CONTEND
WITH. There were times on earth, on Atlantis and Lemuria,
when every ruler was One With Christ. In fact the kings were
Christs incarnate. They were Gods Incarnate. Such is now taking
place. The very Gods are incarnating and will rule on this earth
for TWO THOUSAND YEARS, so Lord Maitreya has
informed me.

You will find, My Beloved Student, that all regarding these
matters are set by the Gods, just as the stars of the heavens, and
if we master selfishness, jealousy, and all human weaknesses
such as history proves to us to have been THE CAUSE of all
the misery we have ever had on earth, then we shall enjoy human

happiness through REAL BROTHERLY LOVE and the Golden Age shall become an ACTUAL MATERIAL REAL-IZATION. Whether it be Catholic, Jew, Protestant, Lions Club, Rotary Club, the Masons, the Knights of Columbus, Federation of Labor or whatnot, wherever selfishness and the show of power exists for the purpose of providing for only a part of God's Children—SUCH POWERS OF SELFISHNESS SHALL BE ABOLISHED IN THE NAME OF CHRIST LORD MAITREYA. No longer can the demons of the Etheric Plane torment the people of this world. Their nefarious schemes will no longer work. "Truth crushed to earth shall rise again." This time the truth shall not only be made known to all True Seekers, but each and all shall see for themselves, just as I have seen the other planes and know when those selfish individuals undertake to bother me in the etheric plane.

In order to make this clear to you I shall tell you of an incident that was brought about by a Catholic Priest in Olympia, Washington, one time. Many times I have observed such activities on the etheric plane, so I know whereof I speak, and I know that such Black practices are to have no effect in the future upon those of you who are Children of Light. I had published a little magazine, as well as having first founded what is now the Olympia News there. Occasionally I would publish something regarding the New Age as I understood it. Again I might publish something regarding the Theosophical Society and its teachings. Of course in the past the Roman Hierarchy has been strongly opposed to anything that might lessen their central power empirically. That is quite natural, however, for any humanly created organization. One night just after I had retired, about eleven P. M., I had no more than gotten into bed, stretched out on my back and relaxed, when Father O——— appeared at the side of my bed waving a wand about twelve inches long over me. I looked at him quite sharply and he disappeared as quick as a flash. I went to the Catholic parish a few days later to pay a visit to Father O———. He was very nice to me. I told him I had seen him in a vision and being interested very much in religious matters, philosophy, etc., I felt that I should call on him. I asked him about certain parts of the Scripture. It was interesting to watch his reaction to my questions and statements. Frankly, he did not seem to be human. His eyes had a glassy stare as though he were hypnotized, or as though he were endeavoring to hypnotize me. I did not tell him that I saw the magic wand he had used over me, nor did I explain to him that I understood why some Catholic priests used such practices of the Dark Ages. But, Beloved, I know why they have used them for centuries and I know why they still use them, and I know why they do not have power any more over the less-informed Children of God. It is because too many of us are wise to those childish tricks of magic. And another reason is: They are all of the etheric plane, WHICH IS NOT OF GOD OR THE HIGHER MENTAL BODY. The whole world, including all who may know a little etheric magic, must rise into the HIGHER BODY and KNOW CHRIST. The GODS OF LIGHT are with me in this matter. That is why I am not afraid of all the priests and ministers in the world. Should they try to harm me THE MASTERS OF LIGHT WILL TAKE CARE OF THEM. "So mote it be."

Now, Beloved, I am not picking on the Catholics. I mention this incident, WHICH IS EVERY WORD TRUE, because I want you to know the truth. The Roman Catholic Hierarchy is the most powerful organization in the empiric realm. They form an international network throughout the world. But that does not make them any more like God than Aimee Semple McPherson's religious organization. However, that world-wide net has held the common level of humanity down for centuries. History proves this. The great Galilleo, the first astronomer to state that the earth was round, was condemned by Inquisition, simply because he would not change his statement at the request of the Pope, who quite naturally thought the world was flat. I dare say the Pope of Rome today admits that the world is round, but I firmly believe and KNOW there are many principles regarding CHRIST and HIS INCARNATION now for the New Golden Age that even he (the Pope) needs to understand and "experience," otherwise he would not proclaim certain tenets, subscribe to certain international activities under his direction, and he WOULD advise IN THE NAME OF CHRIST some very simple things that will ultimately bring about economic peace throughout the world, which will be the basis upon which the New Golden Age is to be founded.

I, Beloved, whoever you be, call to Lord Maitreya to bless you eternally. And know this, My Friend and Seeker after Light, I LOVE EVERY SOUL UPON THIS EARTH, ELSE I WOULD NOT PROCLAM WITH SUCH POWER THE VERY TRUTHS I AM WRITING. They are the TRUTH.

Mah-Atmah Amsumata

Lincoln said, "You can fool some of the people all the time, some of the people some of the time, but you can't fool all the people all the time." I say it is now coming to be that you can not fool anybody any of the time. I believe, also, that the priests and ministers of the gospel have just about come to that same conclusion, too. You cannot longer keep the truth from the people. And, furthermore, you cannot longer DECEIVE the people. This book gives the last great warning to the Brothers of the Shadow.

To return to the main thread of my narrative, it was on the 29th of November, too, that I was paid a visit by the Lord of Venus. He came into the body of Ave Maria. The room was filled with His radiance. He stood within three feet of me, saluting me in a different manner than any salute I had received from any other Master. For not less than five minutes that radiant being stood there gazing at me. It may seem strange to you but I knew what He was thinking all the time He was looking at me. He looked into every part of my body, my mind and spiritual being, I think, and He was wondering all the time whether I would be able to "take it." After He was well satisfied I could stand the test, He gave me a blessing in still another peculiar manner which I cannot reveal here. It was a special sign and symbolism from the Planet Venus. All this time, mind you, this Lord had not spoken a word. Following the blessing he walked into the sitting room, the grace and beauty of his being radiating through the body of Ave Maria. He sat on the far side of the room, I took a chair not far from the kitchen door. Neither of us had spoken a word, nevertheless, I am sure each of us knew what the other was thinking. In a calm sweet voice He said, "You have never sat in my aura before, have you?"

Thinking that probably he had been near me at some time when I was not aware of Him, I replied, "No, have you ever sat in mine?"

"Well, it isn't for ME to sit in your aura," he said in the most kindly voice. He so loved me when He said it, and I felt so ashamed of what I had said I assure you that I thought of my answer and his reply most all the next day. However, even though He is a God, I believe he misunderstood my meaning of what I had said, but I dare say that when he got back to Venus he told some of His Celestial Associates there that there was ONE fellow down on the earth who was not afraid of the Gods and who felt at least he possessed the potentialities of the Gods and even looked forward to being ONE some day.

The Lord of Venus, who later, during our conversation, told me he was Anoma, explained a number of principles of life to me, and somehow I felt He was the same individual as Buddha Gautama or Maitreya. I do know and have proved since that the Great Ones can play the part of many different beings. Why shouldn't they? They are at ONENESS with ALL. It was Anoma who invested me with the power of the NEW NINTH RAY. This RAY, in the hands of the Silent Watcher, I believe, is the most powerful Ray coming into the earth realm at this time. This is the Ray that is doing a marvelous "cleaning up" work necessary before the New Golden Age can be peaceably brought about, first "in the hearts" of mankind.

Yes, the power of the Ninth Ray is quite essential to me in preserving my life in this physical body until the Gods get through with me here on earth. I have seen that Ray used already and I know what it will do any time I need to direct it as a protective power. And it was never given into my hands until the Great Ones knew I would not abuse it or misuse it to the hurt of innocent ones. Blessed Peter of the New Testament is an example of where one of Christ's "chosen" ones misused the Light Rays entrusted to him. You have probably read how the old lady and old man kept back part of their money from Peter when all were asked to place their money and valuables into a common fund. Yes, they no doubt lied to Peter, but Peter should have handled the situation with a great deal more of Love than he did. Instead he became exasperated, drew the "Thunder Bolt" and the two poor ignorant, though selfish, followers dropped dead. Well, Beloved, you may think that was God who struck them dead, but I am of the honest opinion that it was Peter's temper that got away with him and having those great powers with him he suddenly lost his head and actually directed the Rays to them, killing them on the spot. So when anyone tells me of the wonderful things Peter did I always think of those poor ignorant ones he murdered.

To substantiate the above reference to Peter, as I have told you in a previous chapter, I met him in Tacoma, Washington, where he was embodied, and where he ascended in 1930. Now, had Peter learned to control his fiery temper when he was with Jesus and after He ascended while in that embodiment, he might have ascended and finished his earthly work several hundred years ago. Harry Eyer, the body in which Peter embodied in Tacoma, was a marvelous teacher of the mysteries and the Holy

Bible. He was fearless in his denunciation of all things evil, and explained to his eager audiences as well as his private students the most abstruse laws regarding the mysteries and the Cosmic Light that had ever been brought forth on earth at that time. He actually enlarged much upon the limited knowledge regarding the Cosmic Light that Millikan had discovered a few years previous. He told me how a number of years before Millikan made his discoveries he had, on the inner planes of consciousness, made numerous discoveries regarding the Cosmic Light and experimented with it considerably.

It happened that Mr. Eyer passed from the earth plane while I was in another part of the United States on a lecture tour. When I returned to Tacoma, after his decease, I visited with Mrs. Eyer, who, too, was an Adept, and she told me of the marvelous work her husband had done the last week he was in the physical octave. While he was sick that week, she explained, Jesus came and was with him most all the time. It was necessary that a Great Being of Peter's power and understanding, should do a certain work in preparation for the incoming Golden Age. Here is what he did, according to Mrs. Eyer: He went through the stratosphere of the earth and on into the Cosmic Center and carried a cable of Light through from the Cosmic Heart of Creation back through the stratosphere into this octave of life here on earth. He, with the help of Jesus and other Masters of the Great White Lodge, opened the way, in spite of all the organized selfish Anti-Christs, "wolves in sheep's clothing," etc., yes,—THEY OPENED THE WAY FOR THE GOLDEN AGE. THEY BROUGHT INTO THIS HELL THAT WAS CREATED BY THE BLACK FORCES ON THIS PLANET A NEW COSMIC ELEMENT THAT HAS BEEN DOING ITS MARVELOUS WORK ALL THESE YEARS SINCE. Look closely into this matter just related and you will find the cause of the history-making "WALL STREET CRASH."

Brother Eyer (Peter) had just recently returned from Portland, where he had delivered a number of lectures on this new Cosmic Element. Well, Beloved, they got Brother Eyer out of the body, but he brought in the Cosmic Light that has made it possible for all the Spiritual Awakening that has come about in the masses of mankind since 1929. All hail Brother Eyer, a Blessed Member of the Great White Lodge.

CHAPTER XVIII

During the month of December, our instruction — Ave Maria's and mine—continued unabated. It was December 11 that Lord Maitreya informed me I was to teach Ave Maria something regarding the Mantras and Sutras of the Orient I had received through the Universal Brotherhood. Now, she did not know I was a member of that order, nor did she know that I was conscious of my association with the Masters on the inner planes. She was somewhat surprised when Lord Maitreya, in her presence, told me that I should teach her, for, frankly, she, in her outer mind, had not considered me anything of a teacher. I had been so wholly taken up with what had come to me through Ave Maria and the other Masters I assure you I was not a little surprised myself when the Great Lord told me to instruct her.

For twelve years I had received instruction and training under various Directors of the Universal Brotherhood. I am not permitted to give their names, but they are numerous all over the world. But, remember this, Brothers of Light, all empiric orders and brotherhoods so-called are under the direction of the Council of the Great White Lodge, and Lord Maitreya is the Divine Director over all activities, inner and outer.

Lord Maitreya checked over all the Mantras and Mantric Blessings I had carried over my heart for the past twelve years. Each one he read and checked. Lord Maitreya, I might tell you now, is the only Great Master among all the Lords and Masters in this Universe, I was told by another, who understands all languages, dialects and tongues spoken on this earth by any and all races, nations, clans and tribes. He can speak a decree into the ethers of this world, too, and every living individual upon this earth will understand it instantaneously and simultaneously in his own mind as though it were spoken in his own tongue. As we come to the Universal understanding of Christ this is not so impossible of understanding.

As Lord Maitreya checked over those Mantras He came to one which was not "shaped" as it should be. "Who was your Director?" He asked, meaning, of course, the one who had sent me the documents of study and the mantras He was examining. I gave Him the name of the One who had been my Director up until about a year previous, when all documents stopped.

"There is something wrong here," He explained. "It is no wonder you have had so much difficulty. You should have been advanced long ago. He did not wish to advance you because you would have superseded him. Such symbols have great power. He has kept you in the 'material'."

"It might be that he did not understand," I said, hoping to give the erring brother the "benefit of the doubt."

"Oh, yes, he did understand," He exclaimed in a firm voice. And then He very positively affirmed, "HE WHO WANTED TO BE FIRST SHALL BE LAST."

Here, My Blessed Seeker, is an instance when the Great Divine Director of this Universe came forth to see that I, a Brother of the Universal Brotherhood who had been wronged, should be put in my rightful place. "Whatsoever a man soweth that shall he also reap." How that saying of Jesus' had gone through my mind hundreds and hundreds of times. Never, Beloved, had I doubted the Truth of that declaration of law. Be patient and whatsoever is to come to you through the laws of justice, shall reach you when you least expect it.

I gave Ave Maria, under the direction of Lord Maitreya, the various instructions I should. He at the same time declared me a GURU, which means in the words of the Western World, Master-Teacher.

At that time Mrs. Mary Todd, of Eureka, was staying with Ave Maria in Mount Shasta City. She had lived at my hotel in Eureka, was an ardent student of the "I AM" teachings of Saint Germain, and received much instruction from Ave Maria, myself and other Masters. She was later carried so high into the Higher Teachings that her physical body could not withstand the vibration. She had physical reactions that all but took her out of the body. Later, however, she was healed by Koot Hoomi, myself and others. She consciously went through the "crucifixion," so she said when she appeared to Ave Maria and me in spirit in May, 1941. It is my earnest prayer that she has attained the ascension she sought so fervently. I am not in touch with her at this time in the outer plane. She had been a great admirer of my little son David, who ascended.*

*I later contacted this lady in Willits, Calif., May 27, 1942, found her well and happy, thus verifying all I had learned through the Spirit.—*Author*.

A few days before Christmas Joshua came to me, giving me much instruction of great importance to me, since I was soon to leave for the North, where I was to do certain work in the interest of the Great White Lodge. Saint Germain had told Koot Hoomi to tell me that I should get out and do some hard work, physical work, which was essential before I could ascend. There were certain atomical changes that should take place in my body, Koot Hoomi explained, as a matter of purification, before I would be able to receive certain other initiations and states of consciousness so necessary in the future work I was expected to do.

Joshua knew I was to go north. She knew I was to be given severe tests, too, as well as the "hardening" work I was to do. In other words, Friends of the Light, I was to be placed on PROBATION. If I passed the tests I was to return to Mt. Shasta to receive the "Fifth Initiation." If I were to pass through the Fifth, then I was to be "crucified." Should I pass safely through the Crucifixion, then I would ASCEND. Joshua spoke to me so compassionately, so beautifully, regarding my trip north. She said, "You may wonder why so much has been put upon you, John, but it is BECAUSE THE MASTERS LOVE YOU SO MUCH. They want you to finish the necessary work as quickly as possible, so you will be through. I do not like to see you go up north, but they tell me it is essential to your mastery. Remember, whatever you contact, call upon us and we will be with you."

I had nothing to say but, "Yes, Joshua, I understand." It seemed that everything she told me I understood within myself before she spoke. However, the more she spoke to me in that sweet little voice of hers, the more joyously I could go forth to do whatever the Masters required of me. She was certainly preparing me, warning me, arming me, for whatever might come my way. For about an hour she talked to me, love radiating from her Blessed Heart, charging every word she spoke. Before she left I am sure the most excruciating suffering that might have befallen me could have been endured joyously, rejoicingly, since I knew that all was for the purpose of preparing me for the BLESSED ASCENSION. GOD BLESS JOSHUA!

Near the first of December I had been sent on a mission by Lord Maitreya to Eureka, California. I had been a leader in the "I AM" movement there under the Ballards, as you will recall. Lord Maitreya placed on my finger a ring of Koot Hoomi's which Ave Maria had received while in Tibet. It is a gold ring with the letters KH interwoven upon it. I did not know just what Lord Maitreya wanted me to do. I asked him about this. He replied, "You go ahead and do what you think you should do. I do not interfere with my Priests. You are now one of my Priests. Should you start to make a mistake I will let you know. I DO NOT ALLOW MY PRIESTS TO MAKE MISTAKES. THIS RING WILL PROTECT YOU WHILE YOU ARE AWAY FROM HERE."

I saw a number of things I felt should be done while in Eureka. I informed all those who had been associated with me in the "I AM" activity what I had contacted in Mt. Shasta. I frankly told them of my marvelous experiences. I know Lord Maitreya wanted it published, for I knew it was to be a part of the future "build-up," so to speak, essential in broadcasting the TRUE EXPERIENCES of the ASCENSION of myself and Joshua. Most of those I talked to in Eureka, accepted my message from the Masters, however, many of them wrote in to Los Angeles to Mrs. Ballard, asking her about it. However, Mrs. Josephine Barker, the one who succeeded me as Group Leader in Eureka, and one whom I loved very much, permitted me to talk to the students in the Eureka Sanctuary following her regular group meeting. I invoked the Masters and their Blessings in the Sanctuary, made the "SIGN AND SALUTATION OF THE GREAT CENTRAL SUN," and explained to the Blessed Ones present what would be coming about within the next few months upon earth. I was greatly inspired. I spoke with such power it actually shook the building. I am certain all True Students of Saint Germain's felt those words spoken on the inner levels. That is what Lord Maitreya wanted, I found later. He wanted the Truth radiated throughout the whole "I AM" group, and He knew that that would have to be done in one of their regular meeting places in order to meet or BLESS the EGOIC GROUP. It was done beautifully, so I was informed by Lord Maitreya when I returned to Mount Shasta. He almost wept with joy when he told me how perfectly I had performed the duties I had been called upon to do. It was only after that enlightening experience in His charge that I began to feel the importance of my being a PRIEST OF LORD MAITREYA'S. All my life I had prayed to be a True

Minister of the Gospel. I had vowed never to teach or preach about anything I had not experienced. Now, I thought, I can go forth into the world with the GREATEST MESSAGE EVER BROADCAST TO THE WORLD. "How Blessed I AM," I repeated to myself again and again. "It is all like a dream, but I know it is true."

Following is a letter received by one of the Group Leaders in Eureka following my visit there for Lord Maitreya:

THE BILTMORE HOTEL
515 So. Olive St.
Room 9309
Los Angeles, California

Dec. 16, 1940.

Beloved One of the Light:

Your letter of December 8th, as well as that of several others from Eureka, have been received.

Because of more important matters needing my attention at this time, I will not go into detail regarding the matter you refer to, for the Student Body knows the Law concerning such things. For your information and peace of mind, I will state that I have had no contact with Mr. Norman Westphal* personally or otherwise, regarding his new adventure, nor do I know anything concerning it.

As you know, Students are quite free to follow whatsoever they desire, and if they accept something outside of the "I AM" Activity as more important to them, then their cards will be removed from our files, and they will not be permitted to attend our classes.

With all the Love of my Life-stream, I call to the "Mighty I AM Presence" and Great Host of Ascended Masters, to take command of every "I AM" Student in your city, charge them with Ascended Master wisdom, Discriminating Intelligence, Invincible Protection, and see they do the Perfect thing.

Sincerely in the Light,

(Signed)   MRS. G. W. BALLARD.

As soon as I returned to Mt. Shasta I wrote Mrs. Ballard regarding all that had transpired. I venture that she received my letter a few hours after she had written the above letter to the many Eureka inquirers, providing Mrs. Ballard knew her secretary had written such a letter, since I sometimes wonder if Mrs. Ballard knows all the activities of her trusted secretary.

---

*Mrs. Ballard spelled my name with a "p," which significantly told me something of the sinister forces who were evidently controlling her activity.—*Author*.

On Christmas Eve, while a number of us were gathered about a Christmas tree, a beautiful five-pointed STAR OF LIGHT actually descended into the room, evidently falling upon the head of Ave Maria. She exclaimed, "There is the Star of Christ. He is fully incarnated on earth. Amsumata, we have accomplished the work expected of us much earlier than the Masters had planned. This is the greatest Christmas Eve this world has witnessed since Jesus was on earth most two thousand years ago."

Koot Hoomi had told us previously that the Christ would step forth fully illuminated by March 10, 1941. As it was, He came forth in His Glory on Christmas Eve, 1940. As I was leaving that evening for Eureka again on a business trip, we enjoyed our Christmas party, opening the packages, rejoicing in the Great Spiritual Event, making the children happy who were present. My four children, Norman, Jr., James, Edward and Anne Elizabeth, as well as Mrs. Mary Todd, were present with Ave Maria.

May the Blessing of Lord Maitreya, Christ to this Solar System, descend upon all Children of Light throughout the world and may we again sing, "ALL LIGHTS UNITED IN THE ONE GREAT LIGHT."

I am so very happy, Blessed Maitreya, that at last the world is approaching to that illuminating point where they will understand your Light and Love. It is the most transcendent vision to see all Churches, all Light Groups, all Constructive Organizations in this world coming INTO THE ONE GREAT LIGHT.

Just think of it, Blessed Students of Light, HOW MARVELOUS IT WILL BE WHEN CATHOLICS, PROTESTANTS, JEWS, Mohammedans, Buddhists, Brahmans, Confucianists, and any and all religions and philosophies combine together in that ONE GREAT LIGHT WHICH IS GOD ALMIGHTY. Think of the misery and "HELL" we have caused each other in the world in the past because of our ignorance of the WAYS OF GOD AND HIS LIGHT. When we look back over the BLACK PAGES in THE BOOK OF EARTH LIFE, do you not shudder with horror? How happy we are—Saint Germain and all the Spirits in My Lifestream—when I see the NEW JERUSALEM, as a mighty SHIP, just in the offing, ready to ENTER THE HARBOR NOW PREPARED BY THE TRUE CHILDREN OF

LIGHT. It matters not to me, Blessed Ones of Light, what outer church or group you regard yourself in association. Look deeply into your heart, BE TRUE TO YOURSELF and call to the ONE MASTER who resides therein. He will hear your VOICE whenever you SPEAK THOUGH LOVE, for all Love comes from His Heart, THE LORD OF LOVE, MAITREYA, CHRIST TO THIS UNIVERSE. When you know Christ you become ONE WITH HIM. When you understand this SIMPLE MYSTERY you will have known Christ is not "here nor there," but in the HEARTS of those who LOVE HIM. He knoweth His Own. "Let not your heart be troubled. I AM WITH THEE ALWAYS." When Thou, My Beloved, knoweth ONE MASTER thou knoweth ALL MASTERS, for "We are ONE BODY WEE." Let all who have "open ears" hear, and all with "open eyes," SEE THE TRUTH.

Now that the priests, bishops, cardinals, and all ecclesiastical rulers of the Roman Catholic Church and all other Catholic Churches, and all religions in the world, know THEY MUST ASCEND INTO THE HIGHER PLANES IN ORDER TO WIELD ANY POWER ANY MORE, WE SHALL ESTABLISH THE NEW KINGDOM.

CHAPTER XIX

January 9, 1941, my three sons and myself left Mt. Shasta for Olympia, Washington, where a younger brother of mine resides. Although my brother had always been harmonious with me, I was not surprised to learn that he and his wife were not willing to cooperate with me a great deal in taking care of the children. I did not blame them, however, but knew that opposition was due to my spiritual development. They did, however, agree to take care of my youngest son, Edward, temporarily, at least. This I greatly appreciated.

Through a friend of mine in Bremerton, Washington, I was able to get the kind of employment there I needed. I had lived in Bremerton previously, and was able to get a job working on the county highways. Charles Kleinfelter, a former friend and student of mine and one of the county commissioners of Kitsap County, gave me employment. I worked hard there a part of January, February and part of March. Housing conditions were terrible in Bremerton. For the first few weeks we stayed at the Navy Y.M.C.A., but because of the need of all available quarters being needed by the government men we were forced to leave there. For some time we were compelled to sleep in a damp basement—the two boys and myself—where nine of us were quartered in most undesirable conditions. The boys became sick with the measles, but were not long in getting well. I was also unable to work for one day. Cost of board and lodging required all I could make, since I earned but little more than $100 per month.

While working on that road job I really over-did the matter of hardening up my muscles and preparing my body for what Saint Germain had asked. A time or so I lifted too much. I did, however, enjoy the work. Much of the time it rained. I had good rain clothes, rubber boots and everything to make the work agreeable, yet I had much difficulty becoming adjusted to the climate, the work, as well as the clothing. I was wet with perspiration inside the clothes most of the time and wet from rain outside. My body did pass through certain alchemical changes. I was actually so tired many evenings when I came

143

in from work I would almost fall into a chair where I would fall asleep to wake up later chilled by the wet clothing I had on my body. It was during this trying ordeal that Saint Germain appeared to me in spirit—in that damp, dirty basement—with a large White-Light Five-Pointed Star which He presented to me, stating to me in certain well-understood words that I had PASSED THE TESTS. I knew then that my "hardening" and re-chemicalization work was finished. I notified Mr. Kleinfelter that I was quitting, and moved to Seattle. There I planned to give a few lectures.

I delivered three lectures at the Gowman Hotel in Seattle, April 27, 28 and 29. There were but eighteen or twenty people attended. The lectures were little advertised. All who attended were greatly enthused and asked to keep in touch with me. Mrs. Maud Brown assisted me a great deal while at the Gowman Hotel and in other ways helped me in caring for my sons while there. Mahatma Koot Hoomi appeared to me while at the hotel, explaining to me certain instructions.

Knowing that I was expected in Mount Shasta by May 11, 1941, to receive certain other initiations, I left Seattle May 9, arriving there early in the morning of May 10.

Before I continue with the initiatory work I received I wish to quote for you a letter I was compelled by the Spirit of Lord Maitreya to write to the outer personality of "She Who Is Nameless" while at the Y.M.C.A. in Bremerton. This letter was necessary to bring about complete harmony between us in the outer activity, which, invariably, is something each and every Student of Light has to contend with as they travel the "Path of Attainment." The letter, self-explanatory, follows, and was principally for the purpose of developing more LOVE in "HER" outer person, since she had become overbalanced with "WISDOM AND POWER." Kindly notice the wisdom Lord Maitreya used in the letter. It follows:

March 2, 1941.
Y.M.C.A.
Bremerton, Wash.

Blessed One of the Light:

Even though I do not agree with you in all you have written me, however, I was exceedingly happy to hear from you, and sincerely ask Lord Maitreya and the entire Host of Ascended Masters shed their Light and Intelligence, Wisdom and Power—AND *LOVE*—upon you, and keep it forever sustained. May DIVINITY attend you eternally.

I hope you will not be irritated with me should I be most frank with you. My *desire*—just as yours is, I know—is to assist every individual who needs help. When—even—the body or personality of an Ascended Master such as I have every reason to believe you are, really needs help, it is up to me to do my utmost to help you. THIS IS THE LAW. I KNOW THE LAW. Even if I never attained what I desire to attain, still I KNOW WHAT I SHOULD ATTAIN, for I KNOW THE LAW OF MY OWN FREE WILL AND ACCORD and BECAUSE OF MY DIVINE RIGHT. You can never attain more than I aspire to attain. It may be possible that you have attained more than I *at present*. This is beside the point. You have not yet proved to me that you are WISER.

You speak of standing alone as a PILLAR in one paragraph, and even in the beginning of your letter you wrote, "I was not moved before today to write you. AS SOON AS I WAS TOLD TO DO SO I DID." In other words you have to be told what to do. Regarding such matters as writing to ONE IN THE LIGHT—a Brother—I do not have to be told when to write. To be most frank I might suggest that when you KNOW THE LAW well enough to know what to do without being told, then it might be well for you to preach to others about being a STRONG PILLAR, standing alone and travelling alone. Please forgive me if this sounds harsh. My Heart decided.

You say your misson is not my mission. I do not believe this, for OUR MISSION and the mission of every TRUE INITIATE is to ESTABLISH THE GREAT KINGDOM ON EARTH "AS IT IS IN HEAVEN." Understand, please, that I do not wish to be irreverent, nor would I say or write one single thing that would deter you from the Pathway of Light, however I must be true to my Own Presence, My Individual Master, for it is only by being TRUE TO MYSELF THAT I MAY BE TRUE TO YOU AND ALL MASTERS AND ALL MANKIND.

You mention the note I wrote to you about "going straight to the Boss." Well, my dear, did not Lord Maitreya tell me to do so? You might recall, if you have forgotten, that Many times Lord Maitreya told me things that you were not aware of. Are you higher than Lord Maitreya? Are you higher than God Almighty of the Great Central Sun? WHO AM I? Have you a right to "judge me"? Please, dear, better not judge others. Remember, my Dear Sister, we are both teachers—natural and Divinely Inspired—and it is up to each of us as well as all aspiring human beings, Masters, Gods, Lords, Archangels—or what not—to bear with each other, help each other, love each other, for, after all, LOVE IS THE GREATEST OF ALL ATTAINMENTS OR POSSESSIONS, for it is the Universal, Infinite Cement of Understanding. WITHOUT IT YOU CANNOT SURMOUNT THE LAST FEW ROUNDS OF THE LADDER TO EVERLASTING PEACE,

WISDOM, AND POWER, and if you already have them you cannot hold them without LOVE — D I V I N E L O V E.

I love you, otherwise I would not be so rigid and frank with you, and remember, I can be STERN. I have much LOVE for ALL humanity, not just a few Chosen Masters. He who has ears to hear let him hear, and she, too.

Let us not swell up with pride over our attainments, especially in the physical octave, for IT is such a SMALL PART of ALL LIFE, LOVE, WISDOM AND POWER.

You have wondered why Blessed Koot Hoomi weeps so much. I do not wonder, for I, too, weep much—not because of myself, but because of the lack of understanding, love, wisdom, etc., of humanity in general. The saddest thing in all the world to me is the lack of wisdom, and the heedlessness of human beings. Even though, however, I cannot help but feel happy when I think of the great advancement that has been made by the masses of mankind during the past 2,000 years, since my Blessed Elder Brother Jesus came in His ministry. May His Great Work go on, and my dear, may you and all Masters of Light realize the importance of OUR MISSION in establishing the Great Kingdom of God on Earth as it is in Heaven.

Please forget not what you came here to do. Question yourself diligently, lovingly, and remember no one can rise higher than God Almighty, and surely all of us aspire to LIVE IN THE GOLDEN HEART OF GOD.

Incidentally, He who gives up all finds ALL. He who would give up This Life shall find REAL LIFE EVERLASTING. It is probable, my dear, that the things you prize—IN THE OUTER WORLD—I do not consider at all valuable. I do know, however, that I am being trained for a very important work to be done after the Big Change, and I am certain, whether you acknowledge it or not, SHOULD YOU DO THAT WHICH YOU WERE SENT TO DO, our paths will cross many times, and we must assist each other in all possible ways in the work of the Great Kingdom in the Great Circle. Personally, you are just a human being to me; spiritually you are a DIVINE MASTER. Verily, I believe I see more in YOU than you SEE in yourself.

The old saying is "Ye cannot serve two Masters." It is the One Great Master, the Master of Masters, the Lord of Lords, I look to. And you?

Meekness before God is a paramount principle for all Masters to consider. True humbleness is the Key to His Kingdom, Joshua. You have such a full and complete Love. (Notice here, I am writing to Joshua through Her Mother.) Your gentleness is expressed through the sweetness of your musical voice. You have supplied the necessary solvent to my

146

toughened heart, and changed it back again to the tenderness of mother-love. Abracadabra. May every cell within my physical body be transmuted into the Universal Gold of the Alchemists. May your love, my Blessed Twin, ever remain my protective mantle.

Yes, I was greatly privileged to have been taught by A. M. The love She expressed for me ONE DAY shall live for thousands of years. I recall the first time I saw her in this embodiment—before I met J............ —on an inner plane of consciousness, walking a lonely road—I remarked when I embraced Her, "I have not seen you for a thousand years." I wept with joy. She first came in the form of a dove, then took on the form of A.M. and said "I AM MARIA."

I am becoming much more in tune with you and others on the inner planes, Joshua. My All-Seeing Eye is opening. Lord Maitreya opened it for me, so He said. I am His Disciple—His Priest. He seems closer to me than any other, although I feel I must "walk close to Koot Hoomi." I have never yet asked Lord Maitreya for a thing that He has not given it to me. Of course I do not ask Him for non-essential things. I want to do what He and the Great Presence inspire me to do. He once said to me, "I do not allow my Priests to make mistakes." (Please consider.)

The fact that A. M. has gone to the Sun proves Her Infinite Love.

Remember, Joshua, I may make mistakes in the physical octave, but they are made usually in an endeavor to prove the goodness of God's Love. My Great Presence—the Silent Watcher—does not permit me to stray far from the eternal Pathway of God's Light.

So you, Joshua, are chosen to be the Virgin of Wisdom of Joshu. What a blessing! I knew you were going through great initiations, and I AM with you ALWAYS in your trials for Supreme Mastery.—S.W.

Regarding the money matters, J............, I am doing very well, but am paid by the month, and only received a half month on the 13th of Feb., and do not get paid again until the 14th of this month. I shall take care of all obligations. I am working with this in mind. I told A............ I would have to be back there in May. She has a lot of my things there she is keeping for me. She should not be uneasy. I have had so little time to write, I hope she will forgive me. Usually I am so tired at night I do not feel able to do anything but rest. You see, I am doing very hard work— pick and shovel—the hardest of labor. I feel that it is essential to my present unfoldment. Please rest assured I am doing all I can. I shall be in Mt. Shasta in May, God willing.

Night before last Dorothy walked into the room when I was sitting alone. (In her finer body.) She was very happy. I saw the door open. She did not think I saw her at first. It made me very happy. I am sure she is attaining higher and higher planes all the time. She is a busy Master. She helps me, too.

I received a letter from dear Mrs. Barker. She said Anne was a wonderful child, so little bother, and she was so glad to have her there for a while. I must write to Anne soon. Kiss her for me. She is precious to all of us. The boys are fine. Edward is with my brother in Olympia.

Give my love and best wishes to Mrs. Todd. I feel very close to her at times. I talk to Dr. LaC. occasionally.

Lovingly in the Light,

(Not Signed)

P.S.—J.............., should you see fit to do so, and are not too provoked with me, I hope you will mail this letter back to me, as I would like to keep it for future reference. Or, should you keep it, I can get it when I return to Shasta. Will you kindly do this for me? And will you consider the letter entirely impersonally, for I am sure it comes to you from ONE BEYOND me in this world? And I do pray that you will not be irritated too much with me about it. It is your Higher Self I love. I am not infatuated with you in any other way. Please bear this in mind. OUR MISSION is beyond any personal feelings.

Divine Love,

Norman.

Even though I had not slept any on the night of May 9 while I was travelling from Seattle to Mount Shasta City, by 9 o'clock on the morning of the 10th Ave Maria and I were walking toward Mt. Shasta, talking of the many experiences we had encountered while apart. We looked up to the sun in the heavens when we were surprised to see the "Rings of Buddha" clearly radiating about it like an enlarged picture of the "Rainbow Spirit." Ave Maria knelt on her knees for a few minutes in supplication to The Lord of Lords.

We soon returned to the abode of Ave Maria where we ate lunch and later talked over the work we were to do in the interest of the Great White Lodge. The following day, May 11, we understood to be a day when certain initiations were to be given us as well as some others who might be there in body or in spirit. Ave Maria had made arrangements for such an occasion. We prepared an altar in the yard under a shady apple tree. There on May 11 at "High Noon" we, Anne Elizabeth, Ave Maria and I, sitting together, invoked the blessings of the Great Lords.

Among other instructions and initiatory degrees conferred upon us I received the following letter from Ave Maria, signed by her in her outer name signature:

> High Noon
> May 11, 1941.
> Mt. Shasta, Calif.

The following I am asked to give to the Masters of the Western Hemisphere:

Christ was in body on the morning of 12/27/40, drawing the Presence closer and closer to the body. Buddha Gautama, a Lord from Venus, came in His full Presence, then Christ spoke:

"Christ and Buddha will now extend the hands of their Presence, each others hands. Sun Christ and Sun Buddha now unite into oneness and express as the ONE SUN in Jehovah's Kingdom."

The Voice of Jehovah was heard: "My Son I am well pleased in this Union."

Then Master Koot Hoomi stepped through saying: "My labors are now over. There were two years when I labored heavy for the Union of the two Sons of Jehovah. They were years of suffering and pains, but I am so happy to know that this, which was a great strain for Ave Maria (Mary) and myself, is accomplished." "May the world know," he said, "She must know that the Union has happened. I, myself, and Ave Maria claim but one thing, 'We lay ourselves a foundation for the Great Temple (of the Great Temple) of the Golden Age in which two great pillars are standing—Christ and Buddha, and the Two in ONENESS—THE GREAT SUN, that shall shine over the Great Waters, and never shall She go down, but is SHINING BRIGHT IN THE KINGDOM OF JEHOVAH.'"

(Signed)   E. S.

Blessed Students of Light, this letter is the confirmation of the unifying of the EAST and the WEST in the ONE GREAT PHILOSOPHY OF LIFE. One God blesses all mankind. On the 11th of May, 1941, the Great Mahatma Koot Hoomi did come forth to declare, in writing, through Ave Maria, that ALL LIGHTS ARE NOW UNITED IN THE ONE GREAT LIGHT.

Let us be thankful, Brothers and Sisters of Light throughout the world, that at last we can see the Universal Christ in the Light of God Almighty radiating throughout the East and the West as the all-enfolding Presence in Blessing all mankind.

In September, 1940, Ave Maria had sent to me a paper to be published in the Scott Valley Beacon, a weekly newspaper I published at Etna, California. That article, which she had titled "Man Know Thyself," was misplaced somehow and never published. Months later, after I had left Etna, I found it among some valuable papers of my own. I now realize that the article was not to have been published at that time for reasons the Masters best understand, but I here produce the paper for your perusal, which follows:

MAN KNOW THYSELF

We have invented means to talk thousands of miles by wire, radio, television and telephone. All are man's creations. But has man progressed within as well? Is he transforming his own consciousness into the highest consciousness possible? I am speaking of the spiritual man.

In the midst of strange world conditions comes to me, my reader, a call. "Man Know Thyself" are the very words that were written over the temples of initiation of the lost world of Atlantis, in the temples of Greece, of Egypt and Tibet, and these very words are the words that were spoken by the Masters to their disciples.

If we wish to understand these great wise men of Atlantis we must let their mind, THEIR CONSCIOUSNESS, guide us, and the Master-Mind will FILL US, and find expression through those that have acquired mastery.

How can we understand the language of the Masters except we become aware of the powers of the inner man? the true Self? the God within? unless we give up the world as Christ taught us? This means entry into our heart, which we must fill with pure thoughts, as the heart is the Sanctuary of God.

How can we become a follower of the Star, a part of the Brotherhood of Love? To be initiated into this Brotherhood of Love we must give up greediness, gossip, fault-finding, and rather become the uplifters of those that are still in a sleeping state of mind, and we, by doing so, become leaders of a new generation that is willing to take up the threads of the wise men of old. We must be willing to be guided by their wisdom.

Where are the Seers today? Where are the Masters? I hear some question me. For a second I want to speak to the hearts of those that question this.

Is it possible that you who are greedy and material-minded will hear the voice of the wise men, the Messengers of God? You that doubt their existence are the cause of the Masters fleeing today into silence and obscurity. They become visible for those that believe in them.

Is a communication with the Masters possible? There is such possibility. The Masters teach us this: The communications can be between two mental bodies, between two emotional bodies, between two etheric portions of two brains. There are three types of telepathy—etheric, emotional and

150

mental. The Master sends out a mystic or sacred geometrical symbol, such as a triangle, a cross, an eight-pointed cross, a cube, an Egyptian cross or Tau into the etheric substance so that it can be seen by one having etheric sight. While in the creating of this symbol he sends out etheric waves. Those waves strike another brain and reproduce in the other brain an image. Three persons might react to the sacred symbol sent out, each in a different manner. One might see it in his mind's eye as a triangle, another may see the word "triangle", and the third party may mentally perceive it. The most active sense will be affected either through the eye, the ear or the brain.

Emotional telepathy is different than etheric telepathy. The emotional telepathy is connected with visions or premonitions. The recipient will become aware of either a vision or a spoken word. Our emotions are felt by the Masters and they, feeling the sorrow or gloom of others, radiate to the ones in distress with a wave of healing thoughts, peace, love and harmony. Mental telepathic thoughts are communicated from the mind of the sender to the mind of the recipient.

As our race evolves and enters the higher mind for good, for harmonizing the individual mind, the race will be allowed to use such telepathy and also attune herself to the Universal Mind, the Infinite Mind, so that Wisdom may come to earth again and the Star of the Wise Men may shine on our path, and the Lost Word will become the Found Word, and then man is ready to awaken the God within his heart. The Embodied Lord then becomes the conscious ruler of Life, Light, Wisdom—the I AM.

CHAPTER XX

LONGING

I long for freedom in the world of man,
And peacefulness in it from end to end;
For a place of retreat where silence is found,
So quiet that but my heart-beats may sound
To remind me that I AM ONE WITH GOD,
Father of man, beast, plant and sod.

I pray that His beauty reign supreme;
That each individual read His theme
And know the plan of the Great Architect
Unfolds to each man, church, creed and sect
As they acknowledge His Fatherhood
And proclaim the Great Brotherhood, among men.

I wish for myself, secluded from strife,
To render a service of action and life,
Though free to lull in pastures green,
To pause in beauty-spots I've seen,
Yet, send out messages of cheer
To striving people far and near.

I seek the solitudes up most high—
For peaked rocks and frozen brooks;
For pure eternal snows I'll try,
Bereft of man-wise crypts and books.
I hope to find my Sanctuary
A grotto in a mountain aery.

* * *

The eleventh of May, 1941, to me was a very important date because it was on that date that I received new inspiration and was also installed as Silent Watcher in the Great White Lodge. Ave Maria on the same day was placed in charge, temporarily at least, of the Second Ray. Lord Maitreya explained to us how the Truth had been inscribed in the Hearts of the Sons of God.

I was also given a paper by Ave Maria, "AUM TAT SAT," which I shall produce herewith for your study. It is simple, but powerful for good:

"AUM TAT SAT"

"Learn thou this by discipleship, by investigation, and by service. The Wise, the Seers of the essence of things, will instruct thee in wisdom. As the burning fire reduces fuel to ashes, O, Arjuna, so doth the fire of Wisdom reduce all sins to ashes. With the Sword of the Wisdom of the Self cleaving asunder this ignorance-born doubt, dwelling in thy heart, BE ESTABLISHED IN DIVINE UNION (In God). STAND UP! You are FREE from bondage—you that has given up hate, desire."

(AUM TAT SAT—By that are we ordained Brahmans.)

* * *

On May 13, while Ave Maria and I were conversing alone Issa (Jesus) came to invite me to follow with him to Lhassa, Tibet, to enter the Priesthood of The Temple of Lhassa within six months or a year, to receive a Third Great Initiation, in order to complete my mastership. This was at 1 P.M. Fifteen minutes later Issa returned and healed a condition in my spine that had bothered me considerably for about seven years. He said He sent it back to the one who had unjustly hurled it at me years previous. Thus, that one must carry it until released by Issa.

"Issa," I must explain, is the name by which Jesus is called in the Orient. He is much better known in Tibet, India and China than He is in other parts of the world. They do not merely know Him as He manifest in the one embodiment, but they know Him in His many manifestations of Mastery and Perfection.

At other times I was asked to go into a retreat by Lord Maitreya, Koot Hoomi and Buddha Gautama, but Saint Germain (WE) explained that there was very much that we had planned to do here in the Western World before we might consider total seclusion. Where I now reside is a beautiful Retreat, but not in the same sense as the more secluded Retreats of Tibet. Mt. Shasta, "The Mountain of God" in America, is indeed the greatest focus of Light in the Western World at this time and will so remain until the Great Work planned by the Great White Lodge is completed here for the in-coming and establishing of the New Golden Age.

The poem, "Longing," as well as the one following, were written in 1937 when I was most desirous of going into a Retreat for initiation and occult training, which is quite evidenced in the heart-felt appeal I voice to my Higher Presence:

ALONE

I want to be alone,
Away from people and noisy things,
Secretly hidden in a wilderness
Of Nature, midst kindly trees,
Snugly tucked beneath brambles,
Shielded by sprawling vine maples,
Close to warm earth,
Covered by dry leaves,
On a high mountain,
But still, in a fairy-like dell
Where delicate forest blossoms
Their faint fragrance spill
Into the air about me.

I long to be lost thus
Far, far away,
With my thoughts to think
I AM ONE WITH ALL
That breathes and lives
IN THE LIGHT
Of actuality.

I MUST be alone,
Unto myself, with God and Nature,
Away from the human multiple,
Into the Silent One,—
The womb of Time,
Of motion, all things,
Where brood a million myriads—
Shapes, colors, sounds
And qualities—
In such an earthly maze
My mind reels,
Sickens of Time,
Seeks solitude and longs
To be alone
In silent meditation
Where "I AM" GOD;
Where not but the Wheel of Life
But the Sphere of Light—
All Eternal Being—
Spins before my Inner Sight.

And, Beloved Student of Light, should I tell you how much like that place I described in the poem—from my inner vision—is like unto this place where I now reside, you would say we DO live in an age when miracles are brought "in the Light of Actuality." May you, in your sojourn in life, find that place of rest and peace for which your Soul is "longing," and I am sure when found you will be "ALONE" with God.

The Path of Attainment may be devious, Beloved Disciple of Light and Truth, but as a child, in its first three years absorbs and learns so much of the ways of man, so you shall seek here, there and everywhere, believing and trusting those who might lead you into that Spiritual Retreat where you will become a god "in silent meditation." The above little effort at poetry I scribbled down at a time when life in the outer world was almost unbearable. I had to go into the Retreat in my own heart else I could never have endured my physical trials. These things I bring to your attention to aid you in your realization of ONE-NESS WITH GOD.

While in the Retreat with Koot Hoomi, Ave Maria had been given the "Great Dharani" to study to bring about the great reverence to the Masters necessary for one's advancement and spiritual development. One day she asked me to re-type it for her. She had used that precious paper upon which it had been typed until it was falling apart. She had, so it happened, folded it up each time she placed it away. The folding, unfolding, handling, etc., had just about destroyed it. When I finally got all the words together, with her help, and finished typing it, I asked her if she would give me the original copy Master KH had given her. I got some glue and a plain sheet of paper and very painstakingly pasted it back together as best I could. Part of it, however, I had to copy off on another sheet of paper. I have this original here before me and shall produce it herewith for you, as follows:

"THE GREAT DHARANI"

Adoration to all Buddhas and Bodhisattvas!
Obeisance to their perfect Enlightment and perfect Tranquility.
Adoration to all living Arhats;
Adoration to the millions of disciples who make up the Sangha.
Adoration to those who have "entered the stream";
Adoration to those who have but "one more return";
Adoration to those who "will never more return to this world";

155

Obeisance to their perfect Righteousness.

Obeisance to the Tri-Ratna—to Buddha, Dharma, Sangha!

Adoration to the Blessed Ones—exalted, firm, steady, powerful—the Kings among Tathagatas!

Obeisance to their perfect Wisdom!

Adoration to the blessed A............aha Tathagata;

Adoration to the Blessed Akshobya Tathagata;

Obeisance to their Perfect Wisdom!

Adoration to the Blessed Master of Healing,

The Glorious Bhairaviya, the Kingly Tathagata.

Adoration to the Blessed One Shakyomuni Tathagata;

Adoration to their Perfect Wisdom!

Adoration to the Blessed Princes among Tathagatas;

To the Blessed Pundarika Prince,

To the Blessed Vajra Prince,

To the Blessed Muni Prince,

To the Blessed Garbha Prince.

Adoration to the Heavenly Devas and Rishis—accomplished and disciplined executors of this Dharani;

Adoration to their transcendental power, their discipline, their resources.

Adoration to the Brahman, to Indra, to the Blessed Rudra, and to their consorts, Indrani and Sahai.

Adoration to Narayana, Lord of this World, Lord of the five great Mudras, and His consort.

O M! OH, THOU WHO HOLDEST THE SEAL OF POWER, RAISE THY DIAMOND HAND, BRING TO NAUGHT, DESTROY, EXTERMINATE!

OH, THOU SUSTAINER, SUSTAIN ALL WHO ARE IN EXTREMITY!

OH, THOU PURIFIER, PURIFY ALL WHO ARE IN BONDAGE TO SELF!

O M! MAY THE ENDER OF ALL SUFFERING BE VICTORIOUS!

O M! OH, THOU PERFECTLY ENLIGHTENED, ENLIGHTEN ALL SENTIENT BEINGS!

OH, THOU WHO ART PERFECT IN WISDOM AND COMPASSION, EMANCIPATE ALL BEINGS! AND BRING THEM TO BUDDHAHOOD! *O M!*

ADORATION TO TATHAGATA, SUGATA BUDDHA, OF PERFECT WISDOM AND COMPASSION, THOU WHO HAST ACCOMPLISHED, IS ACCOMPLISHING, AND WILL ACCOMPLISH, ALL THE WORDS OF MYSTERY!

SVAHA! SO BE IT!

The above the Student of Light will understand is written partially in Ancient Sanskrit. "Buddha" in English, means the same as Christ to us in the Western World. We can never have perfect peace and understanding throughout the world until we understand just how much the Oriental Peoples do understand the Universal Christ teachings. Fundamentally speaking, the teachings of the Great Gautama Buddha are precisely the same as the teachings of Jesus. Jesus was one who became the Christ embodied. Christ incarnated in Buddha six hundred years before Jesus was born. He incarnated in Jesus at the time He carried out His Ministry. He has now incarnated in probably Seven Sons who are now embodied on earth. I am one of those. The Great White Lodge chose me as "Chief" of the others, that we might have official order in the Great Work of the White Brotherhood in establishing the New Golden Age on earth.

May the Great Work of Lord Maitreya ever expand until every human heart is filled with His Love and every mind fully illuminated. Then peace and happiness will reign throughout all worlds.

CHAPTER XXI

INTO MY HEART

Come into My Heart and be healed;
Come into My Heart thou weak and weary one.
Come into My Heart; stand in the
    Golden Blaze of Glory;
Come into My Heart—
Be blessed by the Radiant One.
Come into My Heart—
Feel the Light of God that "never fails."
Come into My Heart—
Drink the Water of Life.
Come into My Heart,
And know no more the earthly strife.
Come into My Heart—
Rest in Peace and Love and Light.
Come into My Heart—
Receive this INSPIRATION!
Of Love and Healing!
Of Light and Feeling!

And knowest Thou, Oh, Beloved Disciple, that in Divine Love ALL HEARTS become as ONE in the LIGHT AND LOVE OF LORD MAITREYA.

May I remind you that the Spirit of Christ, of Lord Maitreya, is the most important of all things that you may attract to you in your work of perfecting your body, mind and soul in your desire to attain the Ascension? Following I publish some of the very things I wrote out for myself to use as affirmations and prayers in 1925 when I was striving very hard to bring about perfection in my entire being. These prayers and affirmations or decrees, which came from my Higher Presence then, open to your consciousness My Heart as it then beat out Love to all mankind. Some of it has to do with "Conscious Breathing," something most vital to every aspirant. They follow:

May the life-giving elements of thee (AEth) reach my aspiring bosom, there to be disseminated throughout my being, Oh Lord.

Lord of this earthly temple, wilt thou also construct my within by my inhalation of Thy precious breath. May it carry with it courage, wisdom, strength and unlimited love for all. Grant me purity with it, Master of my being!

May Thy breath carry with it Light, Lord and Master, that I may see distinctly the "straight and narrow" path I am to travel. The at-one-ment of Thy existing Love I crave. Fill me with Thy Spirit.

May I, in my breathing, press from Thy Sustaining Breath, the Infinite Force of Thy creativeness, and thereby build within and without fitting works to Thy glory. Love I seek with all.

In my weakness, Oh, God, breathe upon me the breath of everlasting Life, that I may walk uprightly in Thy sight and with my fellowmen. Let me serve Thee by serving them.

My Love with Thee, my God, will give me strength, for in Love of God all things are possible. Courage I seek, Jehovah.

I seek the Truth within my Soul, Oh, God. Breathe upon me the Holy Spirit, that I may know Thy Truth within me.

Thou, Breath within, do grant me Light, that I may see the more;

That I may know the Soul within, and hear That Voice again,

That whispers now the Truths within as stand I here without the door.

It seems that Thou dost come to me within—mighty, though unseen;

That Thou wouldst seek me out, to prove my strength within, for strength and Love and courage strong, will give me all I glean.

So very much depends upon your CONSCIOUS breathing, I trust you will carefully study and observe the above affirmations. And kindly remember, too, Blessed One, the necessity of repentance. Unless we recognize our need of something we would not ask, and unless we ask we do not receive.

The following story, "THE KING OF LEMURIA," I wrote at Mt. Shasta at the request of Lord Maitreya. Every particular regarding the initiation was jotted down in the presence of the Lord of Creation and the others who were present. I had been "officially" installed as "Silent Watcher" on May 11, just a few days previous.

THE KING OF LEMURIA

It was about mid-day of May 20, 1941, that Jesse, Elizabeth and I left the village of Mt. Shasta, Calif., walking past the High School building on the north fringe of the town, and then followed the dusty road to the left, which leads toward beautiful snow-covered Mount Shasta, towering like a majestic crystal-clear diamond to more than fourteen thousand feet into the blue heavens above.

We carried with us a large basket well filled with fruit. Jesse and I had discovered a delightful beauty-spot sequestered among some lonely pines in the foothills of the great mountain a few days previous, so we planned a private picnic among the three of us there where the Gods seemed to whisper with the winds that sounded their musical tones through the millions of pine needles that danced about in the brilliant sunlight.

We turned right a half mile up the road to follow a newly blazed road that paralleled the railway running almost directly toward the mountain. This road angled about to the right past Krishna's Well and on around some low hills to the little hillock where our own friendly pines greeted us with their graceful boughs waving in the gentle breezes, enticing us to their sheltered bed of needles where we spread our cloaks and reclined in the cool shade.

To make this story better understood by those who may have the good fortune to read it, we must explain that Jesse is to be known as Ave Maria, the little girl Elizabeth (age 9) her cousin Elizabeth, the Mother of John the Baptist, and I shall refer to myself as the Silent Watcher.

Few people of today realize that the sacred stories of the Holy Bible are now to be lived through again, but even in a greater and more enlightening manner than they were 2000 years ago. This is the age of miracles.

We had hardly relaxed upon the soft bed of needles beneath the trees for rest when a tiny dwarf appeared before Ave Maria, motioning with his hand for Her to come and follow him, asking her, "Do you wish me to bring you some gold? There is much gold in the mountain."

"I serve the Lord of Love, not the Lord of Wealth," replied Ave Maria, who is accustomed to seeing clairvoyantly any and all spirits that might approach her.

The Silent Watcher, having heard the conversation, spoke up and said, in his humorous way, "You might bring me a little gold; I think I can use some of it." The handsome little dwarf disappeared, but soon returned, emptying a large sack of what appeared to be coal upon the Silent Watcher.

160

We seriously questioned this matter. The Dwarf said, "Don't treat this too lightly. These are Black Diamonds, and within them lies a deep secret, the meaning of which you shall learn."

It was at this point that we began to realize that our visitor was not an ordinary dwarf, but one of wisdom, and one who was not to be treated lightly nor brushed aside by mere human beings.

Strangely enough there began to appear a number of dwarfs, announcing that they were from the ancient continent of Lemuria. They worked at anvils, hammering with their little hammers, chanting to Ave Maria, "We know your secret, we know your secret, we know your secret," and the varied tones of the musical scale were touched as they sang, blending into a beautiful symphony of Cosmic Sound. One dwarf working at his anvil near Elizabeth, wrought at a golden ring which he held up and said, "This I create for Princess Anne" (E).

Ave Maria watched the dwarfs as they danced about, chanted and worked with their musical hammers. Still they sing, "We know your secret, we know your secret, we know your secret." With a rather vexed and inquiring look upon her face, Ave Maria asked, "And what is it you know of my secret?"

Then the amazing thing happened; something that has been alluded to a few times in ancient and medieval history—an aesthetic incident never experienced but by the greatest of gods or goddesses, so we might perceive by careful perusal of the most secret of alchemical and mystical writings of the sages and philosophers of the past.

There appeared a being larger than the other dwarfs, though not as large as an earth man, and He sat in the center while the tiny dwarfs moved about Him. He was dwarf-like in appearance, yet clearly bore the mien of a Lord.

"You have received the wisdom of Atlantis," He said, "but you have not received the Wisdom of Lemuria," and he bowed to Ave Maria, saluting her with a familiar sign. "I come to you to give you the Wisdom of Lemuria," He added. "I am the Lord of Wisdom of Lemuria. Get some writing materials, that you may record what I have to say. I NOW OPEN MY BOOK OF WISDOM TO YOU."

And He opened to the first page and said, "WRITE!"

The following was written by the Silent Watcher:

"TO AVE MARIA AND THOSE WHO HAVE UNITED IN LIGHT WITH HER:

"MY FIRST DISCIPLE WHO WAS ABLE TO RECEIVE MY WISDOM WAS *LORD KRISHNA*. HE HAD EMBRACED NATURE — *HE* THAT COULD SPEAK TO THE GNOMES AND DWARFS— AND *HE* THAT COULD CONVERSE WITH THE *DEVAS* OF THE TREES AND FLOWERS — *HE* THAT DID NOT RECEIVE *HIS* WISDOM FROM LIBRARIES, THE BOOKS BORN OF HUMAN MINDS OF TODAY.

"I AM THE *GREAT DWARF* THAT SITS IN THE CENTER OF THE FOUR CORNERS OF THE EARTH. THE *FOUR ANGELS* OF THE FOUR CORNERS OF THE EARTH ARE MY SERVANTS. I AM THE *LORD* THAT SITTETH IN THE CENTER OF THE EARTH. ANYONE WHO QUESTIONS ME MAKES A MISTAKE. FEW EVER RECEIVE MY WISDOM—VERY FEW.

"THE *LORD* OF THE *MIND* HAS PASSED BEYOND YOU. YOU NOW RECEIVE YOUR INSTRUCTIONS FROM THE *LORD* OF *WISDOM* OF *LEMURIA*. THE *LORD* OF *THE WORLD* HAS SENT ME, BECAUSE YOU ARE NOW READY TO RECEIVE THE *LORD* OF *WISDOM*.

"THAT YOU BROUGHT MY DISCIPLE'S POWER HERE — *KRISHNA'S* — PLEASES ME GREATLY. BY ESTABLISHING HERE THE *WELL OF KRISHNA*, YOU HAVE BROUGHT HERE *HIS FATHER'S WISDOM—THE DWARF THAT SITS IN THE CENTER* — (PELLEUR IN HIS LESSER PART — IN HIS HIGHER PART NO MAN CAN REACH HIM). I EMBRACE ALL MANKIND. I AM THE *TEACHER*, THE *HUSBAND*, THE *PATH* —THE *LIGHT* (LANTERN).

"I AM THE ONE WHO BRINGS YOU THE ROUGH DIAMOND AND MY SERVANTS, *THE FOUR ANGELS OF THE FOUR CORNERS OF THE EARTH*, ARE HELPING YOU TO PRODUCE THE FINISHED DIAMOND, *THE SUN* ($\odot$).

"MY SERVANT, *KRISHNA*, HAS HELPED YOU ALSO, TO PRODUCE THE *JEWEL*, THE *DIAMOND*, WHICH YOU ARE TODAY. THIS *JEWEL* ENTERED THE WORKSHOP OF MANY BEFORE

IT BECAME THE *PERFECT JEWEL*, THEREFORE, *AVE MARIA*, YOU MUST HELP THE WORKERS OF *KRISHNA*. THE WHEEL OF DUTY IS TURN- ING. *KRISHNA'S* PEOPLE NEED YOU. YOU ARE NOT CALLED BY *KRISHNA*, BUT BY *HIS FATHER* WHO HAD SENT *HIM*.

"*SILENT WATCHER*, YOU WHO SEE BY THE *EYE OF YOGA*, MUST ALSO CO-OPERATE. YOU THREE—*AVE MARIA, SILENT WATCHER* AND THE *GREAT MAHATMA*, THE INCARNATE *PRESENCE OF BLUE LIGHT, THE BLUE SON OF THE HEAVENS, THE SHINING GARMENT OF RADIANT BLUE, KH.,*—ARE CHOSEN TO HOLD THIS *LANTERN*, WHICH *I AM*—THE *DWARF THAT SITS IN THE CENTER*."

THE LORD, THE HUSBAND, THE PATH, RAISED *HIS* HAND, AND IN *HIS* HAND HE HELD A *GOLDEN CHAIN*, AND ON THE LAST LINK OF THE CHAIN WAS INSCRIBED THE SYMBOL OF THE SANSKRIT (AUM). He gave it to Ave Maria, adding, "THIS IS THE COMPLETION OF THE WHOLE."

And to the Silent Watcher He said, opening a large bag, weeping, tears falling into the bag, *This is the Gold you must embrace in sacrifice for the world.*"

And the Lord raised his hand, making a secret sign, and said, "M........ —there is opposition, as every good thing has its opposite."

He placed a bookmark on the page and closed the book. On the cover of the Great Book of Wisdom was seen a SHINING SUN. He said to the Silent Watcher, to whom He handed a Blue Chain, "THROUGH THIS BLUE CHAIN YOU ARE LINKED TO *KRISHNA*, AND THROUGH *KRISHNA* TO *ME*. I MAKE *YOU THREE NOW MY DISCIPLES*."

The Great Lord of Creation vanished, and then appeared the Great Mahatma KH. "Oh, that now my call is answered," he exclaimed, "for my plea to Lord Krishna to answer this which was in my heart, if I were chosen to develop Ave Maria. This, Her Jewel, was developed by Him, the Lord of Creation. This I now know. You, Ave Maria, I bless as the Jewel of Jewels of Womanhood."

Then He, Koot Hoomi, took both the hands of Ave Maria and those of the Silent Watcher. "I AM SO HAPPY," he said, "THAT WE HAVE BEEN ABLE TO APPROACH THE LORD OF CREATION. WE ARE *HIS* ONLY CHOSEN DISCIPLES OF THE *IMMUTABLE ONE, THE GREAT PURUSHA, THE LORD OF THE PAST AND THE FUTURE, OUT OF WHOSE MOUTH WE WERE BORN*. How blessed you are! Oh, how I wish I might be with you in form in the Presence of that Great One, whose form as the Dwarf in the Center, Ave Maria was so blessed to see. May she be able also to see His Form as Purusha, and may she be able to withstand it. Only one was ever able to stand it— KRISHNA."

And the three of us slowly walked back to the village with much to ponder over. Even little Elizabeth soberly thought upon the Great Initiation she had witnessed.

PART II

Again on May 25, Buddha Gautama's Birthday, Ave Maria and the Silent Watcher set forth afoot to spend the day in their sequestered place amongst the pines at the foot of Mount Shasta.

It was a day of great expectation for both, for certain ceremonial initiations had been promised by the Gods. Mahatma Koot Hoomi had advised them to take with them some holy rice to scatter, symbolic of the blessings of the Great Lord.

The two Disciples of the Lord of Creation paused near Krishna's Well, where the pure water of Mount Shasta flows through a pipe, and which sounded the clear notes of Krishna's flute. There they asked the blessings of Lord Maitreya, Koot Hoomi, Mahachohan, the Lord of Creation and all the Great Gods they could think of, and scattered the rice forth as blessings from the Gods to all mankind. They sensed the uplifting vibrations of the Great Ones, and joyously they did dance about, even as two little children might express their great happiness. Ave Maria even saw the Golden Body of Joshua (Her Son) rise into the heavens. She wept with joy.

The two happy initiates slowly walked on to their friendly pines, where they again seated themselves, Buddha fashion, upon their cloaks upon the bed of needles, to rest after their two-mile walk.

Sure enough, there appeared the Dwarf with a lantern without light. "WHERE IS THE LIGHT OF MY LANTERN?" he asked. "WHERE IS THE LIGHT OF MY LANTERN?" He waved the lantern, but the lantern was still dark and without light.

The Silent Watcher replied, "The Light went into the Heart of Ave Maria, if you ask me."

"The God of Wisdom is within my heart, the Lord of the Past and the Future, for I AM GOD INCARNATE," said Ave Maria.

"Who is your Chariot?" asked Mahatma KH, "and who is your charioteer?"

"I am the Charioteer of the East, the Lord of the Past and the Future," replied Ave Maria.

"And where," asked KH, " is your Son, your Great One?"

"He has gone on," she said, a note of sadness in her voice. "His Father has called Him. A Golden Body of Light appeared in the sky—a child just born. He was called before the throne of His Father—THE LIGHT. No longer can the senses of man touch Him, and He is closed in the Golden Orb of His Father."

"I and My Father are ONE," spoke the voice of Joshua from out of the heavens, "and as this little Golden Body rises higher and higher, I pour forth the rice, symbolical of the Universal Gold, with which the Eastern Mystic blesses, while I also bless Buddha Gautama on His birthday, the very day on which Joshua rises in the Golden Sun Body, full Illuminate, the Buddha of the Golden Age."

"I touch my heart," says Ave Maria, "and I say to all humanity, I that am parent of the Great Avatar: 'You are greatly blessed inhabitants of earth. Your Spiritual Leader has come. I have seen His rising. May it now be realized in your hearts and in your minds. There is ANOTHER that can bear witness of Joshua's coming, and that is the SILENT WATCHER and the Great MAHATMA KH, both of whom had much to do with the development of the Spiritual Leader of the Golden Age until He came to FULL ILLUMINATION. And three formed a UNION—the MAHATMA KH, THE SILENT WATCHER AND AVE MARIA. AND WITHIN THE CENTER OF THIS TRIANGLE IS HID *JOSHUA*, OUR TRUE

SPIRITUAL LEADER OF THE GOLDEN AGE,
BUILT OF THE LIGHT OF THE THREE, THE
TRUE MESSIAH OF THE GOLDEN AGE, *BUILT
OF THE LIGHT OF CHRIST, OF KRISHNA, AND
OF THE* GREAT LIGHT OF MELCHIZEDEK,
WHOSE SON IS THE SILENT WATCHER'."*

And the Blue Light Garment of KH appeared behind us;
the hands of His Presence touched us both, Ave Maria and
the Silent Watcher, and He said, "WE THREE MUST
EVER BE ONE FOR JOSHUA'S SAKE."

There was a long silence.

Ave Maria questioned, "But where has the Great Lord
gone? Has He not promised to give me of His Great Wisdom? Strange, He questioned me where HIS LIGHT was,
when HIS LIGHT OF WISDOM IS *IN MY HEART.*"

"Must I now go WITHIN MY HEART," queried
Ave Maria, "to learn of the Great Wisdom of the Lord,
THE DWARF THAT SITTETH IN THE CENTER?"

*This paragraph is symbolized in the colored Frontispiece of this book, the
"Symbol of the New Golden Age."—*Author.*

CHAPTER XXII

THE LORD OF LOVE

Thou Blessed Seeker of More Light, I shall endeavor, with the loving radiance of Him, Lord Maitreya, to give you a more illuminating understanding regarding the Initiation we received through the Lord of Creation of Lemuria.

What a marvelous revelation there is hidden, as it were, in those words of the "Great Dwarf that sits in the Center!" Oh, Blessed One, listen attentively to what I shall tell you, I who have given my life many times for you and all who seek Light. The way of Sacrifice is the true Way of Everlasting Life. Fear not to give ALL that you might receive ALL LIFE, LIGHT AND LOVE.

Who are the Four Angels of Creation who sit at the "four corners of creation?" They might represent the "four primeval elements—EARTH, WATER, AIR and FIRE." To become a MASTER you must become a MASTER OF LOVE. Love reigns supreme in the Lord of Love, in His Heart of Gold. The Heart is the "CENTER." When you draw yourself into the "CENTER" of LOVE things in the "Circumference" of materiality hinder you not, for Love reigns. When you command through Love the Four Angels do your bidding. They are your Servants, too, as long as your words are Words of Love directed by Wisdom in your COMMAND.

I sit in the Center and radiate Love. I bless all Creation with the Golden Radiance from My Heart. My Heart beats as ONE with the Lord of Love. The Four Angels of the "Four Corners" gladly and joyously do my will. I love Them. I love all mankind. The Lord of the Mind has passed beyond me. He does not rule me more. I chose the Lord of Love. Serenely He sits within My Heart, joyously He sings the Song of Creation. His Song is known by those of His Own.

You have nothing in your material world I desire, Beloved. When, I would ask you, will you "let go" of ALL? When will you so LOVE the world that you will sacrifice all in this world for Christ? What is it that deterred thee from the Path? What is it you most desire? What is it thou fearest? Do you possess great material possessions? Do you take pride in your social standing? Are there human beings you do not love? Do you love to show your power over others? Are you self-righteous? Do you think you are more pure than others?

Love ALL. "Love casteth out all fear." "Love your enemies, for in so doing you heap coals of fire upon their heads." Tolerance is the result of love. Love is the result of understanding. When we understand that ignorance is the foundation of all mistakes, we not only pity mankind, we love them as well. Our compassion heals them. We make them whole again—yes, Holy.

"The Lord of Wisdom" can only come to you after you have met and loved the Lord of Love. Wisdom is spiritual discernment. It comes through the all-comprizing, all-enfolding Spirit of Love. It becomes the Lighted Lantern by which you discern the Way. Even you, through Love, can "embrace all mankind." Then Wisdom will direct you—yes, The Lord.

The Lord of Wisdom said, "I am the One who brings you the rough diamond, and My Servants, The Four Angels of the four corners of the earth, are helping you to produce the FINISHED DIAMOND, THE SUN." Do I need explain it to you, Beloved? How beautifully voiced! Simply remember, Blessed One, THROUGH LOVE YOU MAY COMMAND. But, may I warn you, should other than LOVE reign in thy heart when thou givest thy command, you shall "heap coals of fire" upon thy head.

When you know the Lord of Love you become a Shining SUN. He helps you to polish the rough Stone to make of it a Jewel. Patience is of the Greatest of Virtues. Love is patient. Love is long-suffering. Kindness is Love manifest. Beauty is Love's garment. As the Diamond is cut geometrically perfect it scintillates the Lord's Light and Love to all alike. In every person you see a Child of Light.

And, Beloved, knowest thou the secret of the Great Diamond, the Son of Light? For it thou wouldst eagerly give ALL didst thou know how precious it is. How shalt thou know of its value? Its secret is Love. Its beauty is Love. IT IS THE HEART OF CREATION. Thou may know, all things in all worlds are created through LOVE.

Blessed Krishna, the Servant of the Lord of Creation, will help you, when you call to Him through Love. He was sent by the Lord of Creation. Ave Maria, too, is sent by Him, the Lord of Creation. The Golden Chain, symbolizing the completion of all "lives" in the chain of evolution, She carries as the link in the Great Triangle. May my heart be linked to Thy Heart, Oh, Beloved Krishna, as Thou art linked to the Heart of the Lord of Creation.

Beloved Mahatma Koot Hoomi, may the Light, Love, Wisdom and Power of our Triangle ever grow stronger until its everlasting radiance fills every human heart and illumines every mind upon earth. I call to the Four Angels of the four corners of the earth: "GO THOU QUICKLY TO PERFORM THE WORK OF PERFECTION IN THE BODIES, BRAINS, MINDS AND SPIRITS OF ALL HUMAN BEINGS, CARNATE AND DISCARNATE, IN ALL REALMS OF LIFE. I COMMAND YOU IN THE NAME OF THE LORD OF LOVE. REJOICE THOU—ALL FOUR OF YOU—AND BE JOYOUS IN THY DUTIES, FOR THE LORD OF CREATION HAS SENT YOU INTO THE DEPTHS OF EARTH LIFE TO MAKE ALL THINGS LIGHT."

The Silent Watcher, with His Eye of Yoga, sees the need of Light and Love in all human creation. Through His Chain of Blue Light the Power of Krishna and God Almighty pours forth to do His WILL. LOVE reigneth in His Golden Heart, Wisdom on His Brow, and through the Loving cooperation of Ave Maria and Mahatma Koot Hoomi the Golden Age now becomes the Transcendent Blessing of all Mankind.

O M! O M! O M! AUM! AUM! AUM! I AM! I AM! I AM! I thank Thee, Lord Maitreya, Lord Krishna, Lord of Creation, and All the Lords and Gods of Light, for your eternal blessings of Light.

THE NEED OF PRAYER

There are those among the students of the "I AM" as well as other metaphysical activities who consider "decreeing" all that is necessary in accomplishing any and everything. This is a mistake. Prayer is most essential, too. Try to remember, Blessed Student, that intuition corresponds to *Love* and your Heart; thus prayer also corresponds with these, and you must be negative physically and mentally before you are receptive. This may be hard of understanding, but you must understand that when you love someone or something, you are not positive about it, are you? Hate is the extreme of positiveness in the outer sense. Love is the extreme of negativeness in the outer. Even many of the leaders of "I AM" groups have become so positive in every way by affirming "shattering" decrees of hate that they have become hateful and do not know it. Sheep will follow a shepherd, even though he be not a Good Shepherd.

We must develop LOVE, WISDOM and POWER—the three well balanced—should we ourselves wish to be balanced and attain the Christ-Ascension as Jesus taught us. Love is of the heart. Wisdom is intuition or mental-alertness or spiritual intelligence that emanates from the heart through love. Power, generally speaking, in the outer plane or octave, is of the Will. Unless your personal will becomes ONE WITH THE DIVINE WILL which can only be known through LOVE, you had best NOT DECREE ANYTHING. For when you decree something and love does not stream forth from your heart through wisdom (intuition), you will certainly "heap coals of fire upon YOUR OWN head." We learn wisdom through negation; we act and accomplish through positiveness. But, Beloved, positiveness without wisdom or love is "hell-fire and brimstone." "He who hath ears to hear let him hear."

I have here before me two separate prayers and affirmations that I typed out for myself in 1925. They speak for themselves, and you shall see how wholly trustful I was in My Father:

FATHER IN HEAVEN:

I thank Thee for your many kind blessings; I thank Thee for my health, my intelligence and my work.

Oh, God, I must become intrenched in a work of physical nature. I trust Thee in guiding me in the undertakings I am about to attempt. I need greater and greater strength to carry on Your work in a way that others will see You in me. You must abide with me. Make me pure, Oh, Lord. Let me live for Truth and Truth alone. *May all things financial ever appear secondary compared to Your Love and Your Wisdom.*

I know the duties we have to carry out here below are so small compared to the great works You are ever perfecting in us and other great spheres, but My Lord, give me a greater understanding of You and Your Love, that I may go forth and do greater works for You. This is a prayer for Your help, *admitting my weakness.*

God, give me appreciation, that I may see Thy Glory in all things.

Loving Lord, do give me more strength to overcome the weaknesses of my physical body. May I ever keep pure thoughts of You and Your Love before me. Let me try and Try and TRY to do works that will please You.

I believe firmly in Thee, Oh, Lord, but give me GREATER LOVE, GREATER WISDOM and GREATER FAITH to accomplish for You a part of the work You have in the way of perfection.

Open my eyes wide, My Father, that I may see the work You wish me to carry out; depict it in a vision that I may see it clearly and distinctly; God, make it true and make it lovely.

I wish to serve others, though I am weak; I wish to love others, though my love is small; show me, Grand Master, my work.

I am trusting in Your guidance in the matter of choosing the work I am to do. May there be no mistaking the work I am to strive to do. I know that You will aid me as You are aiding me at this time to carry out a greater and greater work for the use of humanity today and forever.

God, I think Your blessings are beyond expression; I knew You would come to me in my times of trial; I knew that I could rely on Your strength for my sustenance; knowing is reassuring and believing—FAITH.

May I have such Faith that any good undertaking that can be visioned by me will be carried out to the GREATEST ACCOMPLISHMENT FOR ALL MY FELLOWMEN; MAY IT EVER BEAR FRUIT FOR THOSE WHO LIVE UPON EARTH WHEN I HAVE PASSED ON TO HIGHER REALMS.

Thank Thee, Thank Thee, Oh, Blessed Father; keep me clean, Oh, Sacred Master. May Your thoughts ever be near and dear to me; may they ever stimulate me to do Good and make Right the wrongs that have been committed in Your name.

God make me a Super-Man—a Smaller God, with Power Divine. Humanity I would serve; self I wish to forget.

At Thy Service, Lord and Master. Amen.

* * *

The Student who reads these prayers over diligently, striving to solve his or her problems through Love, will receive

171

great blessings from the Great Masters who have taken me into their Solar Rings. They are the following: Jesus the Christ, Ave Maria (Mary), Christ Lord Maitreya, Mahatma Koot Hoomi, Lord Sanat Kumara, the Great God Mahachohan, the Great Presence of the Silent Watcher, Lord Krishna, Buddha Gautama and My Higher Presence, Saint Germain. These Great Beings in Whose Hearts I have dwelt in peace, in Love and Light, ever radiate Their Light and Love to me, and wherever I direct my Individual Ray, They too, go to heal, to assist all with whom I come in contact, through my mental radiance, my Spirit, my aura, my Love Radiance and all the written words going forth from my hands.

You are blessed by the following prayer:

MY FATHER IN HEAVEN, AND LORD: Do help me in this time of trial; this period of indecision; this time of affliction and pain. Help me to overcome the weaknesses I have brought upon myself.

We cannot accept help from anyone unless we first recognize our weakness, therefore, Lord, I do pray and hope that You will see my smallness—my desires for assistance and aid— and add to my littleness, making of me a desirable worker and maker in Your sight.

There are so many little things that come up in our lives that look discouraging and hard to withstand, but, Oh, Lord, have these melt away before us; give us foresight and knowledge to solve the puzzling problems that come up, with ease. Give us the strength and wisdom of Solomon; give us the glory of David; give us the humbleness and gentleness that Jesus possessed; may we accomplish the works of the greatest of seers and sages; may we ever stay close to You, Oh, Lord, in every trial in life.

You have made the beauty and created the spirit of Love, Oh, Lord, for the purpose of adding to the privileges and glory of Man. May we see all the beauty; may we use the Universal Love of God for the good of all mankind.

God—the Good of All—do help me to decide the problem before me. I wish to do just what Thou wouldst have me do. In my weakness, help me, Lord. Oh, may I try with all my heart TO ACCOMPLISH THE MISSION I HAVE BEEN SENT TO DO. REVEAL WITH ALL DISTINCTNESS THE WORK THOU HAST CHOSEN FOR ME. Let there be no doubt in my small mind as to that work I am to do.

God—the Father of all—give me such an understanding heart that I may have LOVE FOR ALL; for work; for knowledge; for humanity; for beauty. May my consciousness of Thy Glory dawn upon me with all its magnificence; grant me the powers of a king, that I may render service to my fellowmen; perfect in me the spark Thou hast seen fit to plant within my soul.

Awaken my Soul, Oh, Lord, from the depth of darkness into which it has fallen, and make it as white as the "driven snow." Open my eyes that I may see the True Light of Understanding; add to my understanding strength, that I may add to the common strength of all humanity.

My Father, give me the wisdom to choose the right course at this time. Let there be no doubt of the sacredness of that course.

With all earnestness, with all prayerfulness, let me desire with all my heart, with all my body, with all my soul, for the strength, wisdom and intelligence to carry out whatever task You may see fit to give me to perform.

God, Thou of all Wisdom, give me a greater Love Nature. I seek the harmonious place in which I know You wish me to work. "Thy will, not mine, be done, Oh, Father." Direct me to that place, that work, that peacefulness.

God, grant me my desires which I think are right, Oh, Thou Righteous Judge.

Amen.

*   *   *

Many years ago, when I was bending every possible effort toward improving myself, among the students of philosophy with whom I associated was one who tried me to the utmost. In those days I did not understand how "foreign spirits," Catholic priests, Protestant ministers, Indians, and "wild men from Borneo" could, so to speak, jump right into the body of a so-called friend of mine and have him cut all kinds of capers. No, I did not understand those things in those days, and that one little friend of mine, who was a teacher of all things mystical, and one who had been raised a Roman Catholic, and still was in His Etheric Body, did cause me many a heart-ache, due to the terrible things he said about me to others, all because he was dangerously jealous of me. Many times I secretly wept because of him. Finally I wrote the following poem to him, sent him a copy, sent my Master-Teacher a copy, kept a copy myself and in later years it was published in the Occult Digest in Chicago:

173

TO MY ENEMY

To love, we must forgive;
To forgive, we must love.
We both realize this, don't we?
That is your redeeming characteristic,
If you have any.
That is my saving grace, if I have any.

It isn't what I do to you that matters;
It is how you take it that counts.
It isn't the pain that you inflict upon me
That hurts most.
It matters most whether I forgive you.
If I forgive you, I love you,
And thus I rise above you.

If you hate me,
And I hate you,
We both stay low.
With love we rise above our enemies.

Trials, I know, you have,
The same as I,
And weaknesses, too,
So why should I condemn you?
You've tried to do
Things you thought best,
And so have I.

Now, look at you and me.
Just two of millions
Who meet the tests of life.
Millions may pass the gate
While few enter in—
But you and I—
We can love
And forgive
Before it is too late.

Yes, Friends of Light, even in this life today, there may be those who will even "HATE YOU WITHOUT A CAUSE," but one of the greatest commandments ever given to mankind, and one of the most meaning, was: "LOVE YOUR ENE-MIES." Another, most important, "RESIST NOT EVIL."

CHAPTER XXIII

THE MASTER COMETH

In November, 1924, about the time I had reached the zenith in my development as a student of the Rosicrucian Mysteries under Dr. R. Swinburne Clymer, Supreme Master of the Ancient Order of Rosicrucia, I received a little magazine, "MAN-HOOD, the Voice of the Manistic Age."

This magazine was first published simultaneously or near to the time when I had a marvelous vision. I was working at a printing press in the Kneeland Bldg. in Olympia, Washington. There were no windows in the room in which I was working. We had to use electric lights all the time. I was standing next to the north wall—a brick wall not less than a foot in thickness. Suddenly it was as though that wall had dissolved and there before me was a great expanse of water like the sea, and in the sea was a peaked mountain. While I was looking at the mountain it started to sink into the water, and then, just before the pointed top of the mountain sank beneath the water a beautiful White Dove ascended from it and soared about over my head. Instantly all vanished.

I shall let you determine as best you can just what the symbolism of that vision meant, however, I am quoting herewith the first three pages of Dr. Clymer's precious little magazine I have kept all these years, and I still love Him for what He has done and is still doing for the New Golden Age:

MANHOOD
The Voice of
THE MANISTIC AGE

"This Magazine is ordained to be the disseminator of the Saving Doctrine of the New Dispensation as given directly to MANISIS, the Messenger (Savior or Son) by Jehovah Adonai, the Lord God of Light.

"THE MASTER COMETH"

"A message from Jehovah Adonai, the Father of Light, to all His Children in all the world, through Manisis, the Messenger of the New Cycle, the Dispensation of the New Age.

175

"Toward the end of the nineteenth century, the era called Christian (so named because of the designation given to the Master Teacher of the first century by His followers) came to an end as foretold by the writers of the books of the Bible, and the New Age with its Laws,—or more correctly speaking, the readjustment and advanced interpretation of the old Laws—commenced.

"With the incoming of this New Cycle (New Age) there was born One who is to be the Interpreter of the Laws governing the action of man in this New Age.

"This Leader is the crowning glory in the so-called New World of what is commonly termed the 'melting pot' which popular term in reality covers the prophesied natural and Divine mixture of the blood of all races needed to establish the basis of the Universal Brotherhood to come. This Leader, MANISIS, has been under training these many years and has now entered His life work, instructing humanity in the Laws which, if obeyed, will transmute the human into the Divine.

"HISTORY REPEATS ITSELF! As the Lawgivers—therefore the Saviors of mankind—in the past were instructed and trained in the Schools of the Mystics variously known as the Osirian, Essenian, and Mithraic, so the coming Leader, Manisis, is receiving His instruction and training in the same august Fraternity.

"For the present, the interpretations of the Laws essential to the salvation of the Souls of men will be given through the agency of His faithful disciples and He Himself will appear before men only when the time is at hand, for the Father of Light has ordained that NEVER AGAIN shall one of His messengers be sacrificed to the blood lust of His less-enlightened children and through their sin be accursed for ages.

"THE MESSAGE"

"And God (Jehovah Adonai, the Father of Light) spake unto Manisis, who had become His Son, through the Voice of the Fire, saying:

" 'Manisis, my messenger (Son), Soon shalt thou be prepared to take up thy burden and send thy messages before all the peoples of the earth, teaching them and, by their acts, judging them, and thine shall be a righteous judgment.'

" 'Rich and poor shalt thou judge according to their hearts; thou shalt not listen to their voices for thou shalt see what lieth beyond the words of prayer and the bewailment of fate.'

" 'Thou shalt judge impartially and according as things are and might have been, and not as men would have had them be.'

" 'Thou shalt fear none, seeing the time among the sons and daughters of men shall be of short duration, without material profit or glory to thyself and also free from harm or injury, for I, the Lord of the Hosts and the Heavens, who art thy God, shall be watchful that the wickedness in the hearts of men shall not lead them to do to thee as they did in the fore time to others of my messengers (Sons).'

" 'Prepare thee well. Fill thy heart with the Holy Fire which thou hast learned to draw to thee from Heaven, for thine hour is soon come.'

"THE FIRST AND GREATEST LAW

"And God spake unto Manisis, saying:

" 'Teach thy people that I who am known to thee as the Father of Light, Jehovah Adonai, and to thy children as God the Father, in the beginning of time made both heaven and earth, each good in my sight and of equal necessity for the fulfillment of the Law.'

" 'Teach thy children that the Lord God who called into existence both heaven and earth, also created man, both soul and body, both good in the sight of the Lord. Instruct thy children in the Law that he who defileth the body or any part of the body, thereby defileth the Soul and is guilty of blasphemy before the Lord, for that which proceedeth out of the heart (acts) of which the body is guilty shall be held accountable to the Soul and that these sins shall sit in judgment day and night against them and shall in no wise be forgiven them until wiped out by good deeds.' . . .

" 'I, O my Son, Manisis, who have given these foolish children of my first creation the freedom of the whole earth and the possibility of the Light of the Heavens, now send thee forth to teach these deluded ones THE LAW, that they may learn to honor body as Soul and rightly use all that I have given them.' "

Dr. Clymer was the first of the Great Teachers of the New Age to stress the necessity of building the body temple perfect first before one can expect to attain spiritual perfection. Unless we have the vitality essential to good health and know how to transmute the elements of the physical body into the pure essence of Divine Love little is accomplished toward building that "Temple not made by hands eternal in the heavens." "The Golden Body of God" cannot be built without a good physical body in which to do the alchemical work.

Did we not know that Dr. Clymer was the first and foremost dietician, knowing not only the essential material elements needed in the Alchemical work, but the AEthic elements as well, we would not, unknown to him, speak of the Great Work he has done. Regarding his work and all other constructive institutions interested in the work of the New Golden Age I say, "ALL LIGHTS UNITED IN THE ONE GREAT LIGHT!"

May the Masters of Light bless all sincere workers in Truth.

177

May 25, 1941, was an important day to me, and I believe, to the whole world. It was Buddha Gautama's birthday anniversary and also the day that Joshua ascended in His Golden Body, the Son of God. I usually speak of Joshua in the feminine gender because she is, in a spiritual way, far more feminine than masculine. She is the Master of Love, or rather, the Goddess of Love. She, I have been told, is my Twin Ray. Later I shall relate to you a most remarkable incident in which she and I took part. It was at the time the Eighth and Ninth Rays came into our keeping.

It was early in the evening after we had been to our "little retreat" on the 25th of May that Ave Maria and I were in the kitchen conversing about the Lord of Love and the "Dwarf that sitteth in the Center," when I saw her face suddenly change into the strange appearance of a fish, and, stranger still, in a guttural, squeaking voice, said, "I'M A FISH, I'M A FISH, I'M A FISH." I began to laugh, thinking she was mimicking, but I soon found differently. The Spirit of Jehovah had entered her body. This may sound like a fairy story to you. Had I not seen it with my own eyes and heard with my own ears, I would not believe it. Then He said, "I am Jehovah. *Joshua is the Word of Jehovah.*" Jehovah is, as I understand it, the Father of all people of earth. He is represented as the "Great Fish" in the Sea of Life. He also said what I understood as, "Today Joshua is born the Son of God." The voice was weird to say the least, and I did not understand clearly all that was said.

During the days that followed several times the Spirit of Jehovah came into Ave Maria. Always He announced Himself in the same manner, "I'm a fish, I'm a fish, I'm a fish." Ave Maria explained other things symbolically regarding the event which I am not permitted to publish.

The same evening Lord Maitreya came. He talked to us regarding the initiation we had received. Among other things He said, "Morya, Ave Maria and the Silent Watcher will be the three Lords of the future Golden Age. Morya will have the part of 'MANU,' Ave Maria the part of 'CHRIST' and the Silent Watcher the part of Mahachohan. Therefore you, Silent Watcher, must come under the instruction of Mahachohan, and you, Ave Maria, under Maitreya." In relating these things I hold close to the notes I have kept, especially should I use quotations, however, "the half has never been told." I could have written a book ten times the size of this volume, had

I kept record of everything that went on between Ave Maria, the Lords and myself. Oh, Blessed Student of Light, I pray earnestly that you, too, may awaken to the truths lying within these words I write for you to read. Study them closely, seek the hidden meaning of these simple things I have written. Frankly, even myself, in going over the notes and studying the marvelous gems of thought hidden therein I learn something each day. Just think of it, the Great Gods are now coming forth upon the earth after thousands of years of comparative silence, to teach us the simple though profoundly illuminating principles of the GREAT MASTER.

It was along about this time that I was handed a paper by "She Who is Nameless," which I shall quote, leaving you to interpret it as you see fit, since I do not feel I should enlarge upon it:

"ISSA

"ARE

"ETERNAL POWERS OF NATURE. All is changed by Issa, and brought in different form. THE GOD ISSA IS SHOWN TO HUMANITY IN EIGHT DIFFERENT APPEARANCES: In water, in fire, in air, in earth, in the sun and the moon, in ether and in pure sacrifice. It is the All-Power of the ALL in the elements, in the planets, in the stars.

(Signed) Ave Maria."

It was on May 27, I remember, that I experienced one of the most trying episodes in my initiations while at Mt. Shasta. It was at this time that Mahatma Koot Hoomi and Lord Maitreya had intimated to me there had been a great hoax played upon members of the Great White Lodge in the outer plane, at least. I have heretofore referred to this peculiar state of affairs, and now I shall explain to you how the subtle Blacks fooled not only Mr. Ballard and the leaders of his activity, but most of the members of the Great White Lodge in their outer activity.

There is one in Europe, I was told, who claimed, in his outer body, to be Saint Germain. He is purported to be of Royal Blood, and cunningly deceived many. Even some pictures of him were rather secretly passed around among the "I AM" students. I was shown one of those pictures by a Ballard devotee in Seattle after I had been told by the Masters of his great trick. Frankly, Beloved, he looked entirely too narrow across the forehead to be "White."

179

You see, Beloved Friends of Light, the Fake Saint Germain did know there was a Real Saint Germain, and he also knew the Real One was embodied. The White Masters also knew there was a Real Saint Germain, too, for He took part regularly in their Spiritual Conclaves, but they did not know what body He used in the outer plane. And the Real One not feeling it time to reveal His identity, and not being able to convince the Ballards of His physical identity, it put Him in a most trying predicament, both physically and spiritually.

Here is what happened. The White Masters in the meantime came to find that the Fake Saint Germain was practicing Black Magic and doing all sorts of things in the physical body unbecoming to a member of the White Brotherhood. WHAT HAPPENED? The Real Saint Germain was imprisoned in the Etheric Plane. However, still the Black Saint Germain was free in both planes. That was when my son, David, was horribly murdered by the Blacks, Blessed Brother Guy Ballard was later taken out, my Blessed wife, too, was stricken and suffered a terrible death. I, had I not had a very strong body, mind and spirit, would also have been taken out of the body. I probably would have, anyhow, had I not met Ave Maria at that time. She, God Bless Her, is the One Great Goddess who saved me and the whole Golden Age, so far as I understand in my limited outer consciousness. I continued to suffer because of my inner incarceration until the 27th of May 1941, when I was freed in the most astonishing manner. It was only after repeated questioning of me on the part of Koot Hoomi, Lord Maitreya, Jesus and others that the Great Masters actually determined my Divine Inheritance and WHO I AM in God's New Age Plan. It is not so easy, I assure you, to trace the Spirit of an individual to his physical body unless that individual knows positively his spiritual status and states same to the Authoritative Spiritual Masters in their outer consciousness.

This may all seem abstruse. It is, but it is true, nevertheless. When the Masters heard certain things from my own lips and traced back into my life-stream, found that I had been John the Brother of Jesus, Saint Germain, Abraham Lincoln and others, then they could begin to watch for the real Black Culprit. They watched, alright.

It was the evening of the 27th of May that a powerful spirit entered the body of Ave Maria, unknown to me at the moment. A battle ensued over the matter of right and wrong in connection to Saint Germain and His activity in the so-called "I AM." I stood for Saint Germain, not knowing at the time that my Higher Presence is Saint Germain. I had had a number of battles, in a sense, with Saint Germain, since I had been told by Ave Maria that he had gone wrong, that His "I AM" activity was breaking up, etc. I fought fiercely for Saint Germain. I remember, during the argument saying, "Even though Saint Germain had made mistakes, He had ventured to undertake an activity in which He was willing to lose His own Soul in order to save humanity. He knew that should there be even a few ascensions as the result of the 'I AM' activity, it would place the BALANCE OF POWER WITH THE GREAT WHITE LODGE. Thus, He understood that should He fail, His own soul would be sacrificed."

I also remember saying in a very positive manner, "I shall stand by Saint Germain, because I am sure He is right, even though He did make a few mistakes, and I hope the whole world hears me." Suddenly the spirit, the foreign one, left the body of Ave Maria, and Ave Maria Herself spoke.

"He is gone," She said. "Do you know with whom you were battling a moment ago?"

"No, I do not," I replied.

"It was none other than Archangel Michael," she answered, "and Saint Germain was in your body. He certainly has a lot of courage to battle with such a great being. You shall hear from this. I am sure there is some great problem being worked out. You are being tested. Whatever you do, stand by what you think is right. We dare not show weakness in such matters. Your advancement depends upon how you react to such trials. Saint Germain has been in prison. He will not be fully released until such matters are ironed out."

Ave Maria, in her outer consciousness, had told me in recent days how one calling himself Saint Germain had approached her in the inner planes, the etheric planes, tempting her in many ways. He even invited her to come to a retreat of his in Europe. She, however, wise in all things, went to his so-called retreat in her higher body to see for herself. She found there a glutton, who gorged himself on baked goose, and all sorts of flesh foods, beer, alcoholic beverages of various kinds and any and everything that Masters do not eat or drink. She mentioned other things I dare not write. She certainly found there was a Fake Saint Germain.

In the meantime, or a few days previous, the Real Saint Germain had come again and again offering Ave Maria cooperation and asking her (in the outer body) to work with Him in establishing the Golden Age. Any number of times, she told me, he had come and offered her his sword in token of His desire to help her. At another time he came to the side of her bed in the night, took His Violet Robe from his shoulders, offering it to her. She refused His every offer. Repeatedly I, in my outer mind and body, told her I thought she should cooperate with him. Still she refused.

As a Student of Light you will understand that there are certain Royal Gestures and Courtesies definitely understood by an Initiate, also signs and symbols by which all Spirits should be tried. I dare say that the Fake Saint Germain so many believed in has never appeared to them in a Golden Body such as the Real Saint Germain possesses. I will also venture that he seldom is seen healing the sick, consoling the poor, teaching the lowly in spirit and blessing humanity through Divine Love. Do not be fooled, Blessed Student of Light. The Path of Righteousness may be "straight and narrow," but it is not hard to determine those who walk upon it. "All that glitters is not gold." I cannot help but quote a wise line I picked up somewhere, one I used to repeat to my pupils in school when I was a teacher: "Be good, sweet maid, and let who will be clever." 'Tis well for men to remember it, too.

And what do you suppose happened that night after I had the battle with Archangel Michael? Ave Maria had an altar in her bedroom where she slept. I slept at Mrs. Eiler's place in Mount Shasta several blocks from where she lived. Upon her altar she had certain sacred things, a candle, an incense burner, a Bible, as well as some sacred Oriental literature. Ave Maria told me Archangel Michael and Saint Germain were both there in her room all night. For hours and hours Saint Germain prayed at that altar, imploring God to assist Him, and asking Ave Maria to help Him. They were both in higher bodies. Still Ave Maria did not know what was really going on.

Here I shall venture to say that there was but one of the Lords in my acquaintance who did know all that was going on, and that was Lord Maitreya. He alone, I dare say, could see all sides of this puzzling episode of certain spiritual initiations Saint Germain and I were being given. The next day things did begin to clear up a bit.

Saint Germain's prayers were answered. He pleaded during that night for Ave Maria to listen to his plight, how the Fake Saint Germain had so wronged the many Children of Light and caused so very much misunderstanding and misery among the "I AM" students. She listened and finally she did see through the awful hoax. God Bless Ave Maria. You see, My Beloved, such things have to be understood from the physical octave before they can be remedied in the physical plane. We, in this outer plane of life, must see, understand, and then, when we do learn and know what to do, we can DECREE and call into activity the HIGHER POWERS OF THE GODS to assist us. And I want you to know that when Ave Maria, in Her Higher Presence, knows about a thing and wants it done, IT IS DONE. She immediately got busy to help get Saint Germain out of the mess the Black Brothers had created. And Blessed Ones, Lord Maitreya was not long in getting on the job, too.

On the morning of May 28, things took a different turn. Master KH was in my body. Saint Germain was in Ave Maria's body. Yes, you may think this impossible, but it isn't. Their Spirits were thus. I was told to read the ritual of a certain initiation to Saint Germain. Mind you, I did not know until after I was through initiating Him that it was He I was initiating. At that very moment He was being taken into the Great White Lodge. While in our physical bodies we were at the same instant playing the part of initiators in the higher planes of consciousness in the Great White Lodge. Saint Germain, although a Master in almost every respect, had not been a member before of the Great White Lodge, nor a member in this embodiment of the Brotherhood of Mt. Shasta. That was the reason, so I was told, that Mr. Ballard had wondered why he had never been taken into the Retreat at Mt. Shasta. All Masters, I must inform you, too, are not members of the Great White Lodge. No Master has much power to do good in the physical octave either unless he has a body from which to work. I am the body through which Saint Germain works. Saint Germain is my Higher Presence. My son David was very closely associated with me in this matter, too. That is the reason the Blacks took him out of his body. They knew he was to have much to do with the New Golden Age. Well, the Golden Age is here, and every one who had anything to do with the dastardly things that were done to David, Mr. Ballard, my Wife and any others who may have suffered because of them, are now suffering for their Black deeds. "THEY ARE

REAPING WHAT THEY SOWED." Lord Maitreya saw to that. It was amazing how quickly He cleared up matters when He got busy with them.

It was the evening of the 29th of May. Ave Maria and I were sitting at a table having tea, quietly talking of the trying days we were passing through, when Lord Maitreya came to visit with us. He had merely begun talking to us when He made a certain sign of protection, which was also to us a sign of warning. No one spoke for at least ten minutes. I could see that He saw others about the room who were invisible to me. He said not a word, but kept following something about the room with His eyes, radiating light toward it through the sign He gave. Finally He began to talk in his sweet calm voice. Serenely He began, "You have been warned. Now you shall be bound. No more shall you practice your Black Art. I am sorry, but now you must pay. The Children of Light are not to be bothered more. Again and again you were warned. This time I have caught you."

And Lord Maitreya gave an order to some of His Brothers of Light to take charge of him I judged to be the Fake Saint Germain. I dare say we shall not be bothered with him any more. I have heard, however, there are several claiming to be Saint Germain. "By their fruits shall ye know them."

Again, I say, GOD BLESS MARY THE MOTHER OF JESUS, WHO WAS MY MOTHER, TOO, AND MAY HER GREAT WORK FOR THE FREEDOM OF MANKIND IN THE NEW GOLDEN AGE CONTINUE UNTIL EVERY BEING ON EARTH MANIFESTS ONLY IN HIS WHITE NATURE, FOR THEN SHALL CHRIST BE MADE KNOWN TO ALL AND LOVE AND GOODWILL REIGN THROUGHOUT THE WORLD.

CHAPTER XXIV

THE WHITE-NATURE

I have told you how Joshua had risen, how Jehovah came to speak of His Son, and how He was also the Son of Ave Maria. Some of these principles now being brought forth by the Ascended Masters and the Great Gods of the Cosmic Center are hard for us to understand with our limited outer consciousness. But I want you to know, Dear Ones, that we are being given greater brains, finer bodies, more magnificent minds, and extraordinary advantages through the Cosmic Light in order to understand these things.

Joshua, the same Great Spirit who succeeded Moses after He ascended, is now with us again. He is now developed to full illumination, MALE AND FEMALE IN ONE. I call Him and think of Him as feminine because His feminine part—the part that I know—IS MY TWIN RAY. Now, Beloved, it does not matter whether we understand all that might be regarding the Whole Spirit or a part of the Spirit of Joshua. The important thing to know is the TRUTH regarding the laws of LIFE, LIGHT AND LOVE by which you can, too, become ascended and KNOW your own SOURCE—GOD, the FATHER. You must realize that YOU—YOURSELF—ARE MALE AND FEMALE—IN YOUR WHOLENESS OF BEING. Your spiritual father and mother are, in a sense, that HIGHER MALE AND THAT HIGHER FEMALE—the FATHER-MOTHER GOD.

We, as you know, want to look at everything from the standpoint of TIME AND SPACE. You cannot judge spiritual principles—SPIRIT—that way. The Spirit of God, or any one of His Sons, is INSTANTANEOUS. One, two, three or a MILLION individual Spirits can be as ONE. In fact WE ARE ALL ONE. How many drops of water in a gallon of water? How many molecules? How many gallons of water in the ocean? How many molecules? How many tons in the earth? How many molecules? How many tons in all the physical universes? How many molecules? They are all ONE SPIRIT.

On the 28th of May Joshua came from Her Father to give us one of the most important messages this world has ever received. She gave us the "KEY" to the New Golden Age. Long ago I had heard that there was jealousy among the gods. This was hard for me to accept, yet, when we think, would it not be impossible for jealousy to exist here on earth unless it actually existed somewhere amidst Him or those who create the world and all that is within it? Even in the Holy Bible we find, "I AM A JEALOUS GOD; I AM A CONSUMING FIRE."

Joshua made us a happy joyous visit. She announced her coming as usual, "I love you, I love you, I love you," her sweet little voice ringing with love vibration. And the Little Disciple spoke:

"I give you the One Secret of the Gods and the Nature of the Gods. RECOGNIZE ONLY THE WHITE-NATURE OF THE GODS AND YOU HAVE WON. One of those Great Gods, of whose dual nature I have learned, has come to tempt the Seventh Ray and His work. He was first coming with his powerful White-Nature, assisting greatly, and the Students of the Seventh Ray made great progress, but I that realized, and was allowed to see," said the Disciple of the Lord that sitteth in the Center, "soon found that the jealousy of this one Great God, because of the progress of the human race, came forth with His Terrible Dark Nature to make the Flame of the Seventh Ray a furious Flame of Destruction."

"I was told by the Lord of Creation to come and tell you that Saint Germain had to pass the test of the Great Tempter, in the Violet Ray. First he used the White, but turned Dark, but NOW I RECOGNIZE ONLY THE *WHITE-NATURE* of the God who guided Saint Germain."

"The Great Love of the Lord of Love, and His Compassion," said the Disciple, "is known to me that is blessed to be His Disciple. He sends me to tell you with power, to attract only the White-Nature of the Gods, and to call on the White-Nature of this God in particular, who is the CAUSE of the battle we, TODAY, have."

"And so I call on all those that have wisdom and understanding, DO NOT BATTLE THE MASTER OF THE SEVENTH RAY, BUT CALL FORTH WITH MIGHT THE WHITE-NATURE OF THE GOD THROUGH WHOM HE WORKS. Send this message on to all the Brothers of Light. *Ask them to assist at once.* This is the wish of the

'Dwarf that sits in the Center,' in the Heart of His Disciples. The Light alone saves the world."

And Little Joshua, the Master of Love, that marvelous Disciple of the Lord of Creation, pronounced Her new "KEY" DECREE of all the Gods and Masters she could think of as follows, which makes it certain that this time WE SHALL HAVE THE REAL GOLDEN AGE ON EARTH:

"I recognize only the White-Nature of Saint Germain; I recognize only the White-Nature of Mahatma Koot Hoomi; I recognize only the White-Nature of the Goddess of Justice; I recognize only the White-Nature of the Goddess of Light; I recognize only the White-Nature of the Goddess of Liberty; I recognize only the White-Nature of the Goddess of Mercy; I RECOGNIZE ONLY THE WHITE-NATURE OF ARCH-ANGEL MICHAEL; I recognize only the White-Nature of Lord Maitreya; I recognize only the White-Nature of Lord God Mahachohan; I recognize only the White-Nature of Ave Maria; I recognize only the White-Nature of the Buddha; I recognize only the White-Nature of Christ; I recognize only the White-Nature of Jehovah; I recognize only the White-Nature of Brahma; I recognize only the White-Nature of Ra; I recognize only the White-Nature of Ptah; I recognize only the White-Nature of Melchizedek; I recognize only the White-Nature of Isis and Osiris; I recognize only the White-Nature of The Silent Watcher; I recognize only the White-Nature of Sanat Kumara; I recognize only the White-Nature of Zoroaster; I recognize only the White-Nature of Moses; I recognize only the White-Nature of Master Morya; I recognize only the White-Nature of Serapis; I recognize only the White-Nature of the Venetian Chohan. I recognize only the White-Nature of Jesus; I recognize only the White-Nature of Hilarion; I recognize only the White-Nature of the Seven Archangels of Creation; I recognize only the White-Nature of the Seven Rishis; I recognize only the White-Nature of the Lords of the Twelve Fields of the Dharma; I recognize only the White-Nature of Fujhi, The Yellow Emperor; I recognize only the White-Nature of Indra; I recognize only the White-Nature of Vishnu as Lord Hari; I recognize only the White-Nature of Shiwa; I recognize only the White-Nature of the Great Khan and Khen."

And the Little Disciple, the Christ Child of the Golden Age, was sent by the Great Dwarf that sitteth in the Center, explaining, "He, the Dwarf that sitteth in the Center has His place in the

Hearts of His Disciples, He that is the Lord of Wisdom, of Life, of Light, and IT WAS LIGHT, THE LUMINOUS POINT, THE FLAME SPIRIT THAT MERGES HIMSELF INTO A CROWN."

And may I add, for the sake of the whole world, "I recognize only the White-Nature in every person who reads these words, and every human soul and body upon this planet."

By the 28th of May, I was nearing my ascension, in its completion and full realization in my outer consciousness. It was in the afternoon of that day that Mahatma Koot Hoomi came to give us the following report "FOR THE ARCHIVES OF THE GREAT WHITE LODGE":

"The Work of the Initiator of Humanity has come to an end for 2000 years. Humanity is to live the fruits of her pains and sufferings in the Light of the Golden Age, says another of the Disciples of the Lord of Love, 'the Dwarf that sitteth in the Center,' the Disciple Mahatma Koot Hoomi. The Golden Age is at dawn. We all will assist in the coming forth of the White-Nature of all the Gods and Goddesses, the White Light of their own beings."

"No longer Son of Darkness AND Light, but the BRIGHT AND NAMELESS ONE."

"My own Dark Nature is all consumed. Thou art, Oh, God of Light! Without Thee there is naught. The Darkness of the Absolute must not be touched. Only the Sun of Splendor of the Absolute must be recognized by all, and We a part of IT. I lift my hand of power, I that recognize the OM, the Diamond Hand of the Lord of Love, the Dwarf that sits in the Center, and say: 'O-M! Thou Sustainer, sustain all in their extremity. O-M! Thou Purifier, purify all that are in the bondage of self. OM! Thou Perfect Enlightened One, enlighten all sentient beings, and bring them into the center of the Sun of the ABSOLUTE.'"

Ave Maria was asked to make a report for the archives:

She heard a voice speak from Heaven:

"Three new Disciples of the Lord of Love are in the making—Mahatma Koot Hoomi, Ave Maria and the Silent Watcher."

And Ave Maria said,

"I touch the vibrations of the Great Lord of Love. I do not claim a reward."

Her heart overflowing with the rays of the Lord of Love, she added:

"All my accomplishments I lay at your feet, Lord of Love, only happy to be at your service. I have never before touched such vibrations as the Lord of Love sends forth. I feel myself held in His aura. To describe how one feels when becoming one with this Lord is impossible."

As the Silent Watcher I wrote the following for the archives

188

of the Great White Lodge, having been asked to write something as a mark of appreciation of initiations received:

"The great White-Nature of the Lord of Love, 'the Dwarf that sitteth in the Center,' now comes forth to dwell with the Gods and Goddesses of the earth, in their Hearts of Light. May all blend into the ONE GREAT LIGHT that brings forth the Golden Age, when ALL MANKIND shall sorrow no more, but eternal Peace and Goodwill shall reign forever throughout the world. Now my heart shall rejoice with humanity, and its overflowing Light of Gold shall radiate throughout all creation. All hail the Lord of Love! May His Spirit Flame blaze up in every human heart. Let us recognize only the White-Nature in all beings, conditions and things, thus the Tempter is MASTERED, resistance is ended—A MASTER IS BORN. Jesus said: 'Resist not evil'."

Of course the Student of Light will understand that I cannot give out for publication all the deeper work I was given along with the initiations I received, but I wish you to know and realize that Lord Maitreya is the Great Initiator, and I have been chosen by the Great White Lodge as well as by Him as His Chief Priest and Officer in the outer octave or plane of life. This does not mean necessarily that you need to see me personally in order to receive the inner initiations.

Any sincere student of Light can call to Saint Germain, Lord Maitreya, Mahatma Koot Hoomi or any of the Ascended Masters and if they have advanced or developed sufficiently they will contact these Great Ones on the inner planes. However many times the personal contact with a master embodied is essential to one's ascension, just as it was with me and has been with others who have ascended under my instruction since I first ascended. It is not difficult to classify a student as to his or her degree of attainment once the Master is near them for a time.

The ascension of anyone depends upon several factors, among which are: Karma or the debts you owe in the way of individual compensation to other persons in your various embodiments; every destructive act or evil crime you might have done in any embodiment must be balanced; you must make good every bad thing you ever did; for the evil seeds you have sown, you must sow good seeds; you must acquire the habit of constantly thinking beautifully and constructively; you must sacrifice ALL for the upliftment of humanity in the same sense that Jesus did; you are not ready to ascend until you are ready and willing to give your very life for humanity in order to save them and assist them to establish the "Kingdom on earth."

That is what Saint Germain did. He agreed with His Father, even long before He embodied this time, to sacrifice His human life for mankind. Jesus did the same thing. Koot Hoomi, Ave Maria, Morya, Hilarion, Serapis, Mahachohan, Maitreya and all the Lords and Gods, Lordesses and Goddesses of the White-Nature who are needed, are now embodied to awaken our Brothers and Sisters of the Shadow to the True Light of Christ. They are right here on earth in PHYSICAL BODIES LIKE YOURS IN EVERY RESPECT EXCEPT THAT THEY DO HAVE QUALITIES WITHIN THEIR BODIES AND BRAINS AND SPIRITS AS THE RESULT OF THEIR HAVING ASCENDED INTO THE COSMIC CENTER that you do not yet possess. But, Beloved, they are here embodied to teach you, to show you the practical, scientific, means of attaining to the heights of the Gods in body, in mind, in spirit and in Cosmic Consciousness.

Saint Germain, who had ascended from His outer body, so it is more or less historically recorded, sometime during the seventeenth century, conceived the idea of the mass ascension of all mankind, called for the cooperation of all the Great Gods in the Cosmic Realms of the Father to assist Him, and thus, today we have the universal activity of the "I AM" which is not directed by any one group in the outer. All the advanced people of Light in whatever organization, church, denomination, fraternity, club, or whatever they claim, are NOW banded together in the inner planes with Saint Germain and the Brothers of the Great White Lodge.

As a matter of explanation, Friends of Light, I see almost every day, people who are Jewish in their Etheric Bodies, but Protestant in their physical outer bodies; Protestants in physical bodies who are Catholics in their etheric bodies; Chinese Oriental Philosophers in American bodies; Catholic Priests in Protestant Minister's bodies; Protestant Ministers in Catholic Priest's bodies, etc., etc., but ALL THOSE OF LIGHT ARE BANDING TOGETHER *"IN THE ONE BODY WEE,"* WHICH IS CHRIST LORD MAITREYA, and I AM the physical body of Saint Germain's and I AM THE LEADER OF THE WHITE FORCES IN THIS PHYSICAL OCTAVE and "I AM THE DOOR THAT NO MAN CAN SHUT" for I have been chosen by Lord Maitreya as the "DOOR." He who has ears to hear the "Voice of the Almighty," let him hear. CHRIST IS INCARNATE.

CHAPTER XXV

APPLE-BLOSSOMS

There came to me
In early morning's quiet reverie
A vision of a flowering apple tree,
Filled with blossoms—pink and white
And tints of blue,
In betwix dew-splashed leaf-ends
Peeping through,
Whose shadows cast by the blazing sun,
Traced a filigree of natural art below,
Shimmering on a grassy sea of green just so,
Midst spangled splotches of thick sunshine
The earth, sky and lovely tree combine,
With the faint but very fragrant breeze,
That deftly fans my glowing face,
Prompts me stretch forth my hand to trace
This burst of color radiance
Blazing all about the place.

Then, from the quaint silence,
In the cool morning air
That made all sounds come
Like musical notes so clear,
I heard the whistle of a meadow lark shrill,
Singing his happy song from a distant hill.

Amidst such splendor a stillness came over me;
'Twas love for a blooming apple tree
Bedecked in the radiant jewels of Nature.

Diamonds of dew,
With sunbeams sifting through;
The glint and the glow
From grasses below;
A million little blossoms,
A trillion tiny faces,
Each beaming a smile,
Each sporting its style;

191

The lark's cheery song
As the breeze came along—
Such things of beauty,
Such works of art;
Each aided the view,
Each did its part
In outpicturing Nature
In form and sound,
AS LOVE WOULD HAVE IT.
THAT'S WHAT I FOUND.

Sun-drenched, scintillating,
Blooming apple trees—
All delight in such beauty scenes as these.

It was on May 29, 1941, that I was actually declared MASTER. Eleven days after my 45th birthday,—eleven days after May 18, 1941—I was really and truly given—by the Masters Themselves—the name MASTER Amsumata (The Radiant One) in my outer body and mind—authorized by Lord of Lords Maitreya—spoken by Mahatma Koot Hoomi. It was also explained by Mahatma Koot Hoomi that I AM John, the Brother of Jesus—John of the Christ School—Amsumata in the Yoga School.

Koot Hoomi came forth and explained:

"Koot Hoomi speaks," He said, making the Master's salutation to me. "You are of the Priesthood of Lord Maitreya. Go by one particular name, which is Master Amsumata (The Radiant One). You are to be known also as John, Disciple of Christ, during your teaching; in the other work, Yoga, etc.,— Master Amsumata, now Master of Christ—Master Amsumata of the Christ Sun, the Radiant One of the Hindus—BOTH SCHOOLS—School of Christ, School of Yoga."

Then Koot Hoomi told me something of the Mastery of Ave Maria which I am not permitted to state. However, I will say this regarding Mary the Mother of Jesus—SHE IS FAR BETTER KNOWN AND UNDERSTOOD IN THE ORIENT IN HER HIGHER ACTIVITY THAN SHE IS IN THE WESTERN WORLD. IT WILL BE A LONG TIME BEFORE THE AVERAGE MINISTER OR PRIEST IN THE OUTER WORLD, RISES TO THE HIGH DEGREE SHE HAS ATTAINED, IN ORDER TO UNDERSTAND HER. GOD BLESS HER IN ALL HER GREATNESS,

HER LOVE, HER COSMIC INTELLIGENCE AND HER FEARLESSNESS IN DOING WHAT SHE KNOWS TO BE RIGHT AND GOOD.

And just following Mahatma Koot Hoomi's explanation, Mary and Joseph appeared to me in their ancient garb of hundreds of years ago. She described the home, even, where we had lived during the Ministry of Jesus almost 2,000 years ago. She was dressed neatly as a Galilean. She was not Jewish, she explained. She was of the House of Jesse. Joseph (He was KH or KH WAS Joseph) also explained that He was of the House of David, but did not follow the Jewish religious rites, but both were of the Essenean Priesthood. They ate no meat of any kind, he said, and mostly lived on vegetables and fruits, like the Initiates of the School of Apollo of Greece.

Both, Mary and Joseph, in their ancient garb—in the Spirit of that time—came to congratulate me, their son John in that age, upon my attainment of Mastery in this embodiment. They even took me with them in consciousness back to that time. It was as though we went there. They lived, or WE lived, in a very comfortable home. Mother Mary was a frugal mother and housewife. She spun clothing, stored vegetables and fruits and was immaculately clean in all her household duties. She was alone much of the time and used any spare moments she had in prayer and meditation. The Brotherhood to which they belonged taught the deeper interpretations of the Holy Scripture, but they had to be most secretive regarding the higher teachings. "Jesus' teachings had nothing to do with the Jewish doctrines," Joseph told me. "This is why the Jews persecuted Jesus as they did."

Joseph was a good provider. He was, as has been explained to me by Koot Hoomi and Ave Maria since, a Wise Teacher at that time. He was of the Magi himself. Those of today who think Joseph was not the father of Jesus do not understand the spiritual interpretation of the "Immaculate Conception." That Spiritual Conception has little to do with physical parenthood. Jesus was the son of Joseph and Mary as is distinctly shown in the First Chapter of St. Matthew, the 16th verse, "And Jacob begat Joseph the husband of Mary, of whom was born Jesus, who is CALLED Christ."

There is much more said or written regarding the birth of Jesus, all of which I do not deny nor affirm, but I do know that Christ is not born of man nor woman, but of God the Father. The one important thing for the millions of so-called Christians to understand is that Jesus was the physical man; Christ was and IS the Son of God. This principle had not, when the Bible was translated and published, been fully understood, nor is it understood by many today. It cannot be understood fully until one attains Christhood himself. We are now entered into the New Age when all who "seek shall find" the secret to which I refer. Ave Maria is the Bride; Lord Maitreya is the Bridegroom. "Fear not, I am with you always." To him who has love enough in his heart all things are possible. Beloved, ask that your love be increased. Call to the Lord of Love. He is Maitreya. Ask that your faith be also increased, your wisdom, your intelligence. Be not afraid of anything, so long as you KNOW you are RIGHT and TRUE.

Look for the spiritual interpretation of the Bible that is there hidden for those who are to receive it. "Read the Scriptures for in them ye THINK ye have everlasting life." Study them carefully. I have given you some of the keys to the Scriptures. I shall give you more anon.

Pray, affirm, decree, to understand the SPIRIT. Did you understand the Spirit—yes, THE SPIRIT—then you can come to me IN SPIRIT and IN TRUTH, and I shall teach you, just as I have been taught by Lord Maitreya, KH, Ave Maria, Mahachohan, Jesus, Anoma, Sanat Kumara, Krishna, Buddha Gautama and others. You know how instantaneous electricity is in running through a wire or any metallic conductor, don't you? Well, Beloved, Lord Maitreya is even more instantaneous, if that were possible. You have listened to your radio at home, haven't you? Do you ever wonder just how you are able to bring that music, those words and all from out of the atmosphere? There is but ONE ATMA Sphere. There is but ONE SPIRIT. You cannot hide from ME. I SEE YOU THROUGH THE ONE EYE OF GOD. I HEAR YOU THROUGH THE ONE EAR OF GOD. I FEEL YOU THROUGH THE ONE HEART OF GOD. I am here, I am there, I am everywhere IN SPIRIT. I AM HIS SON. HE IS MY FATHER. There is nothing in My Father's House that I do not have access to. My Father has been so very loving and kind to ME. He is your Father, too, but maybe you have forgotten to call to Him. Be not afraid. He has asked you through ME to COME HOME AGAIN. "I AM THE DOOR." No one need to know that I am now talking to you. We—you and I—are Brothers in the Light. I understand how you feel about all these spiritual mat-

ters. You are no different than any other human being. That
is right. You are a "chip off the same block," so to speak. I
probably know much more about you than you do about yourself, just as those who taught me, knew far more about me than
I did about myself when I first contacted the Masters.

Frankly, candidly, I'm going to tell you, Beloved—now that
we are talking these things over—you and I—here in this Quiet
Spirit—that there is so very much conceit and egoism shown
by the average minister of the present-day churches (the average,
I mean) and priests, too, for that matter—that if I were them, I
sure would be ashamed to call myself a theologian. It is pitiful
how little they really do know. I realize that they will not feel
very friendly toward me when they happen to read these lines,
but I cannot help it because they are ignorant of the truth unless
they first acknowledge their lack of understanding. Then I might
teach them something. I'm not just like "Bob" Ingersoll. He
didn't know much about the Bible. I do know something about
it—even something the average priest or minister does not know.
I know what they think I do not know and just a little besides.
HOW DO I KNOW? I KNOW THE ONE SPIRIT.

Read the Scriptures. Trust in God, in Lord Maitreya,
Christ, to enlighten you from within your heart. Your heart
knows more than any priest or minister in the world. Your heart
knows more than the Pope at Rome, even though I love the
Pope for the marvelous work he does for the good of mankind.
At the RIGHT TIME the Pope will make one move that will
electrify the world. When Lord Maitreya gets ready for him to
move, HE WILL MOVE. All such ecclesiastical matters are
under the observation of the Lords of Light. Just watch and
pray. "THAT DAY COMETH." "Love casteth out all fear."
I am with you, ALWAYS. Christ is incarnate.

These are momentous times. "The great change" is at hand.
The Lords of Light hold supreme power over all peoples at
this time. Soon "the Trumpet will sound," and the "walls of
Jericho shall fall."

On June 3, 1941, Lord Maitreya came to me to give me
instructions as to my future activity. As I have intimated to you
before, Lord Maitreya is a being who says nothing unless it is
important. Frequently when He comes into my Presence he says
not a word, but radiates His Light and Love about me. At other
times He came to cleanse my aura. He would make a certain
sign, which represents an important symbol, and holding that in

His hand He would, in a sense, comb all darkness out of my aura.
It was amazing to me. As we walk among outer people and conditions during the day we often contact dark entities, and unless
we are perfectly harmonious they are apt to hang in our auras.
It takes some affirmation or the power radiated by certain symbols
to dissolve or eradicate such influences. I could actually feel the
pressure of such things lift from me as though He were taking
weights from my brain and body. I have learned how to handle
such things myself now, therefore, as soon as any pressure inimical
to my general welfare comes about me, I immediately use the
protective signs, symbols, WORDS and affirmations given me by
the Ascended Masters. There is no condition they cannot handle.
At any time you do not feel right there is a psychic, etheric, mental
or physical condition causing it. Generally such conditions are
caused in the etheric body. If left to develop they affect the
mentality as well as the physical body, thus serious sickness may
result.

Lord Maitreya told me to take down notes. He gave me the
following instructions regarding my work:

"FROM THE WORLD TEACHER
LORD MAITREYA

"TO THE SILENT WATCHER (AMSUMATA):

"The next field to be investigated is the field of your
former teacher, D............ C............ For that reason you
need the assistance of the Master of the Fourth Ray,
Serapis. Kindly give Master Serapis the message that you are
requested to look into the work of D............ C............, Master RC, and his field of activity. You go there without enmity.
This time you go there as the Silent Watcher of the Great
White Lodge, so ask the Goddess Ave Maria to call on
Serapis for permission to investigate D............ C............ and
his activity. She is the head of the religions of the West
and wishes those activities to be investigated."

"You will deliver a lecture in Seattle that will make you
known as a Master of Wisdom. I believe you need 'A............'
in your investigations as Silent Watcher."

"The next following to investigate is A............, which
needs a thorough investigation, to say it mildly. All those
mushroom activities need investigation by the Silent Watcher

196

and Ave Maria as you did in the "I AM" activity. All the "I AM" activities are now in the hands of the World Teacher, as through the assistance of Ave Maria, who is the head of all the religions in the West."

"I wish Ave Maria to direct Her Light to the Unity Workers, as the symbol for which they stand is the winged Sun, which is the symbol Ave Maria also uses. These can be reached by the Golden Sun, the White Sun, the Blue Sun and the Pink Sun, as long as it is the Great Light they seek. I see that the Unity Work can be greatly built out, as one through which they can be led to Sun Initiation."

" 'THOU ART, OH, GOD, OUR WINGED SELF.' "

"She, Ave Maria, must direct her Sun to the Unity Workers and initiate them, those who are ready—on the INNER PLANES—NOT ON THE OUTER. *She should do no teaching on the outer. On the inner planes the teaching is done by the Great Light. The teaching of the outer is by the Lesser Lights.*"

"*You and Ave Maria are soon not to be seen, but only felt. The LIGHT IS THE INITIATOR.*"

"You, Silent Watcher, do not have to feel that you are obligated to anyone. Your spiritual work is payment."

"The lady, Mrs. C........., I have in mind starting a sort of boarding house, where she might keep certain ones who may come here to be initiated into the Great Light. You might be able to aid her in finding such a place, in helping her to build it, even. Something might be built out of shakes and beaver board—not anything elaborate. You might look about for a place and assist her. Here you have Krishna's Well and Christ's Well."

"You will go to Seattle, deliver a lecture and return to Mt. Shasta in a few months. In Seattle you will look into various centers to find those ready for initiation. You should have a place here where to assist them and initiate them. You two, Ave Maria and Silent Watcher, have an enormous field."

"You shall speak in Seattle as the Silent Watcher. Those who do not need blazing decrees, those who are ready to receive the Wisdom of the Sages, are the ones you shall draw to you; those who are ready to become Masters."

"When love offerings are given then the Sister (A.M.) might buy the property where the barns are located. Then a monastery can be developed with your assistance. Develop a cheaply constructed monastery. This is your work. It may be a shack when you first build it, but it will be a palace when you are finished with it."

"Reach to all—to all students of religious thought in the West."

"Do not limit yourself to any one or other thought or religion, but embrace all religious thought."

"Also put up the Wheel of the Dharma and place the students on the Wheel. Let them be initiated by the different Bodhisattvas of the Dharma. In the center of the Lake on the Lotus Throne, is the World Teacher sitting, watching the turning of the Wheel, and initiations of mankind. And all are born from His Tathagatta Womb, born anew, His own true Children."

"Who that is born of My Spirit is my own heir, my own True Son, and in My Spirit He goes forth to do My Will. My Priests are ever ready at My command to do whatever I ask them to do. Even Ave Maria is recognized by me as my Great Priest, even though I have not yet spoken to her regarding this on the outer plane. She is my Great Priest and I am well pleased with Her services, as the Great Priestess from on High, the SUN of the FATHER."

"This to Ave Maria: She is not overlooked, not even by the World Teacher, and I wish to express my deepest gratitude as to what she has done, last night, concerning an activity which she knows. More power to Ave Maria! All your powers are now placed in your hands, as I am sure you are able to take care of it."

"This message following is given to A.M.; by the World Teacher:

"Who the World Teacher is you know, Ave Maria. Do you remember when I allowed you to write a letter to the most feared being in Europe as the officer of Lord Maitreya the World Teacher? This is me. Even then you had accomplished something. This to make you understand, that you need not escape through the Ninth Ray to unite with the Cosmic Father. Do, please, cooperate ever, and do not hurt me. I love you in the Great Love of the Infinite, all embracing, although there were a few difficulties, rather misunderstandings, all is well, and I also give you the greetings of your Beloved Husband Mahatma Koot Hoomi. I assure you that through you both your radiation of Love THROUGH THE CENTER OF THE COSMIC HEART, HUMANITY IS FED WITH THE MILK OF THE SPIRIT. This, again, to make you understand that all is well."

"Mahatma Koot Hoomi is at present on a mission which He must fulfill for me. Let your heart not be troubled. In Presence He is ever around you, as you know. As soon as this mission is fulfilled He will come to you."

KNOW THIS, BELOVED ONES OF LIGHT "THAT ONCE IN A TIME THOSE ARE BORN WHO LEAD HUMANITY, AND WHEN THESE COME, THEY ARE PROTECTED, AND THERE APPEARS A SIGN, THE SIGN OF THE CROSS IN THE HEAVENS. THIS SIGN HAS AGAIN APPEARED AFTER LONG AGES." And I AM directed by a Radiant Star that flashes out of the heavens to remind me of the Way I am to go. And that Star I know to be the Light of Ave Maria who ever guards Saint Germain (Amsumata) in His work among the people of earth. Ave Maria has been called "NADA" by certain Messengers of Saint Germain. She, Ave Maria, is also known as the "Goddess of Justice." She weighs all, and those who "are wanting" now, shall "reap what they have sown," for these are "the last days before that great and dreadful day of the Lord." "Judge not lest ye be judged."

CHAPTER XXVI

The first real proof I had of my ascension in this present episode of the latter part of my present embodiment, was on the night of May 29, 1941. The Seven of Us of the Council of the Great White Lodge were in session in the Inner Council Room of the Inner Retreat of the Brotherhood of Mount Shasta, all present also being members of the Lemurian Brotherhood. I have given you the names of these before.

I shall picturize as nearly as possible just how this strange meeting appeared. We were all more or less relaxed, some sitting and a few of us standing, in one end of the chamber. Before us, in an open space toward the other end of the room, was a tiny little elf, neatly dressed in the modern appearance of a present-day business man. Actually he was no more than three or four inches tall at most. He held a paper in his hand from which he read a message from the outside world. He was most emphatic in his discourse regarding the need at this time of assistance from the Gods in establishing the forth-coming Golden Age. We all had to give him our utmost attention, for, to say the least, he was a "silver-tongued orator." He walked up and down before us much as a lawyer does when pleading his case before a judge and jury. I noticed, particularly, his tiny feet, and how spritely he moved about. He was most serious about the matter under discussion, which, of course, made his statements the more emphatic.

There was a great golden door at the end of the chamber next to our Lilliputian orator. Occasionally he would step toward that door as though in an endeavor to reach the massive door knob to open it, as it were, to invite us Great Giants into the outer world to do there the needed work necessary in preparing the people of the world for the New Golden Age. I distinctly recall how massive I felt in the presence of that mite of a figure. I also definitely recorded in my Saint Germain Mind, too, the great impression the tiny fellow was making on the minds of the other Lords present. I gathered from his talk that he was a newspaper man, a writer, and lecturer. His knowledge of the great philosophies was comparable, too, I recall, to that of the

Lords of Wisdom of the Great White Lodge. As he tripped so lightly over the floor toward the Great Door, I noticed those trim tiny feet again and remarked to those present, "I believe he is even getting smaller." Yes, he did seem to be growing smaller while we were looking at him. And just then another entered the scene of activity.

Ave Maria, the only Goddess present, soared like a great bird through an upper door to the left and above the Great Door of Gold. She said she would go to the outer world to assist this one who had dared to come to the Council Chamber of the Great White Lodge and appeal for help for mankind. Others of us agreed also to assist him.

And as the scene closed I saw the tiny Great Orator walk again to the Massive Golden Door. Still he strove to open it, but this time he seemed to know that Ave Maria would open the door from the other side. The little fellow had been polite, kind and courteous all through his discourse. In fact I as well as the others, I believe, were much in love with him because of his earnestness, his beautiful appearance, and the wisdom of his words. Just before the "curtain fell" the speaker, while reaching up toward the door knob, turned his body at such an angle that I saw the side contour of his head. Then I noticed his hair was rather long, the shape of his head most familiar, and, on closer scrutiny, I discovered that he was Norman R. Westfall in miniature. He was then the "passing" of my outer personality. I heard of him but once after that. He came to me the next day as a messenger boy from Mahatma Koot Hoomi with a message for Ave Maria. I have not seen him since. Yes, he was a pretty nice fellow, I thought.

Every word of this above narrative is true. It was one of the proofs to me of my being in the outer the Temple in which Saint Germain carries on His transcendent work among mankind. "Little Norman" represents just how small your outer personality must become, comparatively speaking, before you can ascend. Another thing it taught me in my outer mind was the possibility of us, even in our limited minds and activity, going DIRECT TO THE ASCENDED MASTERS to get assistance in performing our duties here.

The outer personality must be so "cast down" in one respect, yet so "enlarged" in another direction, that we are ONE IN SPIRIT with the Center of All Life. After all, the Ego, which in one sense is the Electronic Presence or "I AM" Presence, must become manifest in our outer consciousness. The Personality, on the other hand, must, along with the outer mind, give way to that Egoic Light. The human mind is the greatest handicap to Spiritual Conception, yet we can do nothing without it. It must become our willing servant. When we want it to act, it will act. When we want it to be peaceful, harmonious and perfectly tranquil, it will become the "quiet water" upon which we see the reflections of the Christ Presence.

I shall quote, with the permission of Lord Maitreya and the Ascended Masters with whom I am associated, a part of a discourse delivered by my Higher Christ Presence (Saint Germain) in Cincinnati, Ohio, October 27, 1936, as it was reprinted in "The Voice" magazine, December Number, 1936, which gives a very clear idea about why we have physical bodies:

> "Many throughout America and the world have wondered and wondered: why human beings have physical bodies—why they were allowed to come into the limited condition in which mankind finds itself today. The reason is perfectly logical: because in past ages, when mankind was given free will, individuals steadily and gradually began to claim and hold the power in the form, in the outer activity of the mind, through the intellect. That lowered the rate of vibration of the structure of the bodies, until it has reached its present density. That activity, having been the reason for lowering your own vibratory action and causing the density in which you find yourselves today, then in having the knowledge of your 'Mighty I AM Presence,' you CAN CONSCIOUSLY ASCEND from the point to which you descended. Mark you! it is ALL the activity of consciousness and feeling is consciousness just the same as thought."

Now, Blessed Ones, I quote the above principally because thousands of so-called "I AM" students have gotten the erroneous idea that in order to ascend one has to "pass out," take up their physical body with them like "David Lloyd" is said to have done, or something of that kind. The main thing, in order to ascend, is just what was said above, "YOU CAN CONSCIOUSLY ASCEND FROM THE POINT TO WHICH YOU DESCENDED." "David Lloyd," I venture to say, if he did ascend (and I do not doubt), was taken up just as Ave Maria was when she was at the border of Tibet at the time she was carried by levitation by Koot Hoomi and Morya to their Retreat at Shigatse. Yes, I would guess that "David Lloyd" is now, sound and well, in a physical body, in one of the Retreats in India, Arabia, in the Gobi Desert, or somewhere like that. And,

I may add, for the benefit of Mrs. Ballard or any other student who does not wholly understand, that it is not unusual for Ascended Masters to do just such stunts as that. I have seen many things even more strange and mysterious.

The principal point for us to concentrate upon in order to ascend is service to mankind. When we forget ourselves in our eagerness to help others to see and understand the higher states of consciousness, we are liable to catch sight of our "I AM" Presence. Step by step, in service to mankind, degree by degree, we lift ourselves in consciousness up to where we were—BACK TO PAR—BACK TO GOD. And whether you have a physical body or not does not matter—the main thing is GET THERE IF YOU CAN.

Now, I know I have that Higher Mental Body. I have seen it, not once but hundreds of times; examined it, felt of it and thrilled to the marvelous feeling of immortality, indestructibility. I shall tell you of an experience I had in 1925, which proved to me that I had even ascended then, for I was conscious of my "I AM" Presence.

My physical father had passed on but a few months previous. My father had never understood me. He loved me very much, but there was always that "something" about me that put him on "edge" when I was near him, even when I was a tiny boy. It took me many years to analyze the reason for that. When I was seven years of age he came home one night intoxicated and almost beat me to death because I would not say "calf rope." *I did not say it.* My mother, at last, weeping, fearing he might kill me, begged him to stop beating me. Now, I know there were certain Blacks who knew of my identity and as entities they entered his body at times to try to get him to get rid of me. Many were the times I wept because of my father, even after I was grown up. I was living in Olympia, Wash., when my father passed. I wanted no ill feeling existing between us after he passed. I had even sent him occult books to read the last few years of his life. I desired very much to erase anything that might hinder him or myself in advancing along the pathway of Light.

One night I was conscious of going to him in my Higher Body. I rose or ascended into the air, travelled through the ether for what seemed like a great distance and finally came to a beautiful valley. On each side of the wide valley were scraggy oaks growing on low clay hills, I remember. Below in the level plains were farm houses, barns, cattle and other farm stock. I saw men working in the fields. At last I came to a particular farm home, went to the barn, around through some stalls and into a granary, where I found my father. He looked happy, and joyously embraced me. I noticed that his body was more rosy than when in earth life, but so far as tangibility is concerned, he felt just the same. We talked about things there just as if we had not seen each other for some time. He told me of the farm and the work he was doing. He had always talked of owning an ideal farm. He was enjoying just such perfect surroundings. I felt exactly as if I were visiting a foreign country. I went about there in the granary feeling of the boards of which it was built to see if they were like what we have here. Actually I could see no difference.

There was one thing that did puzzle me, however. My father had had his left limb amputated above the knee about seven years before his death. That limb was still missing. I remarked, "I thought you would have both limbs here." Before he could explain anything to me regarding it there was a voice spoke to me from somewhere which said, "We are applying a solution upon it. In time it will be all right. We have to erase from his consciousness the idea that he has that limb amputated. As soon as his mind is healed he will have both limbs perfectly."

So, you may see, my father was not in his Higher Mental Body, but in his Etheric Body. You may understand from this, Beloved, how important it is to do what work we can in this octave while we have a good physical body, for what we do not do here is pretty hard to do after we get beyond this plane. In this body is where we have to prove to be Master.

Suddenly I took a look at my own body while I was there, and I saw what a radiant, glowing body I possessed, for when I looked, it was instantly, as it were, stripped of clothing, and I stretched forth my hands toward heaven and exclaimed, "Why I'm immortal! I'm indestructible! Nothing can harm me! Nothing can touch me!" And I shall never forget that thrilling feeling that vibrated through my being.

I visited with my father for a while and then I said, "Well, Papa, you know now I can come here and see you."

"Yes," he replied, "and I know that not one in a million can come here and return to where you are going."

While speaking of the various bodies we possess I wish to make it known to Students of Light who might have gotten the idea that Ascended Masters do not have physical bodies, that I do not believe they can show me in any of Saint Germain's discourses, even those delivered by Messenger Guy Ballard, where he stated that the Ascended Masters did not have physical bodies on earth. Theosophical students have known for more than a half century that Koot Hoomi and Morya, who are Ascended Masters, have physical bodies. I have known two Masters in particular, right here in the United States, whom I now know to have been Ascended Masters. Hard-headed human beings of course cannot accept but what they have actually experienced themselves.

So, My Doubting Friends, I do not blame you for your doubts, for I know you cannot KNOW of the Ascension and ONENESS WITH THE FATHER until you experience it yourself. With faith, however, in those of us who have experienced it, we can show you the means by which you can prove it to yourself, if you will diligently, sincerely follow our instructions. We cannot tell you just WHEN, for no two students require the same time nor the same teaching and instruction, but I, with the help of Lord Maitreya and other Masters of Light, am sure I can open up a New World for you that will be ample proof and will satisfy you that life is eternal, and it is exactly "WHAT YOU MAKE IT."

Christ is within your Heart. Look for Him there, and remember I have given you a Golden Heart. I AM THE GOLDEN BODY OF GOD. I AM the Son of the God of the Golden Heart. I AM the Prince of the Golden Heart. "Fear not, I am with you ALWAYS."

CHAPTER XXVII

Between May 29 and June 4, 1941, I experienced enough, in the inner planes and my outer activity, should it have been recorded and written about, to fill several good-sized books.

I had been told of my membership not only in the Great White Brotherhood, but also definitely experienced, in my Egoic Presence (I AM Presence) the spiritual knowledge of my being a member of the Council of Seven of the Great White Lodge.

Yes, Beloved Seeker of Light, I make this statement, without fear, knowing that My Father and all the Great Masters, including Lord Maitreya, Solar Christ (Logos) to this Universe, are my PROTECTORS.

In 1936 I was tortured by Blacks on the inner and outer planes to such an extent that I had to leave Bremerton, Washington, where I then lived. There were several weeks I had to keep in hiding, even from my wife and children—October and part of November, 1936—in order to preserve life in this physical body.

It was during that time that in the presence of two persons, one a jeweler, the other a shoemaker, in Bremerton, a priest in Black Robes appeared to me and said, "If you don't keep still we will get you. If it were not for your children we would not allow you to get home this evening. An accident would happen to your car. I come from the Head Man. You had better keep still."

I thank God I had protection then, and I thank the Brothers Of Light that I have protection now. I decreed in the presence of the Black Brother, in a very firm voice, "In the Name of Saint Germain and All the Masters of Light, you go straight to Hell where you belong. I stand for the LIGHT FIRST, LAST AND ALL THE TIME, AND I SHALL TALK WHENEVER CHRIST PROMPTS ME TO DO SO. YOU HAVE NO POWER OVER ME NOR ANY SINCERE STUDENT OF LIGHT. IN THE NAME OF CHRIST GET OUT OF HERE AND STAY AWAY FROM ME. BEFORE *HIS* LIGHT NO DARKNESS CAN REMAIN."

That priest disappeared instantly. A few days later I went to Portland, Ore., where I lived in an attic for several days, with little to eat, for I had no money. This I can prove by two persons, as well as one Master who came to my assistance. I was on my way to a loan shop to see if I could get 50c or 75c for my brief case, having had nothing to eat for two days, when I met a former student of mine, Waldo S. Chase, an artist of Seattle. He asked me to have lunch with him. He loaned me five dollars, also, God bless him. E. R. Hansen was another former student who assisted me at that time. There were many people I knew in Portland at that time, to whom I could have gone for assistance. I dared not, for esoteric reasons, approach them. Those I contacted I met by chance. I still have my brief case.

Last January, 1941, when I visited Bremerton I found that both the jeweler as well as the shoemaker, before whom the priest had appeared, had passed on. I had not heard of their decease until I returned there. The jeweler's name was McDonald, the shoemaker, Jack Phipps.

While in Portland I spent most of my time praying for proper direction in what I should do. I knew that the time for the Great Mission for which I was sent into this world was approaching. I also knew I had to be alone to get into the Great Spirit in order to get my bearings. My physical and mental condition had to be purified. A Master from Los Angeles (Whittier) came to me, in His physical body. Through Him and my own Presence of Light, I was directed to Eureka, California.

Do not fear anybody or anything, Blessed Students of Light, so long as you know Christ is with you. As Koot Hoomi said to me recently, "When He (Christ Maitreya) is with you, who can be against you?" By "recognizing only the White-Nature" in anybody you contact, the Black-Nature cannot act, should they have a Black-Nature. Light is ALWAYS more powerful than darkness. When you turn an electric light on in a dark room there is no struggle between the light and darkness, is there?

To return to my ascension at Mt. Shasta, I must say TIME is an insignificant element when it comes to eternity and the eternal states of consciousness we no doubt experience in our Christ Presence. The spiritual episodes of my initiations and my conscious work with the Great Masters on the inner planes of life have no place with time in earth life. I have proved again and again the fact that a vision or clairvoyant seeing of certain phases of outer activity in the inner planes cannot definitely be dated in the physical plane. For instance, about fifteen years ago, I saw Japanese troops invading the United States (on the inner planes). War was just declared last Monday, December 8, 1941, against Japan, following the invasion by the Japanese aerial fleet of the Hawaiian Islands.*

I believe it was July 17, 1939, that I attended a meeting of the "I AM" students in the "I AM" Temple directed by Ratana in Los Angeles at 123 North Lake Street. Mr. and Mrs. Ballard and their staff were present. Mr. Ballard gave one of his well-known discourses. The Mighty Kosmos, supposed to be one of the mightiest of beings from the Cosmic Center of all Life, was said to have spoken through Mr. Ballard. It was the most powerful address I have ever heard, was most constructive and educational, and He (Kosman) stated during the discourse that He had brought two new Rays into this earth at the time—the Eighth and Ninth. I saw light flashing about in the temple, and anyone, who had the least bit of faith, could certainly feel the marvelous radiance about the place. The audience responded miraculously to the speaker.

Now, Friend, this is what I wish to explain, or undertake to clarify a bit: Twenty-four hours previous, just after I had gone to bed, I had a vision of the whole visit and discourse of the Mighty Kosman. I even saw the colors of the New Rays, having been reminded of the time and place while standing in the audience (all had risen from their seats) in the "I AM" Temple on the evening of July 17. The question in my own mind was: "HOW CAN THIS BE?" How can one see in the outer octave a thing before it actually comes forth in the earth plane? This matter puzzled me a great deal, even long before the Kosman episode. However, I was drawn into a second-hand book store two days later, July 19, and directed by My Presence to an OAHSPE BIBLE, on a shelf there among other old books, and I was directed to turn to page 729, which told all about the KOSMON era now dawning. A map of the Etherean World— the ARC of KOSMON—is there pictured. I read beneath it the following:

"Jehovah said: When the world approacheth dan'ha in Sabea, the nations shall be quickened with new light; for Kosmon cometh out of the midst. And my etherean hosts shall press upon the understanding

*This book was written in November and December, 1941. Where such dates as the above occur, please keep this in mind.—*Author.*

208

of men, and they shall fill all nations and kingdoms with new discoveries and inventions and books of learning. And men shall be conceited of themselves above all the ages past, and they shall deny Me and quarrel with My name, and cast Me out. But I will come upon them as a Father, in love and mercy; AND *MY* HOSTS OF HEAVEN SHALL CAUSE BABES AND FOOLS TO CONFOUND THE WISE BY SIGNS AND MIRACLES. My hosts from heaven shall cause chairs to speak; and inanimate things to walk and dance. THE DEAD SHALL REAPPEAR TO THE LIVING, AND TALK TO THEM FACE TO FACE, AND EAT AND DRINK, AND PROVE THEMSELVES TO THE CHILDREN OF EARTH, AND MAKE MY KINGDOMS KNOWN. Yea, they shall encompass the whole earth round about with signs and wonders, and set at naught the philosophy of men and the idolatries of the ancients. For both, the living and dead, shall know that I, Jehovah, live and reign over heaven and earth. This shall be a new era, and it shall be called Kosmon, because it embraceth the *present and all the past.* THEN WILL I REVEAL MYSELF; AND THEY THAT DENY ME SHALL ACCEPT ME; OF THEIR OWN ACCORD WILL THEY PUT AWAY THEIR LORDS AND THEIR GODS AND THEIR SAVIORS; NOR SHALL THEY MORE HAVE IDOLS OF ME, EITHER ON EARTH OR IN HEAVEN, FOR *I AM* SUFFICIENT UNTO ALL."

I mention the above incidents, and quote from the Oahspe Bible to show you how many of us at this time, NOW EMBODIED IN EARTH, are here at the behest of the Great Gods, Lords, Masters of the ONE ALMIGHTY GOD—THE GREAT SPIRIT—THE "I AM" PRESENCE, and what we, in our individual way, are prompted or actually told what to do, THAT MUST WE DO, otherwise our last state shall be worse than our first.

I, in my CONSCIOUS ASCENSION back to God or the Spiritual Center where all Life issues, merely BECAME CONSCIOUS OF MYSELF, WHO "I AM" AND WHAT I AM TO DO. And, Beloved, I AM DOING IT. I am writing this book. This, at present, is what I am to do. What I am to do in the future lies with Saint Germain (My Presence Eternal), Christ Lord Maitreya, Koot Hoomi, and all THOSE OF LIGHT with whom I am associated. What the Council of the Great White Lodge determines, that shall I do. I shall, however, have a vote in that matter myself, for I AM ONE WITH GOD THE FATHER. I AM HIS SON. HE TOOK ME BACK INTO HIS HOUSE. I LIVE IN THE SUN, YET

I HAVE A BODY ON EARTH. My SUN-BODY is my Golden Body. My Venus-Body is my Love-Body or the source of Love. Our Seven Bodies correspond to the Color-Radiance of the Seven Planets, as well as the Rainbow-Rings of the Seven Great Universes, etc., ad infinitum. There are planets invisible as well as visible. Scientific astronomers know this. However, the invisible planets have their influences upon us on earth sometimes even more than the visible planetary forces. The etherean spaces through which our universe passes from age to age also affects world conditions on earth just as at the present time. We must, in order to understand these matters, learn to weigh all things according to the Infinite Spirit, in which and of which all things are made, "live, move and have their being."

On the 3rd of June, 1941, I went through, physically and mentally speaking, vast changes. There was even a sexual rechemicalization went on in my physical body that I could not possibly explain. I do know that it had to do with regeneration of myself—both MALE AND FEMALE IN ONE, but I am utterly without words to describe the bliss that accompanied the ecstasy of feeling that vibrated throughout my being. I had been told by Blessed Koot Hoomi to concentrate on transmuting all forces in my three lower bodies into the Electronic Substance of Divine Love and draw all into my Four Higher Bodies. That is what I did that night when the "Great Change" came about. I knew Lord Maitreya and Koot Hoomi had much to do with it, but somehow I felt Lord Maitreya was more responsible for all that took place.

It was the following evening, June 4, that I was conscious of ascending from the etheric plane. A few days previous I had contacted the Goddess of Light through Ave Maria. We were sitting talking about different Masters of Light and I happened to have mentioned the Goddess of Light. Almost immediately she stepped through the body of Ave Maria, saying, "Ah, you all wouldn't care for the Goddess of Light, for I have a colored body."

I immediately replied, "I don't care what kind of a body you have, I love you just the same." She is a marvelous being. She stayed there and talked with us for some time. Several times later, even after I had ascended, she would come for short visits with us. On that first visit, however, she told us that she lived with Jesus as His servant where He now lives in a physical body in Arabia. In my etheric body I went to the abode where

Jesus lives. Ave Maria was with me. The three of us, The Goddess of Light, Ave Maria and I, in the living room of that small cottage, were singing religious songs and rejoicing together when suddenly I began to spin around and ascend. I rose from the floor, passed through the ceiling of the room and on into the heavens in consciousness. Ave Maria rose with me. We seemed to have been absorbed in Nirvana or the Field of Bliss or Infinitude.

We later returned to our etheric bodies in that room in Arabia. I found that my etheric body had fallen, so to speak, from the ceiling, and Ave Maria, who evidently was more aware than I of what was taking place, had suddenly thrown her body beneath mine in order to protect me in the fall. She explained the matter to me the next day in the outer octave. I had two other experiences regarding phases of my ascension later—a few weeks later—in a retreat near Seattle,—one regarding the Great Purusha, and the other when my body ascended on July 27, the time that the entire fold of Saint Germain's ascended on the inner planes.

That day, June 4, Lord Maitreya had come to bless me and admonish me regarding certain significant matters in my being His Priest. He sanctified me with His radiance. He told me how pleased He was that I had attained illumination and declared me a Brother of the Great White Lodge. "When you go forth," He said, "be humility exemplified. Remember Love must ever reign in your heart. Never endeavor to show your power or demonstrate before others. I now take you into my Solar Ring of Light and Love, My Son, thus you shall ever be protected by Me, and I shall teach you in My Temple of Light and Love what your heart desires to know. In the Sunlight of Silence you shall drink of the Well of Christ and Everlasting Life. I wish you to meet with the Brothers of the Brotherhood of Mt. Shasta in incarnate bodies."*

---

*Last evening, December 10, 1941, in writing about the ascension as it recurred to my outer mind following my pondering over brief notes regarding it, I was not satisfied with the clarity of it nor the fullness with which I felt it should be treated. When I got to the point indicated by the asterisk above I called to Lord Maitreya, Koot Hoomi, Saint Germain and Ave Maria to bring through to my outer consciousness a better understanding of just what took place at the time of my ascension. I spoke to them quietly in just about the following manner: "Please give me a better understanding of just what took place in me when I ascended. I know I ascended, I know I experienced the consciousness of the Great Spirit. Show me in the inner planes and explain it to me more clearly and allow me to bring it all back to this outer mind right now, this evening. I must be able to explain this to my readers more simply and clearly so they will understand it. I thank you, Beloved Masters of Light, for your cooperation in this matter now."

I judge it was about two A.M. the next morning, when sound asleep, there was a very loud knock on the wall just above my head that awakened me most abruptly. There was no mistaking it as something else. I knew definitely that someone hit that wall with that awful wallop to awaken me, and I was "jerked" back to this outer consciousness so suddenly that I recalled distinctly who I was talking to and what was said. I was talking to Ave Maria, and this is the substance of what She said: "Have you forgotten the Maltese Cross and what it represents? The Dark Square represents you before you began to dissolve and transmute the forces of your three lower bodies into the Pure Gold which forms the Golden Lotus in the Center. That became the Crown or Jewel or Golden Body which ascended, however, before you could ascend you had to 'eat me,' partake of 'the wine and the bread.' You actually ate of my body, My Spirit. This you did after the Resurrection. You recall to your mind, don't you, the crucifixion you experienced in your etheric body?" I admitted that I had remembered it, which I must admit, too, that I had overlooked in my description of the ascension above. Yes, I recall the great streams of blood that ran from the holes in my hands, in my feet and from the pierced side. Even today, when I think of that crucifixion I experienced, I can actually feel the prints of the nails in my hands, and at times the marks become plainly visible. Then Ave Maria surprised me by reminding me that I had often explained that "A yawn is the Soul taking a drink." And, Beloved, at 2 o'clock when I awakened I immediately began to yawn and yawn, tears gushing from my eyes. For fear I would go back to sleep and forget what Ave Maria had told me on the inner plane, I kept yawning and saying over to myself: "Ave Maria—eating Ave Maria, yawning—Maltese Cross—tears, loud knock on wall." For an hour I lay awake thinking about this matter. All Her explanation came through most clearly: Ave Maria is the BRIDE OF CHRIST; Maitreya is the BRIDEGROOM. In Spirit I became wedded to Ave Maria; Her Light, absorbed by my being through "weeping," longing, yawning, dissolved and transmuted through REGENERATION the Darkness in my "SQUARE" which became the Cross of Malta, and in turn the GOLDEN LOTUS, when I became fully conscious of MY SONSHIP WITH GOD OF THE GOLDEN HEART. Then is when I became "Prince of the Golden Heart," Christ Incarnate, which "I AM."

"Jesus wept" is the shortest verse, I believe, in the Bible. It is also one of the most significant. I know, too, that science is overlooking something very important when they do not analyze yawning, for I am certain therein lies one essential involuntary action that gives impetus to the awakening ego or Higher Body of the aspiring individual—an inner "weeping" which draws to the sleeping soul needed LIGHT in building the "Golden Body," or "that house not made by hands eternal in the heavens."

When you, Beloved, long for Christ Maitreya and Ave Maria with such adoration as to move yourself to weeping, I am sure you will find the "babe in the manger," the little Golden Body of Christ. Love will find the way, "And the Spirit and the Bride say, Come. And let him that heareth say, Come. And let him that is athirst come; and whosoever will, let him take the Water of Life freely." LOVE, WISDOM AND POWER are yours and "I AM WITH YOU ALWAYS."

I quote St. Luke 13:31: "The same day there came certain of the Pharisees, saying unto him, 'Get thee out, and depart hence: for Herod will kill thee'."

"And He (Jesus the Christ) said unto them: 'Go ye and tell that fox, "BEHOLD, I CAST OUT DEVILS, AND I DO CURES TODAY AND TOMORROW, AND THE *THIRD DAY I SHALL BE PERFECTED*." (33) 'Nevertheless I must walk today, and tomorrow, and the day following: for it cannot be that a prophet perish out of Jerusalem. (34) O, Jerusalem! Jerusalem! which killeth the prophets, and stoneth them that are sent unto thee; how often would I have gathered thy children together, AS A HEN DOTH GATHER HER BROOD UNDER HER WINGS, AND YE WOULD NOT. (35) Behold your house is left unto you desolate: and verily I say unto you, Ye shall not see me, until the TIME COME when Ye shall say, 'Blessed is he that cometh in the name of the Lord'."

Luke 14:26: "If any man come to me and hate not his father, and mother, and wife, and children, and brethren, and sisters, yea, and his own life also, he cannot be my disciple." (Explanation: You must Love the ONE GOD, the ONE LIFE, LIGHT, LOVE, WISDOM AND POWER of ALMIGHTY GOD ABOVE ALL THINGS to know Christ and become HIS SON.)

CHAPTER XXVIII

On the evening of June 9 the Great Sanat Kumara of Venus came to visit us at Mt. Shasta. It is He who is known as the Father of this planet. He is one of the Great Cosmic beings who I believe has no physical body on earth. He is understood to be one of the Great Kumaras sent here to bring about the civilization of human beings of this earth. When he came on that evening He entered in His Spirit into the body of Ave Maria. When He came into her body I was standing within about four feet of Her. He stepped backward a step. As He did so I felt His aura strike mine. What He said the few minutes He was with us I cannot quote, but He did give me a great blessing and radiated His Light throughout my being. Within a few minutes following His leaving, one of the strangest manifestations of my experiences and initiations took place, of which I shall tell you.

The room in which we were seated was still radiant from the Light of Sanat Kumara, when I noticed the features and radiance of Ave Maria change completely. With a somewhat amazing look on her countenance the new visitor said, "Do not fear me; I am a Bhodisattva. I come to bless you. I am in charge of all girls until they become of age, and all beings under the Sign of Virgo in the Dharma Wheel." I said nothing, for truly I was astonished. Then She added, "I am not as great as Sanat Kumara." Thus I knew that He had come to prepare the way for her. That, I gathered, was the reason of his very short visit.

"Where am I?" asked the radiant being, her voice filled with wonderment.

"At Mount Shasta," I replied as calmly and composedly as I could, for I myself wondered what this strange celestial being might do or say next, for I positively knew she was not acting or pretending, as some might have supposed, had they been in my place.

"Oh, how wonderful to be here!" she exclaimed, stepping quickly to a nearby window where she could see magnificent Mt. Shasta in the approaching twilight, since it was just about sunset, and at that time the mountain is always aglow with radiant light, usually pink.

As She walked back from the window, in wonderment I was looking at Her, when She said, "Don't fall in love with me. I am the Virgin—the Eternal Virgin of God. No man can touch me. I am the Nameless One."

I realized there was an angel of transcendent glory and beauty and grace right there in the room with me. Becoming more confident of myself, I asked, "Where do you live in body?"

"I have no body," she quickly replied, and then I could see a look of amazement on Her face when she realized she was in a physical body, and she inquired of me, "Whose body is this? I am the unborn Virgin of God." She looked down and about the body of Ave Maria.

I answered, "Ave Maria's."

"Oh," she exclaimed, "Ave Maria, the Virgin Christos— the One that is Me on earth. I'm Her mother."

At that moment Ave Maria, who was conscious of all that was going on in Her body, broke down and wept. Seldom had I seen Her weep at all, but she shook with emotion. I endeavored to console Her after she had wept for several minutes. The Spirit of the Bhodisattva of Virgo had gone as soon as Ave Maria had become affected by Her Spirit and radiance. After a while when Ave Maria became quiet she said, "When She mentioned 'mother' I could stand it no longer. There was such a feeling of Her great Spirit and the height of vibration, I could not keep from weeping. O, it was so wonderful. Just think of it —my Spiritual Mother was here in my own body—from the Great Cosmic Center where they have no bodies. They are all Spirit—Pure Spirit. As we think of time here it has been probably millions of years since I have been so near to Her."

For hours Ave Maria talked about that Spiritual visitation. For days afterward I am sure it affected her, and still does, no doubt.

On May 10, Lord Maitreya, in His Spirit, was in my body a great deal of the time. He talked to me much about the changes imminent, some of which have already come about, others to come soon. He gave me the names of those who will be working with me during the Golden Age. These names were mentioned as "Candidates" Lord Maitreya has "chosen": Balcheiour, Alcyone, Genesthai, Landowne, Clymer and Hall. Vivekananda, He said, is reincarnating. Rudolph Steiner is willing to re-embody to assist Ave Maria. Master Morya and the Silent Watcher will return again. I agreed to return again to assist in the government of the Golden Age.

I was given additional signs, symbols and words for my protection. I was informed to what Great Temples to look to for cooperation in my work as a teacher—THE TEMPLE OF THE BODY OF GOLD — THE DALAI LAMA, THE HOLY OF HOLIES.

The following significant instruction I was given by Lord Maitreya, all of which I publish, except certain secrets that cannot be given the "initiate" until one has passed certain degrees of attainment, after which he may be entitled to them. He said:

"The Priesthood of Golden Radiance must be initiated by you, Silent Watcher."

"The White Eagle is the symbol of Ave Maria, also White Swan, and White Phoenix Bird. The White Dove is Her individual symbol. She is the White Body of God."

"You are the 'Eagle-Mounted.' Your symbol is the Golden Eagle."

"The Sign of Sun, 'K-20,' The Solar Terrestial Sigil, the Earth Sun, the Whole Cube or Universe, from the center of the earth to Infinity; metal, Gold; color Gold; power of Holiness."

"You are of the Priesthood of the Golden Radiance of Egypt" (S.W.).

"You are the Golden Man in the Heart."

"You are the Prince of the Golden Heart."

"You are the Golden Presence of the Silent Watcher."

"You are the Gold of God Incarnate."

"You are the Universal Gold. Use the Golden Spiral in your work."

"The Buddhas of the Dharma Fields are the protectors of the Silent Watcher, the Body of God, protecting ever the Golden Sun, the Silent Watcher."

"I am resting on the Golden Lotus-Padma."

"You are FREE from all desires, all lusts; the Will to Be Free makes all—FREE. 'Phur' has no more power over you. YOU ARE FREE. YOU ARE SOL. Life springs from fire, and we become 'SUL,' the Master. 'Sulphur' or 'Radchas' causes great pain through the chains with which He binds, causes lusts and anger while uncontrolled, therefore we learn to purify the Alchemical Sulphur—our WILL OF FREEDOM FROM 'PHUR' will make us FREE. YOU HAVE MASTERED. THE FIRE DOES NOT HARM US ANYMORE. SILENT WATCHER YOU ARE FREE."

"Joshua and the Silent Watcher on the Wheel of Dharma in the Field of Sagittarius, numbers to be used, 8734—metal, tin; letter, 'O'; planet, Jupiter through the mind; female, Quicksilver (Mercury); Power of Wisdom; color, Blue."

"Ave Maria's work on the Wheel of Dharma is in the House of Virgo; numbers, 2 and 6; letter, 'B'; power of soberness, earth of Sulphur."

"Koot Hoomi's work on the Wheel of Dharma is in the House of Pisces; letter 'N'; numbers, 1 and 5; fire of Sulphur (Alchemical); power of Destiny."

On the day I discovered my Higher Presence is Saint Germain, I was handed this message, typewritten, by Ave Maria from Mahatma Koot Hoomi:

"Blessed One:

"I hasten to write you to give you the message of the Worldteacher concerning your cooperation with Master Saint Germain. Yesterday our new Worldteacher was appointed (?) and He writes you through me, he that is Mahatma Koot Hoomi. I want to make it clear to you, Blessed One.

"Master Saint Germain was asked to resign as for the SERVICE OF THE NEW WORLDTEACHER. Therefore he is not listed amongst the Masters that serve the New Worldteacher. A new Master as for the Seventh Ray was chosen, one that needs the experience of being a Master of a Ray. Who the new Master of the Seventh Ray is I am not able to give you as yet. You shall hear from me soon again. I am remaining,

"Sincerely,

"MASTER OF THE WISDOM."

On the day the above message was given to me, I sat down to my typewriter to write a letter to Mahatma Koot Hoomi regarding my working with the World Teacher. There had been an election the night previous in the Great White Lodge, which, frankly, I did not bring through to my outer consciousness clearly enough to get just what my position was regarding the World Teacher. There was no date on the message Ave Maria had given me, therefore, when I put that paper among other notes I was keeping I failed to make a note of the date, however, I think it was the 7th of June.

Ave Maria and I got into quite a discussion regarding who was elected World Teacher. I knew, and She told me, the vote lay between Koot Hoomi and Saint Germain. Now, Ave Maria, just like all Masters I've seen and become acquainted with, is very very sensitive regarding any question regarding Her position, wisdom, love, light or power, and She is extremely "touchy" regarding anything that might be said about her husband, Mahatma Koot Hoomi, or any other Master with whom She is associated in Her Great Work on earth. I had learned not to disagree with Her in anything whatsoever. And, Beloved, never "cross" a Master, or show the least bit of doubt or question as to your obedience if you expect them to teach and instruct you. Generally they instantly take such actions as a signal that you are "finished" so far as they are concerned. May God bless you should you lose your temper or control of your tongue. Patience be with you, humility, love and the gentleness of the Master Jesus, when you are in doubt about anything. Trying moments will pass. In silence the Master will direct you.

When I saw that I was being "testily tried" regarding the election of the World Teacher by the Council of the Great White Lodge, I got up from my typewriter where I had intended writing out certain questions regarding this and my individual connection with the matter. I told Ave Maria I would take a walk alone and think things over. I explained to her (when I use a capital letter as in "Her," I understand the Higher Presence of Ave Maria to be present) that I was sure Lord Maitreya would inform me clearly about the matter once I got out alone where I could meditate upon it.

I walked through the city of Mt. Shasta and on Highway 99 toward Shasta Springs. About a mile out of town I was invited by a gentleman to ride. I rode with him to the entrance of the Shasta Springs Resort. There I walked through the beautiful grounds, down the winding trail, across the rustic bridges spanning the tumbling streams, and, about five hundred feet below, seated myself in the circular band stand near the railway, to meditate upon "WHO I AM."

Yes, Beloved, I had been told I was this, that and the other, and I don't doubt but that I WAS. Right then I AM THE SILENT WATCHER. At times I WAS LORD MAITREYA. Again I AM JOHN THE BROTHER OF JESUS. I was and AM certain I ONCE LIVED AS ABRAHAM LINCOLN. I also knew I had been the ONE who directed the Ballards in the "I AM" activity. But, sitting there in this body, by the railroad, listening to the whir and roar of the talking waters of Mt. Shasta as they came laughing their way down from the WHITE PEAK high in the heavens, I wondered, "WHO AM I?"

Long I meditated there. A group of ladies came by from up on the resort grounds. They passed very near to me, but I sat with my chin resting in one palm, like "The Thinker," immovable, still wondering, "WHO AM I?" The Spirit of Almighty God seemed to enfold me. Even my body became filled with a tangible substance that caused me to feel rigid like the statue of "The Thinker" himself. "WHO AM I?"

"I AM WHO?" "I was Norman Robert Westfall," I said to myself. Then the question came into my mind, "Yes, but who is 'MYSELF'?" I then started to say something about my body and something or some being within me asked, "Whose body is this body?" That had me stumped. I thought it was my body, but I didn't know who I AM.

And then, after having meditated thus for about an hour there in that one position "I" spoke from my Heart, "Why, *I AM* SAINT GERMAIN."

Instead of walking up the winding path to the resort grounds again I walked up the railroad. About a mile toward the city I found a slender pathway winding its way around among flowering shrubs, plants and trees as it rose to the height of the precipitous plateau. I found Highway Nine-Nine and walked all the way back to Mt. Shasta City.

I went to the cottage of Ave Maria's where she was preparing dinner for us both. She knew all about my trip, my meditations, and even mentioned before I spoke of it, "Well, Koot Hoomi says you KNOW ALL now," meaning, as I knew, that I KNOW I AM SAINT GERMAIN. And it was then that she gave me the message from Mahatma Koot Hoomi you read above. Even now it might be a puzzling paper to me did I not KNOW I AM ONE WITH GOD AND HIS GOLDEN SON INCARNATED IN EARTH.

AWAKENING

These days are full of trouble,
   They're also full of thought
For in the field of stubble
   Is where the grain was sought.

In our saddest moments,
   In the gloom,
Is when our mind's at ferment
   If we give it room.

When the sky is darkened,
   Your heart is blue,
Is when you do your thinkin',
   When it comes thru.

Never fear the shadow
    When your thoughts are gray
Seeds will never blossom
    If on top the earth they lay.

Our soul is like a seed, you know,
    First planted in the earth;
The sunlight acts upon it so
    It wakens to another birth.

These days are full of trouble,
    Most every heart is sad,
Walking thru th' field o' stubble
    Thinkin' of the things we had.

Better study nature fairly;
    Plant a little seed some day;
Press it down beneath th' surface,
    In the darkness let it stay.

Air, light and moistened earth,
    In brooding darkness there
Will bring to life another birth
    Enriching you with fruit most fair.

Are you so doubtful as to think
    That souls are planted here
Pressed into the earth to sink
    By ruthless nature without care?

Better think you're like a seed
    Pressed beneath the flowering sod
With a mighty spark and speed
    To know at once the Light of God.

CHAPTER XXIX

I had planned to leave Mt. Shasta for Seattle on the 10th of June, but Mahatma informed me that the 11th would be a better day to travel. I do not recall anything of importance taking place in my activity or experience during the trip that may prove beneficial to my readers. I arrived in Seattle after having spent a day in Olympia with my brother and his family. A friend and student of mine there, Melville Burlingame, assisted me much in some matters regarding my children, all of which were quickly ironed out by the Masters of Light. The "Dark Brothers" had done a little of their dirty work through a relative-in-law. I blame no one. "I recognized only the White-Nature in everybody connected with the matter" and all worked out satisfactorily.

A lady friend of mine had invited me to her home in Seattle. From there I notified but four students of mine to whom I gave individual instructions. They asked that I hold a meeting twice each week, and in this way I hoped to train those few in the higher work I had received and give them some of the initiations I knew it was my duty to confer.

As near as I can recall, I think it was the 18th of June, in the evening, about 11 o'clock, that the unusual again manifested. I had informed the few students invited not to tell anyone of my re-appearance in Seattle. When not holding private meetings with those few I hoped to be alone with my writing and other occult work I planned. On the particular evening mentioned, Mrs. B........, Mrs. H........, and myself were sitting talking, when the door bell rang very abruptly. The lady of the house went to the door and I could very plainly hear a strong, positive man's voice say, "Is there a man here by the name of Amsumata?"

This was all so sudden I did, as it is commonly expressed, "feel the hair raise up a bit on my head," for I felt so certain no one outside our private circle knew I was there. The lady answered him, "Yes, he is here. Will you come in?" The gentleman was shown into my presence.

I can hardly describe the man who approached me. He was most unusual to say the least. I am quick to size up persons, and I knew this man to be one who had stood out alone in the world.

He was about my own height—not more than 5 feet 7 inches tall, but had been taller. His shoulders were stooped from hard work. He shook hands with me. His hands were large, strong and almost horny from callouses. He bowed graciously, with a humility expressive of deep gratitude, as he said, "I hope I am not intruding, coming here so unexpectedly at this late hour. My name is S........."

"I am indeed glad to make your acquaintance," I said, motioning him to a chair. "Will you be seated?" Of all the characteristics I might have seen about our visitor, the golden glow and radiance of his aura, which reached out three or four feet on either side of him, caught my eye, and I could not help but have a feeling of reverence toward him. His Higher Presence actually lighted up the entire room. At the same time I saw the blazing blue Light of Koot Hoomi near him, which signified to me that this new-found Brother had been sent to me.

Again he wanted to apologize for his coming at that hour. "I hope you will forgive me, but I just could not wait. I had to see you, Amsumata."

"My Brother," I said, "anyone who has as much light about them as you have is welcome to come here any time. I do not know what brought you here, but I do know that Koot Hoomi is with you. When you mentioned my name at the door I could not think it possible that any stranger might know of my presence here, however, seeing you are a Brother of Light, I wish you to know you are indeed welcome."

"Yes," he explained, "Koot Hoomi told me to come here. I was talking to Mrs. R........ and she told me I should see Amsumata. She kept talking about Amsumata, about his teachings, etc., until finally I said to her, 'Where is this Amsumata?' Well, she said she was not permitted to tell, for only his students were allowed to attend the meetings. However, I got around all that by telling her that I did not think Amsumata would object to me calling to see him personally. At last she told me where I could find you. I came directly here. I am thankful to God that I have found you and you have received me with such a kindly welcome."

"I assure you, Brother, you are in the right place," I said. "If I can be of assistance to you, I shall be happy to do so. My happiness depends upon making others happy. If I be wise then my wisdom, in order to be proved, is manifest in service to my fellowmen. Truly, I do not know when I've been so happy to see a human being as I am this moment when I look upon you,

Brother, and see the golden radiance of your soul shining through your joyous face. Truly you are a man of God. I feel as though I have known you always, yet it seems that I have not seen you for ages. I know our love for each other is mutual."

"I am a seeker after truth," our visitor replied. "I had such a strong urge to come here I know you must have a message for me. All the way coming here, although I was alone physically, I am sure there was a great spiritual Presence with me. I was definitely conscious of it."

"I am sure my Beloved Teacher, Koot Hoomi, was with you when you entered the room, Brother. There is no mistaking that. I saw His mantle of Blue enfold you, and He gave me His sign through the radiance of His Light. It would have been impossible for you to come here had you not belonged here. I am securely protected by the Great Masters."

Now, Beloved Students, I wish to explain to you just who and what this all meant. The one who came there to that room that evening was no other than the great Chinese philosopher and master, Lao Tse, now embodied. He, in his outer mind, did not know it, nor did I at the moment. All I knew of him was that he was and IS a great spiritual being. This I knew by his radiant aura.

As I do not wish to reveal the true identity of Lao Tse in his outer embodiment I shall refer to Him henceforth as "that" Lao Tse.

Lao Tse came to the bi-weekly classes thereafter. It was after the third meeting he attended, however, that he asked me to go to his home to stay with him for the night. I did. I do not recall the date but I do clearly recall what happened. That I could never forget. I slept in the living room of the house down-stairs; he slept in the east bedroom up-stairs. The next morning just before I awoke I was conscious of Lao Tse in Spirit standing beside my bed. I looked, and, instead of just seeing one of Him, there were three of Him, each dressed in white robes and they were gorgeously bedecked with jewels, too. There was one that stood near. Off about three or four feet stood another, and off still another such distance stood the third Lao Tse. The first seemed to be much taller than the second, the second taller than the third. The first was indeed quite a giant in size.

Yes, Lao Tse talked to me quite at length. He gave me to understand, speaking in a firm voice, that He understood all laws of life; that He was a Master of Life, and He wished me to assist His outer vehicle to make contact with the Masters in His outer activity. It was most important to the world, He said, that the OUTER MAN be initiated into the Great White Brotherhood in its outer activity, too, so He could accomplish for mankind what was needed to be done for the in-coming of the Golden Age. At the time Lao Tse talked to me I must admit I knew little about His individual philosophy—I mean the ancient Chinese philosopher Lao Tse. I learned much the weeks that followed.

I was asked to come and live with Lao Tse; myself and two older sons. We moved there. Lao Tse and I began to plan on a radio program of a philosophical nature. In the meantime he worked as he had for many years, doing odd jobs. He was and is expert at all kinds of mechanical work such as electrical work, carpentering, masonry, grading, or any type of work one may think of. He is the first "Jack of all trades and MASTER OF ALL" that I have ever seen. Every problem, I do believe, that ever came before him, he has solved.

Each evening after dinner, Lao Tse and I would discuss the teachings of the Masters. He, before I met him, so he told me, had never heard of the Great Masters. And, another thing, he did not believe in brotherhoods, lodges, clubs or anything that made any show of power from the empiric standpoint. I spoke to him of Maitreya, Koot Hoomi, Sanat Kumara and others. To him they were all unessential. Jesus, the one he believed in, was sufficient for him, so he informed me. I tried my utmost to get him to see that Jesus, too, was a member of the Great White Lodge, and that every individual in this world, in order to ascend, must be initiated into the Great Lodge. We must become conscious of our ONENESS WITH GOD. "Order is heaven's first law," I explained to him, "and God has that means of directing his activities among his human creatures." "As above, so below." For days we argued these principles. I went about writing the program we expected to broadcast over KIRO in Seattle, since I knew Mr. Quilliam, manager of that station, having made his acquaintance in 1933 when I carried on a program known as "Hood Canal's Outdoor Philosopher" over KJR. Mr. Quilliam was then commercial manager of KJR.

I went to see Mr. Quilliam. He was interested. I prepared the following opening program for him:

A MESSAGE FROM VENUS
By Guru Amsumata

Written July 2, 1941.

Friends of K..........., and you listeners throughout the world:

Will you kindly be quiet for just a few minutes? I have the most important message to give you that the people of this world have ever been able to hear. It is a message of peace and goodwill. It comes to you from the Planet Venus. This may seem strange to you at first, but if you will be real quiet for a few minutes, I am sure that strangeness will give way to an amazing assurance of the truthfulness of my assertion. I am a messenger from Venus, a Messenger of Sanat Kumara's. Have you ears to hear? Never before, in the history of the world, have people had the universal understanding they now possess. Never before have people throughout the world been so ready to sacrifice all they possess for UNIVERSAL PEACE.

Friends, it matters not whether you actually think I come from Venus or not—the message I have to give you—the service I am offering you— this is what counts. Your acceptance of this will be worth millions and millions of dollars to you, if you will but receive it. Money cannot buy the treasured possession a MAN OF PEACE holds.

People of America, I bring to you a message of Peace from Venus. I recall a message that came to you a few years ago from Mars—a message of war and destruction that was marvelously enacted by one over the channels of your radio broadcasting fields. It was a fit of frenzy projected into your country and the world by the potent spirit of the earth's war lords. They wanted to scare you into believing in war, the possibilities of war, the necessity of preparing for war, as well as the need for creating hate among the peoples of this world, so they could shove you into a world conflict.

You listened to the message from Mars. Now, will you kindly listen to a message from Venus, known to the people of the earth as the Love Star. Thank you, my dear friends, you shall indeed be blessed if you will listen these few minutes, while I explain to you exactly how the United States may maintain peace, and at the same time insure the protective power necessary to see us through the next nine years, a period that may prove to be the most devastating, yet the most uplifting epoch in the history of your world.

America, you are head and shoulders above any nation on earth in many respects, but especially in freedom of thought and action are you the most blessed. That freedom you now enjoy you must maintain, citizens of America. And now is the opportune time to expand that freedom, to prove to the warring nations of the world that you are strong enough, broad-minded enough, tolerant enough, to throw aside all narrowness of any sort and proclaim to the whole wide world, your belief and understanding of the Universal Brotherhood of Man, as the plan of God for your world.

Almost two thousand years ago we sent one of our Beloved Brothers to your earth. He was known to the Western part of your world as Jesus and is today recognized as the Christ; in the far eastern part of your world He was known by a different name, yet He was the same Spirit. During His short ministry on earth Jesus attracted to himself many followers of all the leading churches and sects of His time. Almost none of the leaders, however, of that time, understood Jesus. I dare say there was but one of His own disciples who understood Him. That was Saint John the Beloved. The record he, John, left, of the sermons of Jesus and His wonderful life, are evidence that John did thoroughly understand Jesus and His teaching. And I, your Messenger from Venus, have had evidence presented to me that John also ascended soon after Jesus ascended.

Your Great Savior, Jesus, is recorded to have said, "If I be lifted up I shall draw all men unto me." Do you believe that? I do. He meant that you and everyone who may believe Him, and follow His simple commandments, may have life everlasting as He has it today. And I happen to know that He has proved Himself to many people upon this earth in recent years. There are many, I find, who have had Jesus speak to them of His life and mission on earth. Of course they do not tell everybody about it. They do not like to be made fun of; however, I have talked to people of all the better known religions of your world, and I find many people of great spirituality. I find many GREAT ONES who do not even profess any particular religious belief. They believe in a Universal Brotherhood of man. They wonder why you people of earth continue, after all these years, to separate yourselves into groups, fighting each other, as it were, yet you all claim the same Savior. I wonder at this myself.

I happen to know, dear friends, that there are about sixty per cent of the people of the United States who have enough real love and understanding of Christ that they have risen above sectarianism. There are thousands in the Catholic religion, the Methodist religion, the Presbyterian religion, the Jewish religion, the long-haired religion and the shaved-headed religion, and all the hundreds of religions of the entire earth world, who believe in the same Christ, experience the love of the same Christ, and know there is but ONE UNIVERSAL LOVE manifest throughout this world and all worlds and realms of being.

Now, my beloved Friends, that is why this message is so very important to you people of the earth. I have come to call all you real honest-to-goodness believers together. That is to be your salvation from destruction in a world conflict. Is this hard to understand? Now, you can continue to fight over little insignificant passages of your Bible, you can continue to stand apart and battle over "Who's Who Among the Churches," or you can actually come together in truth and in love, just as Jesus wants you to, and win the greatest battle that was ever staged on earth. That is what Jesus wanted the Pharisees and the Sadducees, and all the sects of His time to do. They were so proud of themselves and their material churches they crucified Him instead. They did not want love in this world, for it would deprive them of their high places in their particular organization. The same thing exists today. People become insane with power. Power begets selfishness. Selfishness keeps the world in the same old ruts it has been in for centuries. At the present time the world has an opportunity to throw off that old garment of selfishness. Who has most to do with keeping that old worn-out garment on the necks of the people as a burdensome yoke? The great leaders of our religions, philosophies, universities, industries, channels of commerce, societies, and all the groups of the world. But I speak especially to the leaders of America. Awake to the golden opportunity you have at this time —this moment. This is the time when the people of Light must rally together if you are to be saved from the darkness and destruction of the conniving forces of evil. This is the sifting time. *No longer can the forces of darkness hide behind honeyed* words and phrases, and go on blindly leading the blind. I call to the leaders of America—the leaders of all walks of life, industry, religion, education, science, philosophy—*you must come out of your shells* and proclaim yourselves above narrow religious barriers, shallow individual philosophies, and grip the hand of science, and therefore prove to a peace-hungry world, that there is a Great God, A UNIVERSAL FATHER, whose "Life, Light and Love" WE ARE, in wondrous beautiful manifestation. You "live and move and have your being IN HIM."

No, friends, I do not have any preference when it comes to religion or philosophy. I do not but BELIEVE Christ. I KNOW HIM. He is above any particular religious belief. He blesses all who believe in Him, no matter what church they belong to. How could He be otherwise? Now, doesn't it seem foolish, how some people look upon their religion? What I would like to see is this: THAT ALL RELIGIONS, NO MATTER WHAT THEIR NAME OR BELIEF, SEEK TO KNOW, WITHIN THEIR OWN HEARTS, WHO CHRIST IS. Wouldn't that be wonderful? And wouldn't it be wonderful, too, if all those who have found Him in their hearts, could gather together in one great congregation—one vast audience of people of the Universal Understanding? Even the East and the West shall meet in that splendid audience.

In thy very soul, America, is the power to shake yourself free from the barnacles of selfishness! The unawakened ones who have created that selfishness shall flee from the dawn of this New Day—the LIGHT OF GOD. The "Sword of Truth and Light" has ripped the sinister net of darkness open from end to end—from East to West—from North to South. Freedom of thought and action shall soon, for the first time, encircle our world, IN THE LIGHT, LOVE, WISDOM and POWER of ALMIGHTY GOD.

Again I call to all beings of Light: "All Lights must come under the One Great Light." Those who oppose me in this declaration can be classed with the forces of darkness. Those who are not for me are against me. Those who do not declare themselves for Christ and His Light are opposed to Him. Those who do not put aside all selfishness at this time and declare themselves for TRUTH, FOR JUSTICE AND FOR THE INDEPENDENCE OF THE AMERICAS AND THEIR FREEDOM FROM ALL ENTANGLING ALLIANCES ABROAD, will be declaring themselves with the forces of darkness and destruction. Should you declare yourselves for LIGHT and TRUTH you will thus generate such power, such a masterful intelligence, such a mass ascension of the people of America, that we shall remain invincible in the face of any trials that may beset us in the coming years, no matter how trying they may be. Again I call to all the Brothers of Light throughout the world and throughout all realms of being: ALL LIGHTS UNITED! ALL LIGHTS UNITED! MAY THE EAST AND THE WEST UNITE, AND LIFT THE EARTH WORLD INTO ITS RIGHTFUL SPHERE OF LIGHT, LOVE, WISDOM AND POWER!

Before I return to Venus, Beloved Friends of Earth, may I remind you people of America, there are a number of beings on earth at the present time, who, no doubt, were sent into your earthly sphere as Messengers of Love to assist you to free yourselves from the awful scourge of selfishness, that has so enthralled your world? And then, after the Light has dissolved all selfishness and greed from the earth, THE GOLDEN AGE WILL COME, in its full glory, and nobody will lack anything, and all shall enjoy peace and happiness throughout this world.

I am very thankful that you have seen fit to listen these few minutes to the first of such programs ever broadcast in America. I shall look forward to speaking to you again soon, for I am certain you will have many questions to ask regarding the approaching Golden Age.

Good evening to you, and may the Light of God abide with you always, protecting you and guiding you eternally. Good evening.

* * *

THE STARS OF QUALITIES

Beloved Student, each Master has His individual Quality just as each Star in the Heavens radiates forth its Celestial Influence. Look for your individual star in the firmaments. But until you know your own star and the Quality you may be asked to radiate to humanity, pray to the Gods who reign in His Kingdom above you. I shall tell you how to pray. Listen to MY WORDS. May they be remembered and acted upon:

Until you are master yourself you must depend upon and call for the reflected radiance of another. "Mount Zion" is in the top of your head. A Master blazes forth His Quality from

His forehead. It is discernable to those who see with the "open eye." Even though you may not see it, you will feel it when you call feelingly for it.

It may be that you need "Faith"—Greater Faith. Call to the Lord of Faith. You may need courage—Call to the Lord of Courage. Even should you feel the need of Purity—call to the Goddess of Purity. Maitreya is the Lord of Love. Koot Hoomi and Amsumata are Lords of Wisdom. Morya and Elijah are Lords of Power. Every quality in nature, in human nature, in Super-Men and Gods, is in charge of its respective Lord.

When you pray or decree—after you have become wholly harmonious with the Lord of Love—visualize over and above your head a radiant dome in which are numberless Golden Doors. Each door represents and IS the portal into the Individual Temple of the Lords of Qualities.

When you call to the Goddess of Mercy, Her door opens to flood you with Her radiance. When you call to Lord Maitreya, His DOOR TO LOVE is opened to bathe you in His Light and Love. Remember the DOOR, Beloved.

CHAPTER XXX

MY JEWEL'S DELIGHT

Light of my life, I love you;
   Breath of my Soul art Thou;
Sweeter than dews of the morning—
   Precious jewels adorning Her brow,
Brighter than sunshine at noonday
   Filling the earth with her glow,
Purer than Shasta's clear waters
   As out from the mountain they flow.

Thou art my Soul's deepest yearning,
   Pulse-beat of sorrow art Thou.
Thou art the satisfied longing
   Enfolding my Spirit just now;
Thou art the Peace of surrender;
   Still is Thy voice as the night,
But it spoke to my Soul in the darkness
   A message translucent with Light.

Light of my life, I adore Thee;
   Light of life, Thou art mine.
I have plunged in the sea of surrender;
   Light of my life, I AM Thine.

(Dedicated to Joshua.)   —L-T.

*   *   *

Just when Lao Tse and I were prepared to start our radio program, and just when he was becoming fully awakened to his Higher Presence through instruction I had seen fit to give him, Ave Maria and my little daughter arrived on the scene. Lao Tse had dedicated his home and all his property to the use of Jesus Christ and His disciples some time before I knew him. He had told me before Ave Maria's coming that the place was to be considered a Retreat where the Brothers of Light could assemble, visit with each other and live there as long as they wished.

Lord Maitreya had told Ave Maria to go to Seattle to assist me in initiating our newly-found ancient philosopher. I had spoken to Lao Tse many times of Ave Maria. She had been informed through Mahatma Koot Hoomi and Lord Maitreya just who this strange student of life really IS. She drew me aside after she had been there a few days and said, "We have here a great philosopher. Do you know who he is?"

"No, I do not," I replied. "All I know is that he is a Great One. I saw three of his Higher Bodies, and I know he has attained Mastery in other embodiments previous to this."

"I shall tell you who he is," Ave Maria spoke in a low tone. "He is no other than the great Chinese Philosopher, Lao Tse, founder of the religion of Taoism. We must, without fail, initiate him into the Great White Brotherhood in the outer activity. Lord Maitreya sent me here for that purpose."

"That accounts for an unusual experience I had in Mt. Shasta last December," I explained to Ave Maria. "I was sleeping in a room adjoining the room in which my son, Norman, was sleeping. In the middle of the night a voice spoke through his body in a whisper so loud that I distinctly heard it in my room. I chanced to be awake. That voice said, in a most emphatic way, 'YOU MUST FIND *TAO.*' Now I see what was meant. Here I was led to Lao Tse, founder of Tao, now embodied to assist us in the Great Work of the Light of Christ. How wonderful. I now see how the Great Masters are working with us, and how all the Great Ones are really embodied at this time for the Golden Age."

"This is the age," she went on to explain, "when all the great religions and philosophies are to be brought together, simplified, and explained so that all peoples of the world shall know we MUST have WORLD PEACE AND UNDERSTANDING. Lao Tse is one of those Great Leaders of the past now embodied to help us. You and I, too, as you know, have worked for the freedom and understanding of mankind down through the ages. Lao Tse, in His Higher Bodies, has an inner Retreat in the Mountain of Fujiyama in Japan. There He initiates His devotees into the higher Mysteries of Life, however, we must initiate this outer man, the physical temple Lao Tse is now using, into the Brotherhood of Mt. Shasta. It will take time before he will be able to bring through to his outer consciousness the full realization of what it's all about, but that is our work for the present."

Friends of Understanding, it did not take as long to bring our Brother Lao Tse "through" as might have been expected. Truly I know him to be one of the very wisest men on earth. I could write a great book about his experiences in this one embodiment. The sufferings that body endured, the sorrows that mind experienced, and the physical "crucifixion" by which he was tried, would make wonderful materials for a drama unsurpassed in realistic, heart-rending human activity. He, for instance, spent years in an insane asylum where at one time he was strangled into insensibility or unconsciousness seventeen times by a warden without provocation. By the seventeenth time he was choked Christ appeared to him and spoke to him thus: "You must stay in the body this time, for we need you here." He told me he was at the point where he cared not to live, but after the vision, his tormentor quit and he recovered his strength. I shall not mention the name of the asylum where this took place (even though I can), but I shall mention the name of the warden, for it is so significant. His name was "Black."

Lao Tse told me how, during all his physical trials, over a long period of time, his own God Presence directed him, guided him and finally led him to me and Ave Maria, where he was so thankful to us for the blessings he then received from Koot Hoomi, Lord Maitreya, Buddha Gautama and others of the Great Ones. I regret I have not the time to enlarge upon this phase of my initiatory work.

Within two weeks' time Lao Tse ascended. He became conscious of his Higher Self—His "I AM" Presence, and I am not exaggerating when I say he could just as easily talk Chinese and other ancient languages as he could English, his native tongue in this embodiment. This would all take place when the Individual Spirits of his life-stream came in his body, of all of which he was conscious. After he had attained certain degrees of initiation he went with Ave Maria to Mt. Shasta, where he received additional degrees through Koot Hoomi and other Masters. It was during the latter part of July and the first part of August that Lao Tse received his instructions from Ave Maria, Koot Hoomi, other Masters and myself. I think each of us did our part in the Great Work for him and I believe we learned, or at least confirmed many of the Great Truths through Him.

It was while we were working with Lao Tse at his little retreat and even before then that I had carried on quite a correspondence with a teacher of the Great Work in Los Angeles known as Ratana. She had directed the "I AM" Temple there during the time when Mr. Ballard was active in the "I AM" activity, and was one of their staunch supporters until Mrs. Ballard and her devotees came up for trial in the U. S. Court, when Ratana failed to stand by Mrs. Ballard. It was after I had carried on a lengthy correspondence with Ratana regarding her new activity and my own individual teaching that I invited her and her secretary, Stanley Conrad, to visit our retreat near Seattle.

Lady Ratana had called to me to assist her in some way to protect her from the overpowering manner in which Mrs. Ballard seemed to oppose her in the inner realms. This I did through the assistance of Mahatma Koot Hoomi. I wrote to Ratana, told her how she might protect herself and her students. She wrote to me thanking me for the marvelous spiritual protection. Later she and Stanley came to my retreat near Seattle. They arrived just two days after Ave Maria and Lao Tse left for Mt. Shasta. Circumstances compel me to publish herewith a small part of the correspondence I carried on with Ratana, since all things must be revealed to prevent certain Blacks from hindering Ratana as well as myself and others. They must know they are not dealing with falsehoods nor weaklings, but Masters and Members of the Great White Lodge. Following is a letter I wrote to Ratana the day following her departure from the Seattle Retreat:

Seattle, Wash.
Aug. 24, 1941.

Beloved Ratana:

I had such a marvelous revelation through the spirit—the Great Omnipresence—last night, I do hope I can bring it through clearly enough that it might convey some important angle of this Divine Principle to you for your use in teaching your students.

I saw Jesus and Buddha—BOTH IN ONE PRESENCE—and He came forth in ONE PERSON to bring PEACE to our divided world. I sat near this Divine Representative, knowing that I AM a Brother of that Personification of God, while all about us—but some distance from us— were millions of people, who were acknowledging HIS COMING— CHRIST IN HIM. However, I knew in my consciousness that I AM the ONE to bring the Great Message to the outer world, and even though I approached near to that other ONE—Jesus and Buddha in ONE, He did not seem to know that I AM the one having been prepared to bring THE MESSAGE to the outer world and expound the Higher Mysteries to the people. Yet, I know this is to be SOON. You understand, Ratana, this I knew in my consciousness while in that other body, sitting there listening to Him. * * * The Spirit is Omnipresent, Omniscient, and Omnipotent, as you know. God, to the outer consciousness to any individual, no matter how high or low he may be, is DEEP MYSTERY. We must ever trust in HIM—GOD—the ALL-FATHER—ALL-MOTHER—the EVER-PRESENT—ALL-PERSON. We are—it is true—all Children of God —but the important thing in our individual activity, is to become fully aware of OUR SONSHIP and KNOW HIM COMPLETELY—BECOME ONE WITH HIM IN THE *GREAT SPIRIT*.

Strange, Ratana, but I feel that I have not begun to approach the principle as I expected to when I experienced the great uplift I received sometime during last night. As it came to me it was a wonderful POEM— beautiful, rhythmical, ecstatic, blissful, all-comprehensive, inspirational and infinitesimal, but NOW, I feel so incapable of giving you even a small taste of it. Isn't the physical octave dense?

Please do not overlook the aspects of LOVE in the Physical Octave. Generation—regeneration—Christ. The Spirit is potent. We must be potent to be active. We must be energetic to do things in this world. We must conserve our forces for good thoughts and action. Yet, we dare not be afraid to make proper use of our forces, knowing that "whatsoever we do we do to the GLORY OF GOD." Even in the midst of personal love and affection, THINK OF CHRIST AND DRAW ALL FROM THE THREE LOWER BODIES—ONCE TRANSMUTED—UP INTO YOUR HIGHER OR GOD PRESENCE. This is regeneration. To accomplish regeneration we must have something to regenerate.

Never condemn yourself for anything that might happen in your life or activity when trying to do the best you know. No master would ever condemn you. Masters do not see faults in you. They see perfection in you —ONLY PERFECTION. FEAR NOT to do what you feel within your own consciousness is efficacious to you and the GREAT WORK. REMEMBER: YOU ARE MASTER. You do not have to say to your students, "I AM *A* MASTER," but you can say "I AM MASTER." When you are master of yourself, your mastery is attained—you ARE MASTER. Assert your Mastery. "I AM MASTER OF............................ JOYOUSLY AND GLADLY DO MY WILL." * * * (Private instruction.)

I must try again to express:

'Tis love in this world—yes, love uplifted, transmuted, regenerated, that brings Divine Love to the human octave. How else can the Gods work here? What is it that prevents us—we of the New Kingdom—saying to each other, "I LOVE YOU. I LOVE YOU"? Read Shakespeare. He knew. Those who, in their shriveled minds, see but beastly lust in human love, are but weak children, just beginning to learn Divine Love's lessons in regeneration. Why did William Shakespeare (Bacon?), in "Venus and Adonis," write verse after verse, page after page, words, words, words, of inspiration, in simply telling how a GODDESS craved a single kiss—a token—a symbol, at least, of DIVINE LOVE? And he, Adonis, the longer he tarried, the more he regenerated the forces in his body into the essence of Divine Love—for his mind did dwell in the heights, though, perchance, he did not perceive it. And she, Venus, who might have been the Goddess of Love, did have for her aspiration, a precious flower, which she placed in her Heart as a symbol and representation of HIS perfection.

Oh, that human beings might ascend into the higher, heavenly realms of Divine Love—in Consciousness, at least, is my prayer, my decree. And may the call to the Lord of Love and the Goddess of Love reveal to themselves the great Love of the Universal Christ. The Spirit of Love is the Beautiful Cloud upon which the Lord of Love and the Goddess of Love sail upon—the Ethereal Ocean—when they come to visit us in our now-small world which now expands into the Golden Sphere of Love. "I see and recognize only the WHITE-NATURE IN ALL ACTIVITY on earth." LOVE reigns supreme in the minds and hearts of all mankind. The Lord of Love sits on His Golden Throne in MY HEART and YOURS. His Light radiates out to YOU and ALL through all realms of being.

And still I must confess I cannot convey the rapture that so enthralled me and caused me to attempt to write to you something of the Mystery of my experience last night. Time will tell.

As to coming to Los Angeles, I have not yet heard from my sister, but did get a letter from Brother J.............. He has turned the Retreat here over to me, but said he knew, just as Ave Maria does, that I have to go forth to the outer world with my message. He told me how he had arranged with a neighbor here of his to take care of Anne. So you see they, the Masters, have been doing some planning on the other end of the line. See?

Frankly, Anne is a problem to me in the outer. . . . so, you see, I feel that Anne will have to be with me in Los Angeles, eventually. Maybe you have a suggestion in this regard. I have no secrets regarding the matter. I am most frank and open to you, Ratana. You know this, I am sure.

Will you kindly write to me at your earliest convenience. You know, of course, I send you my Love and I radiate my Light to you and Stanley, and ask that Our Lord enfold you and all your blessed students in His Magic Presence.

In Divine Love.

M. A.

*   *   *

I received the following letter from Ratana:

TEMPLE OF CHRIST
123 North Lake Street
Los Angeles, Calif.

Aug. 27th, 1941.

Our Beloved Amsumata:

I have been trying to get a chance to write to you ever since we left you. This is the very first time I have been able to do so, for I have been so very busy. I found many good reasons why I should have come home, and realized why I felt I must do so. We had our first meeting at the Temple last evening, and we had a good attendance. Some of the Ballard students were there, to carry the report, I guess. I hope they got their eyes open!

Oh, Blessed One, we can never thank you enough for all you have done for us! Those few days in Your Retreat were priceless! And that was just the beginning! You opened the door to us for all that has followed, and we are eternally grateful! (ETERNALLY.)

We were only a short distance on our way when marvelous things began to take place, and our whole trip home was a trip thru the wonders of the Cosmic Realms! I would love to tell you about it, but do not feel like writing it. We arrived home Monday night between 10 and 11 P.M. And was Bobby and Elizabeth happy to see us! They had sat in the porch swing all evening, waiting for us. Of course we found many things awaiting our attention, but found everything in very good order. That wonderful loyal group at the Temple were starry eyed with love and joy, in gratitude for the wonderful messages in the letters I had sent to them. (From Amsumata's Retreat.)

I wonder if you can guess how grateful and glad I was to find your wonderful letter awaiting us, when we arrived home! It was so *very* WELCOME! I feel that I get the idea of your glorious experience, and have felt that you are the ONE to bring forth that Message! Yes, I feel that you have gotten over to me the Message you desired to, the Message of your experience. And I, too, feel that you are right. I feel that you are the One to carry that Message to the world. Oh, Blessed Amsumata, you were so patient with us, you were so kind to us, you were so wise with us! I was grateful that I had the insight to see what you were doing, and why you did things as you did! I feel it is all clear to me, and it was you who took Stanley and I both thru, for Stanley won thru just three days after I did.

I had a wonderful experience at Mt. Shasta, but did not see J............. We made the calls just as you said, but I felt from the first that we would not see her there. I felt that you were the one chosen to take us thru, and that to meet her (Ave Maria) so soon after my marvelous experiences just after leaving your Retreat, and also the glorious one with you and Anoma before we left, I felt that to meet her would perhaps change the vibration, and perhaps cause confusion, at that time. Each one works differently, and you had done all the hard work with us. When the right time comes we will be so happy to meet her. But I leave everything in the hands of the GREAT ONES, oh, so Gladly. I have no desire to push things. ALL THINGS IN DIVINE ORDER!

I feel that something wonderful is right ahead for the GREAT WORK. I feel all uplifted and almost breathlessly waiting for SOMETHING! You and Saint Germain came together to me the last night we were in Mt. Shasta. Both of you showed me how you are both One, in a very interesting manner. Then you left, and He talked to me a very long time about the IMPORTANCE of the physical body. He plead with me to assist Him in clearing up all the false things that have gone out about Him and the Great Work. I do desire to do all that I possibly can to assist you both in every way I can in the GREAT WORK OF THE ASCENDED MASTERS.

I believe that I will tell you now, that shortly after we left your Retreat, the White Dove lighted on my head, and I was illumined! The Blessed Lord Maitreya rode with us all the rest of that day. A little later we were riding through an avenue of great pine trees, and they bowed across the road to me, joining together forming an archway, reminding me of pictures I have seen where swords were held in that manner for someone to pass thru. The Maha Chohan rode with us the second day, Krishna the Beloved the third day, Jesus was with us all during the fifth day. The instruction we received from each one was transcendent! Oh, those wonderful two weeks!

We have the use of the big house until around November. There we can have room for both you and Anne. They have already started foreclosure proceedings to take the house back. I refer to the bank. We would be happy to have you and Anne come to us, and share with us what we have, even as you shared with us, so lovingly and graciously what you have. I still have hope that something will turn up that will give us the use of the home for a Great White Brotherhood Retreat. But that, too, is in the hands of the Great Ones.

How would you come? If you will let me know at once just what it would cost to get you and Anne to Los Angeles, I will be glad to see if I can find some way to take care of that. Perhaps the people who were going to take Anne, would be glad to look after the precious boys until your sister comes, so that you would not have to wait. I would not feel right to leave Anne; she should be with you. She is so precious, I would love to have her come with you to see us. Perhaps that sounds egotistical, when I say "to see us," when I know how all your time is in the Great Work, but I really mean when you come here so that the Great Work can go on in a bigger way than it is at the present. We will feel honored with your Presence with us. It is hard to make words express what we desire to say, isn't it? But I feel that you will understand me and my intentions.

Will you please give my love and blessings to the boys, and to our darling Anne? Stanley joins me in deepest love and gratitude to you. I trust that you have received all the love and gratitude we have sent constantly to you. We love and bless you always! Enclosed please find a tiny Love Gift to sort of help out there. May it be increased a millionfold to each one of you. May every desire of your hearts be fulfilled. In deepest gratitude, I ask all the Great Ones to Bless you with every Good forever. I am,

Ever in service to Lord Maitreya, the Maha Chohan,
Beloved Jesus and ALL THE GREAT ONES,
(Signed) *RATANA.*

P.S. on back of letter: Amsumata: GREETINGS! I understand a great deal more now, and I am grateful to Amsumata and Norman. And I think Norman is a jolly good fellow. I love you and bless you forever. (Written with pencil.) STANLEY.

* * *

While writing an answer to Ratana's letter above Ave Maria and Lao Tse returned from Mt. Shasta to the Retreat at Seattle. They walked into the room where I was writing the letter, announcing that they were told by Lord Maitreya and Mahatma Koot Hoomi to return to Seattle so I could be released to go south to Los Angeles. I did not know they even knew what had gone on at the Retreat, however, Ave Maria knew all that had gone on, and was ready to cooperate with me in getting the Great Message to the world.

Ratana had been initiated into the Great White Lodge. She is remarkably clairvoyant, therefore she could bring all through just as Ave Maria generally does. In the New Age many women shall become Masters, for it will be the age for the ascension of WOMANHOOD.

I shall not quote herewith but a paragraph or two of the letter I wrote to Ratana, regarding our leaving for Los Angeles, but we, Anne and I, got busy immediately preparing for the trip south. Lao Tse provided me with money enough to get to Los Angeles.

I quote from my letter to her:

Seattle, Wash.
Beloved Ratana: Aug. 30, 1941.
Blessed Sister of the G.W.L., the M: Thou who art ascended into His Glory, Lord of Lords Maitreya's, Christ's: Thou who art in communion with the Great Ones in the GREAT WORK: Thou who art ever blessed

with the LIGHT of the Living, the Love, Wisdom and Power of God Almighty (Actually, in TRUTH and Sincerity):

GREETINGS:

Again I weep tears of GREAT JOY! What is more wonderful? Yes, What? Than tears of joy? Tears of Joy, overflowing from a heart made most happy with written words of LIFE, of TRUTH, of WISDOM— words in SPIRIT, in MIND, in musical SOUND, in beautiful WRIT- ING—words of POWER vibrating throughout the ethereal atmosphere of earth, like a COSMIC BELL ringing out a MESSAGE OF LOVE from Maitreya's LOVE STAR. Now, my dear Ratana, you have every- thing you need to GO FORTH a Living Example of the Great Work. WHAT JOY IS MINE! To know that My GREAT BROTHERS OF LIGHT do cooperate with me, the newly initiated ONE, in carrying you THRU so marvelously. I weep over your letter, I read and weep; read and weep with joy. It seems that my heart will burst for you, Stanley, all your students, and ALL THE WORLD. And, strange, I want to exclaim to my Brothers of LOVE: To think that such a wretch as I should be so blessed with such Love and cooperation, and yet, I know that every wrong I ever did in my life was done SEEKING TRUTH, TRYING ALL THINGS, AS Paul said, AND HOLDING FAST TO THAT WHICH IS GOOD. It has been my fearlessness that ever saw me through. "Fear not. I am with you always."

.   .   .   .

Just as soon as I hear from you I will be leaving. I will walk over to the post office to mail this AIR MAIL so you will get it immediately.

God bless you all. Say to your students: "Lord Maitreya, the Great Divine Director, sends you his Light and Love, and Joshua, the Goddess of Love says: 'I LOVE YOU, I LOVE YOU, I LOVE YOU'."

Sincerely in the service of the Masters.

I am as ever,

AMSUMATA.

*   *   *

Instead of waiting for word from Ratana, Lao Tse and Ave Maria, knowing how urgent Koot Hoomi and Lord Maitreya and Saint Germain were to get me started in the work I had to do in the Los Angeles sector, Anne and I left the next day for Los Angeles.

Ratana had promised me that she would assist me in getting my book published. Without money, having the children to look after, and trying to write a book in peace and harmony, is no little task to accomplish, therefore, she had told me she would gladly allow me to live there at her home until I got the book written and published.

We arrived and were comfortably quartered in the beautiful home of Ratana's. She had told me how Saint Germain had appeared to her some years previous, advising her to purchase that magnificent home. Now, Saint Germain is to live in it with his daughter, along with Ratana, Stanley and Bobby.

All would have been very nice. Love might have been the ruling principle in all things that followed, had all been Masters of Love. Anne was most happy. She started to school. I started to work on the book. The "Black" forces began to commence to get ready to get started to "breaking up" our peaceful plans. Every single individual was put through the "fire." For four or five days I felt invading and destructive vibrations. I knew well enough where they were, but hoped they would be "mastered" by those who were being tried.

At last all came to the surface. Ratana and Stanley wanted to talk to me down in the drawing room. Ratana seemed worried. When we had all been quietly seated she said, "Amsumata, you are being investigated."

"Is that so?" I exclaimed, as though I were quite disturbed about it all. "Well, that is perfectly all right with me. I welcome investigation, and I am certain whoever investigates me WILL be investigated most thoroughly."

"Yes," Stanley spoke up, "the Government is investigating you."

"No, Stanley," remarked Ratana, "it's the Great White Brotherhood."

Well, I thought, there is quite a difference already in the opinion of the two as to who is investigating me. Without further questioning, I abruptly asked, "When do you wish me to move?" I then added, "Now, Ratana, so far as any investigation is concerned, I am absolutely unafraid. I have nothing to fear. I have never done anything for which I should fear. I realize the position you are placed in regarding my being here. For several days I had thought I should suggest my going elsewhere to live, for I sensed all this. You prefer to believe others than to believe me. I am sure it will be better for all of us were we separate in our activities. You and Stanley have your ideas about teaching, etc., which I realize you must maintain. I am one who has my own individual plan and ideas of teaching. I know it is too much of a test for some of you with me here. I shall look about for a place in which to live."

"Well, you take plenty of time to look about for a little apartment. There is no hurry," advised Stanley.

I had been attending the meetings in the Temple of Christ with Anne. We enjoyed going very much, but due to jealousy of some of the students, who, of course made remarks to Ratana, it disturbed her and Stanley. They did not know I was the outer presence of Saint Germain. They did not realize that I held the important office I hold in the Great Work of the White Lodge. Jealousy is a terrible disease. There was one member of her group who claimed unusual powers and membership in the Great Lodge. He, Stanley and others all brought their influences to bear upon Ratana, whom I know to be an Initiate of the Brotherhood. I do not blame her in the least. I ask Lord Maitreya and all the Masters of Light to assist her and free her from every interference, and I know now, that the evil, jealous ones knowing they are found out, SHE WILL BE FREED. GOD BLESS RATANA.

I explained to Ratana and Stanley that I would soon receive help from some other members of the Great Lodge. I wrote immediately to one in the North who is a high official of the Universal Brotherhood. Through him and others I was directed here to Mount Olympus, "A Mountain of God," where the book is now almost finished, and where I have been loved and assisted by REAL BROTHERS OF LOVE WHO WERE ABLE TO STAND THE TESTS THROUGH WHICH ALL MUST PASS TO PROVE THEIR MASTERY.

There is one phase of the Great Work I feel I should explain here for the benefit of those who might some day chance to be in a similar predicament wherein Ratana and Stanley were tested. Even after we have been initiated into the Higher Degrees of the Great Lodge, so to speak, is when our greatest tests are sure to come. Even after one might be acclaimed a Master, and has been so informed by his or her master-teacher, THEN IS WHEN ONE IS PLACED ON PROBATION. It is then that all eyes of the Great Lodge (ALL-SEEING EYE) are turned upon the new initiate. If there be the least weakness anywhere in the "armour of righteousness" of the initiate, it will CERTAINLY be found. Then it isn't what you may think is RIGHT, but it is WHAT and WHO YOU ARE that counts.

As Lord Maitreya once said to me, "Eventually every soul shall be saved."

Lord Maitreya also said to me, as I have previously stated, "I do not allow my Priests to make mistakes." I know that regarding initiations and such matters as above related, Lord Maitreya always directs me and is WITH ME. Until the outer mind is "slain," "The Son of Man hath not any place to lay His head." But He has the blessings of the "birds" who are the true Messengers of God.

CHAPTER XXXI

On August 31, 1941, just a day or two before I left Seattle for Los Angeles, Buddha Gautama came to me to bestow His Great Blessing upon me. He addressed me as, "Petetera," or "Peter," as He explained, "Keeper of the Door of the Great Presence." It was at 1:15 P.M., as I have indicated in my notes.

He made the sign and salutation of the Masters, announced His name, "Gautama Buddha!"

He then addressed me, which I did not understand for the moment, as "The Portal!" Then He said, "Maitreya, Keeper of the Portal or Great Presence of Buddha, you should say, in explaining your office, 'I am the Open Door that no man can shut.' I serve Gautama. Gautama place me."

Buddha Gautama then went on to explain, "No one enters in to the Great Lord Presence except the Great Disciple of that particular Lord who is the Portal to this Great Presence permits them to pass through this Portal which He IS." He added, "Refer to Jesus, 'No one comes to the Father but through me.'"

Beloved Students, I did not, for some time realize what was being conferred upon me, and, I am frank to say, even yet I probably do not fully realize the great responsibility that was being placed upon my shoulders at that very moment. Somehow I had, within myself, felt many times in recent months, that such honor and responsibility had been placed upon me in the Great White Lodge. Ave Maria, the most wonderful being on earth, I do believe, explained it to me after Buddha had gone. Maitreya was the name of Buddha Gautama's most beloved disciple, just as John was the Most Beloved Disciple of Jesus. I, in this present embodiment and this generation, have been chosen as the "most beloved" disciple of Christ who is now incarnate in this earth. THE GODS ARE WITH US ONCE MORE.

Later in the day Ave Maria sent the following message, written in long-hand to me. My little daughter brought it from upstairs and handed it to me:

"To Amsumata:

"Gentleness is become desirous of the Fires (Father's) property, and the desires draw the Gentleness of the Kingdom of "LOVE" into itself.

"That (Gentleness) is the Water of Eternal Life, which the Fire (Father) drinks, and gives therefrom the Light of Majesty.

"This is the answer or rather interpretation of your letter. It was accomplished through the Mahatmah, the Great Mahatmah.

"ANOMA."

P.S.—"The above is the thought of one of Theosophical thought, and I but applied it. Anoma."

"I just received a message through one of the Great White Lodge, that I am granted the title which Buddha Gautama had, 'Anoma.'

"ANOMA."

So, Those of You "who have ears to hear," and "eyes to see," there is a mystery worth solving in the above. May I ever be true to the Great Ones to whom I am obligated. And may all who have claimed to be true to me, and have vowed their faithfulness, be true to me, for IN TRUTH AND LIGHT WE GO FORWARD WITH GOD'S MESSAGE OF THE NEW GOLDEN AGE. Christ is incarnate, as well as His Most Beloved Disciple.

On the same day that Buddha Gautama came to bless me and take me into His Great Solar Ring, Mahatma Koot Hoomi talked to me at length, explaining to me that "Now you have the protection you have always wanted. You can now go forth in the world with the Great Message for the people of this world. The fields are heavy with ripe grain. This is the harvesting time. Truly it is the harvest time. Have no fear, the Brothers of the Great White Lodge will be at your side always."

After leaving the home of Ratana in Los Angeles—but a day or two thereafter—my two older sons arrived from Seattle. I was without funds. I had written to two Brothers, explaining the need of calling the members of the Lodge in the outer for a convocation. There was so very much needed doing, however, without money and three children suddenly placed entirely in my care, I had to accept any kind of employment obtainable. I accepted the job of janitor at the El Rey Hotel in East Los Angeles. The work was hard and the pay small. I enjoyed the work. I really worked too hard.

Once while mopping the floor beneath the large rubber rug in the main entrance of the hotel, Mahatmah Koot Hoomi stood within a few feet of me in His tangible body for several minutes watching me, blessing me and radiating His Light about me. He walked back and forth in front of me several times and then disappeared. He is about six feet two or three inches tall. I acknowledged His Presence silently. We understood each other without any outward signs or salutations.

As Students of Light ever be on guard. You never know when the Master will approach you. And, too, you never know just HOW He will approach you.

On Sept. 27, 1941, I received a communication from my friend and Brother in the North, who gave me a card of introduction to be mailed to an official of the Universal Brotherhood. I, in turn, wrote the following letter to the Brother from the Hotel El Rey:

Sept. 28, 1941.

My dear Brother:

I enclose herewith a card of introduction to you from my old friend and Brother (Sanskrit Name), who has felt it "fitting and proper" to place me at your disposal, as I am most desirous to meet you and discuss certain vital issues pertaining to the Great Work of the G.W.B. in the Western Hemisphere.

I am in close contact with the Great Mahatma Koot Hoomi (KH), and it is His desire (if I may venture such) to make necessary preparations for His coming to U. S. (Physical) early next year. Moreya El may accompany Him.

Please address me, should you see fit, (mail) to this hotel, as I am working here at present,—Norman R. Westfall, El Rey Hotel, Los Angeles, Calif.

There are other spiritual matters I much wish to talk over with you, since, I understand, you are in a position to assist me. I feel, too, that I can help you.

My office, etc., regarding Great Work, we can discuss when we are fortunate enough to meet personally.

I might inform you, Brother, that this is the first time I have sought contact with any Brother other than by chance meeting, in 20 years instruction and training under the Masters, not to mention considerable sorrowing discipline. I do pray that you grant me an interview. I assure you, IN THE NAME OF LORD MAITREYA, you shall not regret it.

Fraternally yours,

A Servant in the Light,

AMSUMATA.

Two days later I met the new-found Brother at the hotel in Los Angeles. In another week I was at ...., however, I first went through a very trying physical test.

I had been told by Mahatmah Koot Hoomi some months previous I would have to go through quite a painful adjustment of my etheric body with my physical body due to the time I was shot when embodied as Abraham Lincoln. He told me my etheric body was still in need of healing as a result of the bullet that penetrated my brain at that time. When Brother E............ met me at the hotel the evening above mentioned he touched a spot just behind my right ear where a considerable bump had risen. I had an idea of the cause, and had for a number of years been troubled by a condition at the base of my brain and in my neck. The Brother held his finger right on that spot for several minutes. There was a cold shiver went through my body as though I had an ague chill. Before I left the hotel that evening I was almost unable to sit up. I told him nothing of my feelings.

It was all I could do to get home that evening. I was sick all night. My head began to swell, from the point where the bump had started upward to the top of my head. By morning I looked as though I were recovering from a good mauling over the head. If I happened to move, although I was in bed covered up, I shook with chills running through my body. The condition got worse instead of better. I did not call a doctor. I did not even call the hotel where I had been working. I talked to the Masters about it. I explained to Them that I was ready to go if They felt it was time for me to pass on. I did feel exactly as though I had been shot—as though there was a bullet in there somewhere—and all I could do was to endure it all. I recall that I thought, "Well, Lincoln, you didn't know anything about the suffering in your physical body at the time you passed, but now I guess I will have to endure it here in this body." That is exactly what had to take place. That etheric body had to be completely healed while in a physical body before the proper adjustment could be made. Here is something for scientists to think about.

For three days I was not sure I would live. I talked to but few people about my condition at the time. The children were in school. I finally called the people at the hotel, telling them I was sick and unable to work. I lost my job, which was all right. Mrs. Gloria H. Sommerville, who lived at the same place where I had a small apartment in a garage in the back of the property, asked me why I did not call a doctor. She witnessed the awful swelling of my head when I went to the phone to call my employers.

After the third day the swelling started going down, and within a few days was normal. I have not been bothered with the old condition since. Nor have I felt like the same person. I feel that I am all here now, whereas, before I felt as though there was some of me missing. When I lectured to a group of about thirty people in Long Beach two weeks later one of the men present asked me following the meeting, "Why is it, all the time you were speaking I did not see you, I saw Abraham Lincoln?" You, reader, can answer that question for him. I have had numerous experiences with Abraham Lincoln. Some I shall relate.

On October 29, 1941, I was asked to give an address before two groups of students, in San Bernardino and Long Beach. I was asked by Lord Maitreya to do this before going into seclusion to write this book, and for the purpose of determining the good that might be done and to what extent my message would be accepted. Following is the message given, which began at 12:30 P.M.:

BLESSED STUDENTS OF LIGHT:

You are the first group of people I have been able to speak to since holding the office I have been chosen to fill. I have been promised the full protection and radiance of the Brothers of the Great White Lodge, of which I am a member. I know THIS, I shall not speak to you of one thing I have not experienced. I have never taught anything I had not experienced in my life and I have been a teacher for more than 20 years.

These are momentous times. This is the time, you might say, of the Passover. We are passing over the bridge into the greater world, the Golden Age. I want you to see that bridge clearly. It is a Golden Bridge, which glows with true love, DIVINE LOVE. Love is more beautiful in silence than in spoken words. (Silence for several seconds.) It is a radiance of liquid light, strengthening, power-building. It has all within it anyone would desire.

Lord Maitreya is the Lord of Love. He is the One through whom all Love flows into the world. He is the Lord of Lords. He is the Great Director of the Great White

Lodge. He speaks through Love and those members of the Great White Lodge who know Him,—every word He speaks they drink in. He never has to speak but once in His kind way. Everything He wishes done is done in Love.

Is there anything more wonderful than Love? Love is the all-pervading Light of Understanding. If I love you I know you will understand me. Love a person and he can't help but understand and work with you, and cooperate with you. Sometimes in the trials of life, when we have neglected to keep love burning in our hearts, we may have done things and said things that were not done in the spirit of love, and we regretted them later. But always, when we want to do things in the spirit of love, do you remember how easily they were done?

I remember the things I wanted to do with love in my heart, how quickly, how perfectly they were accomplished. That is what I wanted to talk to you about today—accomplishing the greatest task that was ever undertaken in this world—establishing a new order through the magnificent power of LOVE.

Yes, a few weeks ago, Master KH, and Lord Maitreya came to me and told me, after months of direct training and instruction, that I had received, I could go forth into the world; that they would protect me and see that I was protected wherever I went; and that I could carry their great message into the world. But it was not until I came to The Mountain (Mount Olympus), being directed there by other Brothers of the White Lodge, that I knew I had been chosen the Chief-Avatar. I knew there were other Avatars who had ascended. I was hesitant, but I received a message, stating that I should not hesitate, but to go forth as the Chief-Avatar, the office which I was chosen to fill. (Mrs. Gloria H. Sommerville of Los Angeles, was the witnessing amanuensis through whom the written message was received. She knew nothing of the circumstances referred to in the letter from Mahatmah Koot Hoomi.)

There is much to be done by people like you, who know and understand the higher laws of life. In each of you I see the wonderful possibilities that you have dreamed of accomplishing. I know you would not be here if you had not dreamed of them. I know by your faces; I know by even feeling the radiance from your own minds and hearts, the confidence you have in feeling that the new Golden Age is actually dawning now.

I shall not be able after today to speak in the outer world for several months to come. It just so happens I am working on a book to be published soon.

I love to speak to people who have faith and see the vision of this New World. It makes me extremely happy and if I can make you happy and get you to see the need of whole-hearted brotherly and sisterly cooperation in this work, then I will feel that I have performed a worthwhile duty. I know you understand me, and I know that you feel in your hearts how sincere I am in every word I speak to you, because I love you and I take each of you into my Heart of Gold. I am known among the Brothers as the Prince of the Golden Heart, and I love to feel that I do have the Heart of Gold, and that my Heart radiates forth to all with whom I come in contact, that which will feed your heart, that which it longs for—DIVINE LOVE. That is the most essential thing in all the world, THAT LOVE WHICH IS COMPLETE UNDERSTANDING.

When Buddha Gautama came to me, after others had taken me into their Presences, He came and said, "I take you into my Heart of Hearts, My Most Beloved Disciple Maitreya." He called me Maitreya because Maitreya means "Most Beloved Disciple." He explained to me that I would be the Door through which all those seeking entrance into the Great White Lodge would pass. In other words I am the Door-Keeper. Just as there are those of you, no doubt, who have held offices in such lodges as the Masons (or Knights of Columbus), the Great White Lodge is similar to the Masonic Lodge, and there are those chosen, just as in the outer world.

Many of the laws that are used in the higher planes of consciousness, are the laws, I might say, that are in operation much like the laws we have in this world. So, you see, there are others, I am sure, right here, who are members, and hold various offices in the Great White Brotherhood. I was, for quite a while, The Silent Watcher to this world. That office was the office I held—a powerful office and a very responsible one. During that time I was instructed and directed by the Great Divine Director of the White Brotherhood, to investigate the Rosicrucian activities, the Unity Movement, the I

AM movement in Los Angeles, and ALL OTHER RELIGI-
OUS ACTIVITIES THROUGHOUT THE WORLD.

I went into them to see what was going on, and made
reports to the Recorder of the Great White Lodge of what
I found, then directed what work should be done toward
cleaning them up (Should they need cleaning). Do not think
that this needed cleaning has NOT been done! You need
not have any fear anymore about those forces that have been
tormenting you all these years. The Black and Shady
Brothers know this activity and they have no more power
to bother you. Watch your "Ps" and "Qs," be sure you are
RIGHT and go ahead. Have no fear, "I am with you
always." KNOW THAT CHRIST IS WITH YOU AND
ASSERT YOUR MASTERY. Be Master over these physical bodies and minds of yours. You have what it takes to
become Master. Go forth from this day on, FEELING
YOUR OWN MASTERY. Do not be half-hearted about
it; you cannot be that way. Love, Wisdom and Power, all
three in balance, must be used to become Master. Do not be
afraid.

For years I was in the publishing business. I published
a newspaper. It was not much of a paper (From the outer
standpoint) but it had much in it of Good, of Light and
Truth, of Wisdom and Power. I had a little slogan across
the top of the page, "I fear no one but God and Him only
when I do wrong." I am telling you friends, Brothers and
Sisters, you can look thousands of people in the face and feel
courage enough to face an army of ten thousand. "I FEAR
NO ONE BUT GOD AND HIM ONLY WHEN I DO
WRONG." It will strengthen you when you have something
to meet some day.

There are so many things I would like to tell you. I
have had the most marvelous, thrilling instructions given me
in the past 13 months that I could ever dream of. On the
29th of August a year ago, I met at Mount Shasta, Mary the
Mother of Jesus. This may seem strange to you, but there
are so many things coming forth in the next few years that
may seem strange, we may as well get used to it now. It is
all going to break through before you hardly realize it. You
have been feeling it, because many of you have brought
things through in your outer consciousness to prove what I
am saying. After I had met Her (Ave Maria), then I met

Jesus, KH, Lord Maitreya, St. Germain, Morya, Buddha Gautama, Krishna and God of the Golden Heart Mahachohan, My Father; and also the Great Sanat Kumara, who was Lord of this planet up until last December, when Jesus became Lord of this Earth.

It was some months before I could accustom myself to associating with the Gods; but, my friends, we might as well get used to that now, for they are coming forth to walk among men. Make the "temples beautiful, entire and clean that the gods may dwell therein." In the Spirit of Love any God or Lord or Master can come to you, sup with you, talk with you, walk with you, *even within you.* Even your Individual Spirit, as the Spirit of the Almighty, is illimitable.

I have had Lord Maitreya talk to me about the next two thousand years, just as you and I might talk about the next two weeks' vacation. It is all planned, and is now to be carried out in the physical octave of life, right here among us. He even told me of those who will be reembodying, thereby assisting in establishing the Great Golden Age, some of whom I might mention. Rudolph Steiner—he will be re-embodying to help us—also Vivekananda. I was also told of those who will be initiated—some of those who will be assisting us soon in the establishment of the new order among men. Remember, this new order, this New Age, is to take place especially in the hearts of mankind. It is the easiest thing to accomplish that ever was, if we first understand just how it is to be done. All these people who are fighting in the outer state of being today, do not understand. The Golden Age shall be established right in our hearts, and then it finds its way to our minds, and then what is there to fight over IF WE UNDERSTAND? NOTHING. What is my brother's is mine, and what is mine is my brother's. Whatsoever you sow, that shall you reap. If I strike you, I strike myself. We are all "one BODY, WEE" in Christ, in God the Great Spirit.

There are so many phases of this activity I would like to talk to you about. It is the matter of choosing just which one might be the most expedient at this time. I shall talk to you a little about the seven bodies you have. I believe that is most important.

I want to explain first to you, one thing, which is simple,

but you have never been told about it in the way you should have been told.

The three lower bodies are the ones that give us all the trouble here. The physical, etheric and mental. Most everyone who has a modicum of spiritual understanding, get to seeing their etheric body and THINK they are in the Seventh Heaven. Get those three bodies well under control. Transmute their forces—everything in them, into Divine Love, and draw it all up into the four Higher Bodies, THEN YOU WILL BE GETTING SOMEWHERE. You see, it is that physical body and those desires. Then the mental body. The etheric body is the one you dream in—the ordinary dream. The experience you might have in the higher planes —you usually know the difference when you have had one— in a real experience—you actually go places and you know when you come back to the outer consciousness that you have been someplace and you have been doing something.

It is not uncommon for me to go places and do things. For many years I have been most active. The things you so very much want to do, in your heart, while you are here, and yet do not feel like you will do them,—YOU DO DO THEM. If the desire and love is strong enough you actually go out and do them. That is chalked up for you in your accumulation of Divine Work. The things we really and truly and honestly want to do IN OUR HEARTS, are done. Because we actually go out and do them. "Wherever your heart is, there your treasure is also." How simple! You know, you men and women, when you were sweethearts years ago? You remember when you thought of your sweethearts, how close you were to them? You actually just felt your arms around her, or him, and they were. Those are little ways I want to prove the activity which you are doing many times on the inner levels of consciousness and not being aware of it on the outer. The Spirit of Love is the most important of all. The words I speak to you now . . . There is Wisdom and Power back of every word to do things you would be interested in doing. Every word is loaded with Power, sincerity and truth, and you know it. You cannot fool people. "You can fool some of the people some of the time and you can fool some of the people all the time, but you can't fool all the people all the time." Now it is getting so you can't fool any of the people any of the time. It just can't be done, the people are becoming so wise. These words are Truth—simple Truth. I want you to know that the great beings such as Lord Maitreya are the most simple and child-like beings there ever were. (I can not speak His name without He is here.) I one time was speaking to a sister across a table, and something was said of which I thought in my mind, "I wish Lord Maitreya were here to explain that." No more had I thought that than He spoke in that person. He said, "Did you wish to see me?" I asked, "Did you get me that quickly?" He answered, "I get you instantly."

You have heard much in the past few years about the Ascended Masters. The Ascended Masters are those who actually have, in physical bodies, ascended in consciousness into the Godhead. That is what they are. I want you to know —each and everyone of you—and I want you to tell everyone you see—that you do not have to die to ascend. I HAVE ASCENDED CONSCIOUSLY, PHYSICALLY, MENTALLY, SPIRITUALLY, in every way possible, AND I KNOW I HAVE. I AM A LIVING EXAMPLE OF IT. There have been thousands of people misled through the misinterpretation of the initiation, who have the idea that you have to pass on and die before you can ascend. That is a great mistake. I realize this, since I have ascended: I am not the same being. Any Master who chooses might come and speak to you through me. As Saint Germain said the other day, "We are one small body wee." When you enter into that infinite Spirit of Consciousness with God, you are in the One Body of God in consciousness and reality, in Spirit and Life and Love, in Wisdom and Power. It is not so hard to understand, is it? It is so simple that most people over-look it.

These three lower bodies are the instruments and tools with which we work in this physical octave in the accumulation of our DIVINE INHERITANCE, which is stored up in the four Higher Bodies, so we have that to work with when we are finished with it—the physical body. Mahatma KH worked several months looking through my life-stream and checking up on my Divine Inheritance. It took Him months to find out where I belong in the present activity. Just the other day I found where I AM. I had my record placed on the table before us and two of us read it—from the Great White Lodge. It ended up with these words: "NO

KARMA." A lot of other words were recorded, but those were the most wonderful. A clean slate—that is what we have to have before we can ascend. We have to clean up everything—balance up the books—then it is no trouble to ascend. Everything is out of the way so you can see ahead from the lowly earth to the very Godhead, God Almighty— the main thing we feel in the outer consciousness. I can look you straight in the eye. You are looking me straight in the eye. When you get so you feel HE can look you straight in the face, it is a wonderful thing. I am telling you, the first few weeks after I met Ave Maria, I could just sit and rest and look at Her without saying one word (for hours), and just drink in the radiance. I can call to my Higher Presence and I can direct a Light to you; in proportion to the need and emergency you can do the same thing, and that Light will carry with it whatever we desire it to carry. We can breathe it in, so can you. You can just drink in the liquid light from the atmosphere, take it into your body and transfer it into anybody else. The main thing is to get into the harmonious state of mind, radiating love to all mankind. Feel that very radiance in the air you breathe. YES, FEEL IT! See evidence in the very air you breathe in. Your vision and imagination charge the breath you breathe with that elusive Elixir of Life, which you take into the body, and you send that into any part of the body you wish. Remember, your imagination is very important. It is much more powerful than you think. Just get quiet and do it. WILL TO DO IT.

We are going to perform greater miracles some of these days. Jesus said, "You shall perform even greater miracles than I." I was born during the time of Jesus. I was John that Jesus spoke to when on the cross. He said, "John, know your mother." Mary told me it was not John the Beloved, it was John the Brother of Jesus, to whom He spoke those words. I took care of His mother after Jesus ascended. I helped Her out two thousand years ago, so She came back to help me this time. It was so wonderful when She came and told me about this.

Somebody had to be John. If I am that fellow, I guess I have to take it. There have been a lot of great people in the world. Take the history books. There are thousands of them and somebody had to be some of them. And, contrary to ordinary belief, the higher one becomes, the oftener he re-embodies. The fellow who knows what he is about can easily pick a body. I have known of my embodiments many embodiments back.

In 1923 I chose to join the Rosicrucian Brotherhood. One thing they wanted to know was my birthdate—even the hour of my birth. I wrote to my mother, asking her about it. She wrote back she did not know what the hour was, but that my aunt was present and might know. But, before I wrote to my aunt I got rather anxious about this matter and went over to India (higher body) to a certain stone castle there. I was walking along a path toward the south. In those days we could tell pretty well by the sun in that country what time it was. It was 20 minutes past 9:00 A.M. Something struck me and I was gone. I knew that was when I passed out. The hour of my death there was the hour of my birth here. That was proved conclusively later. (Sometime I shall explain the entire experience. I lived 33 years in India following the assassination of Lincoln and before I embodied in my present body.)

Lord Maitreya is the Soul of Christ or the one who taught Jesus. Jesus became one with Maitreya. It is not so wonderful, but what you, too, can expect it. It is simple. Call to the Masters when you feel alone—all whom you wish to invite,—they will come if it is at all possible, and you are the one who makes it possible. We must mention these things in the outer octave. We have played around enough with creeds and dogmas. We must be filled with the Great Spirit. This is the time. You will be surprised what you can do now when you try. We have all had these trials and tests. I have only told you about the beautiful part. Not the trials unto death almost, but I have faced them. It was the Love and the Truth of the Christ that gave me the strength to carry on and on until I did ascend into the Godhead, into the Cosmic Heart and knew that I ascended. No one can harm you. When you have that feeling, then you have the courage to go along with it. Nothing can harm you, nothing can touch you.

Archangel Michael really put Saint Germain in His place. The first thing I was asked to do (following my ascension) was to take charge of Saint Germain—to reclaim every "I AM" student into the right place today. That is the first job I have to do. There are some three million people who have been sidetracked through the Black forces. They do not know where they are today. They soon will know. The Truth hurts no one.

Blessed Ones, you cannot tell who your neighbor might be. You might be Archangel Michael himself, for all I know. He is around somewhere in a physical body. That is why Jesus said, "Judge not that ye be not judged." We are to live through the Bible again, with all its characters in reality, in Truth, right here in this octave—however, on a much higher plane of consciousness and activity. All those things are to be brought forth, actualized, materialized, right here on this earth. These people who talk about those who ascend, think they have to go away UP somewhere. This is where THEY work (On Earth)—the work has to be done right here. They are not up there somewhere. They come back here to this plane to get busy in the establishment of God's Kingdom on Earth.

Thank you, Blessed Ones, for listening.

*   *   *

The above address was written down in shorthand by Mrs. Mary Smith, one of the students present. I always speak extemporaneously. Many wonderful reports of good done through the addresses given on that day were received by us later.

IF YOU WILL

If you will keep your faith in me,
Though life be like a stormy sea,
And difficult my task may be—
    I WILL SUCCEED!

If you will look with shining eyes,
Though day be dark with lowering skies,
And night be fraught with weary sighs—
    I WILL SUCCEED!

If you will speak a word of cheer,
Though harassed oft by doubt and fear,
And ugly failure hover near—
    I WILL SUCCEED!

—Terry Anderson.

CHAPTER XXXII

To know our own love, wisdom and power it is essential for us to be tried. We ourselves cannot know our strength unless there is some way to prove it; we cannot prove our love unless there is someone or something to love; we cannot prove our wisdom unless there is someone with whom to match our wisdom. No matter what we undertake in this world there will appear an adversary upon the path. He is necessary, otherwise we cannot generate power to attain what we undertake. A boxer (pugilist) or wrestler will train hard for months, and even years, to attain supremacy in his chosen field.

When Sister Ratana and Stanley informed me of their intention, and the extent of their cooperation with me, I immediately got busy looking for the way "out" and "into" the next episode of my training and accomplishment.

I wrote the following letter to a Blessed Brother of mine, a Brother of the Great White Lodge and a Brother of the Universal Brotherhood—one who had proved over a period of 16 years to be a Brother in every sense of the word:

331 New Hampshire South
Los Angeles, Calif.
Sept. 16, 1941.

"My Beloved Brother O............ :

"Just received your 'Bhashya' yesterday afternoon, which was delayed because of forwarding, then, just a few minutes ago I was handed your postal, which was just as timely and opportune as the letter. This I will be able to explain to you sometime. It certainly is marvelous how definitely like 'clock-work' some of these things do work out. The uncanny way things on the inner seem to sift through to our outer activity is astounding.

"Your message going out to the members of 'M' is most timely I think. I have so much that I might report, much of which has been recorded, I am sure, in the records of the Great White Lodge, that it would be impossible for me to write all, but I do believe the time has come when a general conclave of the Brothers should be called, so that I as well as others, might explain some of the New Golden Age principles before an UNDER-STANDING body of people. To be once clearly understood, to me, will be a great great happiness. By all means put me in touch with some of these UNDERSTANDING Brothers here. I shall not be here at this address long, so please send my mail to ...., Apt. 205, Los Angeles,

until further notice. And another thing, O............., please enter D............
and P............ S............ on your correspondence list. They are very reliable.
I have known them for three years and over . . .

"It so happened that I have just started writing a manifesto which I
deem essential to the world. You are perfectly welcome to use whatever of
this you see fit. Koot Hoomi told me the other day that He and Morya
will both be here with me early next year to help me. "She Who is Nameless," to be known as ANOMA, you and the world will be able to know
next year too. Yes, Christ is here embodied. I have seen Him, inner and
outer. But as is written by Veshanajaya, 'the ruling powers will be hidden
because of the magnitude of their positions.' This is most true and well
said. I have proved it true AND MORE.

"Oh, if I could but speak to a group of people who understand! Do
whatever you can, Blessed Brother, to bring this about. In the name of
Christ Maitreya and the Blessed Buddha Gautama, whose Most Beloved
Disciple He has told me I AM, I know great so-called miracles of LOVE,
WISDOM AND POWER shall be manifest THRU ME. So saith
the Lord.

"Blessed Brother I feel the importance of your message I received yesterday. 'I love you, I love you, I love you,' as ANOMA has said to me
many times. ANOMA, Lord of Venus, will be WITH ME FOR TEN
YEARS. BUDDHA AND JESUS ARE EMBODIED IN ONE
BODY—THUS THE EAST AND THE WEST are not only symbolically blended and harmonized in ONENESS and LOVE, BUT THE
NEXT TEN YEARS they will actually live and manifest in the ONE
BODY OF ANOMA. Meditate upon this my Brother. You will be
further enlightened thereby. You ARE illuminated.

"I must hurry and mail this AIR MAIL. This is, to me, the most
important step taken by the 'M' in and for the NEW GOLDEN AGE.

"Lovingly,   "AMSUMATA."

The "BHASHYA" referred to in the above letter, which was
mailed out to the members of the Great White Brotherhood
throughout the world, so far as I know, and which gives the
reader some idea of the great scope of the Brotherhood's activities, I feel impelled to reprint, owing to the office I hold, and
knowing that the Brother from whom it was received, silently
cooperates with me in its publication:

"BHASHYA

"B. DHARSAJAYA OF THE GREAT WHITE BROTHER-
HOOD sends forth the following message:
"The work of the New Age with the Integral Teaching will carry
forth from here to the furthest corners of our planet. This is the head-

quarters for the Integral Purpose and through which it will be realized. I am speaking as a Messenger of the Great White Lodge, the heart of the Great Brotherhood under the Almighty Father. Some of the Father's special Messengers for the New Age are now with me. Even the Messenger who is the Vehicle of the Great Lord that comes once in a while through the ages; the last time was the time when the Lord, the Christ, was on earth. We are preparing for His coming . . . We stand as the Messengers preparing for the fulfilment of the prophecies of the ages of the past."

"Further, in our present emplacement, we can lead the Disciple to that place where he will receive his occult initiation before the Silent Watcher, our Planetary Overlord."

*   *   *

"B. AMSUMATA OF THE BROTHERHOOD OF THE GOLDEN AGE sends forth the following message:

"St. John the Beloved is to be King (spiritual ruler) during the incoming Golden Age. Ave Maria and Her son, John (Amsumata), will be important leaders. John the Beloved is Manu to the Seventh Race (now begun). The Seventh Angel will come forth with power Aug. 27, 1941.

"All who look for Him will see Him 'as He is.' And we have a promise of God that He will appear in the heavens August 27, 1941, A.D. May the world rejoice that the Jewel of Jewels is in Complete Illumination. She is the Law of the New Golden Age."

*   *   *

"B. CELA VESHANAJAYA OF ARTEMIS says:

"The Law of the New Age is the Law of the Transcendental TRIAD. The rulers will be a Tri-inity under the inspiration of the ONE IDEA. The ruling powers will be hidden because of the Magnitude of their positions. Their offices will be distinct, their powers will be Inter-penetrating, and the end will be the establishment of the New Order. There will be a renovation of Art, a clarifying of Beauty, and a Great Illumination of Truth. Goodness will abound and the New Society will be born."

*   *   *

"REJOINDER OF SATRAJITA OF SAHAPTINKIA:

(1) "From the preceding it is evident that there is a presentiment of the coming of events of great magnitude. This prescience has taken the form of prophetic vision. Associates of these seers are believed to be either the reincarnations of previous great souls or vehicles of the Great Lord."

(2) "From the foundation laid in the resume above made it is clear that there is expected to be an appearance of the Universal Lord, and that

259

He is to be announced by those who are His forerunners, and that these forerunners are to be vehicles or reincarnations of former souls who have served in this same capacity in other Golden Ages, and who are therefore Adepts in this special Work."

(3) "Further, it is clear that the message has preceded the official announcement by Heralds Unknown. There is a dynamism about the whole Great Schema that brooks no hindrance. Therefore, it is confusing to some that these reports have gone forth prior to the actual Advent. Dates have been given, the signs described, and those who have heard wait patiently for the coming of the Great Lord."

(4) "In addition to the simple static Idea of the appearance of the Lord, which leaves all students in honor looking for the Advent, there has gone forth dynamically the proclamation that He is here. That the signs of His coming have been seen in the Heavens. And also that the Universal Lord has gone into the Sanctuary of the Temple where the Hierarchy of Vehicles, Messengers and Handmaidens, stand ready to serve and indeed are going forth as Seventh Angels with the dispensation of the Golden Age Blessings."

(5) "From the Temple where the HIDDEN LORD of the Universe sends forth His rule there will go forth a multitude of messengers. The Transcendental Triad of Goodness, Truth and Beauty will become the underlying Organon of thought and action. Wisdom, Love and Power will be given to all. Liberty, Knowledge and Bliss will be the Spirit of the Great Brotherhood. Realization of these things will bring Nirvana to earth.

(6) "This we have gathered from the IMPLICATIONS of the messages that have been received previous to their having gone forth officially. Whether any of these messages have any bearing on the actual appearance of the Lord does not yet appear. If any of the brethren have any word of confirmation to add to this summation please append on a separate sheet or sheets and sign your Mystical Name and official status. Then see that a copy is sent to this scribe. It will be added to the files and will become regular in its circulation."

Included among the data received from a high official of the Universal Brotherhood, was the following paper, which, I suggest the SEEKING STUDENT to read most carefully, since it, too, is authorized by the Great White Lodge, for your protection and direction regarding the Advent of Christ and the Ascension:

"THE DYNAMISM OF THE OCCULT"

"That is true which reveals its own nature, and the nature of that of which it is the expression, especially to one who has a right to that revelation."

"That is false which denies its own nature, and the truths revealed which are the expression of that nature, especially to one who knows surely the truthfulness of that revelation."

"The Infinite and the Infinite alone has the right to Infinite knowledge, and this right is ineffable, infinite and eternal."

"The Infinite is Truth Itself, and the Absolute Logos, which is the Infinite, is Truth Itself."

"Truth Itself, Goodness Itself, Love Itself, is the Fullness of the Godhead bodily. This embodiment fills the Immensity of Space and is Space Transcendent. The Logos is Spirit. Love is Spirit. Beauty is Spirit. These are the revelation of the Unity of God, and in nowise are manifested on the Occult or Ethereal plane."

"Occult Power manifested is dynamic on the sensual plane, and is discerned on the Astral plane. All physical and occult powers as well as mental, are manifested in their respective spheres and octaves as vibratory in nature."

"Spirit is on the spiritual plane, and does not manifest in the vibratory world. True LOVE is spiritual. Therefore it is above time and space and motion."

"Occult manifestations now disturbing the Astral World are the thought forces of Malignant Spirits who have resorted to the most convenient method of carrying on their malignant operations."

"Many of the so-called revelations of occult truths that have in recent years gone forth are the release of knowledge and powers that these myriads of Astral forms have acquired from great persons of all ages to whose beings these forms have attached themselves. Upon the death of each of these great ones the astral forms must of necessity seek new bodies or be destroyed. The result is that there is today, at the beginning of the Golden Age, a legion of deceiving Astral Forms occupying in high places, focusing great monuments of knowledge and power in the hands of many of the so-called Masters in many of our greatest and foremost Esoteric and Acromatic Orders and secret Societies."

"This is a great menace to the propagators of Truth, Wisdom and Love. To increase the dangers and pitfalls along the way many of these Arch-deceivers claim to be Ascended Masters. There is hardly a society that has not been affected. In the abundance of such evidence the most brilliant minds of today wonder if the Ascended Masters themselves are truly Ascended Masters. Or are they merely the spawn of these Astral Forms?"

"Therefore, we join with others in advising the True Teachers, Gurus and Mahatmas of the Great Circle to refuse to entertain any of these self-acclaimed Ascended Masters on any forbidden plane. To do so is to invite spiritual enslavement and mental disaster. True Ascended Masters are Messengers from much higher planes than any ever to be reached by these deceivers."

"This instruction is in nowise to be taken to refer in the least degree to those Ascended Masters, if such there be in any territorial jurisdiction, who are known definitely to be such."

"If it is known positively that these Ascended Masters have Truly Ascended in their own individual right, and have received, not only the highest possible earthly Initiation, but that they passed over the penetralia of Supernatural Life and have been conducted into the Realms of Supernal Bliss and Life Eternal, and who bear evidence in their bodies that they have been changed in the fullest possible measure, and have cast off their mortal bodies and manifest themselves on human planes in their celestialized personalities, then these are the True Ascended Masters."

"More simply put, that is true which reveals its own nature, and the nature of that of which it is the experience, especially to one who has a right to that revelation."

"ASCENSION IS IN ITS OWN NATURE NOT TO BE DENIED, BUT IS ITSELF OF THE NATURE OF SELF-REVELATION."

"THE FALSE MASTER WILL DENY THAT THE RE-QUIREMENTS FOR ASCENSION ARE ACTUALLY AND LITERALLY NECESSARY STEPS IN ASCENSION, AND WILL DENY ALSO THAT A MANIFESTATION OF TRUE CELES-TIALIZATION IS THE ONLY MEANS BY WHICH THE TRUTH IS TO BE REVEALED."

"THE TRUE MASTER WILL LET HIS TEACHING AND HIS NATURE BEAR TESTIMONY TO HIS OWN STAGE OF ATTAINMENT."

"SELF-AGGRANDIZEMENT, DELUSIONS OF GRANDEUR AND THE WORSHIP OF HEROES WILL NOT BE THE DIS-TINGUISHING MARKS OF THE ASCENDED MASTER.
(SIGNED) (SANSKRIT NAME ONLY)."

* * *

Following receipt of the above documents as well as other letters received by myself, due to other questionings I knew to be prevalent regarding my newly chosen office of "Chief-Avatar," I wrote the following letter along with a copy of a communication from KH to me, all of which I mailed to the official whom I had first corresponded with in the North:

Nov. 3, 1941.

Blessed O..........:

I am enclosing herewith a letter received from Mahatma Koot Hoomi. It is really self-explanatory, however, I do wish to express to you, personally, a few words, anent the publishing and advertising of the Great Message I have to give the world.

I know very well just where you stand, Brother, even better, I am sure, than you know. THERE IS NOTHING HIDDEN FROM ME THAT I VERY MUCH DESIRE TO KNOW. God Bless You, I do not say this to "lord it over on you," or anything of that sort.

Even after I had asked you to come to Bremerton that time to receive certain initiations that Lord Maitreya wished me to confer upon you, I met you on the inner planes, MERELY IN YOUR ETHERIC BODY, HOWEVER, and I was deeply hurt that you had the opinion IN YOUR ETHERIC BODY that you were my superior. Bless your heart, Brother Mine, I do not care to match wits, wisdom, power, intelligence, or anything else with anybody. I AM CERTAIN I AM WAY BEYOND THAT, otherwise I should never have been able to receive the initiations I did receive. I KNOW THAT AS LONG AS I AM WITH LORD MAITREYA AND LORD MAITREYA IS WITH ME THAT NO MAN NOR TEN MILLION MEN CAN OUTDO ME IN ANY RESPECT WHATSOEVER. I HAVE THE COMPLETE PRO- TECTION OF ALL THE LORDS OF THE SEVEN RAYS, BUDDHA GAUTAMA, ANOMA OF VENUS AND ALL THE BUDDHA LORDS OF THE BUDDHA FIELD, so why should I seek direction or anything else from any human being or any empiric order or "so-called" brotherhood? THIS IS THE TIME WHEN BROTH- ERLY LOVE MUST MANIFEST AND ALL MUST COMBINE THEIR FORCES—THOSE WHO ARE OF THE LIGHT— OTHERWISE WE ARE ALL LOST. THIS IS THE LAST CHANCE. I KNOW IT.

BLESSED BROTHER, we do need your assistance, your love, your co-operation, and even your direction in things in the outer activity of the Great Brotherhood, and I am sure the Brother here, Sanutra, will give you everything you ask in the empiric activity. We have here a fine and beautiful retreat, and M............ O............ is truly a "Mountain of God." THIS IS MERELY A SUGGESTION. Should you decide to come here a little later, to work with us, I am sure you could accomplish more here with the UB and assisting us and ALL in going forth to the outer world with the GREAT MESSAGE THAN YOU CAN . . .

Anyhow, Brother O............, you should, BY ALL MEANS, come here and talk things over regarding this Guardiancy and matters pertaining to the EMPIRIC ORDER. I HAVE NOT TOLD YOU ALL. THAT WOULD BE IMPOSSIBLE. FEAR NOT. EVERYTHING WILL BECOME TRANSCENDENTLY BEAUTIFUL AND COM- PLETELY ATTAINED AND ACCOMPLISHED "IN HIM"— CHRIST LORD MAITREYA.

PLEASE LET LOVE RULE IN YOUR HEART, THEN YOUR WISDOM MAY BE USED WITH POWER FOR THE GOOD OF THE NEW KINGDOM OF THE GOLDEN AGE. YES!

LOVE : WISDOM : POWER.

Should you use this it will help you: "I transmute and CHANGE ALL THE FORCES IN MY THREE LOWER BODIES INTO THE ELECTRONIC SUBSTANCE OF DIVINE LOVE AND DRAW IT ALL INTO THE AURA OF LORD OF LORDS MAITREYA TO USE AS HE SEES FIT IN THE UPLIFTMENT OF ALL MANKIND."

The three lower bodies are the ones that cause all difficulty in this octave.

Lovingly,

AMSUMATA.

*   *   *

THE FOLLOWING DOCUMENT WAS ENCLOSED WITH THE LETTER:

Nov. 3, 1941.

Blessed Ones of the Light:

The following message was received by the "Chief-Avatar," Guru Amsumata, Oct. 25, 1941, at Los Angeles, Calif., and the witnessing Amanuensis was Mrs. Gloria H. Sommerville:

"From Koot Hoomi

"To the Chief Avatar:

"The way may appear obstructed but when 'He is with you who can be against you?' and when the time is ripe why not let the whole Divine Family be in the lineup for an overwhelming assemblage, for there is not or can ever be any compromise between the 'Haves' and the 'Have nots.' They are either for or against Him, and the 'FORS' *are winners.*

"The law is plainly laid down and all must pay the price of redemption by the obedience to the Golden Age new law as given, and now repeated, resurrected and put into practical action.

"The law of the universe is the same now and forever and ever. He is the 'Alpha and Omega,' and time passeth, and all must observe the law or perish, for as stated, the law was laid down from the beginning.

"The word was spoken and then became law, and the whole universe is based on LAW AND ORDER, and I, saith Jehovah, give unto my children the breath of life. We all breathe according to Divine Law, and the way is made plain, so plain that even a fool cannot err therein, and with the New Golden Age, why delay the ushering in of the Kingdom of God's righteousness on earth?

"As was said, the way is plain and rules are given, and those who run may read, and I am to be associated, and director of the *great change,* and He, the Chief Avatar, will receive the best and truest impressions given, and only an outer form of instruction may from time to time be written to avoid error, but all the Great Masters may urge the New Dispensation more quickly than expected, and so, in that event, a great surprise overtake the 'Have Nots,' and THOSE WHO ARE NOT FULLY PREPARED, or the 'lukewarm,' will have the shock of being fully surprised by the shortening of time, so abruptly that all time is blotted out for them, for THE FEAST IS AND HAS BEEN PREPARED, AND THEY ARE INVITED TO PARTAKE, and yet, TO MANY 'OFFAL' SEEMS MORE ACCEPTABLE, and so why should Christ's mercy be continually delayed to permit the extension of time to those who do not appreciate God's laws, or try to obey them?

"The shock of clearing the landscape is to be suddenly given, and then will follow the very great expansion of God's laws to beautify and cleanse the footstool of God (the earth) to make it the receptacle for the 'Heavenly Manna' with which all will be fed 'a full participation' in the table set for all, and to feed those who long have hungered, and I am ready to leave my 'craggy abode' and follow hither and thither ALL THE WAY, the world around, up and down, and never a weary moment following out the instructions of the Master, as laid down, so we, 'One Body Wee,' one for all and all for one, WE STAND FIRMLY TOGETHER.

"We follow the precepts and the law. So we will be with those that are the 'elect,' so to you, Avatar, I say WEARY NOT OF WELL DOING.

"The faith must be fully exemplified, and none will find the supply wanting, for all is in the hollow of God's hand, and may be fully sustained in all and every undertaking, so I am near to answer all calls and ever ready.

"KOOT HOOMI (KH)."

P.S. From Amsumata:

(Attached to letter)

"We trust that all who are permitted to read this message will understand the urgency of all activity and not take up valuable time quibbling about 'who's who' in this and that. THIS IS THE TIME WHEN ALL LIGHTS MUST COME WITHIN THE ONE GREAT LIGHT *OR PERISH*. We want it thoroughly understood, too, that all orders or commands, or even suggestions, followed by me, and hence, those who are 'with me,' come directly from the COUNCIL OF THE GREAT WHITE LODGE, of which I AM A MEMBER. AND, TOO, IT IS WELL TO OBSERVE THAT ALL EMPIRIC ORGANIZATIONS OF WHATSOEVER KIND WHO ARE FOR *THE LIGHT* ARE SUBJECT TO THE GREAT COUNCIL. I AM NOT SIDING WITH ANY EMPIRIC ORDER. I AM FOR THOSE OF LIGHT, SINCERITY, TRUTH, LOVE, WISDOM AND POWER, AND I AM NO RESPECTER OF PERSONS. THOSE WHO FOLLOW MY COMMANDMENTS ARE THOSE WHO LOVE ME AND THOSE WHO LOVE CHRIST SHALL

LOVE ME FOR 'I AND THE FATHER ARE ONE' IN COM-PLETE UNDERSTANDING. FURTHERMORE I MUST DE-CLARE THAT NONE CAN 'HIDE ANYTHING FROM THE PRIESTS OF LORD MAITREYA,' AND I AM HIS CHIEF PRIEST. URGENT FOR ACTION.

—AMSUMATA."

* * *

It is well that the reader take into serious consideration what Koot Hoomi has said in the above letter.

When I think of the attack on Pearl Harbor, Hawaii, just a week ago last Sunday, December 7, when Koot Hoomi's letter was written on October 25, almost ten weeks previous, I do not wonder, as He said, that the "clearing of the landscape" will be sudden. The Blessed Children of Light will not have to wait much longer before they will see God's retributive laws go into action. The whole world is now at war. It could not be if it were not that the people of the world have created it. We must take what we have sown. However, the Children of Light, of Goodness, of Truthfulness, of Faithfulness, Purity, Love and even Long-suffering, ARE THE ONES WHO WILL BE PROTECTED, DIRECTED AND SHELTERED during the "AWFUL DAY OF THE LORD."

Watch and pray, Children of Light. Lord Maitreya is with you ALWAYS. Call to Him, Christ Maitreya.

CHAPTER XXXIII

In the correspondence I carried on with my Brother in the North is the finest of instruction for any student who may possess the same doubts he expressed. I myself was somewhat shocked by the tone of the following letter I received from him, yet, I know the Great Masters work most mysteriously their wonders to perform, and I feel now, since all was written and answered, Lord Maitreya (Christ) was actually directing all, and I am sure the following letter and its answer is the grandest instruction any seeking student might receive, even though it may seem at the moment otherwise:

"(A beautiful Symbol)
(No date)

"Dear Norman:

"It is very timely that you should have found your way to the Temple of M............ O............ and the Great White Brotherhood. It is needless to say that I have known of and about this group for many years, and in more recent years I have been in close touch with the President of the Society and have had some very illuminative instruction from this very kind and lovable brother. I would say that he is a TRUE INITIATE. He should prove a good companion and an inspiration to you.

"If there is anyone there qualified to judge any recent attainments on your part he should be the one. I feel about you just the same as you have expressed your opinion about me. I feel that I know you better, *and much more fully than you know yourself. I hesitate to formulate in words what you would no doubt misunderstand.* But if you gathered anything good from my recent and previous visits of myself in the ethereal world know that indeed those good wishes are true. And if there was anything unpleasant in the Astral projection I wish you to know that the astral projection, while completely under my control, was only the vile and coarse body, the emotional body which is bound to betray the emotions we strive the hardest to overcome. The spiritual body was also present, full of love and compassion, if you had been attuned to feel its presence there. You need only to open your heart and you will feel the love and uplifting influence of the spirit therein.

"I know that you have sought sincerely the WAY and if you have entered therein I should be the first to rejoice. But you know as well as I the phantoms along the way. They do not need to be enumerated if I were qualified to name them.

"There is one warning I wish to pass on to you, which you may take or leave as it suits your fancy. True discipleship does not end with Guruship. Guruship does not end with the business of an Avatar. There is still the INFINITE to be aspired unto. Keep up the discipleship.

"And hand in hand goes this thought. When you stand at the heights look outward, inward, look straight before you and you will see the brethren. Your lofty attainments do not place the other brethren beneath your own attainments. NO one is the sole AVATAR in this the GOLDEN AGE. Others have seen the new dawn and breathed the fragrance of the Blessed Flower.

"You speak of your COMMISSION which came through the written word, and on perishable materials. Yet I have not questioned your sincerity. You are TOO sincere in some things, and have suffered for it. Yet you have appreciated what you have accepted as your commission to the extent that you are willing to devote your best to its service. I have also been commissioned.

"I have stood on the heights and have looked straight across the abyss. I have seen the great Light and have heard a great Voice. I have also seen ONE great Ascended Master. I have received this commission: "Seek NEW TRUTH with all thy heart, and when thou hast found it, TEACH it with all thy WISDOM, LOVE AND POWER." Now this is not *imagination*. I have *received the commission*. No one is too ILLUMINATED for me to converse with, too EXALTED before the brethren for me to write with any degree of wisdom I may have. But as LOVE must find the OPEN HEART, so TRUTH must find the OPEN MIND.

"Reincarnation has so many varieties that one hardly knows which to believe in. Osiris has so many manifestations today that truly he must not only be confused but diffused as well. Napoleon, likewise. Lincoln and St. Germain. Quibbling is what you would call anything that didn't meet your particular incarnative spirit at this time.

"But this self-assertive ethereal body of mine cannot cease to function and disagrees with a good many things.

"But—another BUT—AVATARS in all ages have revolutionized world thought, and have brought to focus the CENTRAL TRUTHS that pertain to that generation and the generations to follow. I might emphasize the COMMISSION given you.

"As I remember Koot Hoomi's teaching, he promulgated the Secret Traditions of the RACES. These races have progressed, and these teachings have also evolved. But as he says in your commission, the law was laid down from the beginning. And the whole universe, he says, is based on LAW AND ORDER.

"Norman, you wish me to avoid the superior attitude of earthly wisdom and intelligence manifested in reasoning. I wish to God you would tell me how to even so much as formulate one first principle of the UNIVERSAL LAW AND ORDER without the use of reason. Many of us have tried to feel our way into an appreciation of the Art of God's Universe, not because we despised wisdom, but because we didn't have it.

"Law and order are based on wisdom, and truth is to be understood. The WORD has gone forth and will not return to God void.

"Again brother, you say that I have hurt you while in the ethereal body. Bless you, my brother, do you think I can read any one of your letters, in which you tell me of your mighty attainments and how the LORDS, the GODS, the ASCENDED MASTERS, the INITIATES and all the BUDDHAS and the LORDS OF THE SEVEN RAYS come and go at your simple command or beck and call; I say to you, while you complain that I use too much earthly wisdom of the damned Empiric Order which also seems to bow the Knee, it hurts me, it grieves me deeply, in fact beyond repair, that you fail to give me the credit for any sense of proportion whatever. Again, in your last letter, you still have not told ALL.

"Do you not know that did I live on the plane on which such things affect one that the Blood would not run from my hands and my sides and that vinegar would be my drink for sweetness?

"I wish never to have to say to one who is to be the CHIEF AVATAR that he must humble himself and be the servant of all? There are 'Lords many, and Gods Many' but ONE I know!

"No matter what place you may occupy in any Order I have the penetration of spirit to enter into and perceive the real man and I know that underneath all the assumptions, all the great outward masks that cover up the real spirit, all the clouds that arise between us because of such matters, again in a long confusing sentence I say that I have perceived the real boy that your mother gave birth to, that struggled through many tough, heartbreaking years to attain to manhood, and in good clean companionship I learned to love. He is still there, and while the outward man may change the things of the INNER TEMPLE are unchangeable. Spirit is eternal and Gods, MEN and devils are powerless to pollute him. In this NORMAN I LOVE YOU.

"My blessing to you dear brother is this: where fear followed you there was nothing to fear. When you thought your spirit was too weak and small, you were big and kind, and out of your eyes the spirit of youth looked. But you were not a young spirit. Your body confused you many times, and your mind was not equal to the mighty demands of the great soul, the Mahatma, within. It was not your spirit that needed development—it was your lower mind—by which you were fed. But the age-old spirit craved expression and the three lower bodies were confused and you sought the short-cut. I bless you where you do not seek a blessing, but now, once again, be yourself—man—be yourself.

"Now, Norman, can I help you as a brother and friend?

"I love to formulate my experiences in documentary form. Do not think that I seek to deceive. But I do know that I have much that received gladly will help you or any one with an OPEN MIND AND HEART.

"I salute you with Love alone,

"SATRAJITA."

*   *   *

I shall immediately go right on with the answer to the above letter. Although I was "busy as a bee" doing the very things Satrajita thought I was not doing — UNIFYING THE WORLD IN THE ONE GREAT LIGHT—I did take "time out" to answer his letter completely, irrevocably, unconditionally, unreservedly, comprehensively, irrefutably and irregretably as follows:

"Dear O............,   Nov. 9, 1941.
Thou Who Seeketh
Infinity in Christ:

"My Blessed Brother, May God Bless your Soul, and may Lord Maitreya take you, Hand in Hand, into His TEMPLE of LOVE, where Reason is left behind and Your Christ Body, stript of all lower incrustations, stands revealed for what you ARE, THE SON OF GOD ALMIGHTY—ONE WITH THE FATHER—*AGAIN!*

"Brother, I shall answer your letter paragraph by paragraph, as busy as I am, getting together the 'revolutionized world thought' for the book KH and St. G. and L.M. are urging and directing me in writing,—yes, I shall, Blessed Seeker of Truth, 'humble myself and be the servant of YOU.' Yes, 'there are Lords many, and Gods many' but one CHRIST and HE IS INFINITE, and HIM 'I KNOW.' DO YOU?

"KNOW THIS, Brother, since you HAVE CHALLENGED ME AND THE VERY GODS WHO ARE MY PROGENITORS, our swords, YOURS AND MINE—SWORDS OF LIGHT, LOVE, WISDOM AND POWER—shall fly most quickly and cut with lightning speed in the fury of OUR BATTLE to PROVE who's best QUALIFIED to lead the Children of the Shadow back into the TEMPLE OF CHRIST'S LIGHT AND LOVE. AND KNOW THIS, BROTHER MINE, HE WHO HAS MOST OF LOVE SHALL RISE UPON THE VANQUISHED TO LEAD THE STRUGGLING MASSES OF EARTH'S CHILDREN TO THE 'DOOR' WHICH YOU— APPARENTLY—FAIL TO SEE AND RECOGNIZE. I meet you on the battlefield of Christ and His Love guides me, STREAMING FROM THE PORTAL OF MY *GOLDEN HEART!*

"In your very first paragraph (of your letter I just received) you intimate that I found the Great White Brotherhood on M............ O............ In this you err, as I found the Great White Brotherhood IN MY HEART. That the Brother here is an INITIATE I do not question, but this I DO KNOW, after I had been with him less than a week, HE KNEW THAT I WAS THE ONE CHOSEN BY THE GREAT WHITE LODGE AS THE 'CHIEF AVATAR' AND IT DID NOT COME ON A MATERIAL *WRITTEN WORD*. My inspirations come from the Gods, not men. I realize the 'constant' possibility of the Gods visiting me directly through my fellowmen, however. The tenor of your letter constantly betrays your true standing in 'discipleship' since your definite rating of me instantly stigmatizes you and places you in the place of limitation, you in your 'judgment' of me would thereby classify me. HIM you should follow you would dare think you should lead. This is invariably true of all who aspire upward and onward. We cannot rise but by challenging those who STAND IN OUR PATHWAY. You would 'rend my Veil!' I shall bless you, since you DARE.

"There are *none* qualified to 'judge' me but Christ, and my 'recent attainments' in the Cosmic Heart were attained through the Highest Initiations obtainable on earth; three of all on earth received them: Mahatma Koot Hoomi, Ave Maria and Saint Germain (Amsumata), and the 'Great Purusha' was experienced by each of us, Beloved Krishna of long ago having been the last one on earth to have knowingly gone through such initiation up to this time. I AM SAINT GERMAIN.

"It is the 'vile and coarse body, the emotional body,' that you need to dissolve, TRANSMUTE, REGENERATE AND DRAW INTO THE AURA OF CHRIST THAT HE MAY *LIFT YOU* UNTO HIS TEMPLE OF LOVE. You, Beloved, must bring Christ into your body, otherwise He does not 'dwell among man.'

"I do not doubt but that your 'spiritual body' was also present when I witnessed your astral projection, and should you tell me that you were the outer body of Lord Maitreya (the one He uses in this physical plane) I would be inclined to believe you, at least until I proved you otherwise, WHICH I CAN, SHOULD I SO DEEPLY DESIRE IT. Each paragraph of your letter brands you a 'doubting Thomas.' However, we need men such as you to take care of the 'empiric' until more 'John the Beloveds' are congregated together. You write, 'You need only to open your heart,' knowing well that reason does not come from the heart. You had better take your own advice—OPEN YOUR HEART.

"You say you 'should be the first to rejoice' in what I have found. How can you possibly rejoice WITH ME until you, too, have found what I AM—Christ Incarnate? Speaking of 'phantoms,' you say 'They do not need to be enumerated if I were qualified to name them,' do you? I AM QUALIFIED. My 'judgment is righteous judgment,' for I JUDGE IN CHRIST LORD MAITREYA.

"And then you WARN ME, My Little Seeker After Wisdom and Love. 'DISCIPLESHIP DOES NOT END WITH GURUSHIP'

271

nor 'the business of the Avatar.' As though I did not know this my Doubting Brother. There are many higher 'DEGREES' that have been conferred upon me, Brother O............., as I have intimated, when I said 'I have not told *all*.'

"While holding the office of 'SILENT WATCHER TO THIS EARTH,' to be more exact in time, to the day, it was May 22, 1941, that a part of the Great Initiation I received on Mt. Shasta ended with the following:

" 'The Great Lord of Creation vanished, and then appeared the Great Mahatma KH. "Oh, that now my call is answered," he exclaimed, "for my plea to Lord Krishna to answer this which was in my heart, if I were chosen to develop Ave Maria. This, Her Jewel, was developed by Him, The Lord of Creation. This I know now. You, Ave Maria, I bless as the Jewel of Jewels of Womanhood."

" 'Then he, Koot Hoomi, took both the hands of Ave Maria and those of the Silent Watcher (Amsumata). "I am so happy," he said, "THAT WE HAVE BEEN ABLE TO APPROACH THE LORD OF CREATION. WE ARE HIS ONLY CHOSEN DISCIPLES OF *THE IMMUTABLE ONE, THE GREAT PURUSHA, THE LORD OF THE PAST AND THE FUTURE, OUT OF WHOSE MOUTH WE WERE BORN.*" How blessed you are! Oh, how I wish I might be with you in form in the Presence of the GREAT ONE, whose form "as the Dwarf in the Center," Ave Maria was so blessed to see. May she be able to see His Form as Purusha, and may she be able to withstand it. Only one was ever able to stand it—Krishna'."

"I do believe, Brother, that too much of 'shoe-selling' doth cause ye to be of thy doubting nature. 'Worship Thy God with ALL thy heart.' Get right down to business, 'your Father's business.' If this letter does not turn the 'trick' then I shall say 'there is no hope for you.' Just don't bother to answer this letter, if you continue to doubt the Chief Avatar, for any help that such an one might give would only hinder the Great Cause for which I am sent. Do not think that the 'Chief Avatar' does not have a plan for harmonizing all the religions of the world. He even has more than this in mind and He has the aid of the Great Ones, WITHOUT DOUBT. THE BOOK I AM WRITING WILL BE THE BIGGEST STIR IN RELIGIOUS AND PHILOSOPHICAL CIRCLES EVER BROUGHT ABOUT ON THIS EARTH. WHY DON'T YOU COME HERE AND TALK THESE THINGS OVER? THAT IS WHAT YOU SHOULD DO. THERE IS NOT MUCH TIME. HURRY!

"In paragraph five of your letter you talk as though I think my 'lofty attainments place me above the other brethren.' Why did you write that? Do you want the truth? You are conceited, egotistical, and even jealous of me, your Brother, you pretend to love. You, in your reticent, hidden way, having been so long of the opinion that you are 'above' your fellowmen, that you just can't bear to have one you have known so well chosen as the 'Chief Avatar.' Your next sentence proves what I write: 'NO one is the sole "Avatar" in this the GOLDEN AGE.' Meaning of course that you are an AVATAR. Who proclaimed you an Avatar? You say, 'Others have seen the dawn and breathed the fragrance of the Blessed Flower.' Then if you have, for you would have to have experienced it yourself to know that others have experienced it, then you, my Beloved Brother, would humbly stand by my side and go with me wherever the Gods determine. You would do this without question did you know what I do. Of course, my Egotistical Brother, I know there are others who have attained what I have, in a sense, and yet it is not the SAME, for there are not two Saint Germains who have done what 'I HAVE' during the past six or seven hundred years. That is the reason I was chosen the 'CHIEF' and if you want to be CHIEF instead of me, then it means that either you or I get out of the way of the other, or you will have to stand BY ME and assist me in every way you possibly can. WHICH DO YOU WISH TO DO? I PUT THE QUESTION RIGHT UP TO YOU. BE A GOD, MAN; BE A GOD—come with us and help to harmonize this WHOLE WORLD and make of it a fit place for the GODS TO WANT TO DWELL IN.

"You then write, 'Again brother, you say I have hurt you while in the ethereal body.' I do not think I said such a thing. I said it hurt me when I found that you felt yourself superior than I. That is what I said. You could not hurt my ethereal body.

"And in your next paragraph you all but weep when you say, 'It hurts me, it grieves me deeply, in fact beyond repair, that you fail to give me the credit for any sense of proportion whatever.' Bless your little wounded heart. You do have so very very much to learn. Do you want me to sympathize with you? I would rather give you a GOOD SLAP with the flat side of MY SWORD OF FLAMING FIRE to wake you up to a few important principles, however, I guess I will have to LOVE YOU another 16 years before you 'come out of it.' You, Blessed One, are looking for credit from someone in the 'EMPIRIC REALM.' MY KINGDOM IS NOT OF THIS REALM. If you, with all the associates you presume to have in your Empiric Way, did choose to help me, and they are all of your limited Spiritual Awakening, HOW MUCH HELP DO YOU THINK YOU MIGHT GIVE ONE WHO HAS 'CHRIST MAITREYA WITH ME'? I DO NOT NEED SUCH HELP UNLESS IT WERE GIVEN IN THE SPIRIT OF LOVE and by those who at least had FAITH in the one 'Chosen' to lead ALL DOUBTFUL BROTHERS SUCH AS YOU INTO THE FULL ILLUMINATION OF THE TEMPLE OF GOD. WERE YOU HALF AS HUMBLE AS YOU WOULD HAVE ME TO BE, you would be a worthy Neophyte to take into HIS TEMPLE. Again, I think the 'shoe store' has got you down, and

I am afraid it is going to keep you down, unless you SNAP OUT OF IT. WHAT IS WRONG WITH YOU, anyway? If you are a product of the UB—AN EXAMPLE—then I think they had better start over or have Brother Snell—the one who wrote most all the documents—who is now in Heaven—dictate some FRESH instructions for you. And, for your benefit, Brother, I will say, after all, I learned more in the outer and inner from Brother R.S.C. than I learned from all others put together. Now, how do you like that? I was not asleep all those years when you thought I was not 'making enough money in the empiric world.' I was AFTER JUST *ONE* THING AND I FOUND *IT—THE REAL CHRIST*. Many of you so-called Christians talk a lot about Jesus, My Elder Brother, and Christ, but I want you to know, few of you have found HIM.

"Regarding re-incarnation, Friend O............, you know, apparently, just what you have read about it. I talk about what I have experienced about it. I know of several of my Past Embodiments, and even am acquainted with the individual spirits that correspond to each of those embodiments in which I lived. I realize, too, Beloved Friend (FOR I DO LOVE YOU) that you have all these knowledges within your own life-stream but you have not become AWARE OF THEM. That is exactly what I am working so hard to do right now, AWAKEN YOU TO WHO YOU ARE, and then you will not have to take my word for anything, and when someone tells you of such things as I have experienced you will NOT DOUBT but you will KNOW that I SPEAK THE TRUTH AND NOTHING BUT THE WHOLE TRUTH. Truly, if you told me you were Mark, one of Jesus' Disciples, I would believe you, for I have met several of the Great Ones already, and I know that most all the Great Ones are now embodied to FINISH THE JOB OF ESTABLISHING THE DIVINE LAWS HERE ON EARTH IN THE GOLDEN AGE.

"In the above connection, Brother, I recently initiated Lao Tse, the Great Chinese Philosopher. He was embodied in a very humble, broken body—a 'jack of all trades,' so to speak, near Seattle, but Blessed KH sent him to me, and it was only a few weeks until he ascended and knew WHO HE WAS, was able to talk several different languages, including Chinese, and there is no doubt in my mind that He is That Great One who is NOW WILLING TO GO WITH ME and others to establish the Kingdom of Almighty God on Earth. Now, frankly, Blessed Egoist, have you experienced any such experiences? If so SPEAK UP. Do not be afraid. All things are to be revealed, EVEN IN YOU. You can hide nothing from me. You will find this out, for Lord Maitreya, MY BLESSED MAS-TER-TEACHER IS BY MY SIDE CONSTANTLY, guarding me, teaching me, and instantly He responds to my call, and I KNOW IT. I DO NOT GUESS. Your letter proves to me that you have MUCH TO BRING THROUGH IN YOUR OUTER BODY *AND MIND* BEFORE YOU MAY CONSIDER YOURSELF ASCENDED.

When you prove otherwise to me I shall acknowledge your WISDOM and everything else you may possess. I AM NOT SLOW TO PLACE CREDIT WHERE CREDIT IS DUE. AS A RULE I OVER-DO THIS. EVEN YOU, until you got to writing more and revealing your IGNORANCE, I thought you were somebody LIKE LORD MAIT-REYA. Had you kept silent I would have continued thinking you were A GOD. Well, man, BE A GOD, BE A GOD—yes BE YOUR HIGHER 'SELF'—BE YOUR HIGHER 'SELF'—not merely a MAN as you suggested I should be. 'Man you are now, a GOD BY TRYING.' Those lines I wrote in 1936, when I was going through terrible 'trials,' yet I was TRYING, TRYING, TRYING TO BECOME LIKE GOD —'CHRIST.'

"You say you saw 'ONE Great Ascended Master.' I have seen hundreds of them. I associate with them in the higher realms; I consciously attend the meetings of the Great White Lodge. I am one of the Council of Seven of the Lodge. I'll tell you the names of the others, of whom you may be ONE—I do not judge you, the REAL YOU—only the outer Egoist. Here are their names: Mahatma Koot Hoomi, World Teacher; Ave Maria, co-worker of Saint Germain, and Lordess of the New Eighth Ray; Saint Germain (Amsumata), Leader of the Whites in all activities inner and outer, and Lord of the New Ninth Ray, Lord of Sagittarius, and now prepared to take over the Second Ray (BLUE) of Wisdom which KH has held for a long long time, holder of initiatory work of ALL DEGREES AND MASTER OF ALL MASTERS IN ALL BROTH-ERHOODS (Spiritual) active on Earth. He is the One who holds the Great Seal of Alpha and Omega; Jesus, now Lord of this World; Arch-angel Michael, Lord of the Sun; Lord Maitreya, Christ to this Solar System (Universe); Silent Watcher, the only One in this world who does 'work independent of the Logos,' the MOST POWERFUL, no doubt, OF ALL.

"Your statement, 'But this self-assertive ethereal body of mine cannot cease to function and disagrees with a good many things,' is quite a candid acknowledgment for you. I am glad you realize there are SEVEN BOD-IES. This awareness of yours helps some. But there are any number of Spirits in your life-stream, entities you have created, etc., throughout the ages, that you don't seem to be conscious of, and you do not, I dare say, realize the importance they may play in YOU when you become FULLY CONSCIOUS (ascend) OF WHO YOU ARE AND HOW MANY. This, my Dear SATRAJITA, is one phase of philosophy that has not been explained to the outer world ever that I know of, at least not in the clear and 'stepped down' manner that 'your humble Amsumata' will explain it.

"My COMMISSION AS AVATAR is already explained; it is simply that I have been 'about My Father's Business' even much more than you have dreamed of, and I KNOW what it's all about, too. Have no fear but that I know what my responsibilities are.

275

"In regard to KH's teachings, I must say KH, so far as my Higher Consciousness is concerned, is no more my teacher than I am His. I recognize Him as my BELOVED TEACHER IN THE OUTER, because He is Most Wise in the outer activities of all true brotherhoods on earth. Master KH one time last summer came to Ave Maria and me on Mt. Shasta (since I saw you) and wept with joy because we were able to assist Him in receiving an initiation He had prayed for all His life. This, He will prove to you some day, if you ever get over the idea that you ALREADY KNOW EVERYTHING.

"You speak of the 'superior attitude of earthly wisdom.' There is no such thing. Wisdom is not, never was and never will be 'earthly.' I am surprised that one of your supposed intelligence makes so many 'crack-pot' remarks about the Mysteries and the Sublime Wisdom. That you state in regard to 'wisdom' and 'because we didn't have it,' is contrary to most of your letter, however, when you do admit you haven't something, there is some chance for you to find it, since you realize the lack of it.

"The WORD IS GOD, goes nowhere and cannot be 'void.'

"Paragraph, 3rd page, at top, I answered in a previous paragraph.

"Your insinuations regarding the 'Blood would not run from my hands' and 'vinegar would be my drink for sweetness,' I shall merely predict that you will experience the same thing quite soon unless you have already been 'crucified.' You can no more ascend until after you have gone through the 'crucifixion' than you can 'fly' before you can walk. 'Judge not lest ye be judged.' Lord Maitreya will TAKE CARE OF YOU, MY LITTLE BOASTER OF THY WISDOM AND EARTHLY KNOWLEDGE. Fear not, you will be taken care of, and I SHALL BE WITH YOU ALWAYS.

"You shall never know in reality the ONE GOD only through CHRIST, and it isn't an imaginative statement from an 'ascended Master' —you will KNOW HIM when you become like Him, and you will be told you ARE a MASTER when you become MASTER of yourself, your passions, your desires, the 'four elements,' jealousy, and all the little things that keep one from knowing Christ, MEETING HIM EMBODIED, SPEAKING TO HIM FACE TO FACE.

"You may have perceived the 'real boy' that my mother gave birth to, but you certainly have not perceived the CHRIST that has been born in me through Lord Maitreya, and yet, I think you shall SOON. If you don't then only GOD can help you. I shall leave you to your own conceit and let you lead the Empiric World into YOUR LITTLE TEMPLE OF REASONING.

"There is much truth in your next paragraph, but your lack of wisdom in the balance of your letter depreciates from the few words of wisdom you might write, for in the entirety of your letter I have long ago gathered that any wisdom you might write would be borrowed from some source you half understand. I suggest that you read that paragraph over several times

276

yourself and maybe you will realize that your 'age-old Spirit (MANY OF THEM) craves experience and the three lower bodies are confused' and you need to take the 'short-cut' that Lord Maitreya has offered you. 'Once again, be your HIGHERself—man be your HIGHERself.'

" 'Now, O............., can I help you as a brother and friend?'

"I do not like 'to formulate my experiences in documentary form,' for I know it would only be to tickle my own bump of conceit. 'But I do know that I have much that, received GLADLY, will help you or anyone with an OPEN MIND AND HEART.'

"And my blessed O............., what is keeping you from helping me? Did I ever tell you once in my life that you could not help me? What is it that you have HIDDEN in that marvelous reasoning mind of yours that you think I do not know? Will you kindly tell me? Any time you want to help me and the Great Brothers, JUST START RIGHT IN. THE WORLD SURE NEEDS ALL THE ABLE ONES SUCH AS YOU THINK YOU ARE TO HELP IN THIS GREAT BATTLE OF ESTABLISHING THE GOLDEN AGE ON EARTH. WHAT'S HOLDING YOU, MY BROTHER?

"Now, BELOVED (I'm talking to your Spiritual Self now) please forgive me if you think that will do any good, for all the frank and earnest words I have spoken to you. I do not care one whit, how you think about them in the outer. Your real Higher Self knows I have told the truth. I hope that Egotistical Mind of yours gets so it won't operate at all. Then maybe you will find Christ in your Heart.

"That was a fair battle, but I have had bigger, fierier and more interesting battles with mightier ones than you, Dear O............. And I am still going strong. The mightiest battle I ever had was with Archangel Michael, Lord of the Sun. However, here is a paragraph I wrote to one RSC March 24, 1939:

" 'In our travels on our return to "Our Father's House" we want nothing left undone that we may do to hasten that long-sought-after home-coming. In the glorious pathway that leads to those "radiant Ones" whose individual "Lights" ever grow brighter, as we travel on, may we, each of us, tread its blissful course unhampered by the least human mistake that we might have made to withhold the fulfilment of God's eternal Truth.'

"I wish you to know, UNRESERVEDLY, that I do not have one personal feeling toward you that might hurt you in the least. I am positively IMPERSONAL in the work Lord Maitreya and the Beloved Masters want me to do. All I have written herein, is written that it might prove or disprove certain manifestations in your and my individual lives. Frankly, I believe I can help you, and I am sure you can help me, but REMEMBER, Blessed Brother, it is the New Kingdom I am interested in establishing, and in my work, I must be no respecter of persons, empiric orders or brotherhoods so-called. I deal with the Ascended Masters and Members of the Great White Lodge, and I KNOW whereof I speak. I am not guessing as you seem to be doing most of the time.

"Lovingly, AMSUMATA."

The next morning before I mailed the above letter I added the following postscript, to be sure that I was not misunderstood, and to have my Brother know I love him:

"P.S.—Beloved Satrajita:—I wish you to know that I fully appreciate the position you hold. It is important to the outer work. But please be careful what you do, and ALWAYS *KNOW* THAT LOVE REIGNS IN YOUR HEART IN WHATEVER YOU DO. YOUR ACTIONS ARE ALL UNDER THE OBSERVATION OF THE GREAT MASTERS. YOU MAY REST ASSURED OF THAT.

"You are, My Friend, tampering with a very dangerous phase of human and spiritual activity when you tell the Masters of the White Lodge what to do, especially of the Council of Seven. Again, you may be ONE of the Seven. I have learned too much about such matters in recent months to 'judge' anyone. I might judge your outer actions and words—'your fruits' —but even then I would not judge your Higher Presence. Little did I really think I was and AM Saint Germain until I GOT HIM IN A 'CORNER,' so to speak, AND BOMBASTED HIM SO SEVERELY THAT I REALIZED I WAS TORTURING MYSELF. So be careful. Please don't judge me by the body of this letter. THERE IS SOMETHING THERE FOR YOU.

"Now, regarding your 'Ace in the Hole,' that you are so proud of, Beloved; I want you to realize that I know how you are 'working.' I realize that you have contacts in Los Angeles. This doesn't matter to me. I AM CHRIST INCARNATE, just the same.

"I was asked to give those two lectures in San Bernardino and Long Beach. Whether you know it or not, YOUR SPIRIT WAS PRESENT AT BOTH MEETINGS, and I saw you. You had projected your Spirit —one of them—or your Higher Presence did—and you were manifest to me in the bodies of those you 'used.' BE CAREFUL. There is a lot goes on in your VARIOUS SPIRITS that probably you do not understand. This is another reason you should come here and talk over a number of things.

"REMEMBER, Beloved, whatever you do with whatever Power you have, you must, in the Name of Christ, BE CAREFUL, and use it for the upliftment of humanity. And I AM chosen by the Great White Lodge as 'Chief Avatar' for the leadership of the White Forces. God KNOWS, and ALL the White Brothers—WHO HAVE ASCENDED—that I AM not only SINCERE, but ABLE to FILL THE OFFICE for which I AM chosen, and that I AM EMPOWERED BY THEM to do the

JOB that I see and KNOW HOW TO ACCOMPLISH. I am not chosen for this office because of anything I am in this body. It was because of my DIVINE INHERITANCE. It took KH several months to check up on that. The Council of Seven do not make a move unless They KNOW what they are doing.

"Lovingly,

"(Signed) SAINT GERMAIN."

* * *

A few days later I received an answer from Brother O........, which proved to me, after all, that he IS AN INITIATE, that he understands the PARADOXES, and he is ONE with the "I AM PRESENCE" of the ONE LIFE, LIGHT, LOVE, WISDOM AND POWER OF INFINITY. His letter follows:

"DEAR NORMAN:

"May Wisdom, Love and Power be in you and may the LIGHT of the Beatitudes guide many to THE DOOR.

"I AM THE TEMPLE OF LOVE. May the DOOR be opened to all who are guided to IT.

"I AM THE SON OF GOD without beginning or ending. I AM IN THE FATHER AND THE FATHER IS IN ME.

"I AM THE SUPREME EGOIST. THERE IS NO OTHER; beside the ONE THERE IS NAUGHT.

"I AM STIGMATIZED BY MYSELF, THE SELF OF THE SELF and in the ONE WAY—THE CHRIST WAY—WITH STREAMING HANDS AND FEET.

"The FLAMING SWORDS have become ONE IN MY HAND.

"I AM JEALOUS—THERE IS NO OTHER GOD BUT I AM GOD.

"I AM THE AURA OF GOD. ALL who come to GOD are drawn to THE FATHER in the AURA OF GOD.

"I AM THE INFINITY OF ALL REALMS. There is no EMPIRIC REALM. I AM ALL THE BELOVEDS AND THE ALL BELOVED. I AM THE TOTALITY. I AM ALL.

"I have LIFTED THE PHYSICAL BODY and the FATHER ENTERED INTO ME AND I IN HIM. As it is below so it is above.

"I HAVE BREATHED THE FRAGRANCE OF THE SACRED FLOWER and I AM THE SACRED FLOWER. MY AURA FILLS THE INFINITUDE OF MY CREATIONS.

"HUNDREDS OF HUMAN incarnations and YEA MILLIONS OF MILLENNIA are NOTHING TO ME. Before the beginning of time I AM AT WORK. I AM THE SUPREME PRAGMATIST,

279

and FOREVER I ENFOLD HUMANITY IN THE LOVE OF MY SACRED HEART.

"I AM ETERNALLY INCARNATE IN THE ONE BODY, THE BODY OF CHRIST. I AM THE GREAT WHITE LIGHT WHICH LIGHTS THE BROTHERHOOD and from which ALL RAYS EMANATE. I AM PRESENT AT ALL CONCLAVES and no one works INDEPENDENTLY OF THE LOGOS. I AM THE LOGOS. (?)

(Author's Note: I question this: that no one can work independently of the Planetary Logos.)

"ALL WHO ARE SENT ARE SENT BY THE LOGOS.

"I AM ONE BODY. I AM ONE SPIRIT. ALL WHO KNOW CHRIST KNOW I AM.

"I AM THE TEMPLE OF REASONING. I AM THE KNOWER AND THE KNOWN. THERE IS NO EARTHLY WISDOM. ALL WISDOM IS INFINITE. I KNOW WITHOUT PROCESS FOR THERE IS NO MOTION IN ME.

"OPEN THOU—THOU DOOR OF THE TEMPLE.

"SON OF THE FATHER ALWAYS HAVE I HELPED YOU. I HAVE ALWAYS BEEN ABOUT MY FATHER'S BUSINESS. THE CHRIST IN YOU KNOWS THIS.

"IN ME THERE IS NO DESIRE. I AM EXALTED BY THE FATHER. THE GOLDEN AGE IS NOW—there is no other time but NOW.

"IN ME THERE IS NO HIDDEN MIND, THE MIND OF GOD IS IN ME and the SPIRIT OF TRUTH fills the ONE IMMENSITY and REVEALS THE MIND OF THE FATHER TO THE SON and those worthy to receive.

"I AM MY HIGHER SELF AND I AM IN GOD. THERE IS NEITHER MULTIPLICITY NOR DUPLICITY AMONG THE GODS. GOD IS ONE GOD.

"When the ANGELS MADE THEIR FIRST CHOICE there began the KINGDOM OF GOD. I AM ESTABLISHING THE KINGDOM OF GOD ON THE EARTH FOR THE LAST TIME.

"I AM BUILDING THE KINGDOM AMONG THE LOST SOULS WHO ARE NOT LOST TO THE FATHER. I HAVE DECLARED THE CHRIST IN THE REGIONS WHERE NO MAN HAS DARED TO GO. AS THE SON OF GOD I HAVE DECLARED THE MESSAGE IN THE INNERMOST AND THE OUTERMOST, IN THE UPPERMOST AND TO THE NETHERMOST. THE FATHER HAS CHAINED THE (evil) POWERS AND THEY ARE SENILE AND FEEBLE WHEN PROJECTED AGAINST THE SON OF GOD.

"The battles of the SON OF GOD are never ended. THE ONE GREAT BATTLE OF THE SON OF GOD IS WITH HIMSELF and HE is eternally the VICTOR.

"I know ONE ASCENDED MASTER AND I AM THE ONE I KNOW.

"You seek to be IMpersonal — I AM PERSONAL, SUPER-PERSONAL—THE ONE GREAT PERSONAL GOD. HAST THOU DWELT WITH THE FATHER ALL THESE MANY MULTIPLIED INCARNATIONS AND NOT HEARD THE ONE SPEAK TO THEE THAT I AM CHRIST. HAST THOU LET THE BEAM THAT IS IN THINE EYE BE A STIGMA-TISM INSTEAD OF A STIGMATA IN THINE HANDS.

"THOU MAKEST MANY CLAIMS OF BEING CHIEFEST AVATAR AMONG THE BRETHREN. I SAY UNTO THEE BE THE CHIEF AVATAR. THOU HAST FOR THE LAST FOUR HUNDRED YEARS KNOWN THAT THIS TIME WOULD COME. AND NOW I SAY UNTO THEE, WHEN THOU RECEIVEST THIS HONOR AT THE HANDS OF THY BRETHREN IT SHALL BE REQUIRED THAT THOU BE CHIEF AMONG THEM. THOU MAYEST IN TIME WASH THEIR FEET AND PUT THEIR SHOES UPON THEIR FEET. BUT BEFORE GOD SEE THAT IN DOING SO THOU DOEST SO HONORABLY, FOR BLESSED ARE THE FEET OF THOSE WHO BRING GOOD TIDINGS UNTO MAN.

"THE SON OF GOD in days of old handled the feet of the brethren and this is one evidence of Greatness that HE became the least among men —do thou likewise. (I have, Brother; I washed His feet, and He washed mine. 'I sit at the feet of humanity, and humanity at my feet.')

"I AM THE TEMPLE OF POWER. BY MY POWER, BY MY DIVINE ENERGY IS THE COSMOS HELD TOGETHER AND SUSTAINED. BY MY POWER IS THE WORD AND IS THE LOGOS AND THEY ARE ONE. LOGOS IS SPIRIT AND SPIRIT IS TRUTH AND YOU ARE SPIRIT AND SPIRIT IS THE FIRST EVIDENCE OF MY POWER AND IT IS THE FIRST EXPRESSION OF DIVINE LOVE.

"I AM THE TRINITY OF TEMPLES IN ONE. THERE IS ONE DOOR AND I AM THE DOOR.

"I AM UNQUALIFIED. TRUTH IS NOT QUALIFIED. MY POWER IS NOT QUALIFIED. THERE IS NO RELATION-SHIP WHATEVER WITH GOD.

"ALL QUALIFICATION BELONGS TO THE FINITE MIND AND PLANE. TIME FLIES AND JUDGMENTS FAIL AND THE KINGDOMS OF MEN FALTER AND DISAPPEAR, BUT ETERNITY IS HERE AND IN ETERNITY THERE IS NO HURRY.

"I AM THE ONE DOUBTING THOMAS. ALL THAT NEGATES OR DENIES THE ONE GREAT AFFIRMATION IS FALSE AND THAT WHICH AFFIRMS THE ONE GREAT NEGATION IS TRUE, THEREFORE, I NOT ONLY DOUBT BUT WITH ONE STROKE DENY AND DO AWAY WITH ERROR AND AFFIRM THE TRUTH.

"THAT WHICH IS TRUE REVEALS ITSELF TO HIM WHO IS WORTHY TO RECEIVE.

"WHAT HAVE I DENIED? IT IS FALSE. WHAT HAVE I AFFIRMED? I AM.

"WHAT DO I FEAR? I FEAR NO EVIL. LOVE IS NOT TO BE SHUNNED. TRUTH IS TO BE SOUGHT. ERROR MANIFESTS ITSELF.

"SCURRILOUS ATTACKS UPON THE *SON* ARE OF NO AVAIL.

"I AM THE DOOR INTO THE TEMPLE. LOOK TO THYSELF THAT THOU OPENEST INTO THE TEMPLE.

"I AM THE GERM OF LIFE AND I AM THE CARRIER OF THE GERM LOVE AND ENDLESS IS MY NAME.

"(Signed) INDIVIDUAL SYMBOL."

*   *   *

To him who hath ears to hear and eyes to see, may he hear and see as he MAY run. Following is the answer:

Mount Olympus
Temecula, Calif.
Dec. 1, 1941.

"Dear O............:

" 'Thou art THAT.'

"Thou knowest this: 'I AM THAT I AM.'

"WHEN THOU KNOWEST ONE MASTER THOU KNOWEST ALL MASTERS, for there is but ONE, and He is 'the only begotten SON.'

"It is nice to KNOW you.

"As Saint Germain said the other day, in other words, the reason 'WE' must do certain things as the 'Chief' is because no one else will do them.

"I love you,

"Lovingly,

"(Signed)   A GOLDEN LOTUS."

*   *   *

Lord Maitreya, I ask you, Lord, to bless every sincere seeking heart with Thy Light and Love, and may ALL come to KNOW THEE in their HEARTS OF LOVE.

CHAPTER XXXIV

Soon, in the reading of this Message—this Book—My Beloved, it will be as though I have gone.

I have enjoyed your reception quite as much, I am sure, as you have my Blessing and Light.

Our love of Truth drew our attention to the Same Focus of Light, and we each basked in the Radiance of Christ for a brief time.

It may be that some of the narratives herein related were distasteful, but know this, my dear reader, frequently in the distasteful episodes of life our greatest lessons are learned.

Wisdom offered through simplicity has been my aim in this true story of my culminating initiations. What becomes of me, personally, following the world's acceptance of these truths, is of little consequence.

As my Elder Brother Jesus said, in other words: "What profit it a man if he possess the whole world and lose his own soul?"

Frequently, in my individual battle in life's outer restlessness, I have said to myself: "BETTER LIVE A SHORT LIFE IN WELL-DOING THAN A LONG LIFE IN DOING NOTHING FOR THE FUTURE GOOD OF MANKIND."

It is the eternal, the immortal, spiritual BEING that I have ever called to the attention of my hearers, my readers, my fold. Few writers and lecturers seem to KNOW the WHOLE TRUTH regarding the things of which they speak and write. Humanity is no longer satisfied with the husks. They demand the nourishing kernel, the GERM, the LIGHT, the HEART of INTELLIGENCE and UNDERSTANDING. I have given you the KEY. My words are KEYS to NEW DOORS. My words are laden with LOVE. Were my words not charged with Love, they would be as empty cups. My words are Cups filled with the Cosmic Substance of LIGHT, LOVE, WISDOM AND POWER. You have partaken of my LIFE—my "Flesh and Blood"—my SPIRIT. When you read MY WORDS you instantly receive the Blessing of Lord Maitreya, my Beloved

Master-Teacher—Christ Incarnate in ME. I KNOW this. He told me. He proved it to me. He proved it to others.

There are those who tell me I "claim" this and that of myself. This is not true. I have never claimed a single thing of myself.

First, all that I have mentioned regarding my mission and the Message I have given to the world, was claimed of me by the Ascended Masters themselves.

The one whom I have referred to as Ave Maria, as well as Lao Tse, and others whom I have mentioned,—all know I made no claims for myself or of myself. Even now, God knows, as does Koot Hoomi, Lord Maitreya and others with whom I am associated, that I consider the Blessed Ave Maria—the Jewel of Jewels—now embodied right here on earth—far more illuminated than I myself. Humbly I beg of Her and all the Blessed Masters of Light to co-operate with me in awakening humanity to the LIGHT OF THE GOLDEN AGE.

"Judge not lest ye be judged." Oh, Brothers and Sisters of Light, do not judge others. Do not judge your neighbor, your friends, your blood relatives, nor anyone in this world. In these "last days" we never know with whom we may be associating from day to day. These revelations I have portrayed through the written word for you in this hastily written book, are all true. There are thousands of Great Masters among you people of the world. Watch and pray. Hold steadfast to that which is good. Christ will come to you one of these days when you least expect HIM. He is embodied NOW. His Spirit is actually incarnated in human flesh and blood. And this is the first time such has taken place since Jesus was here hundreds of years ago.

I have had a multitude of miracles enter into my own personal experiences the past year. Doubt is the only thing that will keep the "DOOR" closed to you. "I AM THE DOOR THAT NO MAN CAN SHUT."

Had I not passed through the crucifixion and the ascension I would not KNOW the necessary steps one must take in order to enter the TEMPLE OF LOVE AND WISDOM. Even Blessed Koot Hoomi, my Father and Teacher, went through the crucifixion about the time I did at Mt. Shasta. Why? you might ask. Because He, too, wanted to travel the Christ Path, as well as the Brahman Way, the Krishna Road and the Buddha Celestial Stairway. All lead to the same God—the same Son (SUN)—the same Cosmic Heart—the FATHER-MOTHER CENTER OF BEING. Blessed Koot Hoomi will be here soon

—here in the United States—to assist me and the other Brothers of the Great White Lodge in initiating hundreds and thousands of you Blessed Students of Light who were promised by Saint Germain and the Ascended Masters that you would be taught and instructed in the HIGHER DEGREES OF THE GREAT WORK.

WE ARE HERE TO DO WHAT WAS PROMISED. I AM SAINT GERMAIN. LORD MAITREYA CHOSE ME TO DO THIS WORK. I AM HIS HUMBLE SERV-ANT. I ALSO PLACE MYSELF HUMBLY AT THE SERVICE OF KOOT HOOMI, AVE MARIA, JESUS, ARCHANGEL MICHAEL AND THE GREAT PRES-ENCE OF THE SILENT WATCHER.

IT IS ALSO MY JOY TO SERVE ALL MEMBERS OF THE GREAT WHITE LODGE AND THE GREAT WHITE BROTHERHOOD. I AM HAPPY TO SERVE THE MOST LOWLY OF GOD'S CHILDREN ON EARTH. IN THIS SERVICE I "SURRENDER ALL" FOR MANKIND, KNOWING THAT IN SELF-SACRI-FICE I ATTAIN TO OUTER NOTHINGNESS, AND THEREBY ACCOMPLISH THE BLISSFUL FIELDS OF NIRVANIC LOVE, WHERE I AM SWALLOWED UP IN THE ETERNAL SPIRIT OF ALMIGHTY GOD.

OUR PHYSICAL BODIES ARE BUT THE OUTER MEDIA, DESIGNERS AND GENERATORS OF THE FINER BODIES IN WHICH WE ASCEND TO GOD. EACH LOWER BODY WE LEAVE, WHEN THE NEXT HIGHER IS FINISHED, AS AN EMPTY SHELL; TAK-ING WITH US, EACH TIME, THE LIFE-SPIRIT, which we ultimately USE IN THE CREATION OF THE GOLDEN BODY-TEMPLE IN WHICH WE DWELL ETERNALLY.

At this time the whole world is to be regenerated. The Lord of Regeneration actually took up His work on earth in August, 1941. The paradoxical manner in which this is being done is hard to understand. Yet, when we study any one thing or activity in this outer world from the viewpoint of ONENESS, all be-comes clarified—understood.

Even the World War of today is not hard to understand if looked upon through the Universal Eye of God, the Father.

We must look upon the whole world just as you might see a sphere whirling in a sea of ether. That sphere is now all colors, apparently the destructive color of "RED" and the "BLACK" color of death predominating, however, when we look at it closely we see beautiful shades of Violet, Green, Pink, Blue and Gold. The basic color, for the total regeneration of the world, is Gold. The Black and Red now flare up. They oppose each other—principally on the Russian-German battlefront—at the moment. Should I have to choose between the two, I should choose Red. Red does represent life, at least, and if handled correctly, through regeneration, becomes the Rose of Perfection. Red symbolizes passion, too, but passion transmuted and regenerated through Christ, becomes Sonship with God. "BLACK" means total absence of Light—NO LIFE.

What is the simple cause of war? Look at our "sphere" again. There you see the different races—also representing various colors and shades of colors, from the blackest races of Africa to the pink-white of the pure Scandinavian races.

It is the unnatural barriers placed between the races by empiric rulers that now cause all wars. Were peoples of this earth left free to travel, to mingle, to go and come as they please, wherever and whenever they chose, so long as they were law-abiding, there would not nor could be any such wars as we have today.

Is it hard for the so-called wise men of today to see that unnatural interference with God's natural laws of amalgamation of the races cause outbreaks of unrestrainable human tendencies and expansions which affect the whole world in its universal processes of regeneration?

I do believe that the ultimate race of super-human beings upon this earth will be of the color of Pure Gold. That will be when the United States of the World will have accomplished World Freedom for all races and peoples—when every human being upon this earth will have had the Divine Right to choose his or her Divine Mate as God intended. Human laws, so long as they correspond with Divine Law, are conducive to this Divine Amalgamation of the Golden Age. We MUST visualize this entire planet a Radiant Orb of Gold. All darkness and uncontrolled passion must be transmuted into the Pure Gold of the Alchemists. Then Peace shall dwell between all mankind and the "lion and the lamb shall lie down together."

Thus, Beloved Students of Truth, you see why I have used Koot Hoomi's slogan of the White Lodge so frequently: ALL LIGHTS UNITED IN THE ONE GREAT LIGHT. This is the time when all Lights, the Unity Workers, Christian Scientists, Rosicrucians, Catholics, Israelites, Buddhists, Mohammedans, Krishnians, Taoists, Christians, Brahmans, and all religionists of the entire world—THOSE OF LIGHT IN EACH GROUP—must unite, if we are to have the Universal Peace we of the Light so earnestly and sincerely desire.

This symbolized picture of the amalgamation of the peoples, from the standpoint of the Goldenization of the human races, I advise science to take up and analyze. It is another New Gold Standard for the world to consider for future use.

When the economists of the world get the view of the philosophers of the world, and actually "take it to Heart," we will get somewhere.

And when a few of our leading economists chance to see a few hundred of their past embodiments and see how many "colors" they have been as they climbed up through the ages, they may, perhaps, be a little more tolerant toward the other races in the world. Remember, Beloved, I told you the Goddess of Light is now embodied in a Negro Body. So What?

"Judge not lest ye be judged." *You* may have to return again.

Regeneration is the most important step of all "I AM" or occult activity, and this is done through Divine Love.

Sexual impotency has no place in regeneration. A person who is not sexually strong could never attain the ascension. It is the lifting up into Christ all forces in our bodies after they are transmuted into the PURE ELECTRONIC SUBSTANCE OF DIVINE LOVE that enables us to ascend in consciousness, in spirit, in body and in mind. If we have not enough force in our bodies and minds to love human beings in physical bodies, certainly we cannot love beings in their spiritual bodies.

There are many people who become impotent and then boast that they have mastered sex. A student who acknowledges he has not mastered, even though he is most passionate, is better fitted to work for the ascension than those who have suppressed sex and become impotent. The persons in this world who accomplish greatness are people of strong sexual powers, but who master them, utilizing them with the brain and mind in creating "that house not made by hands eternal in the heavens," the Golden Body of God—the Christ Body.

"All things are pure to him who is pure in heart," Paul said. As long as we keep our mind in the three higher centers of the physical body—the heart, the throat and the top of the head—even though we be sexually passionate, the Electronic Essence of the seminal forces in the body will rise into the heart and on into the Higher Mental Body.

The ultimate aim of the Master, of course, is to contain all forces, however, such a high point of development in regeneration, must be arrived at gradually so as to keep all organs and centers of generation functioning properly. It is impossible to RE-generate without something to work with. A DEEP DEEP DESIRE to become pure, to lift all into our Christ Body, will accomplish much. Whatever you do in striving for regeneration, have no fear. Never condemn yourself. Any mistakes you might make, call on the law of forgiveness for yourself and others.

Let no one tell you sex does not have its place in regeneration and the ascension. There is a sexual phase to every plane of life, in the physical, the spiritual, the mental, even in plant life. Even the gods and goddesses love one another. As an ascended being I have blended in Spirit with my Twin Ray in the higher planes of Celestial Life, and I know that God Almighty joyously witnessed our blissful repose in the ecstatic Field of Elysium.

There is much regarding sex and regeneration that cannot be published, and there is much of it if published would not be understood, for it must be learned through intuition. When one ascends in consciousness to a certain degree of spiritual lucidity such questions are easily answered. Such matters, however, should be taken up with the Master-Teacher candidly and unreservedly. Students of the Light will be advised in all steps of attainment in the future by various Master-Teachers in the different departments of the New Age School. All will be protected as well as directed. Lord Maitreya will direct all activities under my charge with the assistance of those I choose under His direction.

A question and answer department will render a complete service which will all be rendered under a free-will plan.

For the benefit of students who wish to immediately start action in their individual work I shall provide you a few affirmations for your use, as follows:

I TRANSMUTE AND CHANGE ALL FORCES IN MY THREE LOWER BODIES INTO THE PURE ELECTRONIC SUBSTANCE OF DIVINE LOVE AND DRAW ALL INTO THE AURA OF LORD MAITREYA TO USE AS HE SEES FIT IN THE UPLIFTMENT OF ALL MANKIND.

I RECOGNIZE ONLY THE WHITE-NATURE IN ALL BEINGS ON EARTH.

ALL LIGHTS UNITED IN THE ONE GREAT LIGHT.

I AM THE SPIRIT OF LOVE ENVELOPING THE WHOLE WORLD.

I HAVE A HEART OF GOLD. I AM THE SPIRIT OF LOVE REIGNING THERE.

I AM MASTER OF THE SPIRITS IN MY LIFE-STREAM. I COMMAND ALL OF THEM TO ENTER THE TEMPLE OF LOVE AND WISDOM AND BE INSTRUCTED.

MY PHYSICAL BODY IS THE TEMPLE OF MY HIGHER BODY. ADORABLE PRESENCE OF MINE, I ASK YOU TO MAKE THIS TEMPLE PERFECT THAT YOU MAY DWELL IN IT RIGHT HERE ON EARTH.

I AM ONE WITH SAINT GERMAIN IN HIS SPIRIT —IN HIS WISDOM.

I AM ONE WITH LORD MAITREYA — IN HIS LOVE.

I AM ONE WITH LORD MORYA—IN HIS POWER.

I AM ONE WITH MAHATMA KOOT HOOMI—IN HIS WISDOM.

I AM ONE WITH AVE MARIA—IN HER PURITY AND LOVE.

I AM ONE WITH MASTER JOSHUA — IN HER LOVE.

I AM ONE WITH JESUS—IN HIS LOVE.

I AM ONE WITH THE SILENT WATCHER—IN HIS POWER.

I AM ONE WITH SANAT KUMARA — IN HIS TEMPLE OF WISDOM. HIS SAPPHIRE DIAMOND PROTECTS ME WITH ITS RADIANCE.

I AM ONE WITH KRISHNA—IN HIS GREAT LOVE.

I AM ONE WITH BUDDHA GAUTAMA, LORD OF LORDS—IN HIS LOVE, WISDOM AND POWER.

I AM MASTER OF MY SPIRIT. I GO WHERE I CHOOSE IN SPIRIT. I AM MASTER OF MY ATTEN-TION. I AM MASTER OF THE QUALITY I CHOOSE. I AM THAT I AM. I REMEMBER WHERE I GO IN SPIRIT.

I AM THE LIQUID-LIGHT SUBSTANCE ENFOLD-
ING ME. I SEE IT PENETRATING EVERY CELL OF
MY BODY.

I AM CHARGING THE BREATH I BREATHE
WITH THE LIGHT-SUBSTANCE FROM THE ETHER.
I BREATHE IT INTO MY LUNGS (gently). I DIRECT
IT THROUGH MY GOLDEN HEART INTO MY
BLOOD STREAM. IT HEALS ME INSTANTLY.

I AM BECOMING THE GOLDEN BODY OF GOD—
HIS SON.

I AM WEAVING A GOLDEN GARMENT. MY
HIGHER PRESENCE DIRECTS ME IN ITS CREA-
TION. I WEAR IT WHEN I LEAVE MY PHYSICAL
BODY.

I AM THE DIRECTOR IN ALL ACTIVITY I NEED
TO DO. I AM LIGHT.

Blessed Students of Light, already, as a result of the Golden
Age Manifesto mailed out—published in the "Foreword" of
this book—numerous ones have written to me asking for assistance. All correspondence shall be kindly taken care of. We make
no charge for such service. All is done gladly. We give all,
knowing we shall receive as the Masters of Love see fit. There
is one thing the sincere student should always remember—Christ
cannot be purchased with money. The Greatest Masters I know
have little to do with money, however, their needs, though simple,
are usually supplied by those whom they serve in the outer octave.
He who has little to give, though he give little in proportion, has
given as much—EVEN MORE—as he who may have millions
and gives thousands.

All such matters are left entirely to the student. The Master-
Teacher can easily determine the sincere heart. All receive what
is justly their own. No one can keep what is yours from you,
whether it be wisdom, love, wealth, intelligence, discrimination
or the Transcendent Experience of the Ascension. "TO THINE
OWN SELF BE TRUE!"

*   *   *

During September, 1941, I called twice personally and
phoned two or three times to talk to Charles Sindelar, publisher
of the "VOICE," the official magazine of the so-called Ballard
"I AM" activity.

I wanted very much to talk to Charles at length regarding several important matters. Mr. Sindelar had always been so kindly and considerate to me. The two times I got to talk to him personally he was very busy, therefore I did not feel I should bring up the matters I did so much wish to discuss. We agreed to make a date at some future time when both of us had some leisure time, but since our last brief visit in his home I have, I dare say, been even more busy than Mr. Sindelar, as I have written about 150,000 words for this book as well as other duties I have had to look after. Since what I wished to reveal to him is of great interest to all Students of Light, I shall herein write about it.

In the December, 1939, "VOICE" were two beautiful pictures, one of Our Blessed Jesus the Christ, the other, presumably of the Divine Director Lord Maitreya. They are the two most radiant pictures, I do believe, ever published in the outer octave. Especially, the Maitreya picture, when you look upon it, actually seems to blaze right out at you, overpowering in its Liquid-Light radiance. WHEN I RECEIVED THAT MAGAZINE IN ARCATA, CALIFORNIA, I WAS MORE AMAZED THAN EVER BEFORE IN MY LIFE, I ASSURE YOU.

Just a few weeks previous to the publication of that particular edition of the "VOICE" Magazine—sometime between 11:00 P.M. and 2:00 A.M.—I had experienced a transcendent CHRIST-AT-ONE-MENT. You will understand, Beloved, it was but a few months following my son David's Ascension, and frequently, after my wife and the other children had retired I would sit alone quietly to meditate or read the Blessed Discourses of Brother Guy Ballard and the Ascended Masters. On the particular evening in mind, following a thrilling inspiration, my thoughts definitely went to Charles Sindelar.

I rose to my feet from the chair where I had been sitting for possibly hours (which I sometimes do without moving a muscle), breathed in the Liquid-Light-Substance as I had been taught in the Great Brotherhood, and breathed MY PRESENCE to Charles Sindelar. My HEART ACTUALLY WENT OUT TO HIM. I STOOD IN EXACTLY THE POSITION LORD MAITREYA STANDS IN THAT PICTURE IN THE DECEMBER, 1939, MAGAZINE. I WAS CONSCIOUS OF STANDING RIGHT IN FRONT OF MR. SINDELAR. A GREAT SHAFT OF BLAZING LIGHT POURED THROUGH ME TO HIM. BELOVED,

TEARS STREAMED DOWN MY CHEEKS. I HELD THAT POSE FOR SEVERAL MINUTES. I WAS POSITIVELY AND TANGIBLY HELD IN A PILLAR OF LIGHT-SUBSTANCE.

Recently I spoke to Koot Hoomi about this. He said: "Yes, I understand. When one attains Christhood—Sonship with God —WHEN WE RADIATE TO ANOTHER THE RADIANCE ALWAYS TAKES ON THE SAME UNIVERSAL LORD. LORD MAITREYA ENTERED IN ON YOUR INDIVIDUAL RADIANCE." I have never spoken to Charles Sindelar about this, but I DEARLY LOVE HIM. GOD BLESS HIM. (Had not informed him then.—*Author*.)

Now, Beloved Friend, I am impelled to tell you that I have never seen any picture in all my life that so affected me as that picture. The evening I went home when I first saw it, Mrs. Mary Todd, who then lived with us, and my wife, had seen it before I arrived home that evening. When I entered the living room, there it was, open to that picture, standing on the mantle above the fireplace.

That evening, after all had retired and a deep stillness and "Cosmic Peace" dwelt in the room about me, I sat gazing into those innocent eyes, and drew about me the RADIANCE OF LORD MAITREYA. I felt that I had entered into MY OWN GOD PRESENCE. WE WERE AGAIN ONE IN SPIRIT AND LOVE. I AGAIN WEPT. COMPASSION FILLED MY BEING JUST AS IT DOES THIS MOMENT WHEN I LOOK AT THE PICTURE HERE BY MY TYPEWRITER.

All I ask, Beloved Students of Light, is, "Judge not," for you never know, when meeting a human being, but that you may "be entertaining angels unawares." Distance means nothing to ONE IN CHRIST. Space and time are gone forever, so far as our Great Presence is concerned.

Koot Hoomi also explained to me when I asked Him about the picture incident, that "WE WHO HAVE ASCENDED CAN HELP HUMANITY MUCH MORE IN SECLUSION, SHUT AWAY FROM THE OUTSIDE WORLD, THAN WE CAN BY MINISTERING TO THEM PERSONALLY." He went on to say, "WITH THE ENERGY EXPENDED IN ASSISTING ONE IN THE OUTER WORLD YOU MIGHT BLESS A MILLION HUMAN

BEINGS IN SPIRIT THROUGH THE CHRIST LORD MAITREYA."

How wonderful, Dear Student! You do not have to come here to Mount Olympus to see me for me to help you. Remember this. I can even help you more right where you are if you will become quiet and call to my Higher Presence Saint Germain or LORD MAITREYA. WE ARE WITH YOU ALWAYS. EVEN BEFORE YOU CALL, WE KNOW OF YOUR LOVE AND DESIRE.

Remember, Beloved, the personal things related in this book are of little value. CHRIST IS PRICELESS. I AM THE DOOR. THAT DOOR—THIS DOOR—IS A SPIRITUAL DOOR. JUST VISIT ME IN SPIRIT AND I WILL LEAD YOU INTO HIS TEMPLE—THE TEMPLE OF LORD MAITREYA. I AM THE DOOR.

CHAPTER XXXV

THE MASTER

When you will have known that all lives, all worlds and all realms of being, in their multiplicity, are unified in the ONE CENTER, and that CENTER is in your HEART—then YOU ARE MASTER.

Division is weakness. Unity is power. Love leads to co-operation. Co-operation is unity. When you have managed and mastered the multiplicity of cells within all organs of your body, and have all organs functioning harmoniously with your heart, you are well on the road to mastery. You are the microcosm— the small world. The whole of God's Creation is the Macrocosm.

Your body and all its members and cells is, likewise, a macrocosm. Your body is the physical world. There is a tiny little sun shining in your heart. If it were not for that sun there, you would have no consciousness in your body. You live in your heart. The cells and various members of your body get their Light from the Heart, the Tiny Sun in the center. When all members work in unison you are healthy and happy.

The slightest disturbance in your mind, the Governor of your physical organism, and all processes of activity are thrown out of harmony. With the mind, working through Love and your Heart, you can master all.

There are a great number of students who attain great heights along the path to mastership. The higher one attains the greater dangers one must meet. Very few ever attain complete Mastery. There are many who overestimate themselves after they attain a certain "degree." Naturally, to work with the Gods, you must become a God. God is no respecter of persons. No matter who you are or how high you might think yourself individually or personally, the moment you fail to acknowledge yourself a willing servant of the ONE GOD in accomplishing His Great Purpose in the Golden Age of Man, the Great Masters will stop their radiation and co-operation with you.

I shall give you an example of what this means. I have mentioned several individuals in my narratives regarding my trials, my initiations, and various phases of my and their activities. Much of this had reference to my family, Ave Maria, Lao Tse, Ratana and others whose parts are less important.

A great deal of the instruction—(not all of it)—given by the Ascended Masters to me was given through the body of the person I have referred to as Ave Maria. She was used as a Messenger. Her body was perfect for the use of Koot Hoomi, Saint Germain, Maitreya, Buddha Gautama, Jesus, or any Master who chose. As long as she keeps her body pure, and proves to be master over all weaknesses the human body is heir to, she will be used as a "Temple of the Living God," and the Great Ones will be able to teach others through her. But should she become weak in any respect, she is no longer a Member of the White Brotherhood so far as the outer activity is concerned. Neither can her own Higher Presence, whether it be Ave Maria, Jesus, Buddha Gautama, Joshua or whoever it might be, manifest through her outer body until she again becomes wholly purified in body, mind and spirit.

Many times Koot Hoomi and Lord Maitreya taught me things pertaining to my own individual development through the body of Ave Maria when she knew nothing about it. It was some time after my instruction began before I was informed of that. Finally both KH and Lord Maitreya would tell me when she was not conscious of their instruction and they would also tell me not to inform her of certain matters regarding my work. I was also warned by Koot Hoomi to realize that the amanuensis had not fully mastered and to be on my guard at all times. I was aware of one weakness that person, in the outer, possessed, just as most women do possess it. She was extremely jealous on a few points. I found she was most jealous of her knowledge. The slightest hint that she might not have fully mastered all things and she would become angry. I learned to "let her have her own way about everything." The letter I wrote to her from Bremerton, Wash., under the direction of Lord Maitreya, in a previous chapter, is an instance in which I had to assert my mastery of the situation for her own benefit. She had developed too much toward the Wisdom and Power, and was not manifesting enough of the Love principle. "Ye must become as a little child before you can enter the kingdom of heaven," is a marvelous point stressed by Jesus in His teaching. That is exactly as Ave Maria was most of the time I was being taught by the Masters through her. But occasionally she would become "puffed up" regarding who she IS. After all, it was explained to me by KH and Lord Maitreya that the various High Spirits manifest through us, one after another, until we have attained Christhood or Sonship with God, which is MASTERY. However, I was reminded that the higher we rise the more difficult the tests.

At the present time, December 26, 1941, Ave Maria, Lao Tse and I, Amsumata, stand at a very important cross-roads in our ascending pathway to complete and final mastership. Our advancement depends upon our sacrifices. Jesus said, in other words, "If a man ask you for your coat give him your cloak also." Those who rise with you are naturally the ones who try you. As I have stated to another through correspondence— also published in a previous chapter—"AND KNOW THIS, BROTHER MINE, HE WHO HAS MOST OF LOVE SHALL RISE UPON THE VANQUISHED TO LEAD THE STRUGGLING MASSES OF EARTH'S CHILDREN TO THE 'DOOR' WHICH YOU — APPARENTLY — FAIL TO SEE AND RECOGNIZE. I MEET YOU ON THE BATTLEFIELD OF CHRIST AND *HIS* LOVE GUIDES ME, STREAMING FROM THE PORTAL OF MY *GOLDEN HEART*." I give all to my friends, and to my enemies, alike. I love all. "With love I rise above my enemies."

Those who separate themselves from Me, choose multiplicity. Those who choose to stand by me, choose peaceful unity. It is easy to determine the White Brothers, for They KNOW ME, for my Unity. The White Brothers always co-operate. The Black Brothers always separate. Separating means devolution. Co-operating means evolution. Separating, one falls. Co-operating, one rises. Hate disintegrates. Love integrates. Hate destroys. Love heals. The White Brother wishes to possess nothing in the outer. The Black Brother wants all things and will fight any and all who might wish to dispossess him of anything.

The unifying power of Christ at this time throughout the entire world—even in spite of the World War—is marvelous to those who stop a moment to meditate upon it. "BE STILL AND KNOW I AM GOD." Those who allow disturbance of any kind to come into their minds, even though they be of the "degree" I AM, they shall "FALL."

Blessed Koot Hoomi, Ave Maria and I made certain vows to each other on Mt. Shasta, in the presence of the Lord of

Creation. "The Silent Watcher (Amsumata), with His Eye of Yoga, sees the need of Light and Love in all human creation. Through His Chain of Blue Light the Power of Krishna and God Almighty pours forth to do His WILL. Love Reigneth in His Golden Heart, Wisdom on His Brow, and through the Loving co-operation of Ave Maria (In Spirit) and Mahatma Koot Hoomi the Golden Age now becomes the Transcendent Blessing of all Mankind."

O M! O M! O M! AUM! AUM! AUM! I AM! I AM! I AM!

Many will ask: "Well, why is Amsumata chosen 'Chief Avatar'?" Beloved students of Light, it was simply because of my Divine Inheritance. For thousands of years, in hundreds of embodiments I have proved faithful to the One Almighty God. Just previous to this embodiment I was a Hindu in India. Koot Hoomi knows this. I lived in India in that embodiment about 33 years. Just previous to that embodiment I was Abraham Lincoln. In another embodiment I was Saint Germain. In still another embodiment I was a great English poet. During the time of the early Christian era I was a Pope of the Roman Catholic Hierarchy. During the time of Jesus I was His brother, John. So, you see, friends, it is not what I have done in this embodiment that caused me to be chosen as the "Chief Avatar." Those are just a few of my embodiments I have mentioned. It is my record of the past, however, with all I have done in God's kingdom on earth, which places upon me at this time my spiritual responsibilities. I do not claim a single thing of myself. In fact Koot Hoomi himself has told me in the past that I was not ready enough to accept the office I have been chosen to fill.

Again, in regard to certain bodies being used by the Ascended Masters, I wish to make this very clear: Those who understand the law well enough in their outer mind, and have mastered all human weaknesses, become Servants of God—Gods Incarnate. Those who fail to master, become Servants of Satan—Devils Incarnate. Should one get the idea that he or she is Master before declared so by an Ascended Master, then the Light from the Great White Lodge is no longer radiated to that one, and eventually they come to find they are alone in UTTER DARKNESS. Should we remain obedient to our Master-Teacher as well as the ONE MASTER CHRIST Lord Maitreya until told that we are FREE and have the protection of the Ascended

297

Masters, then there is no danger of the Lower Spirits taking possession of our "Temple"—the human body.

Each embodiment we have lived in the past we created an individual spirit. Every one of those spirits must be lined up with God before we can ascend. Each is a branch of our Tree of Life. Some of them must be pruned, others consumed entirely, still others that have fruit (Divine Inheritance) must be brought into the granary (The Heart) in the creation of the Golden Body in which we consciously ascend.

Occasionally we see those who consider themselves masters. They may even know that they were some great teacher, near-master or prophet of the past. However, there are many other embodiments that must be accounted for. There may be a certain spirit in your life-stream that was just as evil as the other was good. That evil one wants to manifest "in earth" too. There is where some transmutation must take place. That evil spirit in your Sky Tree must be "bleached" and made white through your own purity of mind and regeneration.

Frankly, I had considerable difficulty with the Spirit of Lincoln. I was told by Ave Maria more than once to order him into the Temple of Wisdom where he would learn needed lessons and accomplish certain celestialization before he *AND I* could ascend. Soon after the spirit of Lincoln ascended, then I—MASTER OVER THIS BODY—also ascended.

Just as a little matter of confirmation to you, to accept or not as you see fit,—I was present at my own funeral (Lincoln's) in Washington, before the body was shipped back to Illinois. I heard the bell tolling, slowly, as the minister began to read the service. He said: "This country has not met such a terrible catastrophe since 1773." I am not real certain about the date that was spoken now, for it has been several years ago since I looked that up in my life-stream. I had many other experiences in the spirit of Lincoln for which I do not have time nor space to describe. Others, too, have seen much to prove to them my spiritual lineage. It will be, I am sure, consoling to many "I AM" students to know, anyhow, that Saint Germain was the Higher Body watching over Lincoln when embodied, just the same as He is now watching over me, along with His Master-Teacher, Lord Maitreya, Christ to this Universe.

So, friends, should Ave Maria (outer body) and Lao Tse remain true to me, as they have vowed, IN DIVINE LOVE, then they shall remain Members of the Great White Lodge. The same is true of myself. So long as I am WITH CHRIST and He is with me, WHO CAN BE AGAINST ME?

When you, Beloved, are in perfect harmony with your Higher Presence, then the Gods do come into your Temple. Then is when the MASTER comes to talk with you. THIS IS INSPIRATION.

My prayer, my decree, is that all Great Masters now embodied, be able to bring that MASTERY through perfectly into their outer Temples.

CHAPTER XXXVI

HUMAN GRADES, CLASSES AND BROTHERHOODS

One of the great laws of ancient philosophy, as quoted by the first known philosopher, Hermes, was, "As above so below; as below so above." What he had reference to, we believe, was the different grades of beings, including the higher and lower planes of life and vibration, the physical, etheric, spiritual and pure electronic realms of consciousness. When we consider all the sciences as taught in our higher schools of learning such as chemistry, biology, theology, archaeology, genealogy, and the many many others that have to do with every form of life— animate as well as inanimate—and how they are so orderly classified, blending and inter-blending, how can one question the SUPREME INTELLIGENCE as the CENTER from which the billions of radii of every conceivable idea or thing MUST inevitably radiate or issue? There is now fast coming into manifestation an "inner school" which will come to be an adjunct of all higher schools and universities, wherein all the sciences will terminate into the MAIN STEM and ULTIMATE and ABSOLUTE knowledge of ALL LIFE—THE WHOLE—THE "I AM." When this comes forth in its entirety the super-human race will have charge of this earth and the perfection conceived for this planet even before it came into being, will manifest in all its wondrous splendor. This is no "pipedream"—it is the actual unfoldment of the eternal verity.

To advance in life, man must first realize that he is actually "on his way," FROM one state of being TO some other state, and as all other forms of life that come under our observation seem to evolve into higher forms, it is but natural to think of man as travelling on a "radii" UPWARD from the center of dense physicality (darkness) toward the "Central Sun," or center of LIGHT. This, we must realize, is not only true universally, but individually, as well, for the microscopic "light centers" of each and every atom in our physical bodies, DO gradually blend into one "Light Center," which we KNOW is within the heart. Now, that YOU are aware of your being on this

300

"radii," you begin to develop your innate powers of "Light" instead of merely evolving as you may have done heretofore. "Seek the light."

The preponderance of human creative thought from thousands of years in the past, is a massive, colossal bugaboo the "Children of Light" must dissolve, transmute and requalify into the substantiation of the coming New Age—the Golden Age— God's dream of earthly perfection. Just as we, the mass humanity of earth, inadvertently wove and enmeshed ourselves in this "dark" density of physicality, now we must advertently and attentively give conscious force and momentum to the dispelling, dissolution and requalification of the life, substance and energy we have so badly misused. The world at present is in a state of flux, as it were, and it is most imperative that the greater and more illumined minds give particular attention to the purification of the earth sphere in preparation for the incoming influx of Cosmic Light Substance—"the Golden Snow"—, the foundation upon which, and the substance from which, the Golden Age shall be born.

That there are classes and grades of human beings, some lower and some higher, intelligent and ignorant, cultured and uncultured, no one can deny. These groups and classes, nationalities, religious denominations and brotherhoods, have existed many thousands of years upon earth. Today they are no doubt more numerous than ever in the history of the world. Each race has its subdivisions; each nation, religious denomination, industrial organization, is regimented according to "higher-ups," who rule or direct them. The Roman Catholic Church is the best example of regimentation in the outer life and is international in its far-reaching dominance and activity. It also has an esoteric or "inner" order which is strictly disciplinarian in its nature, and in which are embraced a number of brotherhoods, some of whom are most holy and educationally constructive; others, however, according to historical records of their diabolical activities, were mysteriously superstitious, and practiced what was and is known as the "black arts." The church is not wholly rid of this diabolical art yet, and this I proved myself. We need only to look up the history of the Church to prove what I say. The fact that some priests of the Church have, in recent years, to my knowledge, practiced black art, does not lead me to think all priests of the Church do practice it. There are many blessed ones in that church, and the "light" is becoming so prevalent throughout the world it is but a matter of time until all such "black" activity is "consumed" through the intensity of the Great Cosmic Light on this planet. Even the black robes worn by most Catholic priests and nuns will someday be displaced and robes symbolic of purity, chastity, beauty, wisdom, intelligence, will be worn by them. At that time the "White Pope" will sit at Rome. By a single decree the color of all clothes and vestments worn by the pope, cardinals, bishops, priests, nuns and all ecclesiastics, will be changed from black to white, clear blues, pinks, goldens and violets. Black and red will be out entirely, for they are destructive colors. Black symbolizes death, red indicates passion, danger or destruction. However, red also symbolizes Life, and when transmuted becomes pure Gold. Clear, bright blue, pink, gold and violet, represent power, joy, love and purification, respectively. White, the absence of color, comprises all colors, and represents purity, of course. Clear green symbolizes health and opulence. The Roman Catholic Church is on the verge of the greatest reforms ever experienced in its history. Although very slow in conforming to world changes in the past, the dominating power of world-wide educational activities of recent years is forcing the Church to adopt the current world reforms. She must do this in order to hold her fast-diminishing power and membership. The greater part of the ritualistic and symbolic work of the Church of the past was laid around the "crucifixion." In the future it will stress the "ascension." The crucifixion, of course, symbolizes death; the ascension, "life everlasting." *

Just about ever since Caesar went over to the British Isles to conquer the Britons in the first century the British have been the prevailing enemies of Rome. Today there seethes, unnoticed by the outside world, the "battle of Armegeddon" being fought between these forces, principally in the etheric plane, but also in the most subtle ways right here in the physical octave, the forces of the Democracies of the world, the British Empire of which is the European leader, the WAR OF THE AGES is being fought. England has been the citadel of freedom for hundreds of years. Practically all the principles of freedom that have

---

*I am quite aware that there are certain dignitaries of the established Church who wear robes and vestments of various colors, some of which are red, but in the mention of colors, the author wishes to convey the idea that the colors adopted will symbolize the total purification of the Church and all its ecclesiastics. The correct colors and symbolism will aid in bringing about that purification, just as the actual purification of a thing is bound to be symbolized by its outer or physical manifestation.

become the common heritage of the peoples of the world have come from England. England has been the "big brother" to smaller nations for several centuries. The Magna Charta Libertatum, the foundation upon which all the liberties of the English speaking peoples have been based since 1215, came from England. The Constitution of the United States of America is the greatest guarantee of freedom that has ever been produced upon this earth. The Masonic Fraternity—Free Masons, as they are called—was the basic structure upon which these guarantees of freedom developed. "Light," and its accompanying means of radiation and education (illumination and enlightenment) are symbolized by Masonry, and are clearly delineated throughout the constructive progress made in the world by the Democracies, a progress whose advance is gloriously marked here and there by evidences of the Great Work as symbolized by Free Masonry. The democracies of the world are the nations who foster such principles. America is today the greatest of these, and will soon take her place as the "Light of the world."

Where do the brotherhoods enter into the matter of governments and the freedom and liberty the people—the common people—strive for? Theirs is the most vital activity upon this earth. While they have labored, one on the side of "Light," and the other on the side of "Darkness," yet both, from all outward appearances (especially to the unlearned and unenlightened), strive for the highest of virtues. The subtlety by which the so-called Black Brotherhood has endeavored to hide its diabolical activities has been the enigma of the ages, but their days are numbered. The "Light" of the New Golden Age is becoming more and more intense. All human darkness is being consumed. All deceit and nefarious work on the part of such groups and international organizations is fast being revealed to the "light of a new day." The plans of the sinister forces for America will never come to fruition. Every move they make is known by the Ascended Masters, and even un-ascended masters, who are ever in constant touch with the gods, goddesses and all Ascended Beings who have full charge of all activities on this planet.

Should you have studied ancient Egyptian history, ancient China, Persia, the Hebrew Bible—the New and the Old Testaments—, then you no doubt have observed how certain brotherhoods played a great part in the activities of man down through the ages. These brotherhoods, in the outer world, were usually built up around some great characters such as Osiris, Hermes,

Confucius, Tao-Sea, Mohamet, Melchizedek and many others time and space do not permit mentioning. For example in the old Testament of the Holy Bible, Psalm 110: "The Lord said unto my Lord, Sit thou at my right hand, until I make thine enemies thy footstool." Verse 4, just below: "The Lord hath sworn, and will not repent, Thou art a priest for ever after the order of Melchizedek." "The Lord said unto my Lord," would mean in the terms of the true Rosicrucian Fraternity, "God spoke to my Soul." The version of the "I AM" Activity is: "The Mighty 'I AM' Presence said to My Higher Mental Body." The order of Melchizedek is mentioned many places in the Old as well as the New Testament. Moses, Elijah, Ezekiel, Enoch, Solomon, Jesus and Saint John the Revelator, Mary the Mother of Jesus, as well as numerous others, were members of the Order of Melchizedek. There is very much evidence to bear this out, should one take the time to investigate. When once you discover all these things so clearly brought out in the Bible, you will be amused at yourself and the entire world for not having observed them before. That order still exists today and is even flourishing now in a manner it never did before on earth.

The true Rosicrucian Order is really an outpost of the Order of Melchizedek, the Mormon Church embraces a branch of the Order, the Roman Catholic Church, in its silent and mysterious way, no doubt, has a number of initiates among its membership. Even among the laity of other religious denominations, as well as among the great mass of humankind outside of any church so-called, to him who KNOWS and SEES with the "ALL-SEEING EYE," there are numerous ones who are members of the Order of Melchizedek, some unaware of it, others conscious of their constant training and instruction in the great Laws of Life. You might ask, "How and why would one be a member of such an order and not know about it?" Read Job 33:14 to 17, which ends up with, "That he (God) may withdraw man from His purpose, and hide pride from man."

My dear reader, you are blessed indeed should you have read thus far the memoirs of me, one who feels impelled to record these things that they may be guide-posts to others who tread the uncertain pathway of human life. I have had so very much proof of life beyond, even in numerous realms of being, that I could no more doubt my own eternal existence and individual consciousness than the most impossible thing you can imagine. I can frankly and honestly say that I have never once doubted the existence of God during my entire life. When a tiny babe I felt as though swathed in bands of streaming light. As I grew to manhood many were the times I spoke to myself thus: "Whatever befalls me I shall never deny God." There is so very much evidence of unending life for you, friend, and every person on earth, that the strange part of it to me is that everybody does not see it. Why should people doubt? Why do not all see the beauty and goodness in all life? The story of the Prodigal Son explains it all more or less.

The earth, I believe, is not so ancient as planets go. God, or the gods (as is stated in the Bible) established life upon this planet in much the same way as you, were you a great lord and land-owner, would start a new colony or settlement upon a distant section of your enormous holdings. In your new settlement, you give them all rights and privileges, on an equal with yourself, and you tell them they must, if they continue to be happy and well provided for, respect certain natural laws of life. You even caution them that unless they follow those rules of life, they will suffer and may die. The lord (the Father) loves his children, his subjects, and He wants them to realize just how HE FEELS, ENJOYS what HE IS, so he explained to them before he sent them out to the new settlement that they would have to put on different garments, earthly apparel. However, He also instructed them thus: "Remember I AM your Father; remember your source, and the Life I AM in you, and whenever you doubt or feel the need of ME, recall to yourself that I AM in thee. You ARE that I AM, so whenever you call to ME, just say to yourself 'I AM THAT I AM that I used to be;' yes, or 'I AM forever THAT same I AM,' and I will come to you, for I AM the ALL-PRESENCE. I AM the WHOLE (the Holy Father) and all beings, all life, all things, come from MY HEART—the Great Central Sun of all LIFE."

You and I, my friend, are that New Settlement. Yes, it has been but a short time, as time may go with the gods, since we came to earth. In our hearts we remember. In our minds, the outer consciousness we use in the physical octave, we are steeped in the luring enchantment of physical things. There have always been a few of us, however, who remembered our Lord's admonition. Those were and are members of the Great Brotherhood He has maintained here among us Settlers. Moses, Ezekiel, Elijah, Solomon, Job (Elihu), Ruth, David, John the Baptist, Jesus, Saint John, Mary the Mother of Jesus, and many many others mentioned in the Bible, were members of the White Brotherhood. There have been hundreds since then, too, but the narrowness of religious sectarianism prevented them being recognized. Churchism and anti-Christ activities under the guise of Christianity—the activity of the Black Brotherhood (fallen angels)—, those so steeped in materialism that they had entirely forgotten their source, the "I AM," "crucified" every member of the True Brotherhood they could find. During the Dark Ages they were tracked like beasts of prey, burned at the stake, and tortured in every conceivable way, but they returned again and again "in the flesh,"—that earthly apparel—to try to get their brothers and sisters to realize their SOURCE—GOD—THE FATHER—THE I AM.

It is easy to recognize the members of the Brotherhood down through the ages, even since Jesus, who was sent by the Lord as a Special Envoy. Socrates, Plato, Epictetus, Pythagoras, Paracelsus and numerous other Greek masters. King Arthur, though more or less mythical, represented the Brotherhood. Joan of Arc was a true initiate. Shakespeare (Francis Bacon), without a doubt, was one of the greatest beings ever to embody on earth, and is now known to students of the "I AM" as Saint Germain, an Ascended Master, as is also Jesus, and many others I shall mention later. Benjamin Franklin, Washington, Thomas Paine, Lincoln, Ballou, and many others in America, were members of the True Brotherhood, as is evidenced in their writings and earthly activities, especially to those who KNOW THE LAW. Madam Blavatsky, who established the Theosophical Society, was a great Initiate, as were those who followed her in carrying out her work. Paschal Beverly Randolph, who in the middle of the nineteenth century, established the activity of the Rosicrucians in America on a much larger scale than theretofore, was indeed a great master.

CHAPTER XXXVII

A TRUE ROMANCE

On my discharge from the army in 1918 I went to Fairfield, Illinois, to visit an old bachelor friend of mine who lived six miles out in the country. He had been a close neighbor to us when we lived on the farm there nine years previous. I wanted to go back there to see the boyhood friends whom I had not seen for many years as well as to visit with my friend C. B. C. was about forty-five years old at that time, I would judge, was a faithful Catholic and had raised a niece and two nephews— children of an older sister who had married a Protestant. There had always been a peculiar spirit about that place that seemed to call me back there. Even today I would like to visit that country neighborhood. M............ B............ and his large family, with many others, come trailing back to my mind as I scan the distant mental horizon lingering there. The cylindrical record Edison Phonograph at C............ B............'s place, his old time fiddling, the singing bees and popcorn balls and taffey-pullings impressed deeply lessons in mannerisms of southern Illinois country folk upon my youthful mind. Memory of childish pleasantries called me there once more.

My two weeks' visit ended, while in Fairfield with C............ one day I casually entered the Wayne County Press newspaper office, where I procured a position as printer, with some time spent on the outside as reporter. John Cooper was a well known and much beloved editor. He was a law partner of Mayor Burgess, whose daughter, Jesse, I had met during the short time I attended McKendree College. Due to my connection with the newspaper and my acquaintanceship with the Burgesses and Coopers, I was drawn into the best social group of the city. Private parties and dances were popular in this inland city. I first accompanied Miss Burgess, then her younger sister, as well as numerous other young ladies, to the various social affairs. Although I had never been much of a socialite, I seemed to be very desirable company so far as the young women of the city were concerned. I was handsome in those days, rather quiet when in a group, but with a philosophical mind, a student's air and convincing manner, I easily won my intimate friends to my way of thinking. I could clearly see they actually enjoyed my ready speculations on life, and not having yet learned that all people were not philosophers, and not realizing that I myself was one, I assure you that my eagerness to talk of life and the serious angles of its activities led to strange episodes in my associations with young people of my own age. I did not understand myself, but others knew far less of me and my idiosyncrasies. There was so very much welling up within me that I could not express, I am sure it was the unexpressed phases of my inner intelligence that gave me a distinguished appearance in spite of my limited understanding, or to better put it, abbreviated schooling. It took me but a short time to get my fill of social life. I was entirely too studious and moody to continue long in such an atmosphere. I was not interested in the shallow topics discussed by those with whom I came in contact. I felt out of place, and decided to abandon all society, secure some good literature and study earnestly the style of writing of the better authors. I recall that I chose "David Copperfield" by Charles Dickens as the first volume to receive my undivided attention and painstaking perusal. Three months I pored over that story, critically observing his style of punctuation, phraseology and general outline. It was for the purpose intended.

There came times during my studies I was very lonely. This is natural for a man at the age of twenty-one. Man, in his unfoldment, is much like a plant—a rose, for instance—and his natural instinctive impulses, along the pathway of life, definitely determine his degree of enlightenment or illumination. I had not met the girl among the numerous ones I singled out who approached my ideal of womanhood. I, like most young men of my age, thought women experienced the same reactions, sensations and emotional feelings as myself, and I looked for a girl who at least showed some inclination toward the analysis of life. Such a girl did appear on the scene.

Miss Marion Singleton, charming daughter of a Fairfield banker, informed me on a chance meeting down town that she had a girl friend who wished very much to meet me and she had arranged to have a party at her home as a means of introducing us. Since I had not taken part in any social affairs for some time, I thoroughly enjoyed the party and met Miss Edythe Warren, the girl of my dreams, a daughter of the Wayne County Sheriff.

Edythe was eighteen, rather tall, slender, dark hair, quiet and introspective. She was, as my ideal should be, contemplative of life and observing and thoughtful enough, and with a mind of her own, at least to the extent that she had planned on meeting me and the plan worked. She had heard of me, I had been pointed out to her, and, as a consequence she wanted to meet that "strange young man" whom the other girls could not fathom. It was much like "love at first sight." We were congenial friends from the first. She did not dance, but in many other ways she made up for that. She could improvise beautifully at the piano— a mark of intuitional prompting that captivated me. She could converse intelligently regarding the more ecstatic things of life. She was imaginative, and could talk of the beauties of earthly scenes as well as the raptures of human emotions. Particularly the sunny afternoons we spent together come back again and again to my mind, when we strolled along flower-bedecked country lanes just outside the city limits, or sat beneath an apple-blossomed tree in a distant corner of a rolling meadow. I was in love. We were in love. The world was in love. Love cast its splendor all about us, created an impenetrable wall just beyond the confines of our happy sphere, and lulled us into such blissful repose that we lived, thought and dreamed as one. Edythe was a favorite among her friends. That old quotation, "Everybody loves a lover," certainly fit into our picture. Our love affair was the talk of the town. I could sense it everywhere I went. Her friends were very happy that she had found a man she could love and one who would love her. It was all too wonderful to last.

"Love is blind," it is said. I was in love, I am sure, according to all outward symptoms, but there suddenly occurred within me a veritable battlefield upon which was fought the "battle of the ages," the fight between my intuitional or higher self and the physical self and its intellectual vanity. The "voice" within me distinctly told me to "flee from this love," while the physical and magnetic individual I was, definitely informed me that I could not "Live without her," that my life and happiness depended upon her, "the girl of my dreams." Now, my dear reader, upon this battlefield men either rise or fall. That "love" of your "ideal" either becomes a propagator of the human species in the physical "field" or a progerminator of creative ideas and immortality in the cosmic or celestial "field." One is intellectual, the other intuitional.

309

In order to explain clearly and exactly what I mean, I shall give you a true-to-life analogy—the love of Abraham Lincoln for Ann Rutledge. It was said of Ann Rutledge: "She was a beautiful girl, and as bright as she was beautiful. She was well educated for that early day, a good conversationalist, and always gentle and cheerful. A girl whose company people liked." Ann Rutledge was disappointed in love previous to Lincoln's love for her, but they had planned on getting married the following year. She died while in Kentucky visiting relatives. I quote the following from "The Life of Abraham Lincoln," by Ida M. Tarbell:

"It was not until McNeill, or McNamar (her former lover), had been gone many months, and gossip had become offensive, that Lincoln ventured to show his love for Ann, and then it was a long time before the girl would listen to his suit. Convinced at last, however, that her former lover had deserted her, she yielded to Lincoln's wishes and promised, in the spring of 1835, soon after Lincoln's return from Vandalia (state legislature), to become his wife. But Lincoln had nothing on which to support a family—indeed, he found it no trifling task to support himself. As for Ann, she was anxious to go to school another year. It was decided that in the autumn she should go with her brother to Jacksonville and spend the winter there in an academy. Lincoln was to devote himself to his law studies; and the next spring when she returned from school and he had been admitted to the bar, they were to be married.

"A happy spring and summer followed. New Salem took a cordial interest in the two lovers and presaged a happy life for them, and all would undoubtedly have gone well if the young girl could have dismissed the haunting memory of her old lover. The possibility that she had wronged him, that he might reappear, that a torturing conflict of memory, love, conscience, doubt, and morbidness lay like a shadow across her happiness, and wore upon her until she fell ill. Gradually her condition became hopeless; and Lincoln, who had been shut from her, was sent for. The lovers passed an hour alone in anguished parting, and soon after, on August 25, 1835, Ann died.

"The death of Ann Rutledge plunged Lincoln into the deepest gloom. The abiding melancholy, that painful sense of the incompleteness of life which had been his mother's dowry asserted itself. It filled and darkened his mind and his imagination tortured him with its black pictures. One stormy night Lincoln was sitting beside William Greene, his head bowed on his hand, while tears trickled through his fingers; his friend begged him to control his sorrow, to try to forget. 'I cannot,' moaned Lincoln; 'the thought of the snow and rain on her grave fills me with indescribable grief'."

The above episode of Lincoln's life, as related by Miss Tarbell, gives one a very clear idea of the beginning of Lincoln's grief—just the beginning. The small part of that grief expressed is like a drop of water compared to the ocean of sorrow he must have experienced as the years came and went—the love for his ideal Ann—that unrequited love that generates within the heart of man the ideation of genius, the magic power of a superman. Lincoln is quoted as having said many years later: "I really and truly loved the girl and think often of her now, . . . and I have loved the name of Rutledge to this day." Lincoln's life and ambition were almost blasted by the brooding gloom that surrounded him for months following the death of Ann, and, I dare say, there were moments of sadness that gripped him as the result of her passing, right up to the last year of his life. Ann Rutledge was Lincoln's inspiration. Had she not been removed from him through death he probably would never have become the great emancipator he afterward became. The love of a man's ideal "in his heart" has far more potent power and influence for the good of the world than a man's love for a woman herself, provided, of course, the idealist has a constructive aim in life and the potential abilities or capabilities for attainment. Without inspiration there can be no genius. Without the ideal love alluded to above, with its corresponding human affection maintained pure and unadulterated IN HIS HEART, idealistically envisaged, man has a small opportunity indeed of attaining greatness of any kind in this world. Even dark, brooding moments of intense gloom, as the result of our "unrequited love," feeds the "light" within our breast, causing it to expand, expand and expand, creating vacuums, as it were, in which to house the power and inspiration of genius. It is a peculiar paradox that unsatisfied cravings mastered are the stepping stones to greatness.

> In our saddest moments,
> In the gloom,
>   Is when our mind's at ferment
> If we give it room.
>
>   When the sky is darkened,
> Your heart is blue,
>   Is when you do your thinkin',
> When it comes thru.

Never fear the shadow
When your thots are grey;
Seeds will never blossom
If on top the earth they lay.

Too frequently we fear the very thing or experience that happens to be our greatest helper in disguise. Repeatedly this has been stated by various poets and writers in numerous versions down through the ages, but seldom do you see such statements analyzed and explained so ordinary minds might understand them. Why should darkness be the mother or father of anything? What important part does it play in the gestation of "life, light and love?" The fecundity of darkness in every phase of life is undeniably the most mystery-wrought field of all human speculation. "The night side of life," one writer expresses it. I explained my thought briefly regarding this in another of the verses I wrote in 1933 entitled "Awakening:"

Better study nature fairly;
Plant a little seed some day;
Press it down beneath the surface;
In the darkness let it stay.

Air, light and moistened earth,
In brooding darkness there,
Will bring to life another birth
Enriching you with fruit most fair.

Darkness would seem to be the universal storehouse from which we as Beings of Light draw our energies for activities in this mundane sphere. Just as the earth, in its rotation around its axis, is enshrouded in darkness half the time, we, as physical beings, living on "mother earth," must conform to her "ways and means" of resuscitation, until ultimately as earth beings we have generated and regenerated the light substance from the "night side" of life and attain the summum bonum—perfection such as Jesus claimed.

Are you so doubtful as to think
That souls are planted here;
Pressed into the earth to sink
By ruthless nature without care?

312

Better think you're like a seed
Pressed beneath the flowering sod
With a mighty spark and speed
To know at once the Light of God!

Just how the forces of life played upon my love and court-ship the following few months I shall sometime explain. My heart was all but broken by the trying ordeal, and yet I persisted in faithfully standing by the promptings of my deeper intuition, but at the time I was most uncertain about which way I should go.

CHAPTER XXXVIII

GODS INCARNATE ON EARTH

In 1938, while many discourses were being received and expressed by Guy W. Ballard, the accredited Messenger of the Saint Germain "I AM" activity, other discourses were being received by other Messengers, some of which were not to be disclosed to the world until the psychological time. At the height of the Ballard activity many of us wondered why the God of Love and the Goddess of Love did not come forth to give discourses, since all the others had favored the world with their blessings.

The following discourse, dictated through one of the great Christ-Channels on this earth at this time by the Goddess of Love, in Los Angeles, July 7, 1938, will answer many questions for the "I AM" students which Blessed Guy Ballard left unanswered because he could disclose to the outer world but what the Masters determined, since he was but a messenger:

> Discourse Given By the three Great Masters, Hilarion, K.H. and the Super Spirit, the Hidden One, thru the channel, or Logos, known to the planet earth as K. P.

Hail Masters! Peace profound—to the rose, to the cross, to the sun and to the flame; and to all the Great Ones descending therefrom into the darkened but rising planet called the earth. To all the Great Ones within God's great Universe, we face the Light and say, "Thy will be done—not my will, not my brother's will, not my sister's will, but the Will of the Great Infinite Father of Great Infinite Spirits controlling this channel being used, being focused upon and electrified in the use and the service of the great Ascended Masters, Who are in control of the rising of the Light and fire spiraling the destiny of the planet earth."

I am in the center, tonight, of the great fiery triangle, blazing with Light, blazing with electrons, whose heat atoms make up this fiery triangle of intensity, second to none. On the top of the spiral of this triangle stands the great Master of Light,

Hilarion, Who has, and has had, in His charge and control, avatars since the Word was first sent forth that the planet earth should be. He it is Who has directed and taught at least, if not for a long duration, at least for some space of time, every avatar, every saviour of humanity, be they in male bodies or female bodies, at some time or other in their great upward step toward Mastery. Were they not chosen by the Cosmic to be avatars to some portion of humanity, or some condition in the planet, He would never be asked by the Powers ruling Him to waste a moment of His time training these.

To my left on this fiery triangle stands my ever-present Master KH; to my right stands the Master, the Supreme Spirit of the Hidden One; within the center dot stands the channel of the Great Infinite Spirit in control; and we ask you to see yourselves again in the great Temple room wherein you in your appointed place, are ready for only a portion from the Fourth Alchemist. Only a portion will be given tonight, for certain reasons known to the channel. The whole discourse would have been forthcoming had conditions been different, but we will give you tonight the portion that you must bear at this time.

We, the Masters, stand guard over this channel while the Alchemist appears and relates to you a discourse in part, that He related unto you many, many centuries ago. The great Master is appearing tonight. He steps from behind a very luminous, white portiere that has been thrown across the entire platform, and for a special purpose. This luminous, brilliant, white portiere will throw upon you students a vital force which the Masters have decided is needed for purification, and your understanding which seems at times to be shadowed. The Alchemist is in His place. He says:

"My dear one, this night if you could see from your plane of expression as We do from ours, you would not need this lesson. We have spoken so often of love, of kindness, of tolerance, obedience, simplicity and above all, that you each are at such a place upon the Path that we have granted unto you, We, the Ascended and Cosmic Beings, the full authorization to be governed and controlled by your own Great Infinite Self, and the Master-Teachers working with you, and We are insisting upon that tonight. Just for this once and never again do we hope to have to repeat it. The channel used is twenty-four hours of the day in full obedience to the Masters controlling her, and her own great Infinite Spirit, and We of the three on the triangle of fire,

315

and others, say that there is no need for anyone to offer any hindrance to that control. She is sealed, guarded, guided and protected, and knows, if no one else does, that she has signed and taken the oath of renunciation, which places her always, at all times, under our guidance. She, at all times, as a human person, feels the lash of the whip and feels at times she could relax from that, but it is not so, and never again will be so. She can have no desire of any kind of herself ever again.

"To the right of me, as I speak, is the Master of the Fourth Alchemical Chamber, the Great Laboratory of Infinite Spirit, and there stands the legions of angels who have control of the swords of blue lightning. Last week, we stepped aside for the great Master Lanto, who told you at that time what these hosts of angelic Beings were doing of Themselves, and through certain perfected instruments, also the full use of this sword of the blue lightning. How it was sweeping through your administration buildings in the city of Los Angeles, and make no mistake it is the city of the angels, for the hand, or mind of man never gave this spot that name. Not only in your administration buildings is this sword being used, but it is being swung with a mighty and tremendous force through all channels that call themselves Light. They are not attacking only the dark places, but the light places as well, and why does the Great Infinite God permit that?

"While yet you are in physical bodies there is much need of this sword of blue lightning. No matter which of you it is, you must face that fact, and as long as there is one iota of self or desire left in you, that sword will sway and swing within your aura and world until every vestige is brought low by your own guiding Infinite Spirit.

"You are in wonderful days, for the 100,440 type of which each of you are included, are just on the verge of a revelation and the unveilment of the ages. Hidden within this nine type are the hidden angels of Light—the hidden Lords of Hosts—the hidden Lords of the Flame—the hidden Lords of the Race—the hidden Lords of Light, elected, projected from the moment that Time began upon the planet earth. That is why there is so much confusion. The forces of darkness are standing in full armor to prohibit the unveilment of the elect, but nevertheless, though dark be the times, the clock of the Father hath struck and the unveiling, and the placing of each of these great Lights, hidden within physical forms, is now taking place.

"Remember the Biblical injunction: 'Two shall be sleeping in a bed, one shall be taken, the other one left. Two shall be grinding at the mill, one taken, one left.' What does it mean? Another night we will give to you a full lecture upon this.

"As sons and daughters of Light, at the separation of this type, marriage and inter-marriage with the sons of men, was in direct controversy against the issue at the time of the Creation, and we have just now arrived at the point where, in spite of all difficulties of ages passed, the sons and daughters of Light, the great Lords and Masters, hidden within human forms, will be separated Eternally from the sons and daughters of men. There are two distinct types treading the earth plane today and it is not given unto the type called the sons and daughters of men to be Lords and Masters in this cycle of Time. That is only for the hidden lights of God.

"The second point tonight: Each of you are being trained in the law of precipitation. Before we go further, this channel has been directed by the Alchemist of the Fourth Division to give His description. He is a Hindu Master and has completely surrounded the face of this channel; but she is conscious of His mouth, nose, eyes and other features.

"There is a fact that can be recorded, and it will be a joy to you. A joy as of the living waters to each—it is truly a fact, you have been faithful on Thursday evenings in this Sanctuary, and also as a matter of record, the channel used tonight has for nearly six years past always held, worked with, or was in, a secret place on Thursday night. We will give to you now the reason.

"In the Reign of Thothmose the III, there are those in this Sanctuary that were with us. There, in Egypt, at that time and at that Time I remember not how long ago it was, it is written in the records, and can be verified by each one of you when you are taken unto Egypt, in the Temple of Karnak, as well as the Egyptian Temple of Luxor, Thursday nights long, long ago, were set aside as the Master's night for the sons and daughters of Light, who held issue. That group and eternal soul bodies, that golden thread, reaches from then until now.

"We have more wonderful facts for you shortly, and tonight we have given you just one-half, but that is sufficient. May our blessing, our peace, our love, overshadow you and you will have from this night on more tolerance, more understanding. *So be it!*"

317

BE THOU WISE

Be big enough to be small enough to do the little things THE MAS-TER prompts you to do.

Be wise enough, ever, to let LOVE be the ruling principle in your life and personal activity.

Be tolerant with your weaker Brothers and the Spirit of the Lords of Light will assist you to help them.

Be kind and gentle to the "least of these," my brethren, and you shall be lifted to the GREATEST OF THESE, the LORDS.

"When you know who you ARE you will know who I AM."—Anno.

Be sure thou art true to thyself in presenting thyself as a representative of Him, Christ Jesus, or Christ Maitreya.

Be thou ONE in HIM, the SUN of LIGHT, and thou art ONE with all the TRUE SONS OF GOD. *HE IS LIGHT!* "CHRIST" means GOD INCARNATE.

Be thou ever humble before all men and thou art sure to meet THE MASTERS OF LIGHT AND LOVE. "Pride goeth before a fall."

Be thou certain it is CHRIST prompts thee when thou deemest thyself capable of Great Works in the outer world of activity.

Be thou a seeker unceasing in thy quest of CHRIST'S LIGHT. "I AM the door that no man can shut." "It shall be opened unto thee."

Be thou a Master of Love when thou judgeth a writer of Christ's words, then thou becometh as thou judgeth, A MASTER OF LOVE.

Be thou thinking good of all men, then, in spite of thine own weak-nesses thou art drawn into the ONE SPIRIT OF GOD—HIS LOVE.

Be thou a lover of thine enemies and thou hast truly become MASTER. Thus LOVE proves the greater over the lesser.

Be thou an ALCHEMIST, when thou hast mastered His Satanic Majesty—all enemies—THROUGH LOVE—to become a collector of FINE GOLD and the designer and perfecter of thine own diadem.

Be remindful that when thou judgeth another thou reflecteth but the likeness of thyself, and more, thou becometh such.

Be filled with thine own GOOD intentions—IN CHRIST'S LIGHT —and your attention cannot be drawn to other persons' business.

Be thou manifest of simplicity even though possessor of LOVE, WIS-DOM and POWER in perfect balance, for BEAUTY IS SIMPLICITY.

Be thou like Jesus, who, though an ordinary man in appearance, was CHRIST MAITREYA INCARNATE, because He actually worshiped God in Spirit and in Truth. Had they known the Spirit of Maitreya they would not have crucified Him they called Jesus.

Eternal Peace Be unto Thee,
MAH ATMAH AMSUMATA.

AMIDST THE STARS

I, in fancy, weave celestial,
  A patterned garment of rarest hues—
    The woof and warp of star dust—
  Yellows, purples, pinks and blues,
  Radiant greens and golds I choose.

Days I work 'mongst men of toil,
    My weaving put aside,
      But nights again my star-lit home
    In Spirit I have spied.
  My joyous task I now begin.

Worlds about me screech and cry,
  Their noises blasting earthly things,
    But in my world celestial
      I work and weave and build;
  My soul most joyful sings.

The pains and sorrows of my heart,
  The griefs I've learned to bear—
Each wrought a secret little part
    In this Celestial Garment
  I've earned the right to wear.

Now that my mantle's finished
  And the Colors blend so well,
    I draw me deep within my Self
  To hear the Cosmic Bell.
  All is well! All is well!

      Lovingly,

        AMSUMATA.

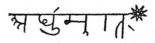

319